Praise from the Expert.

"Michele Burlew's book is one of the best resources for combining and modifying data in SAS. This book provides abundant examples and the descriptions are clear and easy to understand for the beginner or advanced SAS user. As an epidemiologist for the state of Connecticut, I analyze multiple large data sets from the national and state levels that often need to be edited and merged before analysis. This is the most comprehensive book I have found to provide examples of numerous methods for combining data in SAS in a time-efficient manner. It is the ideal book for anyone wanting to manipulate and combine data to fit their specific needs."

Kimberly Nguyen, M.S., M.P.H.
Connecticut Department of Public Health

"This book is indispensable for anyone who handles SAS data sets. As a statistician who prefers analyzing data much more than getting the data into an analyzable form, this book will greatly reduce the time spent mashing up data sets. An exhaustive collection of techniques for the handling of data sets, I frequently found myself saying, "Wow, I wish I had known that a lot earlier in my career." I especially liked the layout of the book. The side-by-side code and commentary will help anyone quickly become a DATA step and PROC SQL guru."

Brian Adams
Regulatory Analyst
Dominion Virginia Power

"In *Combining and Modifying SAS® Data Sets: Examples, Second Edition,* Michele Burlew states the problem, lists the software tools that will be used in the example, and provides some sample data with a little explanation to go with it. Then, and only then, does she provide a sample program to solve the problem.

"Of course every programmer learns early in their career that there is never just one way to solve a problem programmatically! That is why my favorite feature of this book is that most examples are concluded with a section called 'Related Technique(s)' where alternate approaches to solve the problem are also provided and explained.

"I anticipate that this book will be an excellent addition to many personal and corporate bookshelves—starting with my own."

Andrew Kuligowski
FCCI Insurance Group

Combining and Modifying SAS® Data Sets: Examples

Second Edition

Michele M. Burlew

The correct bibliographic citation for this manual is as follows: Burlew, Michele M. 2009. *Combining and Modifying SAS® Data Sets: Examples, Second Edition*. Cary, NC: SAS Institute Inc.

Combining and Modifying SAS® Data Sets: Examples, Second Edition

Contents

Acknowledgments

This book would not have been possible without the contributions and hard work from many people. First, I'd like to thank the authors and designers of the first edition of this book. I had the good fortune to start a second edition from an excellent foundation. I'd like to thank editors, Julie Platt and John West. To Julie, thank you for initiating my working on this book project. To John, thank you for coordinating the development of this book and for working with me on how to focus and organize the examples.

Thanks to the SAS technical reviewers for carefully reading the material and providing thoughtful suggestions: Michele Austin, Amber Elam, Marty Hultgren, Mark Jordan, Lynn MacKay, Charley Mullin, Ginny Piechota, Linda Reznikiewicz, Julia Schelly, Jason Secosky, Jan Squillace, Sally Walczak, and Kim Wilson. And, I'd like to give a special thanks to Amber Elam for reviewing the book several times.

Thank you to SAS Publishing specialists in design, marketing, and editing: Patrice Cherry and Jennifer Dilley for cover design; Candy Farrell for formatting the book; Shelly Goodin and Stacey Hamilton for marketing; Joan Knight for coordinating the indexing of the book; Tate Renner for copyediting the book; and Mary Beth Steinbach for managing the editing of this book.

About This Book

Purpose

Combining and Modifying SAS Data Sets: Examples, Second Edition is a book of examples that show you how to combine, modify, and reshape your SAS data sets. The chapters and examples are organized and titled by task. This structure makes it possible for you to find an example that solves a task similar to the one you need to solve and then adapt the code to your needs.

Is This Book for You?

This book was written for SAS users at all levels from all disciplines who need to combine, modify, and reshape SAS data sets. If you are a beginning SAS programmer, the extensive margin notes that accompany the code will help you solve a task as well as learn more about how to program in SAS. If you are an intermediate SAS programmer, the examples will help you extend your knowledge of SAS and how to apply it to different programming tasks. And, if you are an advanced SAS programmer, you can learn more about how to apply SAS features that you might not have used yet or that you use infrequently.

Many of the examples include both a DATA step solution and a PROC SQL solution. If you are more familiar with one technique, you can adapt that technique to your task. Also, you can learn more about coding the unfamiliar technique by comparing its code to the technique you use more often.

Basic knowledge of SAS programming is necessary to understand the examples in this book. You should know how to write a basic DATA step. If you are more familiar with PROC SQL, you will find that many examples include both a PROC SQL and DATA step solution.

What's New in This Edition

The examples in this new edition were developed using SAS 9.2 and Base SAS procedures. Code in some of the examples is new with SAS 9.2. The book has nearly doubled in size with the addition of several new examples and alternative solutions.

Scope of This Book

The book starts in Chapter 1 with a discussion of the concepts and terminology in combining and modifying SAS data sets.

Chapters 2 through 7 present examples that combine, modify, and reshape multiple SAS data sets in different ways. The examples in Chapter 2 combine data sets vertically by concatenating, interleaving, and appending them.

Chapters 3 through 7 show different ways of match-merging data sets and combining them horizontally. The examples in these chapters show you how to code simple match-merges by value, how to code more complex matches using indexes, how to define and use lookup tables, how to combine summary and detail data, and how to modify SAS data sets in place.

Chapter 8 presents examples that show you how to modify and reshape data in one data set using the SAS language, SAS options, and SAS procedures. Examples included in this chapter demonstrate how to work with BY groups in a DATA step, combine a data set with itself, find unique and duplicate observations in a data set, and obtain previous or next values of a variable.

Chapter 9 illustrates several techniques of modifying data sets using functions, utilities, and the SAS programming language. Some examples show applications of working with character data and SAS dates and times. A few examples explain how to generate random numbers and select observations at random. The last example introduces how to clean data with Perl regular expressions.

Several of the examples include discussions and figures that explain the code and technique in more detail.

Programs and Data Sets Used in This Book

The examples in this book use simple data sets to illustrate the tasks. Input data sets are shown along with brief descriptions of their contents. Resulting data sets are also presented that show how the example code combined, modified, or reshaped the input data sets.

You can access the programs that create the input data sets and that modify them by linking to the author pages for this book at http://support.sas.com/authors. Select the name of the author to display the appropriate author page, locate the appropriate book, and then click the Example Code and Data link for that book.

For an alphabetical listing of all books for which example code is available, see http://support.sas.com/bookcode. Select a title to display the book's example code.

If you are unable to access the code through the Web site, send e-mail to saspress@sas.com.

Author Pages

Each SAS Press author has an author page, which includes several features that relate to the author, including a biography, book descriptions for coming soon titles and other titles by the author, contact information, links to sample chapters and example code and data, events and extras, and more.

You can access the author pages at http://support.sas.com/authors.

Additional Resources

SAS offers you a wide variety of resources to help build your SAS skills and explore and apply the full power of SAS software. Whether you are in a professional or academic setting, we have learning products that can help you maximize your investment in SAS.

Bookstore	http://support.sas.com/publishing/
Training	http://support.sas.com/training/
Certification	http://support.sas.com/certify/
Higher Education Resources	http://support.sas.com/learn/
SAS OnDemand for Academics	http://support.sas.com/ondemand/
Knowledge Base	http://support.sas.com/resources/
Support	http://support.sas.com/techsup/
Learning Center	http://support.sas.com/learn/
Community	http://support.sas.com/community/

Comments or Questions?

If you have comments or questions about this book, you may contact the author through SAS as follows:

Mail:

SAS Institute Inc.
SAS Press
Attn: Michele M. Burlew
SAS Campus Drive
Cary, NC 27513

E-mail:

saspress@sas.com

Fax:

(919) 677-4444

Please include the title of the book in your correspondence.

For a complete list of books available through SAS Press, visit http://support.sas.com/publishing.

SAS Publishing News

Receive up-to-date information about all new SAS publications via e-mail by subscribing to the SAS Publishing News monthly eNewsletter. Visit http://support.sas.com/subscribe.

CHAPTER 1

Introducing Data Relationships, Techniques for Data Manipulation, and Access Methods

Overview

Many applications require input data to be in a specific format before it can be processed to produce meaningful results. Even if all of your data are already in SAS data sets, the data might come from multiple sources and might be in different formats. Therefore, you often have to take intermediate steps to logically relate and process the data before you can analyze them or create reports from them.

Application requirements vary, but there are common denominators for all applications that access, combine, and process data. Once you have determined what you want the output to look like, you must complete the following:

❑ discover how the input data are related

❑ select the appropriate SAS tools to complete the task

Determining Data Relationships

Relationships among multiple sources of input data exist when each source contains common data, either at the physical or logical level. For example, employee data and department data could be related through an employee ID variable that shares common values. Another data set could contain numeric sequence numbers whose partial values logically relate it to a separate data set by observation number. Once data relationships exist, they fall into one of four categories:

❑ one-to-one

❑ one-to-many

❑ many-to-one

❑ many-to-many

The categories are characterized by how observations relate among the data sets. All related data fall into one of these categories. You must be able to identify the existing relationships in your data because this knowledge is crucial to understanding how input data can be processed to produce desired results.

The remainder of this section illustrates the four categories.

One-to-One

In a one-to-one relationship, typically a single observation in one data set is related to a single observation from another based on the values of one or more selected variables. A one-to-one relationship implies that each value of the selected variable occurs no more than once in each data set. When working with multiple selected variables, this relationship implies that each combination of values occurs no more than once in each data set. Figure 1.1 presents an example of two data sets with a one-to-one relationship.

Figure 1.1 One-to-One
Observations in SALARY and TAXES are related by common values for EMPNUM.

SALARY	
EMPNUM	**SALARY**
1234	125000
3333	85000
4876	54000
5489	29000

TAXES	
EMPNUM	**TAX_BRACKET**
1111	0.28
1234	0.33
3333	0.28
4222	0.15
4876	0.25

One-to-Many and Many-to-One

A one-to-many or many-to-one relationship between input data sets implies that one data set has at most one observation with a specific value of the selected variable, but the other input data set might have more than one occurrence of each value. When working with multiple selected variables, this relationship implies that each combination of values occurs no more than once in one data set, but might occur more than once in the other data set. The order in which the input data sets are processed determines whether the relationship is one-to-many or many-to-one. Figure 1.2 presents an example of two data sets with a one-to-many relationship.

Figure 1.2 One-to-Many
Observations in PATIENTS and APPOINTMENTS are related by common values for ID.

PATIENTS	
ID	**DOB**
5MROTF	04/01/1973
AV0LYM	12/29/1944
G7DQTB	2/20/1982
R89CJ7	06/03/1961

APPOINTMENTS	
ID	**APPT_DATE**
AV0LYM	11/14/2008
AV0LYM	12/01/2008
AV0LYM	12/15/2008
R0VZWO	10/08/2008

Figure 1.3 presents an example of three related data sets. Data sets AGENTS and SALES have a one-to-many relationship. Data sets SALES and QUOTA have a many-to-one relationship.

Figure 1.3 One-to-Many and Many-to-One
Observations in data sets AGENTS, SALES, and QUOTA are related by common values for variable ID. Values of ID are unique in AGENTS and QUOTA, but not in SALES. For ID values HE01 and HH01, a one-to-many relationship exists between observations in data sets AGENTS and SALES, and a many-to-one relationship exists between observations in data sets SALES and QUOTA. Additionally, a one-to-one relationship exists between AGENTS and QUOTA.

AGENTS	
ID	**NAME**
GE01	Graham, Emily
HE01	Hall, Elizabeth
HH01	Harris, Hannah
RA01	Ross, Angela
WD01	Wright, Donald

SALES	
ID	**SALES**
GE01	28000
HE01	30000
HE01	40000
HH01	15000
HH01	20000
HH01	25000
RA01	35000
WD01	40000

QUOTA	
ID	**QUOTA**
GE01	15000
HE01	7000
HH01	15000
RA01	5000
WD01	8000

Many-to-Many

The many-to-many relationship implies that multiple observations from each input data set might be related based on values of one or more common variables. Figure 1.4 presents an example of two data sets with a many-to-many relationship.

Figure 1.4 Many-to-Many

Observations in data sets REPAIRS and MAINTENANCE are related by common values for variable VEHICLE. Values of VEHICLE are not unique in either data set. A many-to-many relationship exists between observations in these data sets for values 139 and 593 of VEHICLE.

REPAIRS	
VEHICLE	REPAIR_DATE
139	08/15/2005
139	11/03/2005
139	07/16/2006
139	03/10/2008
414	09/27/2007
593	07/03/2008
593	09/09/2008

MAINTENANCE	
VEHICLE	MAINT_DATE
139	03/01/2006
139	09/15/2006
139	04/22/2007
593	01/08/2008
593	12/15/2008
684	04/15/2008
684	06/24/2008
684	08/15/2008

Understanding the Methods for Combining SAS Data Sets

Generally SAS data sets are combined either vertically or horizontally.

❑ When combined *vertically*, you concatenate the data sets one after another, or you interleave observations from the data sets in order by one or more variables. Observations are not combined side-by-side horizontally nor are they overlaid.

❑ When combined *horizontally*, you usually match data sets by the values of key variables in common or by programmatically aligning observations when they do not have variables in common. The observations in the data sets can be aligned side-by-side and data in one data set can be overlaid by data from another.

You can use these methods to combine SAS data sets vertically:

❑ concatenating

❑ interleaving

You can use these methods to combine SAS data sets horizontally:

❑ one-to-one reading

❑ one-to-one merging

❑ match-merging

❑ updating

Figures 1.5 through 1.11 show basic illustrations of these methods.

The DATA step and PROC SQL can combine SAS data sets. The methods are demonstrated in the following figures primarily with basic DATA steps. A few include PROC SQL code as well.

Although not described in this section, the APPEND procedure and the APPEND statement in the DATASETS procedure can also concatenate SAS data sets. For more information, see examples throughout this book and SAS documentation.

Figure 1.5 shows vertically combining two data sets one after the other with the DATA step and with PROC SQL.

Figure 1.5 Vertical: Concatenating SAS Data Sets

Concatenating appends the observations from one data set to another data set.

ONE	TWO	ALL
YEAR	YEAR	YEAR
2006	2006	2006
2007	2007	2007
2008	2008	2008
2009	2009	2009
2010	2010	2010
		2006
		2007
		2008
		2009
		2010

(ONE + TWO = ALL)

The DATA step reads ONE sequentially until all observations have been processed. Then it reads TWO sequentially until all its observations have been processed.

DATA Step
```
data all;
   set one two;
run;
```

The OUTER UNION CORR set operator in PROC SQL concatenates the two tables.

PROC SQL
```
proc sql;
   create table all as
      select * from one
         outer union corr
      select * from two;
quit;
```

Figure 1.6 presents an example of vertically combining two data sets by interleaving the values of one variable. It shows how to do this with the DATA step and with PROC SQL.

Figure 1.6 Vertical: Interleaving SAS Data Sets
Interleaving intersperses observations from two or more data sets based on values of one or more common variables.

Assume that data sets ONE and TWO were sorted by YEAR prior to the DATA step.

DATA Step
```
data all;
   set one two;
   by year;
run;
```

The ORDER BY clause arranges the observations in the table ALL in the PROC SQL step. It is not necessary to sort the table before interleaving the rows.

PROC SQL
```
proc sql;
   create table all as
      select * from one
         outer union corr
      select * from two
      order by year;
quit;
```

The DATA step in Figure 1.7 combines two data sets horizontally by doing a one-to-one reading of two data sets.

Figure 1.7 Horizontal: One-to-One Reading
One-to-one reading combines observations from two or more data sets by creating observations that contain all of the variables from each contributing data set. Observations are combined based on their relative position in each data set. That is, the first observation in one data set is aligned with the first observation in the other data set, and so on.

The DATA step *stops* after it has read the *last* observation from the *smallest* data set. The fifth observation in Y is not present in XY.

DATA Step
```
data xy;
   set x;
   set y;
run;
```

The DATA step in Figure 1.8 combines two data sets horizontally by performing a one-to-one merge of two data sets.

Figure 1.8 Horizontal: One-to-One Merging

One-to-one merging is the same as a one-to-one reading, except that all observations from the input data sets are read. Compared to Figure 1.7, the fifth observation from data set Y is now present in XY.

The DATA step uses the MERGE statement instead of the multiple SET statements as in Figure 1.7.

X	Y	XY	
XCOORD	**YCOORD**	**XCOORD**	**YCOORD**
25	110	25	110
35	115	35	115
45	120	45	120
55	125	55	125
	130	.	130

DATA Step

```
data xy;
   merge x y;
run;
```

Figures 1.7 and 1.8 show only DATA steps to perform one-to-one reading and one-to-one merging and do not show equivalent PROC SQL code. Conceptually, when PROC SQL joins two tables, every row in the first table is combined with every row in the second table. The result is called a Cartesian product. This kind of join can produce a very large table or report when joining tables in this way. More likely you will want to include ON clauses, WHERE clauses, and set operators in your SELECT statements that subset the Cartesian product.

Figures 1.7 and 1.8 do not contain any common variables that can be used to subset the results. Therefore, no equivalent PROC SQL code is included. Figure 1.9 presents a PROC SQL step that produces the Cartesian product of the two data sets used in both Figures 1.7 and 1.8.

Figure 1.9 Cartesian Product

A *Cartesian product* is produced when tables are combined with PROC SQL and no conditions are specified to subset the results.

X	Y	XY	
XCOORD	**YCOORD**	**XCOORD**	**YCOORD**
25	110	25	110
35	115	25	115
45	120	25	120
55	125	25	125
	130	25	130
		35	110
		35	115
		35	120
		35	125
		35	130
		45	110
		45	115
		45	120
		45	125
		45	130
		55	110
		55	115
		55	120
		55	125
		55	130
		.	110
		.	115
		.	120
		.	125
		.	130

PROC SQL Step

```
proc sql;
   create table xy as
      select * from x,y;
quit;
```

Figure 1.10 presents an example of combining two data sets horizontally by match-merging them by the values of a common variable. It shows how to do this with the DATA step and with PROC SQL.

Figure 1.10 Horizontal: Match-Merging
Match-merging combines observations from two or more data sets into a single observation in a new data set based on the values of one or more common variables.

X	
DAY	**XCOORD**
1	25
2	35
3	45
4	55

+

Y	
DAY	**YCOORD**
1	110
3	120
4	125
5	130

=

XY		
DAY	**XCOORD**	**YCOORD**
1	25	110
2	35	.
3	45	120
4	55	125
5	.	130

Assume that data sets X and Y were sorted by DAY prior to the DATA step.

DATA Step
```
data xy;
   merge x y;
   by day;
run;
```

Tables X and Y do not have to be sorted before submitting the PROC SQL step. The COALESCE function saves the first nonmissing value of DAY from each of the two tables and the resulting column is named DAY.

PROC SQL Step
```
proc sql;
   create table xy as
      select coalesce(x.day,y.day) as day, xcoord, ycoord
         from x full join y
            on x.day=y.day;
```

The DATA step in Figure 1.11 combines two data sets horizontally by updating one data set with information in another.

Figure 1.11 Horizontal: Updating
Updating uses information from observations in a transaction data set to delete, add, or alter information in observations in a master data set.

Assume that MASTER and TRANSACTIONS were sorted by DT prior to the DATA step. Updating a data set with the DATA step requires that the data be sorted or indexed by the values of the common variable. You can update a master data set with the UPDATE or the MODIFY statements.

Note that by default UPDATE and MODIFY do not replace nonmissing values in a master data set with missing values in a transaction data set.

MASTER

DT	MANAGER	SALES
02/01/2008	JHT	10521
02/02/2008	JHT	10761
02/03/2008	IRW	10796
02/04/2008	TRP	10457
02/05/2008	JHT	10729
02/06/2008	LKJ	10850
02/07/2008	JHT	10468
02/08/2008		10646
02/09/2008	UTR	10302
02/10/2008	LKJ	10971
02/11/2008	LKJ	10757
02/12/2008	IRW	10838

+

TRANSACTIONS

DT	MANAGER	SALES
02/02/2008		10845
02/05/2008	LKJ	10976
02/08/2008	UTR	
02/13/2008	LKJ	10754
02/14/2008	IRW	10381

=

MASTER

DT	MANAGER	SALES
02/01/2008	JHT	10521
02/02/2008	JHT	10845
02/03/2008	IRW	10796
02/04/2008	TRP	10457
02/05/2008	LKJ	10976
02/06/2008	LKJ	10850
02/07/2008	JHT	10468
02/08/2008	UTR	10646
02/09/2008	UTR	10302
02/10/2008	LKJ	10971
02/11/2008	LKJ	10757
02/12/2008	IRW	10838
02/13/2008	LKJ	10754
02/14/2008	IRW	10381

DATA Step

```
data master;
  update master transactions;
  by dt;
run;
```

The PROC SQL step performs a full join of the two tables. The COALESCE function saves the first nonmissing value of the columns that are supplied to it. Note that the order of the columns that are supplied to the COALESCE function represents the column from TRANSACTIONS first so that a nonmissing value updates the value in MASTER.

PROC SQL

```
proc sql;
  create table master as
    select coalesce(transactions.dt, master.dt) as date
                       format=mmddyy10.,
           coalesce(transactions.manager, master.manager) as
                       manager,
           coalesce(transactions.sales, master.sales) as sales
      from master full join transactions
        on transactions.dt=master.dt;
quit;
```

Understanding Access Methods: Sequential versus Direct

SAS can access your data either sequentially or directly. When writing a SAS DATA step, your code might enable you to specify which of the two access methods SAS should use. PROC SQL decides for you which method is more efficient to use based on the code and data sets that you have specified.

❑ *Sequential access* means that SAS accesses the observations in your data set in the order in which they appear in the physical file.

❑ *Direct access* means that SAS goes straight to an observation in a SAS data set without having to process each observation that precedes it.

Computer resources such as CPU time, I/O, and disk storage can be conserved based on the access method that you choose.

Using Sequential Access

The simpler and perhaps more common way to process data with a DATA step is to read observations in a data set sequentially. You can read observations sequentially using the SET, MERGE, MODIFY, or UPDATE statement.

Using Direct Access

Direct access allows a program to access specific observations based on one of two methods:

❑ by an observation number in the DATA step only

❑ by the value of one or more variables through a simple or composite index in the DATA step or PROC SQL

In the DATA step, to access observations directly by their observation number, use the POINT= option with the SET or MODIFY statement. The POINT= option names a variable whose current value determines which observation a SET or MODIFY statement reads.

To access observations directly based on the values of one or more specified variables, you must first create an index for the variables. An index is a separate structure that contains the data values of the key variable or variables paired with a location identifier for the observations that contain the value.

If you are using a DATA step and an index, you would then read the data set by using the KEY= option with the SET or MODIFY statement.

With PROC SQL, specific clauses and types of queries and joins can use indexes to access data in your tables. In these situations, unless you specify otherwise, the PROC SQL internal optimizer will determine whether it is more efficient to use an index or not before executing the PROC SQL step.

Understanding the Tools for Combining SAS Data Sets

Once you understand the basics of establishing relationships among data and the ways you can combine SAS data sets, you can choose from a variety of SAS tools for accessing, combining, and processing your data. Table 1.1 lists and briefly describes the primary tools that are featured in this book. The remainder of the section describes in more detail some of the choices to make in determining how to combine and modify your data sets.

Table 1.1 Tools for Combining SAS Data Sets

Class of Tool	Statement, PROC, or Other Tool	Action Performed	Sequential	Direct	Can Use with BY Statement	Comments
DATA Step Statements	SET	Reads an observation from one or more SAS data sets.	X	X	X	Use KEY= or POINT= to access data directly.
	MERGE	Reads observations from two or more SAS data sets and joins them into single observations.	X		X	When using MERGE with BY, the data must be sorted or indexed on the BY variable.
	MODIFY	Manipulates observations in a SAS data set in place.	X	X	X	Sorted and indexed data are not required for direct access or usage with BY, but are recommended for performance.
	UPDATE	Applies transactions to observations in a master SAS data set. UPDATE does not update observations in place; it produces an updated copy of the current data set.	X		X	Both the master and transaction data sets must be sorted or indexed on the BY variable.
	BY	Controls the operation of a SET, MERGE, UPDATE, or MODIFY statement in the DATA step and sets up special grouping variables.	N/A	N/A	N/A	BY-group processing is a means of processing observations that have the same values of one or more variables.
PROCs	PROC APPEND	Adds the observations from one SAS data set to the end of another SAS data set.	X			This procedure is limited to appending one data set to another.
	PROC DATASETS with APPEND Statement	Adds the observations from one SAS data set to the end of another SAS data set.	X			The APPEND statement in this procedure is limited to appending one data set to another.
	PROC SQL	Joins rows from one or more tables and can manipulate the rows in a table in place. The maximum number of tables that PROC SQL can read is 256.	X	X		The access method is chosen by the PROC SQL internal optimizer.
Other	DATA Step Hash Objects	Enables you to quickly and efficiently store, search, and retrieve data based on lookup keys. Consists of two predefined component objects for use in the DATA step: the hash object and the hash iterator object.	N/A	N/A	N/A	Component objects are data elements that consist of attributes and methods. Attributes are the properties that specify the information that is associated with an object. Methods define the operations that an object can perform.
	IORC	An automatic variable that is created when you use the MODIFY statement or when you use the SET statement with the KEY= option.	N/A	N/A	N/A	The value of this variable is a numeric return code that indicates the status of the most recent I/O operation that used MODIFY or KEY=.
	%SYSRC	An autocall macro program that you use in conjunction with _IORC_ to test for specific I/O conditions.	N/A	N/A	N/A	

Understanding the Tools for Processing Information in Groups

Processing BY Groups in the DATA Step

When combining SAS data sets in a DATA step, it is often convenient or necessary to process observations in BY groups (that is, groups of observations that have the same value for one or more selected variables). Many examples in this book use BY-group processing with one or more SAS data sets to create a new data set.

The BY statement identifies one or more BY variables. When using the BY statement with the SET, MERGE, or UPDATE statement, your data must be sorted or indexed on the BY variable or variables.

In a DATA step, SAS identifies the beginning and end of each BY group by creating two temporary variables for each BY variable: FIRST.*variable* and LAST.*variable*. These variables are set to 1 if true and 0 if false to indicate whether that observation is the first or last in the current BY group. Using programming logic, you can test FIRST.*variable* and LAST.*variable* to determine whether the current observation is the first or last (or both first and last, or neither first nor last) in the current BY group. Testing the values of these variables in conditional processing enables you to perform certain operations at the beginning or end of a BY group.

Processing Grouped Data in PROC SQL

The same programming functionality that BY-group processing offers in the DATA step is not replicated in PROC SQL. The GROUP BY clause processes data in groups, similar to the way a BY statement in a PROC step processes data. Tables do not have to be sorted by the columns that are specified in the GROUP BY clause. The ORDER BY clause can be added to arrange the results.

Understanding BY-Group Processing with the MODIFY and BY Statements

Internally, the MODIFY statement handles BY-group processing differently from the SET, MERGE, and UPDATE statements. MODIFY creates a dynamic WHERE clause, making it possible for you to use BY-group processing without either sorting or indexing your data first. However, processing based on FIRST.*variables* and LAST.*variables* can result in multiple BY groups for the same BY values if your data are not sorted. Therefore, you might not get the expected results unless you use sorted data. And even though sorting is not required, it is often useful for improved performance.

Processing Groups with Arrays in the DATA Step

When you want to process several variables in the same way, you might be able to use arrays. Processing variables in arrays can save you time and simplify your code. Use an ARRAY statement to define a temporary grouping of variables as an array. Then use a DO loop to perform a task repetitively on all or selected elements in the array.

Choosing between the DATA Step and PROC SQL

As illustrated earlier, you can sometimes use either the DATA step or PROC SQL to combine data sets. A good understanding of your input data sets and the results you want to obtain will help you determine which tool is the better one to use to combine your data sets or tables. An additional important consideration is which method is easier for you to code and support.

In general, PROC SQL requires more computer resources than the equivalent DATA step. However, you might find coding PROC SQL in certain situations to be much simpler. What you lose in computer resources you might gain in your time to write and support the code.

The DATA step and PROC SQL follow different processes when combining data sets. It is important to understand how the two methods process the input data sets because the results of each method can produce different results.

Many of the examples in this book show how to use both tools. Discussion of efficiency and applicability of both methods is included.

Table 1.2 lists some advantages and disadvantages of the DATA step.

Table 1.2 Advantages and Disadvantages of Using the DATA Step

Advantages	Disadvantages
There is no limit to the number of input data sets, other than memory.	Data sets must be sorted by or indexed on the BY variables prior to match-merging.
Multiple data sets can be created in one DATA step.	When match-merging, the BY variables must be present in all data sets, and the names of the BY variables must match exactly.
With the SAS language in the DATA step, complex logic can be programmed that can include arrays and DO loops, and options in the SET, MERGE, UPDATE, and MODIFY statements.	An exact match on the key values must be found. Sometimes inexact matches can be made if additional programming logic is added.
Multiple BY variables enable lookups that depend on more than one variable.	

Table 1.3 lists some advantages and disadvantages of PROC SQL.

Table 1.3 Advantages and Disadvantages of Using PROC SQL

Advantages	Disadvantages
Tables do not have to be sorted or indexed, but an index might improve performance.	Complex logic can be difficult to code.
Multiple tables can be joined in one step without having common columns in all tables.	PROC SQL might require more resources for a simple join than a DATA step that uses the MERGE statement. For example, even though input tables do not have to be sorted, PROC SQL might perform a sort behind the scenes, which could require more resources than PROC SORT and a DATA step.
You can create tables, views, or query reports with the combined data.	
Combining tables when variable values do not match exactly can often be much easier to accomplish than with a DATA step.	PROC SQL can create only one table from a query.
Matching tables based on the values of variables with different names does not require renaming of the variables as it does in the DATA step.	The maximum number of tables that can be joined at one time is 256.

Choosing between MODIFY and UPDATE

You can use either the MODIFY or UPDATE statement to update a master data set with information in a transaction data set. Chapter 6 includes examples that use the UPDATE statement. Chapter 7 includes examples that use the MODIFY statement.

The MODIFY statement has many applications while the UPDATE statement is limited to updating a master data set. You can use the MODIFY statement to perform the following tasks:

❑ process a file sequentially to apply updates in place (without a BY statement)

❑ make changes to a master data set in place by applying transactions from a transaction data set

❑ update the values of variables by directly accessing observations based on observation numbers

❑ update the values of variables by directly accessing observations based on the values of one or more key variables

Only one application of MODIFY is comparable to UPDATE: using MODIFY with the BY statement to apply transactions to a data set. While MODIFY is a more powerful tool than UPDATE, UPDATE is still the tool of choice in some cases. Table 1.4 helps you choose whether to use UPDATE or MODIFY with BY.

Table 1.4 UPDATE versus MODIFY with BY

Issue	MODIFY with BY	UPDATE
Disk space	Saves disk space because it updates data in place.	Requires more disk space because it produces an updated copy of the data set.
Sort and index	For good performance, it is strongly recommended that both data sets be sorted and that the master data set be indexed.	Requires that both data sets be sorted.
When to use	Use only when you expect to process a small portion of the data set.	Use if you expect to process most of the data set.
Duplicate BY values	Allows duplicate BY values in both the master and transaction data sets.	Allows duplicate BY values in only the transaction data set.
Scope of changes	Cannot change the data set descriptor information, so changes such as adding or deleting variables or variable labels are not valid.	Can make changes that require a change in the descriptor portion of a data set, such as adding new variables.
Error checking	Automatically generates the _IORC_ return code variable whose value can be examined for error checking.	Needs no error checking because transactions without a corresponding master record are not applied, but are added to the data set.
Data set integrity	Data can only be partially updated due to an abnormal task termination.	No data loss occurs because UPDATE works on a copy of the data.

CHAPTER 2

Combining Data Sets Vertically: Concatenating, Interleaving, and Appending Data Sets

When you combine data sets vertically, you concatenate the data sets one after another, or you interleave observations from the data sets in order by one or more variables. Observations are not combined side-by-side horizontally or overlaid.

Data sets can be combined vertically by using the DATA step, PROC SQL, PROC APPEND, or the APPEND statement in the DATASETS procedure.

When using the DATA step or PROC SQL, you can specify conditions under which to combine the data sets. For example, PROC SQL has set operators, UNION, EXCEPT, INTERSECT, and OUTER UNION, that control how to combine the results of queries. These operators find unique rows and rows in common between queries. In the DATA step, you can use the values of BY variables to interleave observations in a specific order when reading multiple input data sets. The ORDER BY clause works similarly in PROC SQL.

PROC APPEND and PROC DATASETS do not have programming features to control how your data sets are combined vertically. However, the advantage of these procedures is realized when you need to conserve computing resources because these procedures do not recopy the base data set to which you are concatenating another data set.

Example 2.1   Concatenating Data Sets

Goal

Concatenate three data sets. Define a variable that identifies the data set from which the observation originated.

Example Features

Featured Step	DATA step
Featured Step Options and Statements	SET statement, IN= option
Related Technique 1	PROC SQL, OUTER UNION set operator and CORR keyword
Related Technique 2	PROC APPEND

Input Data Sets

Data sets SPRINGGRADS, SUMMERGRADS, and FALLGRADS contain lists of biology students who graduated in spring, summer, and fall. The students' final GPAs are included.

The three data sets are also used in Example 2.2.

```
                          SPRINGGRADS

Obs        student        concentration      gpa
 1    Johnson, Allison    Biochemistry       3.86
 2    Davis, Jeffrey      General Biology     3.91
 3    Hall, Daniel        Genetics           3.43
 4    Hill, Courtney      Ecology            4.00
 5    Scott, Tiffany      Plant Biology      3.58
 6    Martinez, Teresa    Zoology            3.21


                          SUMMERGRADS

Obs        student        concentration      gpa
 1    Robinson, Adam      Ecology            3.87
 2    Cox, William        Zoology            3.61


                          FALLGRADS

Obs        student        concentration      gpa
 1    Mitchell, Frank     Biochemistry       3.25
 2    Rogers, Melissa     Microbiology       4.00
 3    Brown, Beverly      Molecular Biology  3.42
```

Resulting Data Set
Output 2.1
ALLGRADS Data Set

```
             Example 2.1 ALLGRADS Data Set Created by DATA Step

     Obs        student        concentration      gpa   graduated

       1    Johnson, Allison    Biochemistry       3.86  Spring
       2    Davis, Jeffrey      General Biology     3.91  Spring
       3    Hall, Daniel        Genetics           3.43  Spring
       4    Hill, Courtney      Ecology            4.00  Spring
       5    Scott, Tiffany      Plant Biology      3.58  Spring
       6    Martinez, Teresa    Zoology            3.21  Spring
       7    Robinson, Adam      Ecology            3.87  Summer
       8    Cox, William        Zoology            3.61  Summer
       9    Mitchell, Frank     Biochemistry       3.25  Fall
      10    Rogers, Melissa     Microbiology       4.00  Fall
      11    Brown, Beverly      Molecular Biology  3.42  Fall
```

Example Overview

The DATA step in this program uses a SET statement to concatenate three data sets: SPRINGGRADS, SUMMERGRADS, and FALLGRADS. The names of the three data sets are listed in the SET statement in the order in which they should be concatenated.

The IN= data set option is added to each input data set to define temporary variables INSPRING, INSUMMER, and INFALL. IF-ELSE statements test the values of these variables to determine the data set source for the observation that is currently being processed and to assign values to new variable GRADUATED. For example, INSPRING=1 when the observation is from data set SPRINGGRADS. When the observation is from SUMMERGRADS or FALLGRADS, the value of INSPRING is 0.

Each of the three data sets contains the same three variables. Therefore, ALLGRADS contains these three variables plus variable GRADUATED, which is created in the DATA step.

If your data sets contain different variables, *all* variables from *all* the data sets are included in the output data set *unless* you specify the variables to keep in the output data set. When concatenating data sets with a SET statement, SAS assigns missing values to a variable for the observations that are contributed from a data set where the variable is not present, but where the variable is present in another data set.

Program

Create data set ALLGRADS.
Concatenate three data sets. Add the
IN= data set option to each input data
set so that the data set origin of each
observation can be determined.
Define a new variable.
Assign values to GRADUATED
depending on the origin of the
observation.

```
data allgrads;
  set springgrads(in=inspring)
      summergrads(in=insummer)
      fallgrads(in=infall);

  attrib graduated length=$6 label='Semester Graduated';
  if inspring then graduated='Spring';
  else if insummer then graduated='Summer';
  else if infall then graduated='Fall';
run;
```

Related Technique 1

The following PROC SQL step creates a table equivalent to the data set that was created by the DATA step in the main example. It concatenates three queries by using the OUTER UNION set operator and the CORR keyword. (CORR is the short version of CORRESPONDING.) Each query creates the same new column, GRADUATED, whose values reflect the origin of the row.

The OUTER UNION set operator concatenates tables. The CORR keyword matches and aligns the same-named columns that were extracted from the two input tables.

Create table ALLGRADS.
Specify a SELECT clause for each
table that you want to concatenate and
specify them in the order you want the
tables concatenated.
Select all columns from table
SPRINGGRADS. Define new column,
GRADUATED.

Concatenate the rows from the next
query to the rows that were selected by
the first query. Include the CORR
keyword to match and align same-
named columns from the two queries.

```
proc sql;
  create table allgrads as




  select *,
         'Spring' as graduated length=6
             label='Semester Graduated'
      from springgrads
      outer union corr
```

Select all columns from table SUMMERGRADS. Define new column, GRADUATED.

Concatenate the rows from the next query to the rows that were selected from joining the first two queries. Select all columns from table FALLGRADS. Define new column, GRADUATED.

```
  select *,
         'Summer' as graduated length=6
               label='Semester Graduated'
     from summergrads
     outer union corr


  select *,
         'Fall' as graduated length=6
               label='Semester Graduated'
     from fallgrads;
quit;
```

Related Technique 2

Using two PROC APPEND steps, the following program concatenates the three data sets SPRINGGRADS, SUMMERGRADS, and FALLGRADS. This procedure adds the observations from one data set to the end of another data set.

When concatenating data sets with PROC APPEND, you cannot add a variable the way you did in the DATA step and PROC SQL step in Related Technique 1.

Other limitations of PROC APPEND to be aware of include how the procedure concatenates data sets that have different variable attributes or different variables. For example, **by default**, PROC APPEND does not append a data set to another under two conditions:

❏ The data set being appended to the base data set has one or more variables that are not present in the base data set.

❏ A variable common to both data sets is character type in one data set and numeric type in the other.

For more information about these limitations and the uses of PROC APPEND, see Example 2.3 and SAS documentation.

The most practical use of PROC APPEND might be when you need to add a relatively small number of observations to the end of a much larger data set. Because PROC APPEND does not read the BASE= data set, you can save processing time compared to concatenating data sets with the DATA step or PROC SQL where all of the data set or table is read.

Delete temporary data set ALLGRADS so that the following steps do not add observations to an existing data set.

```
proc datasets library=work nolist;
  delete allgrads;
run;
quit;
```

Add the observations from data set SPRINGGRADS to ALLGRADS. Create data set ALLGRADS (it does not exist because of execution of the preceding PROC DATASETS step).

```
proc append base=allgrads data=springgrads;
run;
```

Add the observations from SUMMERGRADS to data set ALLGRADS.

```
proc append base=allgrads data=summergrads;
run;
```

Add the observations from FALLGRADS to ALLGRADS to complete the concatenation of the three data sets.

```
proc append base=allgrads data=fallgrads;
run;
```

Example 2.2   Interleaving Observations from Two or More Data Sets Based on a Common Variable

Goal

Interleave the observations from three data sets in order by the values of a specific variable. Define a variable that identifies the data set from which the observation originated.

Example Features

Featured Step	DATA step
Featured Step Options and Statements	SET statement, IN= option BY statement
Related Technique	PROC SQL, OUTER UNION set operator and CORR keyword, ORDER BY clause

Input Data Sets

Data sets SPRINGGRADS, SUMMERGRADS, and FALLGRADS contain lists of biology students who graduated in spring, summer, and fall. The students' final GPAs are included.

Example 2.1 also uses the three data sets.

SPRINGGRADS

Obs	student	concentration	gpa
1	Johnson, Allison	Biochemistry	3.86
2	Davis, Jeffrey	General Biology	3.91
3	Hall, Daniel	Genetics	3.43
4	Hill, Courtney	Ecology	4.00
5	Scott, Tiffany	Plant Biology	3.58
6	Martinez, Teresa	Zoology	3.21

SUMMERGRADS

Obs	student	concentration	gpa
1	Robinson, Adam	Ecology	3.87
2	Cox, William	Zoology	3.61

FALLGRADS

Obs	student	concentration	gpa
1	Mitchell, Frank	Biochemistry	3.25
2	Rogers, Melissa	Microbiology	4.00
3	Brown, Beverly	Molecular Biology	3.42

Resulting Data Set
Output 2.2
GPAGRADS Data Set

Example 2.2 GPAGRADS Data Set Created by DATA Step

Obs	student	concentration	gpa	graduated
1	Hill, Courtney	Ecology	4.00	Spring
2	Rogers, Melissa	Microbiology	4.00	Fall
3	Davis, Jeffrey	General Biology	3.91	Spring
4	Robinson, Adam	Biophysics	3.87	Summer
5	Johnson, Allison	Biochemistry	3.86	Spring
6	Cox, William	Zoology	3.61	Summer
7	Scott, Tiffany	Plant Biology	3.58	Spring
8	Hall, Daniel	Genetics	3.43	Spring
9	Brown, Beverly	Molecular Biology	3.42	Fall
10	Mitchell, Frank	Biochemistry	3.25	Fall
11	Martinez, Teresa	Zoology	3.21	Spring

Example Overview

This program is similar to the main example program in Example 2.1 because both use a SET statement to vertically combine the observations from three data sets. This example differs because instead of concatenating the observations from one data set after another, it interleaves the observations in SPRINGRADS, SUMMERGRADS, and FALLGRADS in the order that is specified by the values of the variables in the BY statement. The two variables that control the interleaving are GPA and STUDENT.

Observations in output data set GPAGRADS are arranged in descending GPA order (highest to lowest). For identical GPAs, the observations are further arranged alphabetically by the student's last name.

As in Example 2.1, this DATA step applies the IN= data set option to each input data set to define temporary variables INSPRING, INSUMMER, and INFALL. IF-ELSE statements test the values of these variables to determine the data set source for the observation that is currently being processed and to assign values to new variable GRADUATED.

Each of the three data sets contains the same three variables. Therefore, ALLGRADS contains these three variables plus new variable GRADUATED.

Three PROC SORT steps precede the DATA step in which the observations in each of the three data sets are sorted in the order in which they will be interleaved.

If a data set has been indexed by the variables in the BY statement in the DATA step, you might not need to sort the data set. This depends on whether simple **and/or** composite indexes have been defined prior to the step. For more information about when indexes are used and not used in accessing observations, see your SAS documentation. In this example, none of the data sets are indexed by GPA and STUDENT.

Program

Sort the observations in the three data sets in the order in which you want to interleave them.

```
proc sort data=springgrads;
  by descending gpa student;
run;
proc sort data=summergrads;
  by descending gpa student;
run;
proc sort data=fallgrads;
  by descending gpa student;
run;
```

Concatenate three data sets. Add the IN= data set option to each input data set so that the data set origin of each observation can be determined.

```
data allgrads;
  set springgrads(in=inspring)
      summergrads(in=insummer)
      fallgrads(in=infall);
```

Specify the order in which to interleave the observations from the three data sets.

```
  by descending gpa student;
```

Define GRADUATED and assign it values based on the origin of the observation.

```
  attrib graduated length=$6 label='Semester Graduated';
  if inspring then graduated='Spring';
  else if insummer then graduated='Summer';
  else if infall then graduated='Fall';
run;
```

Related Technique

The following PROC SQL step creates a table equivalent to the data set that was created by the DATA step in the main example. It concatenates three queries by using the OUTER UNION set operator and the CORR keyword. (CORR is the short version of CORRESPONDING.) Each query creates the same new column, GRADUATED, whose values reflect the origin of the row.

The OUTER UNION set operator concatenates tables. The CORR keyword matches and aligns in the output table the same-named columns that were extracted from the two input tables. The ORDER BY clause arranges the rows in the output table.

The ORDER BY clause interleaves the rows so that the rows in table GPAGRADS are arranged from highest GPA to lowest GPA. The DESC keyword arranges the values of GPA in descending order. For identical values of GPA, the ORDER BY clause arranges the rows arranged alphabetically by the student's last name (STUDENT).

Note that the keyword DESC *follows* the column name that is to be arranged in descending order. In BY statements, the keyword DESCENDING *precedes* the variable name that is to be arranged in descending order.

The only difference between this PROC SQL step and the PROC SQL step in Related Technique 1 of Example 2.1 is the addition of the ORDER BY clause. For details about all other statements in the step, see that example.

Repeat the SELECT clauses from Related Technique 1.

```
proc sql;
  create table gpagrads as
    select *,
          'Spring' as graduated length=6
              label='Semester Graduated'
        from springgrads
      outer union corr
    select *,
          'Summer' as graduated length=6
              label='Semester Graduated'
        from summergrads
      outer union corr
    select *,
          'Fall' as graduated length=6
              label='Semester Graduated'
        from fallgrads
    order by gpa desc, student;
```

Arrange the rows in table GPAGRADS from highest GPA to lowest GPA and within identical GPAs, arrange the rows alphabetically by the student's last name.

```
quit;
```

Example 2.3   Appending One Data Set to the End of Another Data Set

Goal

Add the observations from one data set to the end of another data set.

Example Features

Featured Step	PROC APPEND
Featured Step Options and Statements	FORCE option
Related Technique 1	PROC DATASETS, APPEND statement with FORCE option
A Closer Look	Determining When to Use PROC APPEND
	Using PROC APPEND When a Variable Exists in Only One of the Data Sets

Input Data Sets

Data set YTDPRICES contains 103 observations that record daily closing mutual fund prices. The first ten and the last five observations in YTDPRICES are shown.

Data set WEEK22 contains four observations that record daily closing mutual fund prices for the twenty-second week in June 2010.

```
            YTDPRICES (first 10 observations)

       Obs      tradedate       price    boardmtg
        1      01/04/2010      $80.29
        2      01/05/2010      $85.36
        3      01/06/2010      $81.43
        4      01/07/2010      $79.51
        5      01/08/2010      $83.58
        6      01/11/2010      $79.80
        7      01/12/2010      $80.87        X
        8      01/13/2010      $78.95
        9      01/14/2010      $84.02
       10      01/15/2010      $85.09
                  . . .

       99      05/24/2010      $90.84
      100      05/25/2010      $90.93
      101      05/26/2010      $94.02
      102      05/27/2010      $94.12
      103      05/28/2010      $93.21


                      WEEK22

       Obs      tradedate       price    week
        1      06/01/2010      $95.59      22
        2      06/02/2010      $89.68      22
        3      06/03/2010      $93.78      22
        4      06/04/2010      $91.87      22
```

Resulting Data Set
Output 2.3
YTDPRICES Data Set (last nine observations)

```
    Example 2.3 YTDPRICES Data Set (last 9 observations) Created with PROC APPEND

              Obs       tradedate       price    boardmtg

               99      05/24/2010      $90.84
              100      05/25/2010      $90.93
              101      05/26/2010      $94.02
              102      05/27/2010      $94.12
              103      05/28/2010      $93.21
              104      06/01/2010      $95.59
              105      06/02/2010      $89.68
              106      06/03/2010      $93.78
              107      06/04/2010      $91.87
```

Example Overview

This program uses PROC APPEND to append the observations from a smaller data set, WEEK22, to the end of a larger data set, YTDPRICES. Base data set YTDPRICES contains the closing prices for a mutual fund for each trading day from January 4, 2010, through May 28, 2010. Data set WEEK22 contains the closing prices for the twenty-second week of 2010, which are the trading days June 1, 2010, through June 4, 2010. May 31, 2010, is Memorial Day and not a trading day.

Variable BOARDMTG is present only in base data set YTDPRICES, and variable WEEK is present only in data set WEEK22. A value of "X" for BOARDMTG indicates that a board of directors meeting was held that day. In this example, board meetings were held the second Tuesday of each month.

At the conclusion of the program, YTDPRICES contains the same three variables that it had at the beginning of the program: TRADEDATE, PRICE, and BOARDMTG. PROC APPEND did not copy variable WEEK, which was found only in data set WEEK22, to data set YTDPRICES.

The FORCE option in the PROC APPEND statement does not add WEEK, but it does allow the step to complete. For more information, see the "A Closer Look" section "Using PROC APPEND When a Variable Exists in Only One of the Data Sets."

Program

Specify the data set to which you want to append observations.
Specify the data set whose observations you want to append to the data set named by the BASE= option.
Force the procedure to concatenate the DATA= data set to the BASE= data set even though the DATA= data set might contain a variable not found in the BASE= data set.

```
proc append base=ytdprices

           data=week22

           force;
run;
```

Related Technique

The APPEND statement in the DATASETS procedure and the FORCE option create the same data set as the PROC APPEND step in the main example.

Invoke PROC DATASETS and process data sets in the WORK library. Do not list the names of the members of the WORK library in the output window.
Specify the data set in the WORK library to which you want to append observations.
Specify the data set whose observations you want to append to the data set named by the BASE= option.
Force the procedure to concatenate the DATA= data set to the BASE= data set even though the DATA= data set contains a variable not found in the BASE= data set.

```
proc datasets library=work nolist;


   append base=ytdprices


   data=week22


   force;



run;
quit;
```

A Closer Look

Determining When to Use PROC APPEND

PROC APPEND is most advantageous to use when you want to add observations to the end of another data set and you do not need to add or delete any variables in the process.

Either the DATA step or PROC SQL can append data sets as demonstrated in Example 2.1. However, for efficiency reasons, you might want to choose PROC APPEND when the data set to which you want to append observations is much larger than the data set that contains the observations to be appended. PROC APPEND does not recopy the data set or table as a DATA step but PROC SQL does.

The following DATA step produces the YTDPRICES data set equivalent to that created by PROC APPEND in the main example. Note the DROP=WEEK data set option that is applied to data set WEEK22. This ensures that the output data set YTDPRICES is the same as the data set that is produced by PROC APPEND.

```
data ytdprices;
  set ytdprices week22(drop=week);
run;
```

The following PROC SQL step produces a table YTDPRICES equivalent to the data set that was created by PROC APPEND in the main example.

```
proc sql;
  create table ytdprices as
    select * from ytdprices
      outer union corr
    select tradedate, price from week22;
quit;
```

The CREATE TABLE statement generates a WARNING because the name of the table that is being created is the same as one of the table names in the SELECT statement. However, in this example it does execute correctly.

```
WARNING: This CREATE TABLE statement recursively references the
         target table. A consequence of this is a possible data
         integrity problem.
```

Using PROC APPEND When a Variable Exists in Only One of the Data Sets

By default, PROC APPEND does not execute when a variable found in the data set that is being appended does not exist in the base data set to which it is being appended. The PROC APPEND statement option FORCE overrides this default and allows such a data set to be appended to the base data set. However, the variable unique to the data set that is being appended is not copied to the resulting data set.

To execute, this example requires the FORCE option because variable WEEK is present in WEEK22 and it is not present in YTDPRICES. The program generates the following warning about this condition when option FORCE is in effect. The warning indicates that PROC APPEND did not add variable WEEK found in data set WEEK22 to base data set YTDPRICES.

```
WARNING: Variable week was not found on BASE file. The variable
         will not be added to the BASE file.
NOTE: FORCE is specified, so dropping/truncating will occur.
```

Conversely, if a variable exists in the base data set, but not in the data set that is being appended, you do not need to add the FORCE option to the PROC APPEND statement for it to execute. In this situation, PROC APPEND assigns missing values to the variable for the observations added from the data set that is being appended. The procedure generates a warning when this occurs. In this example, missing values are assigned to BOARDMTG for the four observations that were contributed from WEEK22 because BOARDMTG is not in WEEK22.

```
WARNING: Variable boardmtg was not found on DATA file.
```

Example 2.4   Selecting Unique Rows When Concatenating Tables

Goal

Select the unique rows among two or more tables based on the value of a specific column.

Example Features

Featured Step	PROC SQL
Featured Step Options and Statements	UNION set operator
Related Technique	DATA step PROC SORT, NODUPKEY option

Input Tables

Tables MARCHRUNNERS, APRILRUNNERS, and MAYRUNNERS contain the names and running times for the runners in the month that is specified in the table name.

The three input tables are also used in Examples 2.5 and 2.6.

MARCHRUNNERS

Obs	runner	racetime
1	Sanchez, SO	35:49.4
2	Flores, RX	38:32.8
3	Martinez, KF	36:12.3
4	Hayes, MU	35:24.7
5	Carter, RT	39:38.1
6	Rogers, LX	40:22.1
7	Clark, SQ	40:05.8
8	Taylor, TP	38:30.2
9	Smith, JD	37:03.5
10	Green, TF	37:50.0
11	Brown, GL	35:59.2
12	Lee, AO	39:36.4
13	Jones, LW	37:38.3
14	Smith, KB	38:10.3

APRILRUNNERS

Obs	runner	racetime
1	Martinez, KF	37:55.1
2	Rogers, LX	37:21.7
3	Smith, JD	38:32.7
4	Lee, AO	37:18.8
5	Jones, LW	35:04.1
6	Patterson, BB	38:26.1
7	Smith, KB	37:27.1
8	Alexander, SW	38:55.0
9	Young, SX	37:14.8

MAYRUNNERS

Obs	runner	racetime
1	Lee, AO	35:36.0
2	Williams, JO	40:26.7
3	Martin, JF	39:12.4
4	Jones, LW	36:37.6
5	Young, MX	39:17.6
6	Brown, NV	35:37.6
7	Patterson, BB	36:09.8
8	Johnson, AY	37:37.9
9	Cox, SR	37:16.6
10	Smith, KB	40:12.7
11	Martin, MG	35:37.9
12	Johnson, GR	38:14.6
13	Alexander, SW	36:36.8
14	Martinez, WL	37:06.6
15	Miller, JN	36:40.3
16	Young, SX	37:15.4
17	Wilson, WU	38:53.1

Resulting Table
Output 2.4
SPRINGRUNNERS
Table

```
                    Example 2.4 SPRINGRUNNERS Table Created by PROC SQL

                              Obs     runner

                                1     Alexander, SW
                                2     Brown, GL
                                3     Brown, NV
                                4     Carter, RT
                                5     Clark, SQ
                                6     Cox, SR
                                7     Flores, RX
                                8     Green, TF
                                9     Hayes, MU
                               10     Johnson, AY
                               11     Johnson, GR
                               12     Jones, LW
                               13     Lee, AO
                               14     Martin, JF
                               15     Martin, MG
                               16     Martinez, KF
                               17     Martinez, WL
                               18     Miller, JN
                               19     Patterson, BB
                               20     Rogers, LX
                               21     Sanchez, SO
                               22     Smith, JD
                               23     Smith, KB
                               24     Taylor, TP
                               25     Williams, JO
                               26     Wilson, WU
                               27     Young, MX
                               28     Young, SX
```

Example Overview

The following PROC SQL step combines three tables vertically. The step performs three queries that each select the same column and it returns one row for each unique value of the column.

The UNION operator that connects the queries concatenates the rows that the three queries return. The process that PROC SQL follows is to combine the first two queries, and then combine that result with the third query.

A UNION operator that is used without the ALL keyword removes duplicate rows from the output table. PROC SQL determines uniqueness of a row by the values of the columns in the SELECT clauses.

The program combines tables MARCHRUNNERS, APRILRUNNERS, and MAYRUNNERS by column RUNNER. Each input table records the names and running times for the runners in the month that is specified in the table name.

The goal of the program is to find the names of all runners during the spring season from March to May. Some runners ran only once while others ran two or three times. Output table SPRINGRUNNERS should contain the names of all the runners with no duplicate rows for those running two or three times. There were 14 runners in March, 9 in April, and 17 in May. Output table SPRINGRUNNERS contains 28 rows.

PROC SQL determines uniqueness of rows by the columns in the SELECT clauses. For example, if you expanded the list of columns selected by coding SELECT * instead of SELECT RUNNER, PROC SQL would select all rows from each of the three input tables because none of the repeat runners had identical race times.

Even though the CREATE TABLE statement did not include the ORDER BY clause, the rows in the output table are arranged alphabetically by the runner's name. With the ALL keyword omitted, PROC SQL first concatenates all the rows that are returned by the three queries. Next, it sorts the rows by the column in common, and last, it removes duplicate rows. The result is that the output table is ordered by the runner's name.

Program

Create table SPRINGRUNNERS. Specify three queries. Select the same column from each of the three tables. Find the unique values of the column in the three queries by using the UNION set operator.

```
proc sql;
  create table springrunners as
    select runner from marchrunners
      union
    select runner from aprilrunners
      union
    select runner from mayrunners;
quit;
```

Related Technique

The following program creates a data set equivalent to the table that was produced in the main example with PROC SQL. A DATA step concatenates the three input data sets. Next, PROC SORT sorts the new data set by RUNNER. With the PROC SORT option NODUPKEY specified, PROC SORT saves unique occurrences of variable RUNNER in the output data set SPRINGRUNNERS.

Concatenate the three input data sets. Save only variable RUNNER in data set ALLENTRIES.

Sort data set ALLENTRIES and save the sorted observations in SPRINGRUNNERS.
Do not save duplicate values of RUNNER in SPRINGRUNNERS.
Sort the data set by RUNNER.

```
data allentries;
  set marchrunners aprilrunners mayrunners;
  keep runner;
run;
proc sort data=allentries out=springrunners


                nodupkey;

  by runner;
run;
```

Example 2.5   Selecting Rows in Common When Concatenating Tables

Goal

Select the rows common to all tables based on the value of a specific column.

Example Features

Featured Step	PROC SQL
Featured Step Options and Statements	INTERSECT set operator

Input Tables

Tables MARCHRUNNERS, APRILRUNNERS, and MAYRUNNERS contain the names and running times for the runners in the month that is specified in the table name.

The three input tables are also used in Examples 2.4 and 2.6.

MARCHRUNNERS

Obs	runner	racetime
1	Sanchez, SO	35:49.4
2	Flores, RX	38:32.8
3	Martinez, KF	36:12.3
4	Hayes, MU	35:24.7
5	Carter, RT	39:38.1
6	Rogers, LX	40:22.1
7	Clark, SQ	40:05.8
8	Taylor, TP	38:30.2
9	Smith, JD	37:03.5
10	Green, TF	37:50.0
11	Brown, GL	35:59.2
12	Lee, AO	39:36.4
13	Jones, LW	37:38.3
14	Smith, KB	38:10.3

APRILRUNNERS

Obs	runner	racetime
1	Martinez, KF	37:55.1
2	Rogers, LX	37:21.7
3	Smith, JD	38:32.7
4	Lee, AO	37:18.8
5	Jones, LW	35:04.1
6	Patterson, BB	38:26.1
7	Smith, KB	37:27.1
8	Alexander, SW	38:55.0
9	Young, SX	37:14.8

MAYRUNNERS

Obs	runner	racetime
1	Lee, AO	35:36.0
2	Williams, JO	40:26.7
3	Martin, JF	39:12.4
4	Jones, LW	36:37.6
5	Young, MX	39:17.6
6	Brown, NV	35:37.6
7	Patterson, BB	36:09.8
8	Johnson, AY	37:37.9
9	Cox, SR	37:16.6
10	Smith, KB	40:12.7
11	Martin, MG	35:37.9
12	Johnson, GR	38:14.6
13	Alexander, SW	36:36.8
14	Martinez, WL	37:06.6
15	Miller, JN	36:40.3
16	Young, SX	37:15.4
17	Wilson, WU	38:53.1

Resulting Table
Output 2.5
RAN3TIMES Table

```
                  Example 2.5 RAN3TIMES Table Created by PROC SQL

                          Obs       runner

                           1      Jones, LW
                           2      Lee, AO
                           3      Smith, KB
```

Example Overview

The following PROC SQL step combines three tables vertically. The step performs three queries that each select the same column and it returns one row for each column value found in all three queries.

The INTERSECT operator that connects the queries concatenates the rows that the three queries return. The process that PROC SQL follows is to combine the first two queries, and then combine that result with the third query.

The INTERSECT operator that is used without the ALL keyword removes duplicate rows from the output table. PROC SQL determines uniqueness of a row by the values of the columns in the SELECT clauses.

The following PROC SQL step combines tables MARCHRUNNERS, APRILRUNNERS, and MAYRUNNERS by column RUNNER. Each input table records the names and running times for the runners in the month that is specified in the table name.

The goal of the program is to find the names of runners who ran in each of the three months during the spring season from March to May. Some runners ran only once while others ran two or three times during the spring season. Output table RAN3TIMES should contain the names of runners who ran three times and have one row per runner. Three runners ran three times. The queries select only the RUNNER column.

PROC SQL determines commonality of rows by the columns in the SELECT clauses. For example, if you expanded the list of columns selected by coding SELECT * instead of SELECT RUNNER, PROC SQL would not select any rows for output because none of the three-time runners ran identical times in their three races.

Even though the CREATE TABLE statement did not include the ORDER BY clause, the rows in the output table are arranged alphabetically by the runner's name. With the ALL keyword omitted, PROC SQL first concatenates all the rows returned by the three queries. Next, it sorts the rows by the column in common, and last, it removes duplicate rows. The result is that the output table is ordered by the runner's name.

Program

Create table RAN3TIMES.
Specify three query results. Select one column from each of the three tables. Use the INTERSECT set operator to select the rows in common among the three queries according to the column that is specified on the three queries.

```
proc sql;
   create table ran3times as
      select runner from marchrunners
         intersect
      select runner from aprilrunners
         intersect
      select runner from mayrunners;
quit;
```

Example 2.6   Selecting Observations Unique to Each Data Set When Concatenating Data Sets

Goal

Select observations found in only one data set among a group of data sets based on the value of a specific variable. Concatenate the selected observations.

Example Features

Featured Step	PROC SORT
	DATA step
Featured Step Options and Statements	MERGE statement with IN= option (match-merge)
Related Technique	PROC SQL, OUTER UNION set operator, GROUP BY and HAVING clauses

Input Data Sets

Data sets MARCHRUNNERS, APRILRUNNERS, and MAYRUNNERS contain the names and running times for the runners in the month that is specified in the data set name.

The three input data sets are also used in Examples 2.4 and 2.5.

MARCHRUNNERS

Obs	runner	racetime
1	Sanchez, SO	35:49.4
2	Flores, RX	38:32.8
3	Martinez, KF	36:12.3
4	Hayes, MU	35:24.7
5	Carter, RT	39:38.1
6	Rogers, LX	40:22.1
7	Clark, SQ	40:05.8
8	Taylor, TP	38:30.2
9	Smith, JD	37:03.5
10	Green, TF	37:50.0
11	Brown, GL	35:59.2
12	Lee, AO	39:36.4
13	Jones, LW	37:38.3
14	Smith, KB	38:10.3

APRILRUNNERS

Obs	runner	racetime
1	Martinez, KF	37:55.1
2	Rogers, LX	37:21.7
3	Smith, JD	38:32.7
4	Lee, AO	37:18.8
5	Jones, LW	35:04.1
6	Patterson, BB	38:26.1
7	Smith, KB	37:27.1
8	Alexander, SW	38:55.0
9	Young, SX	37:14.8

MAYRUNNERS

Obs	runner	racetime
1	Lee, AO	35:36.0
2	Williams, JO	40:26.7
3	Martin, JF	39:12.4
4	Jones, LW	36:37.6
5	Young, MX	39:17.6
6	Brown, NV	35:37.6
7	Patterson, BB	36:09.8
8	Johnson, AY	37:37.9
9	Cox, SR	37:16.6
10	Smith, KB	40:12.7
11	Martin, MG	35:37.9
12	Johnson, GR	38:14.6
13	Alexander, SW	36:36.8
14	Martinez, WL	37:06.6
15	Miller, JN	36:40.3
16	Young, SX	37:15.4
17	Wilson, WU	38:53.1

Resulting Data Set
Output 2.6 **RANONCE**
Data Set

```
                Example 2.6 RANONCE Data Set Created by DATA Step

                        Obs     runner
                         1      Brown, GL
                         2      Brown, NV
                         3      Carter, RT
                         4      Clark, SQ
                         5      Cox, SR
                         6      Flores, RX
                         7      Green, TF
                         8      Hayes, MU
                         9      Johnson, AY
                        10      Johnson, GR
                        11      Martin, JF
                        12      Martin, MG
                        13      Martinez, WL
                        14      Miller, JN
                        15      Sanchez, SO
                        16      Taylor, TP
                        17      Williams, JO
                        18      Wilson, WU
                        19      Young, MX
```

Example Overview

The following program match-merges data sets horizontally by the values of a variable common to the data sets. The program starts by sorting the data sets by the common variable. A DATA step combines the data sets and outputs an observation if the current value of the common variable is found in only one of the data sets.

Although the program combines the data sets horizontally, the result is that observations from the data sets are concatenated. Chapter 3 focuses on combining data sets horizontally and match-merging them by values.

The goal of the program is to find the names of all runners who ran only once in each of the three months during the spring season from March to May. Some runners ran only once while others ran two or three times during the spring season. Output data set RANONCE should contain the names of runners who ran only once. The queries select only the RUNNER column.

The program starts by sorting the three input data sets by the variable that is used to match the observations. A DATA step match-merges the data sets by the values of this common variable.

The IN= data set option that is applied to each input data set names a temporary variable whose value indicates whether that input data set contributes data to the current observation. Its value is 1 if the data set contributes to the current observation; otherwise, it is 0. The IF statement tests whether the sum of the three IN= variables is equal to 1 and selects for output to RANONCE those observations with a sum of 1. A sum of 1 indicates that only one of the three input data sets contributed to the current observation.

Program

Sort the three input data sets by the variable that will determine the observations in common.

```
proc sort data=marchrunners;
  by runner;
run;
proc sort data=aprilrunners;
  by runner;
run;
proc sort data=mayrunners;
  by runner;
run;
```

Create data set RANONCE.

```
data ranonce;
```

Merge the three input data sets by the values of RUNNER. Add the IN= data set option to each input data set so that the data set origin of each observation is known.

```
merge marchrunners(in=inmar) aprilrunners(in=inapr)
      mayrunners(in=inmay);
  by runner;
```

Keep only variable RUNNER.
Sum the IN= variables. Execute a subsetting IF statement to save observations found in only one of the three data sets.

```
keep runner;
if inmar+inapr+inmay=1;
```

```
run;
```

Related Technique

The following PROC SQL step creates a table equivalent to the data set that was created in the main example. The step combines three tables vertically and selects the rows found in only one table based on the value of one column common to the tables. An inline view concatenates the three tables with the OUTER UNION operator and the CORR keyword. The outer query selects rows found in only one of the tables, and within that table, found only once.

The CORR keyword overlays same-named columns so that the values of the common column are aligned and values from all contributing tables are processed. Without the CORR keyword and using the CREATE TABLE clause to create a table, only the values from the first table in the inline view are returned.

The GROUP BY clause in the outer query groups the rows that are returned by the inline view by the values of the common variable. The COUNT function on the HAVING clause tallies the number of times each value of the common column is found in the rows that are returned by the inline view. The clause selects the rows where the number of times is one.

PROC SQL determines commonality of rows by the results of the GROUP BY and HAVING clauses and the COUNT function. For example, if you expanded the list of columns selected by coding SELECT * instead of SELECT RUNNER for all of the queries, PROC SQL would select all rows from all three tables because none of the repeat runners ran identical times.

```
proc sql;
  create table ranonce as
    select runner from

      (select runner from marchrunners
          outer union corr
       select runner from aprilrunners
          outer union corr
       select runner from mayrunners)

      group by runner

      having count(*)=1;

quit;
```

Create table RANONCE.
Select one column from the inline view.

Select the same column and concatenate all rows from the three tables. Use the CORR keyword to align the RUNNER column from the three tables.
Group the rows returned by the inline view by the values of RUNNER.
Tally the number of rows for each value of RUNNER. Output the rows where the value of RUNNER is found only once.

CHAPTER 3

Combining Data Sets Horizontally: Match-Merging Data Sets by Value

This chapter presents ways to combine your data sets horizontally by aligning observations side-by-side or by overlaying observations. The examples match observations from the input data sets either by the values of variables in common or by programmatically aligning observations when the data sets do not have variables in common.

DATA steps, PROC SQL, and hash objects in DATA steps can match data sets and tables, and they can combine two or more data sets at a time.

Typically when combining data sets with the DATA step, these data sets are either sorted or indexed by the values of the matching variables. You do not have to sort or index your tables before combining them with PROC SQL, but you might want to so that the step executes more efficiently.

When developing your code to combine data sets horizontally, you need to understand the relationships among your input data sets. Relationships among multiple sources of input data exist when each source contains common data, either at the physical or logical level. For example, employee data and department data could be related through an employee ID variable that shares common values. Another data set could contain numeric sequence numbers whose values logically relate it to a separate data set by observation number.

Once data relationships exist, they fall into one of four categories:

❏ one-to-one

❏ one-to-many

❏ many-to-one

❏ many-to-many

All related data fall into one of these categories. You must be able to identify the existing relationships in your data because this knowledge is essential to understanding how to process your input data to produce desired results.

For an illustration of these relationships, see Chapter 1.

You can also sometimes choose to match your data sets by processing them either sequentially or directly. Programming statements in a DATA step enable you to specify an access method. PROC SQL decides for you the most efficient method to use on your code and data sets. This chapter includes examples of both access methods.

❏ *Sequential access* means that SAS accesses the observations in your data set in the order in which they appear in the physical file. This is achieved with the SET, MERGE, MODIFY, and UPDATE statements in the DATA step.

❏ *Direct access* means that SAS goes straight to an observation in a SAS data set without processing each observation that precedes it. This is achieved with the POINT= option in either the SET or MODIFY statement.

Computer resources such as CPU time, I/O, and disk storage can be conserved based on the access method that you choose.

For more information about sequential access and direct access, see Chapter 1.

Example 3.1   Merging Data Sets by a Common Variable

Goal

Match and merge observations from two data sets based on a variable common to both. To make the new data set more informative, create a new variable whose values indicate the data set origin of each observation, and replace the missing values that result from the merge operation with meaningful values.

Example Features

Featured Step	DATA step
Featured Step Options and Statements	Match-merge with MERGE and BY statements IN= data set option
Related Technique	PROC SQL, FULL JOIN, COALESCE function

Input Data Sets

Data set TASKS contains task assignments for five employees. Data set HOURS contains the available hours for five employees. Some employees have data in only one of the two data sets while others have data in both. Both TASKS and HOURS are sorted by ID.

```
                        TASKS                                         HOURS
                                                                             available_
    Obs    id      name      dept     task          Obs    id      name        hours
     1    DDQ02   Diana      B45    Document          1    DDQ02   Diana         40
     2    FXB03   Fred       B45    Survey            2    FXB03   Fred          35
     3    MRF08   Monique    A12    Document          3    MRF08   Monique       37
     4    MSG01   Miguel     A12    Document          4    SWL14   Steve          0
     5    VTN18   Vien       D03    Survey            5    VTN18   Vien          42
```

Resulting Data Set
Output 3.1
TASK_STATUS Data Set

```
                         Example 3.1 TASK_STATUS Data Set

                                                        available_
        Obs    origin    id      name      dept    task      hours

         1     both     DDQ02   Diana      B45    Document      40
         2     both     FXB03   Fred       B45    Survey        35
         3     both     MRF08   Monique    A12    Document      37
         4     tasks    MSG01   Miguel     A12    Document       0
         5     hours    SWL14   Steve      NEW    NONE           0
         6     both     VTN18   Vien       D03    Survey        42
```

Example Overview

This program demonstrates simple match-merging of two data sets by the values of one variable in common. The two data sets are sorted by the common variable prior to the match-merge DATA step.

Data set TASKS contains task assignments for five employees. Data set HOURS contains available hours for five employees. The two data sets have two variables in common: ID and NAME. The DATA step uses the values of variable ID to match the two data sets by value.

The program has three objectives:

❑ create a single data set that matches each individual with the correct departmental and project information based on corresponding ID values

❑ add a new variable that indicates the origin of that information (i.e., data set TASKS or HOURS or both data sets)

❑ add meaningful information where values are missing

The MERGE and BY statements in the DATA step match and merge data sets TASKS and HOURS by variable ID to create output data set TASK_STATUS. The IN= data set option is applied to both input data sets in the MERGE statement so that the data set origin of the observation can be determined.

The first group of IF-THEN/ELSE statements tests the values of temporary variables INTASKS and INHOURS that are defined by the IN= data set options to determine the origin of the observation and assign a value to ORIGIN.

The second group of IF-THEN/ELSE statements tests if the values of variables that are unique to one data set are missing so that meaningful values can replace the missing values that result from the merge operation.

Program

Create data set TASK_STATUS.

Merge the observations. Add the IN= data set option to both data sets so that the data set origin of each observation can be determined.
Match the observations by the values of ID.
Assign values to ORIGIN based on the data set origin of the observation that is currently being processed.
Assign 'both' to ORIGIN when the employee has data in both data sets.
Assign 'tasks' to ORIGIN when the employee has data only in TASKS.
Assign 'hours' to ORIGIN when the employee has data only in HOURS.
Assign values to DEPT and TASK when either is missing, which occurs when an observation in HOURS does not have a match in TASKS.
Assign a value to AVAILABLE_HOURS when it is missing, which occurs when an observation in TASKS does not have a match in HOURS.

```
data task_status;
  length origin $ 5;
  merge tasks(in=intasks) hours(in=inhours);



  by id;




  if intasks and inhours then origin='both';

  else if intasks then origin='tasks';

  else if inhours then origin='hours';

  if missing(dept) then dept='NEW';

  if missing(task) then task='NONE';


  if missing(available_hours) then available_hours=0;



run;
```

Related Technique

The following PROC SQL step creates a table equivalent to the data set that was created by the DATA step in the main example. A full join by ID combines the two tables.

A CASE expression defines column ORIGIN. The WHEN clauses test whether an ID value is missing in either TASKS or HOURS. When a row from each table is joined by ID, neither value of ID is missing. When an ID value in one table is not found in the other, the output row contains data from only the one table.

The COALESCE function returns the first nonmissing value in the list of arguments that is supplied to it. The arguments to COALESCE can be any combination of column names, text values, or expressions. The last three calls to COALESCE replace missing values with text in the DEPT, TASK, and AVAILABLE_HOURS columns. Replacement with text occurs when a row is found in only one table.

Create table TASK_STATUS.
Define column ORIGIN with a CASE expression.
Assign 'both' to ORIGIN when two rows are joined by an ID.
Assign 'hours' to ORIGIN when an ID value is found only in HOURS, which occurs when TASKS does not contain a matching row.
Assign 'tasks' to ORIGIN when an ID value is found only in TASKS, which occurs when HOURS does not contain a matching row.
Complete the CASE expression by assigning a value to ORIGIN when a row has missing values in both TASKS and HOURS, which does not occur in this example.
Terminate the case expression. Name the column and assign it a length.
Return the first nonmissing value of the pair of columns within parentheses.
Assign a value if the first argument to the COALESCE function is missing.

Select all matching and nonmatching rows by performing a full join of the two tables by ID.

```
proc sql;
  create table task_status as
    select case

            when tasks.id is not missing and
                 hours.ids is not missing then 'both'
            when hours.id is not missing then 'hours'


            when tasks.id is not missing then 'tasks'



            else '?????'




            end as origin length=5,

            coalesce(tasks.id,hours.id) as id,
            coalesce(tasks.name,hours.name) as name,
            coalesce(tasks.task,'NONE') as task,
            coalesce(tasks.dept,'NEW') as dept,
            coalesce(hours.available_hours,0)as
                            available_hours
      from tasks full join hours on tasks.id=hours.id;

quit;
```

Example 3.2   Merging Observations from Multiple Data Sets by a Common Variable

Goal

Combine observations from multiple data sets based on a variable common to each contributing data set.

Example Features

Featured Step	DATA step
Featured Step Options and Statements	Match-merge with MERGE and BY statement
Related Technique	PROC SQL, multiway join with WHERE clause
A Closer Look	Understanding How the DATA Step Processes a Match-Merge

Input Data Sets

Data set AGENTS contains the names and IDs of five real estate agents.
Data set PROPERTIES contains a list of properties that have sold. The agent responsible for the sale is identified by the ID variable.
Data set RATES contains the commission rates for the five agents with the agent identified by the ID variable.

The variable in common is ID. The data sets must be sorted or indexed by the values of ID. Each value of ID occurs only once in data sets AGENTS and RATES, but it might occur multiple times in PROPERTIES. All five ID values are present in the three data sets.

```
                AGENTS                        PROPERTIES                    RATES

       Obs    id     lname        Obs    id      salesprice        Obs    id     rate
        1     991    Wong          1     991    $345,000.00         1     991    0.040
        2     5144   Johnson       2     5144    $80,000.00         2     5144   0.035
        3     8170   Cross         3     5144   $644,000.00         3     8170   0.080
        4     8173   Chan          4     8170    $72,000.00         4     8173   0.060
        5     9381   Ames          5     8170    $64,000.00         5     9381   0.050
                                   6     8170   $426,500.00
                                   7     8173   $198,400.00
                                   8     9381   $278,000.00
```

Resulting Data Set
Output 3.2
PAYOUTS Data Set

```
                 Example 3.2 PAYOUTS Data Set Created with DATA Step

        Obs     id     lname      salesprice      rate      commission

         1      991    Wong      $345,000.00     0.040      $13,800.00
         2      5144   Johnson    $80,000.00     0.035       $2,800.00
         3      5144   Johnson   $644,000.00     0.035      $22,540.00
         4      8170   Cross      $72,000.00     0.080       $5,760.00
         5      8170   Cross      $64,000.00     0.080       $5,120.00
         6      8170   Cross     $426,500.00     0.080      $34,120.00
         7      8173   Chan      $198,400.00     0.060      $11,904.00
         8      9381   Ames      $278,000.00     0.050      $13,900.00
```

Example Overview

The following DATA step demonstrates how to match-merge more than two data sets. The previous examples match-merged only two data sets or tables at a time.

The three input data sets contain information about real estate agents in data set AGENTS, properties that the agents have sold in data set PROPERTIES, and the agents' commission rates in RATES. The variable that links the three data sets is ID.

The objective of this program is to create a new data set that matches each individual with the correct sale and rate based on corresponding ID values. The DATA step match-merges the data sets AGENTS, PROPERTIES, and RATES to create a single data set, PAYOUTS, which contains the variables from the three data sets plus a new variable, COMMISSION. The values for COMMISSION are computed by multiplying SALESPRICE from data set PROPERTIES by RATE from data set RATES.

Data set PROPERTIES contains multiple occurrences of some values of ID, while AGENTS and RATES contain only one occurrence of each ID value. Because values of LNAME and RATE (which are read from AGENTS and RATES) are automatically retained across the BY group, multiple observations with the same value for ID found in PROPERTIES contain the correct values for LNAME and RATE.

Program

Create PAYOUTS.
Combine observations from the three data sets based on matching the values of ID.
Compute a new variable by using information merged from two of the input data sets.

```
data payouts;
  merge agents sales rates;
  by id;

  commission=rate*salesprice;
  format commission salesprice dollar12.2;

run;
```

Related Technique

This PROC SQL step creates a table with contents identical to the data set PAYOUTS that was created in the main example. It performs a multiway join with a WHERE clause to link the three tables by column ID. In processing a multiway join, PROC SQL joins two tables at a time and performs the joins in the most efficient order. The order it chooses minimizes the size of the Cartesian product.

Create table PAYOUTS.
Specify the columns to select from the three tables.
Create a new column by using columns from different tables.
List the three tables to join.
Specify how to link the three tables.

```
proc sql;
  create table payouts as
    select agents.id,lname,
           salesprice format=dollar12.2, rate,
           salesprice*rate as commission
                                 format=dollar12.2
             from agents, properties, rates
           where agents.id=properties.id and
                 properties.id=rates.id;
quit;
```

A Closer Look

Understanding How the DATA Step Processes a Match-Merge

This section shows how the DATA step in the main example creates the Program Data Vector (PDV) and match-merges the three input data sets.

During the compilation phase, SAS reads the descriptor portions of the input data sets and creates the Program Data Vector (PDV). Also, SAS determines the BY groups in each input data set for the variables that are listed in the BY statement. The five unique ID values define five BY groups.

AGENTS	
id	lname
991	Wong
5144	Johnson
8170	Cross
8173	Chan
9381	Ames

PROPERTIES	
id	salesprice
991	345000
5144	80000
5144	644000
8170	72000
8170	64000
8170	426500
8173	198400
9381	278000

RATES	
id	rate
991	0.040
5144	0.035
8170	0.080
8173	0.060
9381	0.050

Program Data Vector

id	lname	salesprice	rate	commission

SAS looks at the first BY group in each input data set to determine whether the BY values match. If so, SAS reads the first observation of that BY group from the first input data set that has that BY value and records the values in the PDV. In this example, all three data sets have the same BY value of ID=991.

AGENTS	
id	lname
991	Wong
5144	Johnson
8170	Cross
8173	Chan
9381	Ames

PROPERTIES	
id	salesprice
991	345000
5144	80000
5144	644000
8170	72000
8170	64000
8170	426500
8173	198400
9381	278000

RATES	
id	rate
991	0.040
5144	0.035
8170	0.080
8173	0.060
9381	0.050

Program Data Vector

id	lname	salesprice	rate	commission
991	Wong			

Because the BY values match in all three data sets, SAS reads the first observation of the same BY group from the second and third input data sets. It moves the variable values for SALESPRICE and RATE from PROPERTIES and RATES to the PDV, computes COMMISSION, and outputs the observation to data set PAYOUTS.

Program Data Vector

id	lname	salesprice	rate	commission
991	Wong	345000	0.040	13800

The first iteration is complete. SAS returns to the top of the DATA step to begin the second iteration and determines that there are no more observations in any of the three data sets with an ID=991. It clears the PDV and examines the next BY group.

Program Data Vector

ID	LNAME	SALESPRICE	RATE	COMMISSION

The next BY group is ID=5144, and there are observations in all three data sets for this BY value. The variable values are moved into the PDV, COMMISSION is computed, and the observation is written to PAYOUTS.

AGENTS	
id	lname
991	Wong
5144	Johnson
8170	Cross
8173	Chan
9381	Ames

PROPERTIES	
id	salesprice
991	345000
5144	80000
5144	644000
8170	72000
8170	64000
8170	426500
8173	198400
9381	278000

RATES	
id	rate
991	0.040
5144	0.035
8170	0.080
8173	0.060
9381	0.050

Program Data Vector

id	lname	salesprice	rate	commission
5144	Johnson	80000	0.035	2800

SAS returns to the top of the DATA step to begin the third iteration. Data sets AGENTS and RATES do not have any more observations for ID=5144, the current BY value. There is a second observation for ID=5144 in PROPERTIES. The variable values for ID=5144 that are contributed from AGENTS and RATES remain in the PDV while the new value for SALESPRICE is moved into the PDV. The DATA step computes COMMISSION by using the new value for SALESPRICE and outputs the observation to PAYOUTS.

AGENTS	
id	lname
991	Wong
5144	Johnson
8170	Cross
8173	Chan
9381	Ames

PROPERTIES	
id	salesprice
991	345000
5144	80000
5144	644000
8170	72000
8170	64000
8170	426500
8173	198400
9381	278000

RATES	
id	rate
991	0.040
5144	0.035
8170	0.080
8173	0.060
9381	0.050

Program Data Vector

ID	LNAME	SALESPRICE	RATE	COMMISSION
5144	Johnson		0.035	

Program Data Vector

ID	LNAME	SALESPRICE	RATE	COMMISSION
5144	Johnson	644000	0.035	

Program Data Vector

ID	LNAME	SALESPRICE	RATE	COMMISSION
5144	Johnson	644000	0.035	22540

SAS continues to match-merge observations until all observations from the three input data sets have been read and written to the output data set.

The five BY values all have matches in the three data sets. If a BY value does not match, SAS will read the input data set with the lowest BY value. The PDV and the output data set will contain missing values for variables that are unique to the other data set.

Example 3.3   Combining Observations When Variable Values Do Not Match Exactly

Goal

Perform a *fuzzy merge* by merging observations from two data sets based on data values that do not match exactly.

Example Features

Featured Step	PROC SQL
Featured Step Options and Statements	SELECT statement with FULL JOIN and ON clause

Input Tables

Table BATCH_ONE contains times and sample numbers for seven samples. Table BATCH_TWO contains times and sample numbers for nine samples.

```
            BATCH_ONE                                      BATCH_TWO

 Obs          samptime    sample      Obs          samptime    sample
  1    23NOV2009:09:01:00    100        1    23NOV2009:09:00:00    200
  2    23NOV2009:10:03:00    101        2    23NOV2009:09:59:00    201
  3    23NOV2009:10:58:00    102        3    23NOV2009:11:04:00    202
  4    23NOV2009:11:59:00    103        4    23NOV2009:12:02:00    203
  5    23NOV2009:13:00:00    104        5    23NOV2009:14:01:00    204
  6    23NOV2009:14:02:00    105        6    23NOV2009:14:59:00    205
  7    23NOV2009:16:00:00    106        7    23NOV2009:15:59:00    206
                                        8    23NOV2008:16:59:00    207
                                        9    23NOV2008:18:00:00    208
```

Resulting Table
Output 3.3
MATCH_APPROX
Table

```
            Example 3.3 MATCH_APPROX Table Created with PROC SQL

   Obs         samptime1 sample1          samptime2 sample2

    1    23NOV2009:09:01:00    100    23NOV2009:09:00:00    200
    2    23NOV2009:10:03:00    101    23NOV2009:09:59:00    201
    3    23NOV2009:11:59:00    103    23NOV2009:12:02:00    203
    4    23NOV2009:14:02:00    105    23NOV2009:14:01:00    204
    5    23NOV2009:16:00:00    106    23NOV2009:15:59:00    206
    6                           .     23NOV2009:11:04:00    202
    7                           .     23NOV2009:14:59:00    205
    8                           .     23NOV2009:16:59:00    207
    9                           .     23NOV2009:18:00:00    208
   10    23NOV2009:10:58:00    102                           .
   11    23NOV2009:13:00:00    104                           .
```

Example Overview

This example joins two tables with PROC SQL by using a full join. It matches rows where the difference in the values of the matching column is within an acceptable range.

Table BATCH_ONE contains times and sample numbers for seven samples. Table BATCH_TWO contains times and sample numbers for nine samples. The goal is to match rows where the difference in time between the two values of SAMPTIME is less than five minutes.

The full join results in an internal table that matches every row in BATCH_ONE with every row in BATCH_TWO. The ON clause subsets the internal table by those rows where there is less than a five-minute time difference.

This join is a full outer join, which returns rows that satisfy the condition in the ON clause. In addition, a full outer join returns all of the rows from each table that do not match a row from the other table, based on the condition in the ON clause. For example, samples 202, 205, 207, and 208 in table BATCH_TWO do not have a match within five minutes in BATCH_ONE and are included in output table MATCH_APPROX. The columns that originate from BATCH_ONE for these rows have missing values. Similarly, samples 102 and 104 in BATCH_ONE do not have a match in BATCH_TWO. The columns that originate from BATCH_TWO for these rows have missing values.

Because the columns have the same names in both input tables, they are referenced with the table alias in the SELECT and ON clauses. The SELECT clause assigns the columns new names. This ensures that the output table has values from both sources and PROC SQL does not overlay any values.

Program

Create table MATCH_APPROX.
Select all columns from both input tables. Rename the columns so that values are not overwritten when there is a match between BATCH_ONE and BATCH_TWO.
Perform a full join. Assign an alias to each table.

Match rows where the absolute difference in SAMPTIME from the two tables is less than five minutes (300 seconds).

```
proc sql;
  create table match_approx as
    select one.samptime as samptime1,
           one.sample as sample1,
           two.samptime as samptime2,
           two.sample as sample2

    from batch_one one
            full join
         batch_two two
    on abs(one.samptime-two.samptime)<=300;


quit;
```

Example 3.4   Combining Observations by the Formatted Value of a Variable

Goal

Perform a *fuzzy merge* by merging observations from two data sets based on the formatted version of the matching variable rather than the stored value.

Example Features

Featured Step	DATA step
Featured Step Options and Statements	BY statement with GROUPFORMAT option
Related Technique	PROC SQL, left join, ON clause with functions

Input Data Sets

Data set PRIZES contains a list of four prizes and the last day of the month in which they are awarded. Data set PARTICIPANTS contains a list of participants who will receive a prize dependent on a completion date.

```
                              PRIZES                                      PARTICIPANTS

    Obs   completed  prize                 Obs   name                  completed
     1    01/31/2009 Restaurant Certificate  1   Moore, Kathryn        12/27/2008
     2    02/28/2009 Audio Player            2   Jackson, Barbara       01/15/2009
     3    03/31/2009 Theater Tickets         3   Brown, Shannon         03/23/2009
     4    04/30/2009 Baseball Tickets        4   Williams, Debra        03/26/2009
                                             5   Harris, Joseph         02/01/2009
                                             6   Brown, Patricia        01/08/2009
                                             7   Johnson, Christopher   02/17/2009
                                             8   Rodriguez, Shawn       03/31/2009
                                             9   Gonzalez, Patrick      01/14/2009
                                            10   Wright, Nicholas       03/02/2009
                                            11   Jones, Robert          02/28/2009
                                            12   Miller, Christopher    03/25/2009
```

Resulting Data Set
Output 3.4
PARTIC_PRIZES
Data Set

```
               Example 3.4 PARTIC_PRIZES Data Set Created with DATA Step

     Obs    completed   prize                    name

      1     DEC2008     (unknown)                Moore, Kathryn
      2     JAN2009     Restaurant Certificate   Brown, Patricia
      3     JAN2009     Restaurant Certificate   Gonzalez, Patrick
      4     JAN2009     Restaurant Certificate   Jackson, Barbara
      5     FEB2009     Audio Player             Harris, Joseph
      6     FEB2009     Audio Player             Johnson, Christopher
      7     FEB2009     Audio Player             Jones, Robert
      8     MAR2009     Theater Tickets          Wright, Nicholas
      9     MAR2009     Theater Tickets          Brown, Shannon
     10     MAR2009     Theater Tickets          Miller, Christopher
     11     MAR2009     Theater Tickets          Williams, Debra
     12     MAR2009     Theater Tickets          Rodriguez, Shawn
```

Example Overview

This example demonstrates how you can match-merge two data sets based on the formatted values of a variable instead of the exact values of the variable.

The DATA step combines two data sets, PRIZES and PARTICIPANTS, by the formatted values of one variable, COMPLETED. The goal is to find the prize to be awarded to a participant based on the month and year in which the participant finished a project. Variable COMPLETED in data set PRIZES is the last day of the month in which a specific prize is awarded. The actual date of completion for a participant is stored in variable COMPLETED in data set PARTICIPANTS.

Only two of the values of COMPLETED in PARTICIPANTS are exactly equal to values of COMPLETED in PRIZES. The values need to be grouped to make matches between the two data sets. A FORMAT statement for COMPLETED formats its values with the MONYY format, which groups the date values by month and year.

The BY statement in the DATA step includes the GROUPFORMAT option. This option causes the matching between the two data sets to be done by the formatted values of the BY variable COMPLETED rather than its internal value. If you omit the GROUPFORMAT option, only two observations in PARTICIPANTS match to an observation in PRIZES. These two observations are the ones with dates of completion on the last day of a month: Robert Jones on February 28, 2009, and Shawn Rodriguez on March 31, 2009.

Note that GROUPFORMAT can be specified anywhere in the BY statement and will apply to all BY variables.

The DATA step creates two temporary variables, INZ and INP, with the IN= data set options on data sets PRIZES and PARTICIPANTS, respectively. IF-THEN statements test the values of INZ and INP to determine how to handle observations found in only one data set.

Program

Sort both data sets by the matching variable.

```
proc sort data=prizes;
  by completed;
run;
proc sort data=participants;
  by completed;
run;
```

Create data set PARTIC_PRIZES. Combine the data sets. Add the IN= data set option to each input data set so that the data set origin of the current observation can be determined.

```
data partic_prizes;
  merge prizes(in=inz) participants(in=inp);
```

Specify the matching variable. Specify with GROUPFORMAT that matches be made by the formatted values of COMPLETED and not its internal values.

```
  by completed groupformat;
```

Group the values of COMPLETED by month and year.

```
  format completed monyy7.;
```

Keep all the observations that are found in PARTICIPANTS whether or not they have a match in PRIZES.

```
  if inp;
```

Assign a value to variable PRIZE when a participant's completion date does not have a match in PRIZES.

```
  if not inz then prize='(unknown)';
```

```
run;
```

Related Technique

The related technique combines the two tables, PRIZES and PARTICIPANTS, with a PROC SQL left join. It creates a table equivalent to the data set in the main example.

The ON clause matches the rows by the formatted values of COMPLETED. As in the DATA step, the PROC SQL step uses format MONYY to group the values.

```
proc sql;
```

Create table PARTIC_PRIZES. Specify the columns to include in PARTIC_PRIZES. Specify the table on the left side of the join as the one from which to return the values of COMPLETED.

```
  create table partic_prizes as
    select p.completed format=monyy7., name,
```

Return the first nonmissing value in the pair of arguments. For rows in PARTICIPANTS without a match in PRIZES, assign the value "(unknown)" to column PRIZE.
Keep all rows in PARTICIPANTS by performing a left join of the two tables.

Match the rows by the formatted values of COMPLETED.
Order the rows in the output table by COMPLETED.

```
      coalesce(prize,'(unknown)') as Prize



   from participants p
      left join
   prizes z
      on put(p.completed,monyy7.)=
                     put(z.completed,monyy7.)

   order by p.completed;

quit;
```

Example 3.5   Combining Multiple Tables When the Matching Column Has Different Attributes

Goal

Combine multiple tables where the matching column has different attributes such as length and can be stored as either numeric or character.

Example Features

Featured Step	PROC SQL
Featured Step Options and Statements	FULL OUTER JOIN COALESCE function Subquery
Related Technique	PROC SORT and DATA step match-merge

Input Tables

Table WEBCLASSES contains information about six classes. Table CLASS_UPDATES contains updates on some of the classes in WEBCLASSES, and it includes new classes. Table WEBCLASS_SCHEDULE contains scheduling information for classes and their section in fall 2009.

Column CLASSID is in common among the three tables. However, it is defined as character with different lengths in tables WEBCLASSES and CLASS_UPDATES, and it is defined as numeric in WEBCLASS_SCHEDULE.

```
                       WEBCLASSES

Obs  classid  maxstudents  class_title
 1     101         25       Web Design 1
 2     201         15       Web Design 2
 3     301         15       Web Design 3
 4     210         35       Increasing Website Traffic
 5     203         20       Web Graphics 1
 6     303         15       Web Graphics 2


                      CLASS_UPDATES

Obs  classid  maxstudents  class_title
 1     101         30       Basic Web Design
 2     201         20       Intermediate Web Design
 3     301         15       Advanced Web Design
 4     220         15       Internet Security
 5     010         40       Keyboarding


                    WEBCLASS_SCHEDULE

Obs  classid  sessionid    startdate
 1     101        A        09/03/2009
 2     101        B        10/05/2009
 3     201        A        10/05/2009
 4     210        A        09/15/2009
 5     220        A        09/21/2009
 6     10         A        09/02/2009
 7     10         B        10/07/2009
 8     10         C        10/27/2009
```

Resulting Table
Output 3.5
ALLWEBCLASSES Table

```
          Example 3.5 ALLWEBCLASSES Table Created with PROC SQL

   Obs classid sessionid   startdate class_title                maxstudents

     1   010       A       09/02/2009 Keyboarding                    40
     2   010       B       10/07/2009 Keyboarding                    40
     3   010       C       10/27/2009 Keyboarding                    40
     4   101       A       09/03/2009 Basic Web Design               30
     5   101       B       10/05/2009 Basic Web Design               30
     6   201       A       10/05/2009 Intermediate Web Design        20
     7   203      none          .     Web Graphics 1                 20
     8   210       A       09/15/2009 Increasing Website Traffic     35
     9   220       A       09/21/2009 Internet Security              15
    10   301      none          .     Advanced Web Design            15
    11   303      none          .     Web Graphics 2                 15
```

Example Overview

This example shows you how to combine several tables where the matching column can have different attributes.

The goal in combining all three tables is to update information in WEBCLASSES with information from CLASS_UPDATES, and then join all the rows in these two tables with the rows in the third table, WEBCLASS_SCHEDULE. The resulting table should have a row for each class whether or not it's scheduled to be held. Classes with multiple sessions have a row for each session.

A PROC SQL step combines the three tables by matching column CLASSID, which has different attributes in each of the tables. CLASSID is defined as character in tables WEBCLASSES and CLASS_UPDATES and as numeric in table WEBCLASS_SCHEDULE. The length of the character version of CLASSID is 8 in WEBCLASSES and 3 in CLASS_UPDATES.

Because all matching and nonmatching rows from all three tables are required in the resulting table, a full outer join combines the three tables. And because a full outer join can combine only two tables at a time, two full outer joins are required to produce the final table. The result of a nested subquery that combines WEBCLASSES and CLASS_UPDATES with a full join is combined with WEBCLASS_SCHEDULE in the second full join.

The matching variable for both full joins is CLASSID. To ensure a length of 3 for CLASSID in the subquery, the LENGTH= option is added to the column definition of CLASSID. Joins can be completed only on columns with the same type. In order to perform the second full join, which is a join based on a numeric column and a character column, one of the columns must be converted to the type of the other. The column from WEBCLASS_SCHEDULE is converted to character by using the PUT function.

Program

Create table ALLWEBCLASSES.
Select columns from the subquery results (alias c) and the WEBCLASS_SCHEDULE table (alias s). Place CLASSID from the subquery first so that the resulting column's attributes are the same as in the subquery. Convert the value of CLASSID from WEBCLASS_SCHEDULE to character because the arguments to COALESCE must have the same type.
Assign the text 'none' to column SESSIONID for classes that are not found in WEBCLASS_SCHEDULE.

Assign an alias.

Perform a full join of WEBCLASS_SCHEDULE and the result of the subquery.

Specify a subquery that joins WEBCLASSES and CLASS_UPDATES and enclose it in parentheses. Apply the COALESCE function to the two CLASSID columns so that nonmatching rows will have a value for CLASSID. Override the length of the first argument to

```
proc sql;
  create table allwebclasses as
    select coalesce(c.classid,put(s.classid,z3.-1))
                     as classid,




                     coalesce(sessionid,'none') as sessionid,

             startdate, class_title, maxstudents
      from webclass_schedule s

             full join


             (select coalesce(old.classid,new.classid)
                     as classid length=3,
```

COALESCE, which is 8, by assigning a length of 3 to the results of the function.

Apply the COALESCE function to columns in common. List first in each call the columns from the table with the updates, CLASS_UPDATES, which ensures new information overwrites old information.

```
            coalesce(new.maxstudents,old.maxstudents)
                            as maxstudents,
            coalesce(new.class_title,old.class_title)
                            as class_title
```

Perform a full join. Assign aliases.

```
       from webclasses old
              full join
           class_updates new
         on old.classid=new.classid)
```

Specify how to match the rows in the subquery.

Assign an alias to the subquery result.

Specify how to match the rows of table WEBCLASS_SCHEDULE and the subquery. Convert the numeric CLASSID column in WEBCLASS_SCHEDULE to character.

```
       c
       on c.classid=put(s.classid,z3.-1)
```

Order the output rows.

```
            order by classid, startdate;
quit;
```

Related Technique

A combination of PROC SORT steps and DATA steps can create a data set equivalent to the table that was created by PROC SQL in the main example.

The following program combines the three data sets by match-merging on variable CLASSID. As with PROC SQL, the DATA step cannot match observations by a variable that has different types without additional programming.

The goal is to match CLASSID in its character form and to define CLASSID as a 3-byte character variable in the output data set. Two steps are taken to accomplish this:

❑ The first DATA step converts the numeric version of CLASSID to a 3-byte character variable.

❑ The match-merge DATA step places a LENGTH statement prior to the MERGE statement that assigns a length of 3 bytes to CLASSID. The MERGE statement lists WEBCLASSES first. By default, the attributes of the first occurrence of a variable in the data sets in the MERGE statement define the attributes of the variable in the output data set. Because the length of CLASSID in WEBCLASSES is 8 bytes and the goal is to output CLASSID as a 3-byte character variable, a LENGTH statement is needed prior to the MERGE statement.

The match-merge DATA step produces the following message:

```
WARNING: Multiple lengths were specified for the BY variable
         Classid by input data sets and LENGTH, FORMAT, INFORMAT,
         or ATTRIB statements. This may cause unexpected results.
```

SAS generates this message because the length of CLASSID in WEBCLASSES is 8 and its length in the other two input data sets is 3. Because the data values are never wider than 3 bytes, this match-merge completes successfully. If you are uncertain about your data in a similar situation, you might want to add DATA steps to convert the smaller length versions of your variables to the longest length.

Create SCHEDULE2 to contain a character version of CLASSID.

```
data schedule2;
```

Prevent the numeric version of CLASSID from being put in the PDV by renaming it.

```
set webclass_schedule(rename=(classid=nclassid));
```

Define the length and type of the character version of CLASSID.

```
length classid $ 3;
```

Drop the numeric version of CLASSID, which was renamed earlier when it was read in.

Convert the numeric values of NCLASSID to character.

Sort the input data sets. Sort the observations in SCHEDULE2 also by STARTDATE so that the observations in ALLWEBCLASSES will be arranged chronologically within each CLASSID.

Create data set ALLWEBCLASSES. Assign a type and length to CLASSID, which overrides the length of 8 that it has in WEBCLASSES.
Name the data sets to match-merge. Add the IN= data set option so that it can be determined whether the current observation has data contributed from SCHEDULE2.
Specify the matching variable.
Assign text to SESSIONID for observations that are not found in SCHEDULE2.

```
drop nclassid;


classid=put(nclassid,z3.-l);

run;
proc sort data=webclasses;
  by classid;
run;
proc sort data=class_updates;
  by classid;
run;
proc sort data=schedule2;
  by classid startdate;
run;
data allwebclasses;
  length classid $ 3;


  merge webclasses class_updates schedule2(in=insched);



    by classid;
  if not insched then sessionid='none';


run;
```

Example 3.6   Combining Rows When There Is No Common Column

Goal

Combine rows from two tables based on specific criteria, even when there is no column common to the two tables.

Example Features

Featured Step	PROC SQL
Featured Step Options and Statements	Full join, WHERE clause with BETWEEN operator
Related Technique	DATA step, multiple SET statements, POINT= and NOBS= options

Input Tables

Tables BUILD_PROJECTS and BUILD_BILLS have no common column. The dates associated with each project in BUILD_PROJECTS do not overlap with any other project.

```
               BUILD_PROJECTS                            BUILD_BILLS

                                                             completion_
Obs   start_date   end_date   project     Obs   workid         date        charge
 1    01/08/2010   01/27/2010  Basement     1     1234      01/18/2010     $944.80
 2    02/01/2010   02/12/2010  Frame        2     2225      02/18/2010    $1280.94
 3    02/15/2010   02/20/2010  Roofing      3     3879      03/04/2010     $888.90
 4    02/22/2010   02/27/2010  Plumb        4     8888      03/19/2010    $2280.87
 5    03/02/2010   03/05/2010  Wire
 6    03/08/2010   03/29/2010  Brick
```

Resulting Table
Output 3.6
BUILD_COMPLETE
Table

```
        Example 3.6 BUILD_COMPLETE Table Created with PROC SQL

                                             completion_
    Obs start_date   end_date project  workid    date       charge

     1  01/08/2010 01/27/2010 Basement  1234  01/18/2010    $944.80
     2  02/15/2010 02/20/2010 Roofing   2225  02/18/2010   $1280.94
     3  03/02/2010 03/05/2010 Wire      3879  03/04/2010    $888.90
     4  03/08/2010 03/29/2010 Brick     8888  03/19/2010   $2280.87
```

Example Overview

The PROC SQL step in this example shows how you can combine two tables that do not have a variable in common.

Table BUILD_PROJECTS contains a list of start and end dates for six home repair projects. Table BUILD_BILLS contains a list of four charges with a completion date. The two data sets do not have a variable in common. None of the start and end dates of one project overlap with another.

The objective of this program is to bill charges to the correct phase of a construction project. A row in BUILD_BILLS is matched to a row in BUILD_PROJECTS when the completion date falls within the start and end dates of a project.

Conceptually, the PROC SQL join results in an internal table that matches every row in BUILD_PROJECTS with every row in BUILD_BILLS. From that internal table, the WHERE clause outputs the rows with a value of COMPLETION_DATE that is between START_DATE and END_DATE.

Program

Create table BUILD_COMPLETE.
Select all columns from both tables.
Combine every row from
BUILD_PROJECTS with every row
from BUILD_BILLS.
Select from the joined rows those where
the completion date is between the start
and end date of a project.

```
proc sql;
  create table build_complete as
    select *
      from build_projects, build_bills


      where completion_date between
            start_date and end_date;

quit;
```

Related Technique

The DATA step in this related technique creates a data set equivalent to the table that was created by the PROC SQL step in the main example. It programmatically combines the two data sets by using an iterative DO-UNTIL loop and SET statements that control how the two input data sets are read. It does not use MERGE and BY statements to do this.

For each completion date in BUILD_BILLS, the DATA step looks for a range of dates in BUILD_PROJECTS in which the value of COMPLETION_DATE fits. All observations from BUILD_BILLS are output to BUILD_COMPLETE. Not necessarily all observations from BUILD_PROJECTS are output to BUILD_COMPLETE.

Each iteration of the DATA step reads one observation from the first data set, BUILD_BILLS, and each iteration also potentially reads all observations from the second, BUILD_COMPLETE. It starts with a simple SET statement that identifies the first data set. The iterative DO-UNTIL loop that follows processes the second data set.

The POINT= and OBS= data set options in the SET statement for the second data set access observations in BUILD_BILLS sequentially by observation number until a match is found or until all observations in BUILD_BILLS have been read. The POINT= option references the index variable I whose value directly accesses each observation in BUILD_BILLS by observation number. The NOBS= option assigns the number of observations in BUILD_BILLS to the variable N. This assignment occurs before the DATA step executes.

The iterative DO-UNTIL loop iterates once for each observation in BUILD_BILLS until a match is found. If a match is not found, the loop stops when it has iterated the number of times equal to the value saved in N.

When a match is found, the DATA step writes the matching observation to BUILD_COMPLETE, and it sets variable FOUND to 1. The condition of FOUND=1 stops the iterative DO-UNTIL loop so that no more observations are read from BUILD_BILLS. Variable FOUND is initialized to zero prior to the DO-UNTIL loop.

This program might be inefficient if the second data set is large because potentially this large data set could be read over and over again.

The program could be improved to include programming statements that write messages to the SAS log when an observation does not have a match in BUILD_BILLS or when multiple matches are found. Neither of these conditions exists in this example.

Create BUILD_COMPLETE.
Read an observation from
BUILD_PROJECTS.

Initialize FOUND whose value is used
to control execution of the iterative
DO-UNTIL loop.

```
data build_complete;
  set build_projects;

  drop found;
  found=0;
```

Read observations from BUILD_BILLS until a match is found or until all observations have been read. Directly access an observation in BUILD_BILLS by pointing to the Ith observation. Save the total number of observations in BUILD_BILLS in variable N. Set the upper index value of the iterative DO-UNTIL loop to N. When the condition is met, set FOUND to 1 so that the iterative DO-UNTIL loop stops, and then write the matching observation to BUILD_COMPLETE.

```
do i=1 to n until (found);
   set build_bills point=i nobs=n;




   if start_date le completion_date le end_date
         then do;
      found=1;
      output;
   end;
 end;
run;
```

Example 3.7   Matching Observations Randomly

Goal

Randomly pair observations from two data sets until a good match is found. Create a new data set that contains the results of the match. Update the value of a variable in the data set considered the master data set with information that was obtained in the match with the other data set.

Example Features

Featured Step	DATA step
Featured Step Options and Statements	MODIFY statement, NOBS= and POINT= options REPLACE statement Random number function RANUNI CEIL function

Input Data Sets

Data set ENGINEERS has the available hours for seven engineers. It is the master data set. Data set ENG_PROJECTS contains a list of six engineering projects and the hours to complete on the project. It is the transaction data set.

```
          ENGINEERS                              ENG_PROJECTS

Obs   engineer   availhours      Obs    project_id    hours
 1    Inge           33           1     AERO041         31
 2    Jane          100           2     BRANDX         150
 3    Eduardo        12           3     CHEM005         18
 4    Fred           16           4     CONTRACTA       41
 5    Kia           130           5     ENGDESIGN2       6
 6    Monique        44           6     ENGDESIGN3      29
 7    Sofus          23
```

Resulting Data Sets

Output 3.7a **Updated Version of ENGINEERS Data Set**

```
                Example 3.7 Updated ENGINEERS data set

              Obs      engineer      availhours

               1       Inge              33
               2       Jane              82
               3       Eduardo            6
               4       Fred              16
               5       Kia               60
               6       Monique           13
               7       Sofus             23
```

Output 3.7b **ENG_ASSIGN Data Set**

```
                Example 3.7 ENG_ASSIGN data set

              Obs      project_id    engineer

               1       AERO041       Monique
               2       BRANDX        **NONE**
               3       CHEM005       Jane
               4       CONTRACTA     Kia
               5       ENGDESIGN2    Eduardo
               6       ENGDESIGN3    Kia
```

Example Overview

The following DATA step shows how to use a random access technique to match observations between two data sets.

Data set ENGINEERS contains a list of seven engineers and their available hours. Data set ENG_PROJECTS contains a list of six projects identified by PROJECT_ID and the hours needed to complete that project. The objective is to match a project with an engineer who has sufficient hours to complete that project, output the project assignments to the new data set ENG_ASSIGN, and update ENGINEER to reflect the hours that remain for each engineer after assignment.

The DATA step reads each observation from ENG_PROJECTS sequentially, and then looks randomly for an engineer in ENGINEERS with sufficient hours available to complete the project. An iterative DO-WHILE loop controls the search process for the engineer to work on the project.

Each iteration of the DO-WHILE loop generates a random integer between 1 and the number of observations in ENGINEERS with the RANUNI and CEIL functions. The RANUNI function generates random numbers from the uniform distribution.

The argument that is supplied to RANUNI in this example is a positive number greater than 0. This causes the function to generate the same series of random numbers each time the DATA step executes, which allows the results of this example to be reproduced. If you specify 0 or less as the argument to RANUNI, the function seeds the random number generator with the time of day and the numbers it generates are not reproducible.

The NOBS= option in the MODIFY statement assigns to variable N the number of observations in ENGINEERS. The variable that is assigned to the POINT= option in the MODIFY statement is RANOBSNO, which is the generated random integer. The value of RANOBSNO determines which observation to read from ENGINEERS.

If the engineer has sufficient hours to complete the project, the program assigns the engineer to the project, updates the engineer's hours in data set ENGINEERS, and stops the iterative DO-WHILE loop. If the engineer does not have sufficient hours to complete the project, the DO loop continues to iterate. The upper limit on the DO loop is 1,000. If the DO loop iterates 1,000 times and does not find an engineer with sufficient hours, no engineer is assigned to the project currently being processed.

For more examples of the MODIFY statement, see Chapter 7.

For more examples of working with random number functions, see Chapter 9.

Program

Open ENGINEERS for update and create ENG_ASSIGN.

```
data engineers eng_assign(keep=engineer project_id);
```

Read an observation from ENG_PROJECTS.

```
   set eng_projects;
```

Initialize a variable to track whether a match for the current observation in ENG_PROJECTS has been made.

```
   found=0;
```

Process observations from ENGINEERS until an engineer is selected for the current project or until the loop iterates 1,000 times.

```
   do i=1 to 1000 while (not found);
```

Generate random values that will be used to access ENGINEERS by observation number. Generate a random number from the uniform distribution. Transform that number so that it ranges between 1 and the number of observations in ENGINEERS.

```
      ranobsno=ceil(ranuni(12345)*n);
```

Find the observation in ENGINEERS whose observation number equals the value of RANOBSNO.

Assign the total number of observations in ENGINEERS to N.

Process this DO group when the engineer's available hours at least equal the hours needed to complete the project currently being evaluated.

Output the project assignment observation to ENG_ASSIGN.

Update AVAILHOURS for the engineer just selected.

Update ENGINEERS with the new value for AVAILHOURS.

Set FOUND to 1 so that the iterative DO-WHILE loop will stop because an engineer with sufficient hours for the project has been selected.

When no engineer's available hours at least equal the hours needed for the current project, write an observation to ENG_ASSIGN to indicate that no engineer was selected.

```
   modify engineers
                   point=ranobsno

                   nobs=n;

   if availhours => hours then do;


      output eng_assign;

      availhours=availhours-hours;

      replace engineers;

      found=1;
   end;


  if found=0 then do;
   engineer='**NONE**';
   output eng_assign;
  end;
run;
```

Example 3.8 Combining Multiple Data Sets without a Variable Common to All the Data Sets

Goal

Combine three tables that do not all share a common column. Each table has one column in common with a second table, but not with the third. Use this relationship to combine all three tables. Compute a new column by using information from two of the tables.

Example Features

Featured Step	PROC SQL
Featured Step Options and Statements	Compound WHERE clause
Related Technique	Hash object in the DATA step

Input Tables

Table MAINTENANCE contains a list of maintenance tasks performed on four vehicles identified by VEHICLE_ID. Table VEHICLES contains a list of customer vehicles. Table MAINTCHARGES contains a list of tasks identified by TASK_CODE and the charge for each task.

Column VEHICLE_ID is found only in tables MAINTENANCE and VEHICLES. Column TASK_CODE is found only in tables MAINTENANCE and MAINTCHARGES.

```
                  MAINTENANCE                                        VEHICLES

       vehicle_   task_                                   vehicle_
 Obs     id       code    discount  mechanic      Obs       id      type       customer
  1     195331    M001      0.00      REW           1      195331   Minivan    Lee, HG
  2     195331    M005      0.05      REW           2      152843   Sedan      Gomez, UR
  3     321551    M003      0.08      PFG           3      321551   SUV        Carlson, BG
  4     371616    M006      0.12      KJH           4      430912   Sedan      Quinn, IP
  5     371616    M003      0.00      JNB           5      371616   Minivan    Monte, YR
  6     911192    M002      0.00      TRA           6      843200   Hatchback  Weeks, CA
                                                    7      911192   SUV        Lane, NH


                  MAINTCHARGES

        task_
 Obs    code    task_desc              charge
  1     M001    Oil change             $25.00
  2     M002    Filters                $30.00
  3     M003    Tire rotation          $40.00
  4     M004    Brake pads            $100.00
  5     M005    Radiator flush        $100.00
  6     M006    Battery replacement   $120.00
```

Resulting Table
Output 3.8
MAINTBILLS Table

```
              Example 3.8 MAINTBILLS Table Created with PROC SQL

        vehicle_                              task_
 Obs      id      customer      type          code    task_desc              cost

  1      195331   Lee, HG       Minivan       M001    Oil change             $25.00
  2      195331   Lee, HG       Minivan       M005    Radiator flush         $95.00
  3      321551   Carlson, BG   SUV           M003    Tire rotation          $36.80
  4      371616   Monte, YR     Minivan       M003    Tire rotation          $40.00
  5      371616   Monte, YR     Minivan       M006    Battery replacement   $105.60
  6      911192   Lane, NH      SUV           M002    Filters                $30.00
```

Example Overview

The following PROC SQL step demonstrates how to combine three tables that do not have a matching column common to the three tables. Each table has one column in common with a second table, but not with the third. The tables are combined with a compound WHERE clause, and new columns are computed that combine columns from different tables.

Data set MAINTENANCE contains a list of maintenance tasks performed on four vehicles identified by VEHICLE_ID. Data set VEHICLES contains a list of customer vehicles. Data set MAINTCHARGES contains a list of tasks identified by TASK_CODE and their charges.

The objective of this program is to join the MAINTENANCE, VEHICLES, and MAINTCHARGES tables to find vehicle information and final costs for each task in MAINTENANCE. The MAINTENANCE table can be linked to the VEHICLES table by column VEHICLE_ID, and it can be linked to the MAINTCHARGES table by column TASK_CODE.

As a result of the join, all columns from all three tables are available to process. By joining MAINTENANCE and MAINTCHARGES, you can compute the final cost for the maintenance task by multiplying DISCOUNT and CHARGES. By joining MAINTENANCE and VEHICLES, you can find information about each vehicle serviced.

Vehicles 430912 and 843200 do not have any maintenance activity and do not have rows in the MAINTENANCE table. Also, no vehicles in MAINTENANCE have task M004. Therefore, no rows for these vehicles or this task is present in output table MAINTBILLS because no conditions that include these vehicles or task satisfy the compound WHERE clause.

Create table MAINTBILLS.
Select specific columns from the three input tables. Specify the origin of the columns by preceding the column name with an alias for those columns in more than one table.
Compute a new column by using column CHARGE selected from MAINTCHARGES and column DISCOUNT selected from MAINTENANCE.
Identify the three input tables. Assign an alias to each table.

Join the tables with a compound WHERE clause. Precede each column name with the alias for the table source.
Arrange the rows in table MAINTBILLS.

```
proc sql;
   create table maintbills as
      select m.vehicle_id, customer, type,
             m.task_code, task_desc,




             (charge-discount*charge) as cost
                    format=dollar8.2




      from maintenance as m,
           vehicles as v,
           maintcharges as c

      where m.vehicle_id=v.vehicle_id and
            m.task_code=c.task_code


      order by m.vehicle_id, m.task_code;
```

Related Technique

The following program creates a data set equivalent to the table that was created in the main example. It creates two hash objects: V loaded from data set VEHICLES and C loaded from data set MAINTCHARGES. The DATA step reads data set MAINTENANCE. For each observation in MAINTENANCE, the DATA step looks up information in hash object V based on the values of VEHICLE_ID. It also looks up information in hash object C based on the values of TASK_CODE.

When each hash lookup finds a match, SAS copies the data part of the hash object into the variables that are specified by its DEFINEDATA method. When a match is found in both hash objects, an assignment statement computes COST.

Because the SAS compiler cannot detect the data variable assignments that the hash objects make, you will see notes in the SAS log about uninitialized variables unless you define the variables with SAS language statements. This example defines the four items in the two hash objects as data variables by supplying them as arguments to the CALL MISSING function.

An improvement to the DATA step would be to add code that handles the situation when matches are not found in one or both of the hash objects. In this example, each observation in MAINTENANCE finds a match in both hash objects.

Create data set MAINTBILLS.
Define the variables saved in
MAINTBILLS and used in the DATA
step.

```sas
data maintbills;
  attrib vehicle_id length=8
         customer length=$15
         type      length=$9
         task_code length=$8
         task_desc length=$20
         cost      length=8 format=dollar10.2
         charge    length=8
         discount  length=8;
  keep vehicle_id customer type task_code task_desc
       cost;
  if _n_=1 then do;
```

On the first iteration of the DATA step,
create, name, and specify attributes of
the two hash objects.
Create hash object V. Load V with data
from data set VEHICLES. Specify one
key variable and two data variables.

```sas
    declare hash v(dataset:"work.vehicles");
    v.defineKey('vehicle_id');
    v.definedata('type','customer');
    v.definedone();
```

Create hash object C. Load C with data
from data set MAINTCHARGES.
Specify one key variable and two data
variables.

```sas
    declare hash c(dataset:"work.maintcharges");
    c.defineKey('task_code');
    c.definedata('task_desc','charge');
    c.definedone();
```

Prevent SAS notes about uninitialized
variables that are data items in the
hash objects.

```sas
    call missing(type, customer, task_desc, charge);
```

```sas
  end;
```

Read data set MAINTENANCE.
Determine whether the current values
of VEHICLE_ID and TASK_CODE in
MAINTENANCE have matches in the
two hash objects. Save the return codes
of the search results in two different
variables.
When both lookups succeed in finding
a match, compute COST.

```sas
  set maintenance;
  rcv=v.find(key: vehicle_id);
  rcc=c.find(key: task_code);




  if rcv=0 and rcc=0 then cost=charge-discount*charge;
run;
```

Example 3.9 Generating Every Combination of Rows (Cartesian Product) between Tables

Goal

Combine two tables that have no common columns in order to produce every possible combination of rows.

Example Features

Featured Step	PROC SQL
Featured Step Options and Statements	Cartesian product
Related Technique	DATA step, multiple SET statements, NOBS= and POINT= options

Input Tables

Table TRIAL_A has the identifiers for a group of patients who are participating in a clinical trial. Table TRIAL_TESTS contains the lab tests for this trial. There are no columns in common between the two tables.

TRIAL_A

Obs	patientid	patientinits
1	KPGY	AHB
2	MWGM	DOH
3	PQZU	LRH
4	FQ82	HCI
5	EYPS	MEF

TRIAL_TESTS

Obs	testcode	testtype
1	L001	Cholesterol
2	L002	Glucose
3	L003	HDL
4	L004	LDL
5	L005	Triglycerides

Resulting Table
Output 3.9 **ALLTESTS Table**

```
              Example 3.9 ALLTESTS Table Created with PROC SQL

      Obs patientid patientinits testcode testtype        result
        1   KPGY         AHB        L001   Cholesterol   Not done yet
        2   KPGY         AHB        L002   Glucose       Not done yet
        3   KPGY         AHB        L003   HDL           Not done yet
        4   KPGY         AHB        L004   LDL           Not done yet
        5   KPGY         AHB        L005   Triglycerides Not done yet
        6   MWGM         DOH        L001   Cholesterol   Not done yet
        7   MWGM         DOH        L002   Glucose       Not done yet
        8   MWGM         DOH        L003   HDL           Not done yet
        9   MWGM         DOH        L004   LDL           Not done yet
       10   MWGM         DOH        L005   Triglycerides Not done yet
       11   PQZU         LRH        L001   Cholesterol   Not done yet
       12   PQZU         LRH        L002   Glucose       Not done yet
       13   PQZU         LRH        L003   HDL           Not done yet
       14   PQZU         LRH        L004   LDL           Not done yet
       15   PQZU         LRH        L005   Triglycerides Not done yet
       16   FQ82         HCI        L001   Cholesterol   Not done yet
       17   FQ82         HCI        L002   Glucose       Not done yet
       18   FQ82         HCI        L003   HDL           Not done yet
       19   FQ82         HCI        L004   LDL           Not done yet
       20   FQ82         HCI        L005   Triglycerides Not done yet
       21   EYPS         MEF        L001   Cholesterol   Not done yet
       22   EYPS         MEF        L002   Glucose       Not done yet
       23   EYPS         MEF        L003   HDL           Not done yet
       24   EYPS         MEF        L004   LDL           Not done yet
       25   EYPS         MEF        L005   Triglycerides Not done yet
```

Example Overview

This example shows you how to produce a table that has every possible combination of the rows in two tables that are being joined. This result is called a Cartesian product.

Note that a Cartesian product of large tables can produce huge tables, and usually you would add code to produce a subset of the Cartesian product. This example does not restrict the combinations so that you can see how a Cartesian product is formed.

Table TRIAL_A has the identifiers for a group of patients who are participating in a clinical trial. Table TRIAL_TESTS contains the lab tests for this trial. The two tables do not have any columns in common.

The goal of the following PROC SQL step is to combine each row in TRIAL_A with each row in TRIAL_TESTS so that there is one row for each combination of patient and lab test. The Cartesian product of the five rows in each table produces 25 rows in ALLTESTS.

The intention is to edit ALLTESTS later as each patient's test results are obtained. The SELECT statement adds one new column, RESULT, which PROC SQL initializes to the text "Not done yet."

While the Related Technique in a later section creates a data set equivalent to table ALLTESTS that was produced by PROC SQL, it is easier to code a Cartesian product with PROC SQL when there is minimal additional processing necessary.

Program

Create table ALLTESTS.
Select all columns from the two input tables.
Add the column, RESULT, to ALLTESTS and initialize its value.
Specify the two input tables.

```
proc sql;
   create table alltests as
      select *,

                   'Not done yet' length=12 as result

                   from trial_a, trial_tests;
   quit;
```

Related Technique

The following DATA step creates a data set equivalent to the table that was created by PROC SQL earlier. If you need the programming capabilities of the DATA step that are not easily coded in PROC SQL, you can adapt this code to form a Cartesian product with the DATA step.

You cannot combine the two data sets with a MERGE statement to produce a Cartesian product because a MERGE statement does a one-to-one match of the observations in the two data sets.

The DATA step uses both sequential and direct processing. It starts by sequentially reading each observation in TRIAL_A with the first SET statement. For each observation read from TRIAL_A, the DO loop iterates the number of times equal to the number of observations in TRIAL_TESTS. The SET statement in the DO loop reads each observation in TRIAL_TESTS by directly using the POINT= option. The OUTPUT statement in the DO loop outputs an observation for each observation in TRIAL_TESTS.

The upper bound of the DO loop is set to NTESTS, which equals the number of observations in TRIAL_TESTS. The second SET statement assigns a value to NTESTS using the NOBS= option. SAS assigns a value to a NOBS= variable during compilation of the DATA step before the DATA step executes.

The POINT= option is set to TEST, which is the index variable of the DO loop. The SET statement in the iterative DO loop directly accesses each observation in TRIAL_TESTS in observation order.

This technique of forming a Cartesian product requires the POINT= option in the second SET statement because this option prevents the end-of-file condition from being set on data set TRIAL_TESTS. By default, a DATA step stops when it detects an end-of-file condition. Without the POINT= option, the DATA step would stop when it reads the second observation in TRIAL_A because it detects that data set TRIAL_TESTS has already been completely read. The DATA step would combine the first observation from TRIAL_A with every observation in TRIAL_TESTS and would produce a data set that has the number of observations found in TRIAL_TESTS.

Create data set ALLTESTS.
On each iteration of the DATA step, read one observation from TRIAL_A.

```
data alltests;
   set trial_a;
```

Execute an iterative DO loop for each observation in TRIAL_A. Name the index variable the same as the POINT= variable in the following SET statement. Set the upper bound of the DO loop as the number of observations in TRIAL_TESTS, which is saved in NTESTS, the NOBS= variable that the following SET statement defines.
Specify the data set to read directly.

```
   do test=1 to ntests;
```

Specify the index variable of the iterative DO loop as the POINT= variable.

```
      set trial_tests nobs=ntests
```

For each observation in TRIAL_A, output every observation in TRIAL_TESTS.

```
         point=test;
```

```
      output;
```

```
   end;
run;
```

Example 3.10 Generating Every Combination of Rows between Tables Based on a Common Column

Goal

Combine two tables that have a common column where the common column has duplicate values in both tables. Produce a table that contains all possible combinations of the rows where the values from the common column match.

Example Features

Featured Step	PROC SQL
Featured Step Options and Statements	Full join with WHERE clause
Related Technique	Hash iterator object in the DATA step

Input Tables

Table MEETINGS contains events to be held on two days and the expected attendance for each event. Table MEETINGROOMS contains meeting rooms that are available for the same two days. The column in common between the two tables is MEETINGDATE with multiple occurrences of the two values in each of the tables.

```
                          MEETINGS

                                                    approx_
Obs   meetingdate              event              attendance
 1    09/14/2009    Civil Engineering Seminar 1       25
 2    09/14/2009    Economics Panel Discussion        150
 3    09/14/2009    Psychology Working Group          15
 4    09/14/2009    Statistics Users Group            45
 5    09/15/2009    Civil Engineering Seminar 2       25
 6    09/15/2009    Energy Solutions Committee        50
 7    09/15/2009    Language Arts Teachers            60
 8    09/15/2009    Management Certification          25
 9    09/15/2009    Transit Planning Hearing          40
```

```
                      MEETINGROOMS

                               room_
Obs    meetingdate    number    capacity
  1    09/14/2009      A140       100
  2    09/14/2009      A020        40
  3    09/14/2009      B200       300
  4    09/14/2009      B220        75
  5    09/14/2009      C030        15
  6    09/14/2009      C125        30
  7    09/15/2009      A140       100
  8    09/15/2009      A120        25
  9    09/15/2009      A200       300
 10    09/15/2009      B110        50
 11    09/15/2009      B220        25
 12    09/15/2009      C050        25
 13    09/15/2009      C070        10
 14    09/15/2009      C125        20
```

Resulting Table
Output 3.10
**POSSIBLE_LOCS
Table**

```
               Example 3.10 POSSIBLE_LOCS Table Created with PROC SQL

                                              approx_   room_
     Obs  meetingdate        event          attendance number capacity
       1  09/14/2009  Civil Engineering Seminar 1     25    A020     40
       2  09/14/2009  Civil Engineering Seminar 1     25    A140    100
       3  09/14/2009  Civil Engineering Seminar 1     25    B200    300
       4  09/14/2009  Civil Engineering Seminar 1     25    B220     75
       5  09/14/2009  Civil Engineering Seminar 1     25    C125     30
       6  09/14/2009  Economics Panel Discussion     150    B200    300
       7  09/14/2009  Psychology Working Group        15    A020     40
       8  09/14/2009  Psychology Working Group        15    A140    100
       9  09/14/2009  Psychology Working Group        15    B200    300
      10  09/14/2009  Psychology Working Group        15    B220     75
      11  09/14/2009  Psychology Working Group        15    C030     15
      12  09/14/2009  Psychology Working Group        15    C125     30
      13  09/14/2009  Statistics Users Group          45    A140    100
      14  09/14/2009  Statistics Users Group          45    B200    300
      15  09/14/2009  Statistics Users Group          45    B220     75
      16  09/15/2009  Civil Engineering Seminar 2     25    A120     25
      17  09/15/2009  Civil Engineering Seminar 2     25    A140    100
      18  09/15/2009  Civil Engineering Seminar 2     25    A200    300
      19  09/15/2009  Civil Engineering Seminar 2     25    B110     50
      20  09/15/2009  Civil Engineering Seminar 2     25    B220     25
      21  09/15/2009  Civil Engineering Seminar 2     25    C050     25
      22  09/15/2009  Energy Solutions Committee      50    A140    100
      23  09/15/2009  Energy Solutions Committee      50    A200    300
      24  09/15/2009  Energy Solutions Committee      50    B110     50
      25  09/15/2009  Language Arts Teachers          60    A140    100
      26  09/15/2009  Language Arts Teachers          60    A200    300
      27  09/15/2009  Management Certification        25    A120     25
      28  09/15/2009  Management Certification        25    A140    100
      29  09/15/2009  Management Certification        25    A200    300
      30  09/15/2009  Management Certification        25    B110     50
      31  09/15/2009  Management Certification        25    B220     25
      32  09/15/2009  Management Certification        25    C050     25
      33  09/15/2009  Transit Planning Hearing        40    A140    100
      34  09/15/2009  Transit Planning Hearing        40    A200    300
      35  09/15/2009  Transit Planning Hearing        40    B110     50
```

Example Overview

This example uses PROC SQL to produce all possible combinations of the rows from two tables that match on a column common to the two tables. And from the product of the two tables, it selects rows that meet a specific condition.

The goal of the program is to create a list of suitable meeting rooms for several events on two days. Table MEETINGS stores event information. Table MEETINGROOMS stores meeting room information. The compound WHERE clause in the SELECT statement matches the two tables by MEETINGDATE, which is the column in common, and it selects matches based on whether the meeting room has the capacity for the event.

Program

*Create table POSSIBLE_LOCS.
Select all columns from MEETINGS,
which has the alias m, and select two
columns from MEETINGDATE.
Combine the two tables. Specify an
alias for each table.
Select rows where MEETINGDATE
matches. Produce all combinations of
rows that match on MEETINGDATE.*

```
proc sql;
   create table possible_locs as
      select m.*,
             room_number, capacity

         from meetings m, meetingrooms r

         where m.meetingdate=r.meetingdate and
```

Select from the rows that match on MEETINGDATE those rows that pass the comparison of APPROX_ATTENDANCE and CAPACITY.	`approx_attendance le capacity`
Order the rows in the output table.	`order by meetingdate, event, room_number;` `quit;`

Related Technique

This related technique uses a hash iterator object in a DATA step to find all the possible combinations of observations between the two data sets MEETINGS and MEETINGROOMS that match by meeting date. The DATA step selects matches that have a value of CAPACITY at least equal to the value of APPROX_ATTENDANCE. It produces a data set equivalent to the table in the main example.

Both data sets in this example are small and each easily fits in memory. A data set that is loaded into a hash table is read only once. Retrieval from memory is fast. The hash table in this example is used like a dynamic array, and it can store an indefinite amount of data.

The DATA step on its first iteration declares hash object ROOMS as a hash iterator object and loads data set MEETINGROOMS into ROOMS. One key is defined and multiple data items for each key value are allowed.

After reading an observation from MEETINGS, the DATA step applies the FIRST method to return the first data item in hash object ROOMS. The DATA step then uses a DO WHILE loop to apply the NEXT method to move through the hash object. When the DATA step detects the end of the hash object, the iteration of the DATA step is complete.

To make key variables available for output and for processing by SAS language statements, you must define them as data variables. The DATA step defines key variable ROOMDATE as data with the DEFINEDATA method so that its values are available for testing in the DO WHILE group.

Because the SAS compiler cannot detect the key and data variable assignments that the hash object and the hash iterator make, you will see notes in the SAS log about uninitialized variables unless you define the variables with SAS language statements. This example defines the three items in the hash object as data variables by supplying them as arguments to the CALL MISSING function.

Create data set POSSIBLE_LOCS.
Specify attributes for the variables that are processed in this DATA step.
	`data possible_locs;`
	`  attrib meetingdate length=8 format=mmddyy10.`
	`    event length=$30`
	`    approx_attendance length=8`
	`    roomdate length=8 format=mmddyy10.`
	`    capacity length=8`
	`    room_number length=$4;`

On the first iteration of the DATA step, define hash object ROOMS.	`if _n_=1 then do;`
Load data set MEETINGROOMS into ROOMS. Rename MEETINGDATE so that its values in the hash table can be compared to MEETINGDATE in data set MEETINGS.	`  declare hash rooms(dataset:` `    'work.meetingrooms(rename=(meetingdate=roomdate))',`
Allow multiple data items for each key value.	`                    multidata: 'yes'`
Specify retrieval of items from ROOMS in ascending order of the key values.	`                    ordered: 'a');`
Declare that ROOMS is a hash iterator object.	`  declare hiter iter('rooms');`
Define the key in ROOMS. ***Define all the variables in MEETINGROOMS as data variables, which includes key ROOMDATE.***	`  rooms.definekey('roomdate');` `  rooms.definedata(all:'yes');`

Close the definition of hash object ROOMS.	```rooms.definedone();```
Prevent SAS notes about uninitialized variables.	```call missing(roomdate, room_number, capacity);```

```
   end;
   set meetings;
```

On each iteration of the DATA step, read one observation from MEETINGS.

Drop variables not needed in the output data set, including the renamed version of MEETINGDATE.

```
   drop rc roomdate;
```

Return the first set of data values in ROOMS, which are in ascending order by the key values. Assign to variable RC the return code that indicates whether the FIRST method was successful.

```
   rc=iter.first();
```

Iterate through ROOMS. Stop the loop when the return code from the NEXT method is not 0, which indicates that the end of ROOMS has been reached.

```
   do while (rc=0);
```

Output an observation when the set of currently retrieved items meets the conditions in the IF statement.

```
      if meetingdate=roomdate and
              approx_attendance le capacity then output;
```

Because the values of ROOMDATE are in ascending order in ROOMS, stop processing the DO WHILE loop if the value of ROOMDATE is greater than the value of MEETINGDATE.

```
      if roomdate > meetingdate then leave;
```

Return the next set of values from ROOMS. Assign to variable RC the return code that indicates whether the NEXT method was successful.

```
      rc=iter.next();
```

```
   end;
run;
```

Example 3.11 Generating Every Combination of Observations between Data Sets Based on a Common Variable When an Index Is Available

Goal

Combine two data sets that have a common variable where the common variable has duplicate values in both data sets and at least one of the data sets is indexed by the common variable. Produce a data set that contains all possible combinations of the observations where the values from the common variable match. Use indexing features to match the two data sets.

Example Features

Featured Step	DATA step
Featured Step Options and Statements	KEY= option in the SET statement Automatic variable _IORC_ and %SYRC autocall macro program
Related Technique	PROC SQL, WHERE clause and subqueries
A Closer Look	Checking for Errors When Using the MODIFY Statement or the SET Statement with the KEY= Option Finding a Match for Consecutive Duplicate Values When the Data Set Is Indexed

Input Data Sets

Data set FURNITURE_SALES contains six sales records. Data set FURNITURE_STOCK contains information about four products. Each product has more than one piece. Variable PRODUCT is common to both data sets. Multiple occurrences of the values of PRODUCT occur in both data sets and some occurences of the values of PRODUCT are found in only one data set.

FURNITURE_SALES is sorted by PRODUCT. Data set FURNITURE_STOCK is indexed on PRODUCT.

```
                      FURNITURE_SALES

        Obs    product      salesrep        orderno
         1       309      J.Corrigan      09173JC018
         2       310      K.Roland        09173KR001
         3       310      Y.Alvarez       09173YA015
         4       312      J.Corrigan      09173JC021
         5       313      J.Corrigan      09173JC031
         6       313      K.Roland        09173KR008
```

```
                          FURNITURE_STOCK

 Obs   product     product_desc          pieceid     piece_desc
  1      310      oak pedestal table     310.0103    tabletop
  2      310      oak pedestal table     310.0203    pedestal
  3      310      oak pedestal table     310.0303    two leaves
  4      311      upholstered chair      311.0103    chair base
  5      311      upholstered chair      311.0203    one cushion
  6      311      upholstered chair      311.0303    two arm covers
  7      312      brass floor lamp       312.0102    lamp base
  8      312      brass floor lamp       312.0202    lamp shade
  9      313      oak bookcase, short    313.0102    bookcase
 10      313      oak bookcase, short    313.0202    two shelves
```

Resulting Data Sets
Output 3.11a
SHIPLIST Data Set

```
                    Example 3.11 SHIPLIST Data Set Created with DATA Step

      Obs  product  salesrep   orderno       product_desc        pieceid   piece_desc

       1     310    K.Roland  09173KR001  oak pedestal table    310.0103  tabletop
       2     310    K.Roland  09173KR001  oak pedestal table    310.0203  pedestal
       3     310    K.Roland  09173KR001  oak pedestal table    310.0303  two leaves
       4     310    Y.Alvarez 09173YA015  oak pedestal table    310.0103  tabletop
       5     310    Y.Alvarez 09173YA015  oak pedestal table    310.0203  pedestal
       6     310    Y.Alvarez 09173YA015  oak pedestal table    310.0303  two leaves
       7     312    J.Corrigan 09173JC021 brass floor lamp      312.0102  lamp base
       8     312    J.Corrigan 09173JC021 brass floor lamp      312.0202  lamp shade
       9     313    J.Corrigan 09173JC031 oak bookcase, short   313.0102  bookcase
      10     313    J.Corrigan 09173JC031 oak bookcase, short   313.0202  two shelves
      11     313    K.Roland  09173KR008  oak bookcase, short   313.0102  bookcase
      12     313    K.Roland  09173KR008  oak bookcase, short   313.0202  two shelves
```

Output 3.11b
NOSTOCKINFO Data Set

```
              Example 3.11 NOSTOCKINFO Data Set Created with DATA Step

             Obs      product     salesrep       orderno

              1        309      J.Corrigan    09173JC018
```

Example Overview

As in Example 3.10, this example illustrates how to make all possible combinations of the observations from two data sets that match by a common variable. Here, one of the data sets is indexed, and the DATA step code uses indexing features. Additionally, both data sets can have duplicates of the values of the common variable.

Data set FURNITURE_SALES contains information about products sold. Data set FURNITURE_STOCK contains information about the products in stock. Both data sets identify the products by the values of variable PRODUCT. Each product has multiple pieces. Variable PIECEID in FURNITURE_STOCK contains both the product number and the piece number.

Product 309 in FURNITURE_SALES does not have a match in FURNITURE_STOCK. Product 311 in FURNITURE_STOCK does not have any sales data in FURNITURE_SALES.

The following DATA step has two objectives in combining FURNITURE_SALES and FURNITURE_STOCK by common variable PRODUCT:

❑ generate a shipping list of items sold, which includes all the pieces for a product

❑ generate a list of ordered items not found in FURNITURE_STOCK

The output data set, SHIPLIST, contains data for each sold product as identified in FURNITURE_SALES and this includes a list of all of the pieces that make up a product as stored in FURNITURE_STOCK. For example, the second observation in FURNITURE_SALES shows that product 310, an oak pedestal table, was sold. Data set FURNITURE_STOCK shows that product 310 consists of three pieces: a top, a base, and two leaves. Therefore, the resulting data set SHIPLIST contains three observations for the second sold item recorded in FURNITUTE_SALES.

The program requires that data set FURNITURE_SALES be sorted by or indexed on PRODUCT and that FURNITURE_STOCK be indexed on PRODUCT. The DATA step reads each observation sequentially from FURNITURE_SALES. The BY statement on PRODUCT enables BY-group processing of the observations in FURNITURE_SALES.

Because there can be multiple observations in FURNITURE_STOCK for one value of PRODUCT, the index on variable PRODUCT does not have unique keys.

A DO UNTIL loop executes for each observation in FURNITURE_SALES. This loop controls the lookup process for a match by PRODUCT in FURNITURE_STOCK. With the KEY=PRODUCT option in the SET statement, the DATA step reads matching observations directly from FURNITURE_STOCK and outputs all matches to SHIPLIST. A SELECT block within the loop evaluates the return codes from the indexed searches by using the %SYSRC autocall macro program. When no match occurs, the loop takes one of two actions depending on whether it has finished processing the current BY group in FURNITURE_SALES:

❏ If the current observation is the last observation in FURNITURE_SALES for the current BY group, the DO UNTIL loop condition is met causing the loop to end and to return processing to the top of the DATA step to read the first observation from the next BY group in FURNITURE_SALES.

❏ If the current observation is *not* the last observation in FURNITURE_SALES for the current BY group, the code resets the automatic variable _IORC_ to 0 and the flag variable MULTSAMEPROD to 1. Resetting _IORC_ to 0 keeps the loop executing and finds the multiple pieces per product from FURNITURE_STOCK. Assigning a value of 1 to MULTSAMEPROD causes the IF statement at the top of the DO UNTIL loop to assign a nonexistent PRODUCT value to the KEY=variable. Changing the value of the KEY= variable to this "dummy" number forces the index pointer to return to the beginning of the index so that multiple matches for one value of PRODUCT are found in FURNITURE_STOCK.

The variable INSTOCK that is defined in the DATA step tracks when a match for the current value of PRODUCT in FURNITURE_SALES is found in FURNITURE_STOCK. The value of INSTOCK is initialized to 0 prior to the DO UNTIL loop. If the value of INSTOCK is still 0 after the loop ends, the program concludes that the current value of PRODUCT from FURNITURE_SALES does not have a match in FURNITURE_STOCK. These nonmatched sales are written to data set NOSTOCKINFO and not to SHIPLIST.

Program

Define an index on PRODUCT for the data set that will be directly accessed. Allow nonunique keys in this simple index by omitting the UNIQUE option in the INDEX statement.

```
proc datasets library=work;
  modify furniture_stock;
  index create product;
run;
quit;
```

Create data set SHIPLIST.
Create data set NOSTOCKINFO. Keep in NOSTOCKINFO the variables found only in FURNITURE_SALES because this data set will contain observations for orders without a match in FURNITURE_STOCK.

```
data shiplist(drop=multsameprod instock)
     nostockinfo(keep=product salesrep orderno);
```

Read FURNITURE_SALES sequentially.

```
set furniture_sales;
```

Specify BY-group processing for data set FURNITURE_SALES.

```
by product;
```

Initialize a flag variable that tracks whether there are multiple occurrences of the same PRODUCT value in FURNITURE_SALES.

```
multsameprod=0;
```

Initialize a flag variable that tracks whether a match is found in FURNITURE_STOCK for the current value of PRODUCT from FURNITURE_SALES.

```
instock=0;
```

Execute a DO UNTIL loop for each observation in FURNITURE_SALES.

```
do until(_iorc_=%sysrc(_dsenom));
```

Specify that it test whether the return code from the indexed search saved in automatic variable _IORC_ equates to the not found condition.

```
if multsameprod then product=0;
```

Assign a value to PRODUCT that is nonexistent in FURNITURE_STOCK when a duplicate occurrence of a PRODUCT value has been found in FURNITURE_SALES. This action forces the pointer to return to the beginning of the index so that later observations in FURNITURE_SALES in the same BY group can find matches in FURNITURE_STOCK.

Search from the current pointer position in FURNITURE_STOCK for a match by PRODUCT in FURNITURE_SALES.

```
set furniture_stock key=product;
```

Direct processing of the results of the indexed search based on the value of the automatic variable _IORC_.

```
select (_iorc_);
```

Execute this DO group when the current observation from FURNITURE_SALES has a match in FURNITURE_STOCK. Set flag variable INSTOCK to 1. Output an observation to SHIPLIST.

```
  when (%sysrc(_sok)) do;
    instock=1;
    output shiplist;
  end;
```

Execute this DO group when the current observation from FURNITURE_SALES does not have a match in FURNITURE_STOCK.

```
  when (%sysrc(_dsenom)) do;
```

Reset automatic variable _ERROR_ to 0 to prevent writing error messages to the SAS log when no match is found. When the search does not find a match, SAS sets _ERROR_ to 1.

```
      _error_=0;
```

Execute this DO group to set flag variable MULTSAMEPROD and reset _IORC_ so that processing of multiple observations of a PRODUCT value from FURNITURE_SALES can occur.

```
      if not last.product and multsameprod=0 then do;
```

Set flag variable MULTSAMEPROD to 1 so that the IF statement at the top of the loop executes to assign a nonexistent key value to PRODUCT.

```
        multsameprod=1;
```

Reset automatic variable _IORC_ to 0 so that the DO UNTIL loop continues to execute and repeat matching the multiple occurrences of the current value of PRODUCT in FURNITURE_SALES.

```
        _iorc_=0;
```

```
      end;
    end;
    otherwise do;
```

For an unexpected _IORC_ condition, write a message to the SAS log and stop the DATA step.

```
      putlog 'ERROR: Unexpected ERROR: _IORC_= '
                              _iorc_;
      stop;
    end;
  end;
end;
```

Output observations from
FURNITURE_SALES that have no
match in FURNITURE_STOCK.

```
        if not instock then output nostockinfo;

run;
```

Related Technique

The following PROC SQL step creates two tables equivalent to the data sets that were created in the main example. A separate CREATE TABLE statement is needed for each table.

The SELECT statement that creates table SHIPLIST performs an inner join of the two tables on the values of the PRODUCT column.

The second SELECT statement specifies a subquery that selects the unique values of PRODUCT from FURNITURE_STOCK. The main query then uses the NOT IN condition test to select rows from FURNITURE_SALES that have values for PRODUCT not in the group of values that were returned by the subquery.

The PROC SQL step does not require that the tables be sorted or indexed. However, your PROC SQL programs might run more efficiently if the tables are sorted or indexed by the matching columns.

While the PROC SQL code is much simpler to follow than the preceding DATA step, it does not provide you with return codes from indexed searches that you can evaluate for error-checking purposes.

```
                         proc sql;
```
Create table SHIPLIST.
Select all columns from both tables.
Assign an alias to each table.
Select rows that match by the values of
PRODUCT.
Create table NOSTOCKINFO.
Select all columns from
FURNITURE_SALES.
Specify a subquery. Select rows from
FURNITURE_SALES that have values
for PRODUCT not found in
FURNITURE_STOCK. Include the
DISTINCT keyword so that the
subquery returns the unique values of
PRODUCT in FURNITURE_STOCK.

```
                           create table shiplist as
                             select * from furniture_sales as s,
                                          furniture_stock as k
                              where s.product=k.product;

                           create table nostockinfo as
                             select * from furniture_sales

                              where product not in
                                  (select distinct product from furniture_stock);


                         quit;
```

A Closer Look

Checking for Errors When Using the MODIFY Statement or the SET Statement with the KEY= Option

The DATA step in the main example reads observations from the indexed data set, FURNITURE_STOCK, by using the SET statement and the KEY= option. The DO UNTIL loop that follows the SET statement examines the return codes that result from the keyed search. The return codes determine the next step the program takes.

When reading observations with the KEY= option in the SET statement or the MODIFY statement, it is important to check the results of the keyed search. Because these tools use nonsequential access methods, there is no guarantee that the keyed search will locate an observation that satisfies the request.

Error checking enables you to direct execution to specific paths depending on the outcome of the keyed search. When you include error checking, you can prevent your programs from ending abnormally. Your program will continue executing for expected conditions and terminate execution when unexpected results occur.

Two SAS tools make error checking easier when using the MODIFY statement or the SET statement with the KEY= option:

❑ _IORC_ automatic variable

❑ SYSRC autocall macro program

SAS automatically creates variable _IORC_ when you use the MODIFY statement or the SET statement with the KEY= option. The value assigned to _IORC_ is a numeric return code that indicates the status of the I/O operation from the most recently executed MODIFY statement or the SET statement with the KEY= option.

Checking the value of _IORC_ for abnormal I/O conditions enables you to detect them and direct execution down specific code paths instead of having the application terminate abnormally. For example, if the KEY= value does find a match, you might want to process the data that were obtained from the matched observation. If the value does not find a match in the data set being searched, you might want to only write a note to the SAS log.

Because the values of the _IORC_ automatic variable are internal and subject to change, SAS created the %SYSRC macro program to enable you to test for specific I/O conditions while protecting your code from future changes that SAS might make in the values it assigns to _IORC_. Using %SYSRC, you can check the value of _IORC_ by specifying a mnemonic, the most common of which are listed in Table 3.1.

For more information about the values of _IORC_ and mnemonics you can pass to %SYSRC, see SAS documentation.

Table 3.1 List of Most Common Mnemonic Values of _IORC_

Mnemonic Value	Meaning of Return Code
_DSENMR	The *transaction* data set observation does not exist in the *master* data set.
_DSEMTR	Multiple *transaction* data set observations with the same BY variable value do not exist in the *master* data set. This return code occurs when consecutive observations with the same BY values do not find a match in the first data set. In this situation, the first observation to fail to find a match returns _DSENMR. Following observations return _DSEMTR.
_DSENOM	No matching observation was found in the *master* data set.
_SOK	The I/O operation was successful. When using the MODIFY statement or the SET statement with the KEY= option, it means a match was found.

Finding a Match for Consecutive Duplicate Values When the Data Set Is Indexed

Much of the logic of the DATA step in the main example focuses on the need to successfully match observations that contain consecutive duplicate values of the BY variable PRODUCT in FURNITURE_SALES with observations in FURNITURE_STOCK that contain the same value for PRODUCT. Unless you reposition the pointer at the beginning of the PRODUCT index for FURNITURE_STOCK, consecutive duplicate values of PRODUCT in FURNITURE_SALES will not be successfully matched.

The SELECT group in the DO UNTIL loop begins this process. When there are no more matches in the index on FURNITURE_STOCK for the current value of PRODUCT in FURNITURE_SALES, your code must determine whether there are more observations in the current BY group in FURNITURE_SALES. If there are more observations to process in the same BY group in FURNITURE_SALES and MULTSAMEPROD has not already been set to 1, assign values to automatic variable _IORC_ and the variable MULTSAMEPROD:

```
when (%sysrc(_dsenom)) do;
  _error_=0;
  if not last.product and multsameprod=0 then do;
    multsameprod=1;
    _iorc_=0;
  end;
end;
end;
```

By resetting the value of _IORC_ to 0, you cause the DO UNTIL loop to iterate again:

```
do until(_iorc_=%sysrc(_dsenom));
  if multsameprod then product=0;
  set furniture_stock key=product;
```

Because MULTSAMEPROD is true (equals 1), PRODUCT is set to 0, a nonexisting, "dummy" value. When the SET statement executes again, the pointer is forced to the beginning of the index on FURNITURE_STOCK because the value of PRODUCT, which is the KEY= variable, has changed. No match is found for PRODUCT=0, so the DO UNTIL loop ends and processing returns to the top of the DATA step. Then the DATA step reads the next observation from FURNITURE_SALES:

```
data shiplist(drop=multsameprod instock)
     nostockinfo(keep=product salesrep orderno);
  set furniture_sales;
  by product;

  multsameprod=0;
```

Because the pointer is at the beginning of the index on FURNITURE_STOCK, the observation in FURNITURE_SALES with a consecutive duplicate value for PRODUCT in FURNITURE_STOCK finds the appropriate match in FURNITURE_STOCK. MULTSAMEPROD is reset to 0 at the top of the DATA step so that its value does not trigger a change in the value of PRODUCT when it is not needed.

Example 3.12 Combining and Collapsing Observations Based on a Common Variable

Goal

Reshape a transaction data set by turning related observations into single ones. Match each collapsed observation from the transaction data set with an appropriate observation from the master data set, based on the value of a key variable.

Example 3.13 also combines and collapses observations based on a common variable, but its transaction data set is indexed on the common variable and it uses index features to combine the observations.

Example Features

Featured Step	PROC TRANSPOSE and DATA step
Featured Step Options and Statements	PROC TRANSPOSE: BY, ID, and VAR statements, PREFIX= option DATA step: match-merge by common variable
Related Technique	DATA step, arrays, RETAIN statement
A Closer Look	Naming the Variables in the Transposed Data Set

Input Data Sets

Data set WEIGHT_LOSS identifies five participants in a weight loss group. Data set WEIGHTS contains the weights for four of the five participants over a four-week period. The variable in common is ID. No weights were recorded for S005. Only one (S003) of the five participants has a weight recorded for each of the four weeks.

```
                 WEIGHT_LOSS

                          goal_
          Obs      id     weight
           1      S001     190
           2      S002     176
           3      S003     136
           4      S004     118
           5      S005     135
```

```
                   WEIGHTS

         Obs      id      week    weight
          1      S001      1       231
          2      S002      1       187
          3      S003      1       154
          4      S004      1       134
          5      S001      2       223
          6      S003      2       151
          7      S004      2       133
          8      S002      3       176
          9      S003      3       148
         10      S004      4       129
         11      S003      4       142
```

Resulting Data Set
Output 3.12
WEIGHT_UPDATES
Data Set

```
        Example 3.12 WEIGHT_UPDATES Data Set Created with PROC TRANSPOSE

                  goal_
    Obs   id     weight  wt_week1 wt_week2 wt_week3 wt_week4

     1   S001     190      231      223       .        .
     2   S002     176      187       .       176       .
     3   S003     136      154      151      148      142
     4   S004     118      134      133       .       129
     5   S005     135       .        .        .        .
```

Example Overview

This example transposes the observations in a transaction data set and match-merges the transposed observations to a master data set. It shows you how to use PROC TRANSPOSE to collapse observations based on a common variable and control how the variables are named and arranged in the output data set. A DATA step then merges this new transaction data set to the master data set.

Participants in a weight loss group and their goal weight are identified in data set WEIGHT_LOSS. Each observation in data set WEIGHTS records the weight for a participant at a specific week.

The goal of the program is to rearrange the observations in WEIGHTS so that all the weights for a participant are in one observation rather than several observations, and then merge the transposed observations to the master data set WEIGHT_LOSS by common variable ID. All observations in WEIGHT_LOSS are to be kept even if there is no match in WEIGHTS.

An *advantage* of this program over the DATA step in the Related Technique is that you do not have to know in advance how many values of WEEK are in WEIGHT_LOSS so that you define the correct number of variables.

One *disadvantage* of this program over the DATA step in the Related Technique is if you have multiple variables to transpose. Within each BY group, PROC TRANSPOSE creates an observation for each variable named in the VAR statement. Data set WEIGHT_LOSS is collapsed into four observations, one for each study subject in WEIGHT_LOSS, because the procedure transposes only one variable, WEIGHT. If two variables were transposed, PROC TRANSPOSE would create an output data set with eight observations and you would have to perform additional processing to get all the information for one subject on one observation.

Program

Sort data set WEIGHTS by ID because the goal is to transpose WEIGHT values for each subject. Order the observations for each subject by WEEK so that PROC TRANSPOSE will define the transposed variables in order by the values of WEEK as they are encountered in the data set.

```
proc sort data=weights;
   by id week;
run;
```

Transpose data set WEIGHTS.
Save the transposed observations in TRANSWT. Drop the automatic variable _NAME_, which contains the name of the variable that is being transposed.

```
proc transpose data=weights
               out=transwt(drop=_name_)
```

Specify a prefix to use in constructing the names of the transposed variables. Do not enclose the text in quotation marks.

```
               prefix=wt_week;
```

For each ID value, create an observation for each transposed variable.

```
   by id;
```

Name the variable to transpose.
Specify the variable whose values name the transposed variables in the output data set. By specifying the PREFIX= option, precede the values of WEEK in the variable name with the PREFIX= text.

```
   var weight;
   id week;
```

```
run;
```

Create data set WEIGHT_UPDATES. ***Combine WEIGHT_LOSS and the*** ***transposed data set TRANSWT by the*** ***common variable ID. Specify the IN=*** ***data set option on WEIGHT_LOSS so*** ***that it can be determined when*** ***observations are contributed from*** ***WEIGHT_LOSS.***	```data weight_updates;
merge weight_loss(in=ingroup) transwt;
by id;```
Keep all observations in ***WEIGHT_LOSS whether or not they*** ***have a match in TRANSWT.***	``` if ingroup;```
	```run;```

Related Technique

The following DATA step creates a data set equivalent to the one that was created in the main example. It requires that you know beforehand the possible values of WEEK in data set WEIGHTS, and it relies on the values of week being sequential from 1 to 4. If the data values of the variable you want to transpose are not sequential, you must modify the code that tests the values so that the values are placed in the proper array elements.

The DATA step places each value of WEIGHT in the WT_WEEK array based on its associated value for WEEK. The elements of the WT_WEEK array are retained across observations. When processing the first observation in an ID BY group, all of the elements of the WT_WEEK array are set to missing. The DATA step outputs observations to WEIGHT_UPDATES only after processing the last observation in an ID BY group.

Both input data sets must be sorted or indexed by ID before executing the DATA step.

The dimension of the WT_WEEK array is the maximum number of observations in a BY group, which is 4. The ARRAY statement is the only location where that value is explicitly specified.

Create data set WEIGHT_UPDATES. ***Combine WEIGHT_LOSS and*** ***WEIGHTS by the common variable ID.*** ***Specify the IN= data set option on*** ***WEIGHT_LOSS so that it can be*** ***determined when observations are*** ***contributed from WEIGHT_LOSS.***	```data weight_updates;
merge weight_loss(in=ingroup) weights;```
Merge the two data sets by common ***variable ID and define BY-group*** ***processing.***	``` by id;```
Define an array that will hold the ***transposed values. Specify as the*** ***dimension of the array the maximum*** ***number of observations in a BY group.***	``` array wt_week{4};```
Retain the elements of the WT_WEEK ***array across iterations of the DATA*** ***step.***	``` retain wt_week:;```
Drop variables not needed in the output ***data set, including WEIGHT whose*** ***values are moved to the elements of the*** ***WT_WEEK array, and WEEK whose*** ***values are represented by the suffix on*** ***the WT_WEEK series of variables.***	``` drop weight week;```
At the beginning of each BY group, set ***to missing all the elements of the*** ***WT_WEEK array.***	``` if first.id then call missing(of wt_week[*]);```

For known values of WEEK, copy the value of WEIGHT to the corresponding WT_WEEK array element.

Output an observation only when processing the last observation in an ID BY group.

```
if 1 le week le dim(wt_week) then
                    wt_week{week}=weight;

if last.id then output;

run;
```

A Closer Look

Naming the Variables in the Transposed Data Set

The PREFIX= option in the PROC TRANSPOSE statement in conjunction with the ID statement control how the main example names the variables that were created by transposing variable WEIGHT.

PROC TRANSPOSE transposes the values of WEIGHT for each study subject into a series of variables that have the prefix WT_WEEK. The suffix for the WT_WEEK variables is the week of the measurement. Because variable WEEK has four values—1, 2, 3, and 4—the data set that contains the transposed observations will contain four WT_WEEK variables: WT_WEEK1, WT_WEEK2, WT_WEEK3, and WT_WEEK4.

The values of WEEK determine the suffix on the WT_WEEK variables. For example, if your WEEK values were 1, 4, 8, and 12, the names of the four variables would be WT_WEEK1, WT_WEEK4, WT_WEEK8, and WT_WEEK12.

The order in which PROC TRANSPOSE encounters the values of WEEK determines the order in which it defines the transposed variables. Subject S001 has a weight value for the first two weeks, subject S002 has values for the first and third weeks, and subject S003 has values for all four weeks. Therefore, PROC TRANSPOSE defines the series of WT_WEEK variables in sequential order: WT_WEEK1, WT_WEEK2, WT_WEEK3, and WT_WEEK4. However, if subject S001 did not have a value for week 1, the order of the variables in the output data set would be WT_WEEK2, WT_WEEK1, WT_WEEK3, and WT_WEEK4.

You could also move the ARRAY and RETAIN statements before the MERGE statement to ensure these variables were defined in the Program Data Vector in a specific order.

Ensure that the variable you name in the ID statement does not contain duplicate values within the BY group. None of the subjects in this example have more than one weight recorded per week. If a subject did have duplicate values for a week, SAS would stop the PROC TRANSPOSE step and issue an error and warning message. If you are aware of the duplicate condition, you could add the LET option to the PROC TRANSPOSE statement. This prevents the error condition and causes PROC TRANSPOSE to transpose the observation that contains the last occurrence of the particular ID value within the data set or BY group.

Example 3.13 Combining and Collapsing Observations Based on a Common Variable When the Transaction Data Set Is Indexed

Goal

Reshape a data set by turning related observations into single ones. Match the collapsed observations from this data set with an appropriate observation from another data set based on the value of a key variable that is indexed in the first data set.

Example 3.12 also combines and collapses observations based on a common variable, but Example 3.12 does not use code that relies on indexes.

Example Features

Featured Step	DATA step
Featured Step Options and Statements	KEY= option in the SET statement Automatic variable _IORC_ and %SYRC autocall macro program

Input Data Sets

Data set KIDS_IDS contains identification information about five pediatric patients with one observation per patient. Data set IMMUNIZATIONS contains 36 immunization records for patients with one immunization per observation and multiple observations possible per patient. The variable in common between the two data sets is ID. Four of the observations in KIDS_IDS have at least one matching observation in IMMUNIZATIONS. ID C1901 does not. ID C0054 is not in KIDS_IDS, but it does have two observations in IMMUNIZATIONS.

```
                   KIDS_IDS

        Obs      id           dob
         1      C0402     07/15/2001
         2      C1593     06/30/2003
         3      C1374     04/23/2007
         4      C3811     02/01/2009
         5      C1901     03/18/2009
```

```
                  IMMUNIZATIONS

   Obs      id      type     sequence    received
    1     C3811     POLIO        1      04/01/2009
    2     C0402     DTAP         1      09/12/2001
    3     C0402     POLIO        1      09/12/2001
    4     C0402     DTAP         2      11/16/2001
    5     C0402     POLIO        2      11/16/2001
    6     C0402     DTAP         3      01/10/2002
    7     C0402     POLIO        3      04/14/2002
    8     C0402     CPOX         1      07/30/2002
    9     C0402     MMR          1      07/30/2002
   10     C0402     DTAP         4      11/20/2002
   11     C0402     CPOX         2      04/15/2006
   12     C0402     MMR          2      04/15/2006
   13     C0402     DTAP         5      08/15/2006
   14     C0402     POLIO        4      08/15/2006
   15     C1593     DTAP         1      09/05/2003
   16     C1593     POLIO        1      09/05/2003
   17     C1593     DTAP         2      10/29/2003
   18     C1593     POLIO        2      10/29/2003
   19     C1593     DTAP         3      01/03/2004
   20     C1593     CPOX         1      08/04/2004
   21     C1593     MMR          1      08/04/2004
   22     C1593     DTAP         4      10/20/2004
   23     C1593     DTAP         5      07/16/2008
   24     C1593     POLIO        3      07/16/2008
   25     C1593     CPOX         2      08/23/2008
   26     C1593     MMR          2      08/23/2008
   27     C1374     DTAP         1      06/28/2007
   28     C1374     POLIO        1      06/28/2007
   29     C1374     DTAP         2      08/22/2007
   30     C1374     POLIO        2      08/22/2007
   31     C1374     DTAP         3      10/20/2007
   32     C1374     POLIO        3      01/22/2008
   33     C1374     CPOX         1      05/03/2008
   34     C1374     MMR          1      05/03/2008
   35     C0054     DTAP         1      07/01/2000
   36     C0054     POLIO        1      07/01/2000
```

Resulting Data Set
Output 3.13
DTAP_KIDS Data Set

```
                      Example 3.13 DTAP_KIDS Data Set Created with DATA Step

     Obs  id          dob dtap_date1 dtap_date2 dtap_date3 dtap_date4 dtap_date5

      1   C0402 07/15/2001 09/12/2001 11/16/2001 01/10/2002 11/20/2002 08/15/2006
      2   C1593 06/30/2003 09/05/2003 10/29/2003 01/03/2004 10/20/2004 07/16/2008
      3   C1374 04/23/2007 06/28/2007 08/22/2007 10/20/2007 06/15/2008          .
```

Example Overview

This example shows you how to link two data sets where the key values are unique in one data set and where the second data set can contain multiple observations for the same key value. The second data set with multiple observations per key value is indexed by the key variable.

The program reads the first data set sequentially while using the KEY= option to directly access observations in the indexed data set. The code shows you how to collapse the multiple observations per key value in the second data set into a single observation and combine the single observation with an observation in the first data set.

Data set KID_IDS contains a list of pediatric patients age 6 and under and uniquely identifies them by variable ID. Data set IMMUNIZATIONS contains immunization information about pediatric patients. Each observation in IMMUNIZATIONS stores the information for one immunization for a child. The variable in common between the two data sets is ID. The variable TYPE in IMMUNIZATIONS identifies the type of immunization. The variable SEQUENCE in IMMUNIZATIONS identifies the shot number in the series of immunizations for a specific type.

The goal of the DATA step is to find all the diphtheria, tetanus, and pertussis (DTAP) immunizations in IMMUNIZATIONS for the pediatric patients in KIDS_IDS. Following pediatric medicine standards, it is expected that the child will receive up to five DTAP immunizations by the age of 6. Therefore, it is expected the value of SEQUENCE can range from 1 to 5 for a child.

The dates of the DTAP immunizations are added to the observations read from KIDS_IDS. Only observations with at least one DTAP immunization are output. The IF statement in the second WHEN block checks that the observation has at least one immunization date before outputting an observation.

Five new variables defined by array ALLSHOTS store the series of DTAP immunization dates: DTAP_DATE1, DTAP_DATE2, DTAP_DATE3, DTAP_DATE4, and DTAP_DATE5. The program copies each DTAP immunization date to the ALLSHOTS array element that is defined by the value of SEQUENCE.

The DATA step starts by reading KIDS_IDS sequentially. A DO UNTIL loop follows that looks for all observations in IMMUNIZATIONS that match by ID. The observations are found by directly accessing IMMUNIZATIONS through a simple index on ID. The return codes from the search operations are tested so that appropriate code paths are followed.

DTAP immunizations are found for three children: C0402, C1593, and C1374. Because child C3811 has only a polio shot, the DATA step does not output an observation for this child. Child C1901 has no observations in IMMUNIZATIONS and therefore no observation in the output data set. Child C0054 has two immunization observations in IMMUNIZATIONS and none in KIDS_IDS so an observation for this child is not in the output data set.

Note that you do not need to sort KIDS_IDS by ID prior to the DATA step. The technique shown does not perform a match-merge that relies on ordering the observations by a BY variable. Instead, matching observations in IMMUNIZATIONS are accessed directly by the key variable ID.

The "A Closer Look" section in Example 3.11 describes in more detail how to use the _IORC_ automatic variable and %SYSRC autocall macro program.

Program

Create data set DTAP_KIDS.
Read data set KIDS_IDS sequentially.
Prepare to collapse up to five DTAP immunization observations from the transaction data set into one observation by defining array ALLSHOTS.

```
data dtap_kids;
  set kids_ids;
  array allshots{5} dtap_date1-dtap_date5;
```

Drop unneeded variables that come from IMMUNIZATIONS and whose values are collapsed into the DTAP_DATE variables.

```
  format dtap_date1-dtap_date5 mmddyy10.;
  drop sequence received type;
```

Execute a DO UNTIL loop until all observations in IMMUNIZATIONS with the current value of ID from KIDS_IDS have been read. Specify that it test whether the return code from the keyed search, which is saved in automatic variable _IORC_, equates to the not found condition.

```
  do until (_iorc_=%sysrc(_dsenom));
```

Read an observation from IMMUNIZATIONS based on the current value of the key variable ID from KIDS_IDS.

```
    set immunizations key=id;
```

Direct processing of the results of the indexed search based on the value of the automatic variable _IORC_.

```
    select (_iorc_);
```

Test if the search was successful by passing the mnemonic _SOK to autocall macro program %SYSRC.
Process only observations of type DTAP.

```
      when(%sysrc(_sok)) do;

        if type='DTAP' then do;
```

Update the ALLSHOTS array element that corresponds to the current value of SEQUENCE for values of SEQUENCE between 1 and 5.
Write an error message to the SAS log when the values of SEQUENCE are invalid.

```
          if 1 le sequence le 5 then
              allshots{sequence}=received;

          else putlog
'ERROR: DTAP_DATE cannot be updated. Value of SEQUENCE
                          is not 1-5.'  /
                    id= sequence= received=;
        end;
      when (%sysrc(_dsenom)) do;
```

Execute this block of code when the indexed search does not find a match, which includes when all observations from IMMUNIZATIONS with the current value of ID from KIDS_IDS have been read.
Because there are no more observations with the current value of ID in IMMUNIZATIONS, conclude that all DTAP_DATE values present for the ID value have been copied to the elements of ALLSHOTS. Write the completed observation to DTAP_KIDS only if the child had at least one DTAP immunization.

```
        if allshots{1} ne . then output;
```

***Reset automatic variable _ERROR_ to
0 to prevent writing error messages to
the SAS log when no match is found.***
When the search does not find a match,
SAS sets _ERROR_ to 1.

***For an unexpected _IORC_ condition,
write a message to the SAS log and stop
the DATA step.***

```
      _error_=0;



    end;
    otherwise do;
      putlog "ERROR: Unexpected error _IORC_=" _iorc_;
      stop;
    end;
  end;
 end;
run;
```

CHAPTER 4
Using Lookup Tables to Match Data

Table lookup programming involves setting up a table of values that a DATA step or PROC SQL step can reference. Your code then finds a value in the lookup table usually based on information in the observation or row that it is currently processing.

A program that performs table lookup typically puts the table of values in one of four structures:

❑ *A data set.* When a data set stores your lookup values, the table lookup process can be coded as a match-merge or join by value as demonstrated in Chapter 3.

❑ *An array.* Your DATA step finds a value in an array that stores your lookup table through use of an array index value.

❑ *A hash table.* Your DATA step finds values in a hash table that stores your lookup values through use of hash keys.

❑ *A user-defined format.* With lookup values stored in a user-defined format created by PROC FORMAT, you can use the PUT function or a FORMAT statement to find a value in the lookup table.

When deciding on the table lookup technique to use, you need to consider the effort and resources it takes to make the table. With a small set of lookup values, it might be more efficient to load the values into an array and write DO loops to find values than it would be to store the values in a data set, and then perform a match-merge. On the other hand, if you have many lookup values, it would not be efficient to store them in an array because of memory usage. When you have complex lookup values, it might be more efficient to program a hash table that can handle the complexity rather than writing a series of user-defined formats and PUT functions.

This chapter demonstrates lookup table techniques that use the four structures listed above. All of the examples show at least two ways of accomplishing the lookup task.

Example 4.1   Performing a Simple Table Lookup

Goal

Find a match in a lookup table for the current value of the key column in the primary table. For observations in the primary table with no match in the lookup table, assign a default value to the lookup column.

Example Features

Featured Step	PROC SQL
Featured Step Options and Statements	Left join ON clause
Related Technique 1	Hash object in the DATA step
Related Technique 2	DATA step match-merge, MERGE statement with IN= option

Input Tables

Table SALARIES contains salaries for four employees identified by column EMPNUM. Table BRACKETS contains tax brackets for five employees. Column EMPNUM is common to both tables.

```
     SALARIES                    BRACKETS
                                          tax_
Obs  empnum    salary       Obs  empnum  bracket
 1    1234    $125,000       1    1111    0.28
 2    3333    $85,000        2    1234    0.33
 3    4876    $54,000        3    3333    0.28
 4    5489    $29,000        4    4222    0.15
                             5    4876    0.25
```

Resulting Table
Output 4.1
NETPAY Table

```
          Example 4.1 NETPAY Table Created with PROC SQL
                                    tax_
           Obs    empnum     salary    bracket     net_pay

            1      1234    $125,000     0.33      $83,750
            2      3333     $85,000     0.28      $61,200
            3      4876     $54,000     0.25      $40,500
            4      5489     $29,000     0.10      $26,100
```

Example Overview

This example shows you how to look up information for every row in a table by linking to another table by the values of a key column that is common to both tables.

Table SALARIES contains the salaries for four employees. Table BRACKETS contains tax brackets for five employees. Column EMPNUM is common to both tables and uniquely identifies the rows in each table.

The goal of this example is to look up the tax bracket for each employee in SALARIES and to compute the net pay for that employee. One employee, EMPNUM 5489, does not have a matching row in BRACKETS.

A PROC SQL left outer join correctly combines the tables because all rows from the master table, SALARIES, are to be output while values for TAX_BRACKET from only matched rows in the lookup table, BRACKETS, are retrieved. On the left side of the join is SALARIES and on the right side is BRACKETS.

The PROC SQL step matches the rows in SALARIES to the rows in BRACKETS by common column EMPNUM. The left join returns the rows that satisfy the condition in the ON clause and the rows in SALARIES that do not have a match in BRACKETS.

The CASE clause creates a column called TAX_BRACKET. When a row in SALARIES matches a row in BRACKETS, the value assigned to TAX_BRACKET is simply the value for TAX_BRACKET in BRACKETS. When a row in SALARIES has no match in BRACKETS, the value 0.10 is assigned to the TAX_BRACKET column in NETPAY.

Because employee 5489 has no row in BRACKETS, and thus no value for TAX_BRACKET in BRACKETS, the CASE clause assigns 0.10 to the calculated column TAX_BRACKET for employee 5489. It is then possible to compute NET_PAY for employee 5489.

Program

Create table NETPAY.
Select specific columns from SALARIES.
Use the value of 0.10 for the calculated column TAX_BRACKET in table NETPAY when a value for TAX_BRACKET is not found in BRACKETS.
Compute the new column NET_PAY by using information from both SALARIES and BRACKETS. Precede column name TAX_BRACKET with the keyword CALCULATED so that the value used is the value that was computed earlier in the CASE expression and not a value taken directly from BRACKETS.
Perform a left join of SALARIES and BRACKETS based on the values of EMPNUM. Assign an alias to the SALARIES table.

```
proc sql;
  create table netpay as
    select s.empnum, s.salary,

          case when tax_bracket eq . then 0.10
              else tax_bracket
          end as tax_bracket format=4.2,


          salary*(1-calculated tax_bracket)
            as net_pay format=dollar10.




      from salaries s left join brackets
      on s.empnum=brackets.empnum;

quit;
```

Related Technique 1

The DATA step in this related technique creates a data set equivalent to the table that was created by the PROC SQL step in the main example. It accomplishes the same lookup task by defining a hash object from which to find the information stored in data set BRACKETS through values of the common key variable, EMPNUM.

A hash object provides a fast, easy way to perform lookups. Data that are loaded into a hash object do not need to be sorted or indexed. Because a hash object is stored in memory, it provides quick retrieval. Using a hash object for this example is a good choice because the lookup data set in this example is small and can fit easily into memory.

The DATA step loads data set LOOKUP into hash object B. It defines EMPNUM in BRACKETS as the single hash key and TAX_BRACKET in BRACKETS as data. For each observation in SALARIES, the DATA step looks for a match in hash object B for the current value of EMPNUM. For those observations without a match in BRACKETS, and for those observations with a match in BRACKETS but no value for TAX_BRACKET, the DATA step assigns a default value to TAX_BRACKET before computing NET_PAY.

Specify attributes for the variables saved in data set NETPAY.

Define a default value for the tax bracket.

On the first iteration of the DATA step,

```
data netpay;
  attrib empnum length=8
         salary length=8 format=dollar10.
         tax_bracket length=8 format=4.2
         net_pay length=8 format=dollar10.;
  retain default_bracket .10;

  drop default_bracket rc;
  if _n_=1 then do;
```

create, name, and specify attributes of the hash object.	
Create hash object B and load the hash object with data from data set BRACKETS.	`declare hash b(dataset:'brackets');`
Specify one key variable.	`b.defineKey('empnum');`
Specify one data variable.	`b.defineData('tax_bracket');`
Close the definition of hash object B.	`b.defineDone();`

```
end;
set salaries;
```

Read data set SALARIES one observation at a time.	
Determine whether the current value of EMPNUM from SALARIES is stored in hash object B. Save the return code of the search results in variable RC.	`rc=b.find();`

When the hash lookup finds a match in hash object B, SAS copies the data part of the hash object into the variables that are specified by DEFINEDATA, which is TAX_BRACKET.

When the hash lookup does not find a match in hash object B, or if the value for TAX_BRACKET that was returned from B is missing, assign a default value to TAX_BRACKET.	`if rc ne 0 or tax_bracket=. then` `        tax_bracket=default_bracket;`
Compute NET_PAY.	`net_pay=salary*(1-tax_bracket);` `run;`

Related Technique 2

This related technique program also uses a DATA step to look up values. It does a match-merge of data sets SALARIES and BRACKETS by variable EMPNUM. Many of the examples in Chapter 3 used match-merges to combine data sets. Match-merging can also be used as a lookup technique. Here, information is looked up in BRACKETS for each observation in SALARIES.

Because the DATA step does the match-merge by using a BY statement, both input data sets must be sorted or indexed by variable EMPNUM. The DATA step uses the IN= option on SALARIES to keep all the observations in SALARIES whether or not the observation has a match in BRACKETS.

Sort the two input data sets by the variable that will match them.	`proc sort data=salaries;`
	`  by empnum;`
	`run;`
	`proc sort data=brackets;`
	`  by empnum;`
	`run;`

Create data set NETPAY. *Merge the two data sets. Add the IN= option to data set SALARIES so it can be determined when an observation is found in SALARIES.*	`data netpay;` `  merge salaries(in=insal) brackets;`

Match the data sets by EMPNUM.
Keep all observations from SALARIES.
	`  by empnum;`
	`  if insal;`
	`  format net_pay dollar10.;`

Assign a default value to TAX_BRACKET for those observations in SALARIES without a match in BRACKETS.	`  if tax_bracket=. then tax_bracket=.1;`
	`net_pay=salary*(1-tax_bracket);` `run;`

Example 4.2 Performing a Table Lookup in a Small Lookup Data Set

Goal

Perform a table lookup based on more than one key where the lookup data set is small and not indexed. Subset the observations from the primary data set into one of two output data sets based on specific criteria that are supplied by the lookup data set.

Example Features

Featured Step	DATA step
Featured Step Options and Statements	SET statement, NOBS= option Two-dimensional arrays
Related Technique	Hash object in the DATA step
A Closer Look	Processing the Two-Dimensional Array WT Understanding Temporary Arrays

Input Data Sets

Data set BTEAM contains data on team members' height, weight, and body type.

```
                            BTEAM

     Obs    lname       gender    height    weight    type

      1     Adams         M         67       160       2
      2     Alexander     M         69       115       1
      3     Apple         M         69       139       1
      4     Arthur        M         66       125       2
      5     Avery         M         66       152       2
      6     Barefoot      M         68       158       2
      7     Baucom        M         70       170       3
      8     Blair         M         69       133       1
      9     Blalock       M         68       148       2
     10     Bostic        M         74       170       3
```

Data set IDEAL shows the ideal weight for males based on one of three body types.

```
                            IDEAL

     Obs    height    small    medium    large

      1       66       126      138       149
      2       67       130      141       154
      3       68       134      145       158
      4       69       138      149       162
      5       70       142      153       167
      6       71       146      157       172
      7       72       150      161       177
      8       73       154      165       181
      9       74       158      169       185
     10       75       162      173       189
```

Resulting Data Sets
Output 4.2a
INSHAPE Data Set

```
                Example 4.2 INSHAPE Data Set

         Obs    height    lname    weight    type

          1       69      Apple     139       1
          2       70      Baucom    170       3
          3       69      Blair     133       1
          4       68      Blalock   148       2
```

Output 4.2b
OUTOFSHAPE Data Set

```
                        Example 4.2 OUTOFSHAPE Data Set

            Obs    height    lname        weight    type

             1       67      Adams          160       2
             2       69      Alexander      115       1
             3       66      Arthur         125       2
             4       66      Avery          152       2
             5       68      Barefoot       158       2
             6       74      Bostic         170       3
```

Example Overview

This example shows you how to look up information for every observation in a data set based on the values of more than one key variable. A DATA step performs the lookup and places the lookup information in a multidimensional array. In this example, an array as a lookup table is a good choice because the lookup data set that fills the array is relatively small and can easily fit into memory. Additionally, the lookup data set is already sorted and organized in the way that is needed to easily fill the array.

The related technique also works just as well in performing this lookup in a small data set.

The goal of the program is to create subsets from the BTEAM data set based on whether a team member's weight is considered to be in shape or out of shape. A DATA step looks up each team member's ideal weight to make the fitness determination based on the team member's height (variable HEIGHT) and body type (variable TYPE). The ideal weights are copied from data set IDEAL to an array that is defined in the DATA step.

Each observation in IDEAL stores the ideal weights for the three body types for a specific height sequentially from 66 inches to 75 inches. The body type variables in IDEAL are SMALL, MEDIUM, and LARGE, which correspond to BTEAM variable TYPE values of 1, 2, and 3, respectively.

The DATA step starts by filling the temporary array WT with all the values from IDEAL. The following "A Closer Look" sections describe characteristics of temporary arrays. The first dimension of the array defines the 10 sequential height values. The second dimension of the array specifies the three body types. Therefore, array WT has a total of 30 elements.

The first IF statement checks that the observation currently being processed is valid for lookup. For valid observations, a second IF statement compares the current value for WEIGHT to the ideal weight for the person's body type and height.

Observations for team members within five pounds of the ideal weight are output to the INSHAPE data set while those not within five pounds of the ideal weight are output to OUTOFSHAPE. For observations that are not valid for lookup, the DATA step writes a message to the SAS log. These observations are not saved in either output data set.

Program

Create INSHAPE and OUTOFSHAPE data sets.

Define a temporary two-dimensional array. Specify the first dimension range from 66 to 75, which corresponds to the heights that were saved in IDEAL. Specify three levels in the second dimension, which correspond to the

```
data inshape outofshape;

   keep lname height weight type;
   array wt(66:75,3) _temporary_;
```

three body types of small, medium, and large, respectively.

On the first iteration of the DATA step, load the WT temporary array with the information that was saved in IDEAL.

Execute an iterative DO loop to read each observation in IDEAL.

Set the upper index of the DO loop to ALL, which is the total number of observations in IDEAL and is defined by the NOBS= option in the following SET statement.

Read data set IDEAL.

Assign weight values from IDEAL to the correct array elements.

Read each observation in BTEAM. Process observations that are valid for lookup.

Compare the team member's actual weight to his ideal weight. Find the ideal weight value in the WT array based on the team member's height and body type. Output an observation to either INSHAPE or OUTOFSHAPE based on the results of the comparison.

Write a message to the SAS log if the observation is not valid for lookup.

```
if _n_=1 then do;


  do i=1 to all;










    set ideal nobs=all;
    wt(height,1)=small;
    wt(height,2)=medium;
    wt(height,3)=large;
  end;
end;
set bteam;
if gender='M' and
   (1 le type le 3) and
   (66 le height le 75) then do;
  if wt(height,type)-5 le weight le wt(height,type)+5
                          then output inshape;
  else output outofshape;




end;
else putlog
        'WARNING: Observation out of lookup range: '
                           _all_;
run;
```

Related Technique

The DATA step in this related technique creates data sets equivalent to the data sets that were created in the main example. Instead of filling an array with the lookup information, it defines a hash object and loads it with this information. A hash object resides in memory and does not require that you sort the data set before loading it into the hash object.

For each observation in BTEAM that is valid for lookup, the DATA step looks for a match in hash object WT for the current value of HEIGHT. For those observations with a match, assignment statements select the ideal weight based on the team member's body type. IF statements compare the team member's weight to that retrieved from the hash object. If the team member's weight is within five pounds of the ideal weight, the code outputs the observations to INSHAPE. Otherwise, the code outputs the observation to OUTOFSHAPE.

As in the main example, the DATA step writes a message to the SAS log for those observations that are not valid for lookup in IDEAL.

Specify attributes for the variables that are saved in data sets INSHAPE and OUTOFSHAPE.

On the first iteration of the DATA step, create, name, and specify attributes of the hash object.

Create hash object WT and load the hash object with data from data set

```
data inshape outofshape;
  attrib lname length=$10
         gender length=$1
         height length=8
         weight length=8;
  keep lname gender height weight;
  if _n_=1 then do;


    declare hash wt(dataset:'ideal');
```

IDEAL.
Specify one key variable.
Specify three data variables.
Close the definition of hash object WT.
Prevent SAS notes about uninitialized
variables with the CALL MISSING
statement. (The SAS compiler does not
see variable assignments in the hash
object and these three variables do not
have explicit assignment statements
elsewhere in the DATA step.)

Read data set BTEAM.
Process observations valid for lookup.

Look up weight classification
information in hash object WT for the
current value of HEIGHT from
BTEAM. Save the return code of the
search results in variable RC.
Execute this DO group for matches
that are found in hash object WT,
which is when the FIND method
returns a code of 0. For matches, SAS
copies the data part of the hash object
into the variables that are specified by
DEFINEDATA.
Determine the ideal weight based on
the value of TYPE.

Output an observation to either
INSHAPE or OUTOFSHAPE based on
the results of the comparison.

For observations valid for lookup, but
without a match in the hash object,
write a message to the SAS log.

Write a message to the SAS log if the
observation is not valid for lookup.

```
wt.defineKey('height');
wt.defineData('small','medium','large');
wt.defineDone();
call missing(small,medium,large);




end;
set bteam;
if 66 le height le 75 and gender='M' and
        type in (1,2,3) then do;
  rc=wt.find();



  if rc=0 then do;




    if type=1 then ideal=small;
    else if type=2 then ideal=medium;
    else if type=3 then ideal=large;
    if ideal-5 le weight le ideal+5 then
        output inshape;
    else output outofshape;
  end;
  else putlog 'WARNING: Height not found in hash
                      object: ' _all_;

end;
else putlog 'WARNING: Observation out of range: '
                  _all_;

run;
```

A Closer Look

Processing the Two-Dimensional Array WT
To help visualize the processing in this example, Figure 4.1 represents the two-
dimensional array WT, beginning with the lower bound of 66. If you compare it to the
IDEAL data set, you can see how it was constructed.

Figure 4.1
Representation of
Two-Dimensional
Array WT

TYPE	HEIGHT									
	66	67	68	69	70	71	72	73	74	75
1	126	130	134	138	142	146	150	154	158	162
2	138	141	145	149	153	157	161	165	169	173
3	149	154	158	162	167	172	177	181	185	189

This statement processes the array:

```
if wt(height,type)-5 le weight le wt(height,type)+5 then
        output inshape;
```

On the first iteration of the DATA step, the first observation from BTEAM is processed:

```
Adams M 67 160 2
```

The cell in the array that is the intersection of column 67 (HEIGHT) and row 2 (TYPE) contains the weight value 141. The IF-THEN statement processes these values:

```
if 141-5 le weight le 141+5 then
        output inshape;
```

Understanding Temporary Arrays

When elements in an array are constants that are needed only during the duration of the DATA step, you can save execution time by using temporary arrays instead of creating variables, as shown in this ARRAY statement:

```
array wt(66:75,3) _temporary_;
```

In addition to saving execution time, temporary array elements differ from variables in the following ways:

❏ They are not written to the output data set.

❏ They do not have names and can be referenced only by their array names and dimensions.

❏ They are automatically retained instead of reset to missing at the beginning of each iteration of the DATA step.

Example 4.3   Performing a Table Lookup in a Large, Non-Indexed Lookup Data Set

Goal

Efficiently combine two data sets when one is relatively large and not indexed and whose retrieved values remain fairly constant.

Example Features

Featured Step	PROC FORMAT and DATA step
Featured Step Options and Statements	PROC FORMAT CNTLIN= option DATA step: PUT function, END= data set option
Related Technique	Hash object in the DATA step
A Closer Look	Using Formats to Perform a Table Lookup Building a Format Dynamically with CNTLIN=

Input Data Sets

PROVIDERS contains information about providers in a healthcare system. The first 12 of 279 observations are presented.

PROVIDERS

Obs	provider_ id	provider_ name	specialty	provider_ type
1	0025	Davis, WU	Family Medicine	MD
2	0032	Miller, KB	Family Medicine	MD
3	0034	Scott, XG	Obstetrics and Gynecology	MD
4	0047	Gray, VO	Family Medicine	PA
5	0064	Sanchez, WY	Internal Medicine	MD
6	0070	Scott, QC	Family Medicine	MD
7	01DZ	White, VA	Family Medicine	PA
8	021C	Parker, YF	Family Medicine	NP
9	02CZ	Scott, BP	Internal Medicine	MD
10	0341	White, GX	Family Medicine	MD
11	03B9	Kelly, NJ	Family Medicine	MD
12	04X4	Foster, SH	Surgery	MD

. . .

PATIENT_LIST contains information about 11 appointments. The value of PROVIDER_ID for Lisa Miller is not found in data set PROVIDERS.

PATIENT_LIST

Obs	patient_ id	patient_name	dob	gender	appt_date	appt_ time	provider_ id
1	Z060B0C4	Allen, Nancy	08/14/1952	F	03/04/2010	8:30	0595
2	07C37865	Brown, Michael	02/12/1951	M	03/04/2010	8:30	X747
3	1D851962	Campbell, Jeremy	03/12/1989	M	03/04/2010	8:30	X5A1
4	Z6928441	Evans, Diane	04/15/1973	F	03/04/2010	8:30	624Z
5	98994892	Miller, Lisa	07/08/1981	F	03/04/2010	8:30	0BBB
6	Y6972399	Lopez, Nicholas	06/28/1969	M	03/04/2010	8:40	C116
7	545Y9722	Mitchell, Lori	01/06/1962	F	03/04/2010	8:40	Z902
8	22D08623	Ramirez, Gail	03/17/1947	F	03/04/2010	8:40	4Z25
9	Y79X9Y64	Walker, Amanda	01/08/2005	F	03/04/2010	8:40	49Z6
10	X3842479	Walker, Patricia	02/01/1964	F	03/04/2010	8:40	3214
11	55090520	Williams, Amanda	09/21/1986	F	03/04/2010	8:40	1C28

Resulting Data Set
Output 4.3
PATIENTS_SPEC
Data Set

```
                        Example 4.3 PATIENTS_SPEC Created with DATA Step

      patient_                                          appt_  provider_
 Obs     id       patient_name        dob    gender  appt_date  time    id     appt_type

   1  Z060B0C4  Allen, Nancy       08/14/1952    F   03/04/2010  8:30  0595   Family Medicine
   2  07C37865  Brown, Michael     02/12/1951    M   03/04/2010  8:30  X747   Psychiatry
   3  1D851962  Campbell, Jeremy   03/12/1989    M   03/04/2010  8:30  X5A1   Family Medicine
   4  Z6928441  Evans, Diane       04/15/1973    F   03/04/2010  8:30  624Z   Cardiology
   5  98994892  Miller, Lisa       07/08/1981    F   03/04/2010  8:30  0BBB   **Provider ID Not Found
   6  Y6972399  Lopez, Nicholas    06/28/1969    M   03/04/2010  8:40  C116   Internal Medicine
   7  545Y9722  Mitchell, Lori     01/06/1962    F   03/04/2010  8:40  Z902   Obstetrics and Gynecology
   8  22D08623  Ramirez, Gail      03/17/1947    F   03/04/2010  8:40  4Z25   Internal Medicine
   9  Y79X9Y64  Walker, Amanda     01/08/2005    F   03/04/2010  8:40  49Z6   Pediatrics
  10  X3842479  Walker, Patricia   02/01/1964    F   03/04/2010  8:40  3214   Family Medicine
  11  55090520  Williams, Amanda   09/21/1986    F   03/04/2010  8:40  1C28   Obstetrics and Gynecology
```

Example Overview

This example demonstrates how a user-defined format can serve as a lookup table. The program dynamically creates the format from the data set that contains the lookup values. A DATA step or PROC SQL step can process a primary data set and apply a FORMAT statement or the PUT function to obtain lookup values from the format.

This technique is efficient when you have a large data set whose retrieved values remain fairly constant and when no index is otherwise needed for the data set. You process the large data set only to create the user-defined format. You do not have to sequentially read the lookup data set to perform a match-merge by value to the primary data set.

The program has three steps:

1. Modify the lookup data set so that it can be an input control data set to PROC FORMAT. The procedure requires specific variables in the control data set in order to define the format.

2. Create the format with PROC FORMAT and specify on the CNTLIN= option the name of the input control data set.

3. Process the primary data set sequentially. Use the PUT function or FORMAT statement to look up values in the format for each observation based on a variable in common between the primary data set and the lookup data set. The variable's values are the values that are supplied to the user-defined format.

For more information about the required contents of the input control data set, see "Building a Format Dynamically with CNTLIN=" in the "A Closer Look" section.

This example creates a temporary format. You can also create a permanent format to use as a lookup table. Defining a permanent format is useful when the values in your format do not change frequently. For more information about working with permanent format libraries, see SAS documentation.

The goal of the following program is to find the healthcare provider's specialty for each of the 11 appointments in data set PATIENT_LIST. Data set PROVIDERS stores information about the providers. The common variable between the two data sets is PROVIDER_ID.

The first DATA step modifies PROVIDERS to conform to the input requirements of PROC FORMAT. The first OUTPUT statement outputs an observation for each observation in PROVIDERS. The IF-THEN block adds an additional observation to PROVFMTS. This additional observation defines the value label to assign when a value for PROVIDER_ID in PATIENT_LIST does not have a match in the format. It sets the input control data set variable HLO to 'O' for the value 'OTHER.' PROC FORMAT recognizes 'OTHER' as a keyword that specifies the text to assign when there are no other matches in the format.

The PROC FORMAT step creates the $SPECLTY format from information in data set PROVFMTS.

The second DATA step processes each observation in PATIENT_LIST. It applies format $SPECLTY to the common variable, PROVIDER_ID, to find the provider's specialty.

*Modify data set **PROVIDERS** to conform to the input control data set requirements of **PROC FORMAT**.*
*Rename the variable that contains the values for the format to **START**.*
*Rename the variable that contains the associated value labels for the format to **LABEL**.*
*Define temporary variable **LASTOBS** to track when the DATA step has read the last observation in **PROVIDERS**.*
*Name the format and save the name in variable **FMTNAME**.*
Keep only the variables that an input control data set can use.
*Output every observation in **PROVIDERS**.*
*When processing the last observation in **PROVIDERS**, output an additional observation that defines a value label for all values that don't have a match in the format.*

```
data provfmts;


  set providers(rename=(provider_id=start
                        specialty=label))



                end=lastobs;


  retain fmtname '$speclty';

  keep fmtname start label hlo;

  output;

  if lastobs then do;
    hlo='O';
    label='**Provider ID Not Found';
    output;
  end;

run;
```

Build the format dynamically and specify the input control data set.
*Create data set **PATIENTS_SPEC**.*
*Read each observation in **PATIENT_LIST**.*
Define the variable that will contain the lookup information.
*Assign values to the new variable by associating the values of the common variable **PROVIDER_ID** with the values of the format **$SPECLTY**.*

```
proc format cntlin=provfmts;
run;
data patients_spec;
  set patient_list;

  attrib appt_type length=$35;

  appt_type=put(provider_id,$speclty.);



run;
```

Related Technique

The DATA step in this related technique creates a data set equivalent to the data set that was created in the main example. Instead of defining a format from the information in PROVIDERS, it defines a hash object and loads it with this information.

For each observation in PATIENT_LIST, the DATA step looks for a match in hash object P for the current value of PROVIDER_ID. When a match is found, the DATA step assigns the value of the data variable that was retrieved from the hash table to variable APPT_TYPE. It assigns text to APPT_TYPE when there is no match.

*Specify attributes for the variables saved in data set **PATIENTS_SPEC** and for the data variable, **SPECIALTY**.*

```
data patients_spec;
  attrib patient_id length=$8
         patient_name length=$20
         dob format=mmddyy10.
         gender length=$1
         appt_date format=mmddyy10.
         appt_time format=time5.
         provider_id length=$4
         appt_type length=$35
         specialty length=$35;
```

On the first iteration of the DATA step, create, name, and specify attributes of the hash object.	```if _n_=1 then do;```
Create hash object P and load the hash object with data from data set PROVIDERS.	``` declare hash p(dataset:'providers');```

Specify one key variable.
 Specify one data variable.
 Close the definition of hash object P.
 Prevent SAS notes about uninitialized variables with the CALL MISSING statement.
	``` p.defineKey('provider_id');```
	 ``` p.defineData('specialty');```
	 ``` p.defineDone();```
	 ``` call missing(specialty);```

	``` end;``` ``` drop rc specialty;```
Read data set PATIENT_LIST sequentially.	``` set patient_list;```
Look for a match by key variable PROVIDER_ID in the hash table. Save the return code of the search results in variable RC.	``` rc=p.find();```
When a match is found, assign the value of the retrieved data variable to APPT_TYPE. Assign text when no match is found.	``` if rc=0 then appt_type=specialty;``` ``` else appt_type='**Provider ID Not Found';```
	```run;```

A Closer Look

Using Formats to Perform a Table Lookup

When you need to perform a table lookup, a common technique is to use a merge operation with the IN= option and the BY statement. However, when you have a large lookup data set and a small unsorted primary data set, using formats can be much more efficient. A user-written format that is created with PROC FORMAT uses a binary search technique to take the input value and match it with the appropriate output value. The binary search requires ```int(log2(n))``` seek operations to find the desired key value. This solution of the two is preferable as the size of the lookup table increases with respect to the primary data set.

When you use a hash table to perform a table lookup, only one seek operation is needed to find the desired key value.

Building a Format Dynamically with CNTLIN=

This example creates input control data set PROVFMTS and specifies it as input to PROC FORMAT with the CNTLIN= option. The procedure converts the observations in PROVFMTS to user-defined format $SPECLTY.

Each observation in an input control data set corresponds to one value specification for the format or informat. The observation can specify a single value, or it can specify a range as you can with the PROC FORMAT VALUE statement.

An input control data set must contain three variables: FMTNAME, START, and LABEL.

❑ The FMTNAME variable specifies a character variable whose value is the name of the format or informat. The value of FMTNAME is constant across all observations that define one format or one informat. The name for a format or informat for a character variable must start with a dollar sign ($). Alternatively, you could add a fourth variable, TYPE, and assign the value "C" to TYPE. This example assigns the text "$SPECLTY" to FMTNAME and does not use the TYPE variable.

❑ The START variable specifies a character variable whose values give the range's starting value. This variable often is used in conjunction with the optional END variable, which specifies the range's ending value. This example did not specify ranges. Each value of PROVIDER_ID forms its own value-range-set in the format. The values of PROVIDER_ID were not assigned in order of specialty.

❑ The LABEL variable specifies a character variable whose values are the text that is associated with the value. In this example, the values of LABEL are the specialty of the specific provider.

There are additional optional variables you can add to your input control data sets to further customize your format and informat definitions. One additional variable that this example adds is HLO. This is a character variable whose values contain range information about the format in the form of eight different letters that can appear in any combination. The example assigns the character value 'O' to HLO. This value specifies that the range is 'OTHER,' which is a keyword value that PROC FORMAT recognizes. In this situation, the value for START is ignored. For more information about how to specify input control data sets, see SAS documentation.

Example 4.4 Performing Multiple Lookups for Each Observation in a Data Set

Goal

Perform multiple lookups in other data sets for each observation in a data set. The lookup values are codes, and full information is found for the codes in the other data sets.

Example Features

Featured Step	DATA step
Featured Step Options and Statements	Hash object in the DATA step
Related Technique	PROC FORMAT CNTLIN= option and DATA step with PUT function and END= data set option

Input Data Sets

Data set SUPPLEMENTS is one of two lookup tables. It contains a list of vitamins and supplements.

SUPPLEMENTS

Obs	suppid	suppname	fullsuppname
1	V001	Vitamin A	Beta Carotene
2	V002	Vitamin B-1	Thiamine
3	V003	Vitamin B-2	Riboflavin
4	V004	Vitamin B-3	Niacinamide
5	V005	Vitamin B-6	Pyridoxine Hydrochloride
6	V006	Vitamin B-9	Folic Acid
7	V007	Vitamin B-12	Cyanocobalamin
8	V008	Vitamin C	Ascorbic Acid
9	V009	Vitamin D	Cholecalciferol
10	V010	Vitamin E	DL-Alpha-Tocopherol
11	S001	Gingko	Gingko Biloba
12	S002	Glucosamine	Glucosamine Sulfate
13	S003	Lycopene	Lycopene
14	M001	Calcium	Calcium Carbonate
15	M002	Calcium	Calcium Citrate
16	M003	Iron	Ferrous Fumarate
17	M004	Magnesium	Magnesium Citrate
18	M005	Selenium	L-Selenomethionine
19	M006	Zinc	Zinc Gluconate

Data set STUDYSTAFF is one of two lookup tables. It contains identification information about the staff members who are involved in a study.

STUDYSTAFF

Obs	staffid	unit	staffname	degree
1	371	Nursing	EN Cameron	RN
2	461	Nursing	YU Garcia	CNP
3	104	Dietary	RD Hong	RD
4	240	Nursing	TR Howe	RN
5	439	Dietary	KA Izzo	RD
6	592	Dietary	HS James	RD
7	387	Dietary	HN Lee	RD
8	391	Nursing	MR Smith	CNP

Data set STUDYSUBJECTS contains information about five subjects in a study. Information for variables SUPP1, SUPP2, and SUPP3 can be found in SUPPLEMENTS. Information about variables NURSEID and DIETICIANID can be found in STUDYSTAFF.

STUDYSUBJECTS

Obs	id	inits	nurseid	dieticianid	supp1	supp2	supp3
1	101	GHY	461	582	V003	V005	V006
2	102	REA	391	592	M002	M004	V003
3	103	PLK	391	387			
4	104	MIJ	461	592	M003		
5	105	NHC	240	439	V004	M005	

Resulting Data Set
Output 4.4
STUDY_SUPP
Data Set

```
                        Example 4.4 STUDY_SUPP Created with DATA Step

     Obs  id inits supplement1 supplement2 supplement3    nurse       dietician

      1  101  GHY   Vitamin B-2 Vitamin B-6 Vitamin B-9 YU Garcia, CNP (unknown)
      2  102  REA   Calcium     Magnesium   Vitamin B-2 MR Smith, CNP  HS James, RD
      3  103  PLK   (none)      (none)      (none)      MR Smith, CNP  HN Lee, RD
      4  104  MIJ   Iron        (none)      (none)      YU Garcia, CNP HS James, RD
      5  105  NHC   Vitamin B-3 Selenium    (none)      TR Howe, RN    KA Izzo, RD
```

Example Overview

This example demonstrates how to look up several items for one observation when processing that observation once in a DATA step. The DATA step loads lookup information into two hash objects from data that are stored in two data sets. Variables in the primary data set link to the lookup tables through the keys that are defined for the hash objects.

The program processes the observations in STUDYSUBJECTS. Each observation contains supplement codes and staff assignment ID codes for each subject in a study.

Here are the two main goals of the program:

❑ Find the supplement name that is associated with the values of each of the three supplement code variables, SUPP1, SUPP2, and SUPP3, in STUDYSUBJECTS.

❑ Find the name and degree of the nurse and the dietician who are associated with each study subject. Their ID codes are saved in primary data set variables NURSEID and DIETICIANID.

On its first iteration, the DATA step defines two hash objects: S, which will be loaded with data from data set SUPPLEMENTS, and F, which will be loaded with data from data set STUDYSTAFF. Each hash object has a single key: hash object S has SUPPID from SUPPLEMENTS, and hash object F has STAFFID from STUDYSTAFF. Hash object S defines one data element, variable SUPPNAME in SUPPLEMENTS. Hash object F defines two data elements, variables STAFFNAME and DEGREE.

An additional entry is added to the S hash table with a key value of missing. The data element that is associated with this row is "(none)". This value is returned when the value of SUPP1, SUPP2, or SUPP3 is missing.

An iterative DO loop looks up the name of each supplement code value in hash object S. It assigns the retrieved supplement name value to one of three new variables: SUPPLEMENT1, SUPPLEMENT2, or SUPPLEMENT3.

A second iterative DO loop examines each of the staff IDs. For each nonmissing ID, the program looks up the person's name and degree in hash object F. For matches that are found in hash object F, the program concatenates the values it retrieves and assigns the result to one of two new variables: NURSE or DIETICIAN. The text "(unknown)" is assigned when no match is found.

This technique accomplishes the lookups in one DATA step. The related technique uses formats to find information in the lookup tables. It requires three DATA steps and two PROC FORMAT steps. Two DATA steps modify the lookup data sets so that each data set conforms to the structure of a PROC FORMAT control data set. Two PROC FORMAT steps create the formats from the modified data sets. The third DATA step performs the lookups.

Program

Create data set STUDY_SUPP and list the variables to save in the data set. Define the variables that will be specified later in the DEFINEKEY and DEFINEDATA methods. Explicitly defining these variables puts them in the Program Data Vector (PDV). If you do not define these variables, SAS generates an error message.

```
data study_supp(keep=id inits nurse dietician
                       supplement1-supplement3);
  length suppid $ 4 suppname $ 15 staffid 4
         staffname $ 25 degree $ 3;
```

Define the two hash objects on the first iteration.
Declare hash object S. Specify the data set to load into S. Define one key variable and one data variable.

Declare hash object F. Specify the data set to load into F. Define one key variable and one data variable.

Initialize to missing the variables defined as key and data in the two hash objects. This action prevents SAS from writing notes about uninitialized variables to the SAS log when there are no explicit assignment statements in the DATA step for the key and data variables.

```
if _n_=1 then do;

  declare hash s(dataset:"work.supplements");
  s.defineKey('suppid');
  s.definedata('suppname');
  s.definedone();
  declare hash f(dataset:"work.studystaff");
  f.defineKey('staffid');
  f.definedata('staffname','degree');
  f.definedone();
   call missing(suppid,suppname,
                staffid,staffname,degree);
```

Add data to the hash object S for the key value of missing.

```
  s.add(key:' ', data:'(none)');

end;
set studysubjects;
```

Process each observation in STUDYSUBJECTS.
Define the arrays that work with the supplement codes and names. The elements of SUPPCODES are from the input data set. The elements of SUPPNAMES are new variables.
Define the arrays that work with the staff IDs, names, and degrees. The elements of ID are from the input data set. The elements of NAMES are new variables.

```
array suppcodes{3} $ supp1-supp3;
array suppnames{3} $ 15 supplement1-supplement3;


array ids{2} nurseid dieticianid;
array names{2} $ 25 nurse dietician;
```

Process each of the supplement code variables.
Look in S for the value of the current element of SUPPCODES. Save in RC the return code of the result of the search.
For matches in S, assign the value of hash data variable SUPPNAME to the current element of the SUPPNAMES array.
For nonmatches, assign text to the current element of the SUPPNAMES array.

```
do i=1 to dim(suppcodes);

  rc = s.find(key:suppcodes{i});


  if rc = 0 then suppnames{i} = suppname;


  else suppnames{i} = '(error)';

end;
```

Process each of the staff ID variables.
Look in F for the value of the current element of IDs. Save in RC the return code of the result of the search.

```
do i=1 to dim(ids);
  rc=f.find(key:ids{i});
```

<table>
<tr>
<td>For matches, concatenate the two
retrieved data variable values and
assign the result to the current element
of NAMES.</td>
<td>

```
   if rc=0 then names{i}=
        catx(' ',cats(staffname,','),degree);
```

</td>
</tr>
<tr>
<td>For nonmatches, assign text to the
current NAMES array element.</td>
<td>

```
   else names{i}='(unknown)';

 end;
run;
```

</td>
</tr>
</table>

Related Technique

This related technique is similar to Example 4.3 because it creates formats in which to look up information. The following program creates a table equivalent to the data set that was created in the main example.

Both lookup tables, SUPPLEMENTS and STUDYSTAFF, need to be modified to conform to the input control data set requirements of PROC FORMAT. The program starts with DATA steps to modify these two tables. Each DATA step is followed by a PROC FORMAT step with the name of the newly created input control data set that was specified on the CNTLIN= option.

The main example specified two data variables for hash object F, STAFFNAME, and DEGREE. These were concatenated to form the staff member's complete name. A user-defined format can look up only one value. In order to map STAFFID to the complete name, the DATA step that modifies STUDYSTAFF for input to PROC FORMAT concatenates STAFFNAME and DEGREE when defining values for LABEL.

The two DATA steps also add observations to the end of the input control data sets to handle missing values and values for which no label has been defined. For the latter, the DATA steps assign a value of "O" to variable HLO. This value specifies that the range is 'OTHER,' which is a keyword value that PROC FORMAT recognizes. Variable HLO is an optional character variable in an input control data set. Its values contain range information about the format in the form of eight different letters that can appear in any combination.

<table>
<tr>
<td>Define input control data set
SUPPFMT by using data set
SUPPLEMENTS. Rename existing
variables to the names that are required
by PROC FORMAT.</td>
<td>

```
data suppfmt;
   set supplements(rename=(suppid=start suppname=label))
```

</td>
</tr>
<tr>
<td>Include the END= option so that code
can test when the last observation in
SUPPLEMENTS has been read.</td>
<td>

```
                      end=eof;
```

</td>
</tr>
<tr>
<td>Keep the minimum required variables,
FMTNAME, START, and LABEL in
the input control data set. Also keep
HLO, which is an optional variable in
an input control data set.</td>
<td>

```
   keep fmtname start label hlo;
```

</td>
</tr>
<tr>
<td>Name the format. Because its values
are character values, define SUPP to
be a character format by preceding the
format name with a dollar sign ($).</td>
<td>

```
   retain fmtname '$supp';
```

</td>
</tr>
<tr>
<td>Include the OUTPUT statement so that
the DATA step outputs each
observation in SUPPLEMENTS to
SUPPFMT.</td>
<td>

```
   output;
```

</td>
</tr>
<tr>
<td>Process this DO group when the DATA
step reaches the end of
SUPPLEMENTS.</td>
<td>

```
   if eof then do;
```

</td>
</tr>
<tr>
<td>Define a value and label for missing
values.</td>
<td>

```
     start=' ';
     label='(none)';
     output;
```

</td>
</tr>
</table>

Define a value and label for all other supplement values not accounted for in SUPPLEMENTS and the missing value above.

```
     hlo='O';
     label='(error)';
     output;

   end;
run;
proc format cntlin=suppfmt;
run;
```

Build character format $SUPP.

Modify data set STUDYSTAFF to conform to the input control data set requirements of PROC FORMAT. Name the input control data set STAFFFMT.

```
data stafffmt;
   set studystaff(rename=(staffid=start)) end=eof;
```

Define variable LABEL to be the concatenation of the staff person's name and degree.

```
   keep fmtname start label hlo;
   retain fmtname 'staff';
   length label $ 25;
   label=catx(' ',cats(staffname,','),degree);

   output;
   if eof then do;
```

Process this DO group when the DATA step reaches the end of STUDYSTAFF. Define a value and label for all staff IDs not accounted for in STUDYSTAFF.

```
     hlo='O';
     label='(unknown)';
     output;
   end;
run;
proc format cntlin=stafffmt;
run;
```

Build numeric format STAFF.

Create data set STUDY_SUPP and specify the variables to save in the data set.

Process each observation in STUDYSUBJECTS.

Define the arrays that work with the supplement codes and names.

Define the arrays that work with the staff IDs, names, and degrees.

Find the supplement name for each supplement code value by applying format $SUPP to the value.

Find the complete name of the staff person that is associated with each ID value by applying format STAFF to the value.

```
data study_supp(keep=id inits nurse dietician
                     supplement1-supplement3);

   set studysubjects;

   array suppcodes{3} $ supp1-supp3;
   array suppnames{3} $ 25 supplement1-supplement3;
   array ids{2} $ 25 nurseid dieticianid;
   array names{2} $ 25 nurse dietician;
   do i=1 to dim(suppcodes);
     suppnames{i}=put(suppcodes{i},$supp.);
   end;

   do i=1 to dim(names);
     names{i}=put(ids{i},staff.);
   end;

run;
```

Example 4.5 Performing a Table Lookup When the Lookup Data Set Is Indexed

Goal

Combine two data sets by using a table lookup technique that directly accesses the lookup data set through an index on a key variable. This lookup technique is appropriate for a large lookup data set.

Example Features

Featured Step	DATA step
Featured Step Options and Statements	SET statement, KEY= option Automatic variable _IORC_ Macro function %SYSRC
Related Technique	PROC SQL, INNER JOIN, ON clause, subqueries

Input Data Sets

Data set INVOICES contains a list of invoices for five insurance policies. Data set POLICIES contains data for 12 policy holders.

Variable ID is common to both data sets. Data set INVOICES contains no consecutive duplicate values for ID. Because the program depends on directly accessing observations in POLICIES by using KEY=ID, POLICIES must be indexed on ID.

```
                    INVOICES

Obs       id       salesdate      amount
 1    JL80SHJ0981I  05/01/2009    $543.22
 2    LZJ4NWZOPH1W  05/01/2009    $910.09
 3    6VIKYDYXMC8I  05/02/2009    $961.73
 4    9VOEB36I3F2D  05/02/2009    $402.63
 5    70QAL1JLV1FF  05/03/2009    $733.54
```

```
                       POLICIES
                                policy_
Obs       id        lname       type     lastpayment
  1   6PP97SYCJ6MR  Aamodt        A       01/10/2009
  2   3K3JWQ1WWCY0  Ababa         A       01/15/2009
  3   70QAL1JLV1FF  Abad          A       10/04/2008
  4   JL80SHJ0981I  Abate         B       03/22/2009
  5   B4ZAM563BAN6  Abbas         B       06/12/2008
  6   WEFSBW6US11T  Abbey         C       07/31/2008
  7   3EB21R22VMPZ  Abbott        A       02/27/2009
  8   CNT2MDT1LP9K  Abbott        B       12/06/2008
  9   6VIKYDYXMC8I  Abel          A       11/01/2008
 10   9XUIQK04MHO8  Abell         A       07/12/2008
 11   E1U1T182R2J9  Abraham       B       02/15/2009
 12   9VOEB36I3F2D  Abraham       C       09/12/2008
```

Resulting Data Sets
Output 4.5a
REBATES Data Set

```
            Example 4.5 REBATES Data Set Created with DATA Step

                                         policy_
   Obs      id        salesdate  amount lname  type  lastpayment  rebate

    1   JL80SHJ0981I 05/01/2009 $543.22 Abate    B    03/22/2009   $43.46
    2   6VIKYDYXMC8I 05/02/2009 $961.73 Abel     A    11/01/2008   $96.17
    3   9VOEB36I3F2D 05/02/2009 $402.63 Abraham  C    09/12/2008   $20.15
    4   70QAL1JLV1FF 05/03/2009 $733.54 Abad     A    10/04/2008   $73.35
```

Output 4.5b
NOTFOUND Data Set

```
            Example 4.5 NOTFOUND Data Set Created with DATA Step

                                        policy_
   Obs     id       salesdate  amount lname type  lastpayment  rebate  status

    1  LZJ4NWZOPH1W 05/01/2009 $910.09                   .        .   NOT FOUND
```

Example Overview

This example shows you how to perform a table lookup in an indexed data set. This technique is useful when working with a large indexed lookup data set.

The DATA step in this program reads one data set sequentially and performs a table lookup in a second data set that is indexed by the key variable. The table lookup uses the index to locate observations in the second data set that have key values that are equal to the key's current value in the first data set.

Data set INVOICES contains a list of invoices for five insurance policies. Data set POLICIES contains policy information for 12 policy holders. Assume the observations in POLICIES are for the first 12 policies in a very large data set of many policies. A small subset is used here for illustration.

The objective of the program is to create two new data sets by reading the observations in INVOICES sequentially and finding matching information in POLICIES for each invoice by direct access. Here are the two new data sets:

❑ REBATES, which are the matches between POLICIES and INVOICES.

❑ NOTFOUND, which are the observations in INVOICES that do not have a match in POLICIES. The variables from POLICIES have missing values.

When an observation from INVOICES has a match in POLICIES, the DATA step calculates a value for variable REBATE based on the current value of AMOUNT from INVOICES and POLICY_TYPE from POLICIES. Matched observations are output to data set REBATES.

When an observation from INVOICES does not have a match in POLICIES, the DATA step outputs the observation to data set NOTFOUND. Data set NOTFOUND includes variable STATUS whose value is "NOT FOUND." This variable is not kept in data set REBATES. Values for the variables in POLICIES might still have values in them from the previous successful lookup. Therefore, code sets these variables to missing for the nonmatches before writing the nonmatching observation to data set NOTFOUND.

The DATA step starts with a simple SET statement that specifies INVOICES. The second SET statement specifies the lookup data set and includes the KEY= option. The value that is specified for the KEY= option is the name of the key variable, ID. This second SET statement reads an observation from POLICIES based on the current value of ID as read from INVOICES by the first SET statement.

The SELECT group evaluates the results of looking for a match in POLICIES for the current value of ID in INVOICES. The expression in the SELECT statement is the _IORC_ automatic variable. This variable is created automatically when you use the MODIFY statement or the SET statement with the KEY= option. The value of _IORC_ is a numeric return code that indicates the status of the I/O operation from the most recently executed MODIFY statement or SET statement with KEY=.

The values of the _IORC_ automatic variable are internal and subject to change. Instead of hardcoding the values in your SAS statements, you can use the autocall macro program SYSRC that SAS has supplied to enable you to test the values of _IORC_ while protecting your code from future changes in _IORC_ values.

The "A Closer Look" section in Example 3.11 further describes _IORC_ and SYSRC.

Program

Create REBATES and NOTFOUND.

Read observations sequentially from INVOICES.

Read an observation from POLICIES directly through the index by using the current value of ID that is provided by the observation from INVOICES.

```
data rebates(drop=status)
     notfound;
  set invoices;

  set policies key=id;
```

Evaluate the return code from the keyed lookup in POLICIES.

When the current observation from INVOICES has a match in POLICIES, calculate a value for REBATE based on the value of POLICY_TYPE. Output the observation to REBATES.

When the current observation from INVOICES does not have a match in POLICIES, set the variables from POLICIES and variable REBATE to missing. This action prevents the values from the observation previously retrieved from POLICIES from being saved in the current unmatched observation from INVOICES.

Output unmatched observations to NOTFOUND.

Reset automatic variable _ERROR_ to 0 to prevent an error condition that would write the contents of the PDV to the SAS log.

In case of an unexpected _IORC_ condition, write an error message and stop execution.

```
  format amount rebate dollar7.2;
  select (_iorc_);

    when (%sysrc(_sok)) do;
      if policy_type='A' then rebate=.1*amount;
      else if policy_type='B' then rebate=.08*amount;
      else if policy_type='C' then rebate=.05*amount;
      output rebates;
    end;
    when (%sysrc(_dsenom)) do;
      lname=' ';
      lastpayment=.;
      policy_type=' ';
      rebate=.;




      output notfound;

      _error_=0;
    end;


    otherwise do;
      putlog 'ERROR: _IORC_=' _iorc_
             '**** Program stopped.';
      stop;
    end;
  end;
run;
```

Related Technique

The following PROC SQL step has two CREATE TABLE statements to create two tables similar to the two data sets that were created by the DATA step in the main example.

The first CREATE TABLE statement creates REBATES by performing an inner join between INVOICES and POLICIES on ID. This table is identical to the REBATES data set that was created in the main example.

The second CREATE TABLE statement creates NOTFOUND by using a subquery to select rows in INVOICES that do not have an ID match in POLICIES. It finds the same row that the main example does, but it contains only the three columns found in INVOICES plus new column STATUS. It does not contain the columns from POLICIES.

PROC SQL does not necessarily use an index when it is available. It evaluates the request and chooses to use an index based on efficiency before it processes the request.

Create REBATES and calculate column REBATE.

Perform an inner join of the two tables.

Create NOTFOUND.
Select all observations in INVOICES that do not have a match in POLICIES. Specify a subquery to find the IDs of the nonmatches.

```
proc sql;
  create table rebates as
    select salesdate, amount, lname, policy_type,
      case when policy_type='A' then .1*amount
           when policy_type='B' then .08*amount
           when policy_type='C' then .05*amount
           else .
      end as rebate format=dollar7.2
      from invoices inner join policy
              on invoices.id=policy.id;
  create table notfound as
    select *,
           'NOT FOUND' as status from invoices
           where id not in (select id from policy);
quit;
```

Example 4.6   Performing a "Chained" Lookup

Goal

Trace the links that associate observations in one data set. Assume there are no breaks in the chain.

Example Features

Featured Step	DATA step
Featured Step Options and Statements	Hash object in the DATA step
Related Technique	DATA step, BY-group processing, RETAIN statement

Input Data Set

Data set FLEET_REGISTRATION contains registration transactions for three vehicles. Variable VEHICLE_ID uniquely identifies the vehicle. The values for REGISTRATION change when the vehicle is transferred. When ACTION= "XFER", the vehicle has been transferred and its new registration ID is stored in variable NEW_REG. There are no breaks in the links between observations for a vehicle because all values of NEW_REG have a match in FLEET_REGISTRATION.

```
                                   FLEET_REGISTRATION

           vehicle_
   Obs        id        action    registration    new_reg    effective
    1      SEDAN0238     XFER         WI008          IL302    05/01/2001
    2      TRUCK0081     XFER         IN082          IL235    01/15/2002
    3      TRUCK0081     XFER         IL235          WI371    03/29/2003
    4      SEDAN0238     XFER         IL302          IL419    07/21/2004
    5      SEDAN0238     TERM         IL419                   11/03/2008
    6      MINIV0761     NEW          IL658                   09/19/2008
    7      TRUCK0081     XFER         WI371          IN454    08/22/2008
```

Resulting Data Set

Output 4.6
FLEET_HISTORY
Data Set

```
                 Example 4.6 FLEET_HISTORY Data Set Created with DATA Step

      vehicle_
 Obs     id     current nxfers history                                                     firstxfer   lastxfer

  1   SEDAN0238            2   WI008; IL302(05/01/2001); IL419(07/21/2004); REMOVED 11/03/2008 05/01/2001 07/21/2004
  2   TRUCK0081  IN454     3   IN082; IL235(01/15/2002); WI371(03/29/2003); IN454(08/22/2008)  01/15/2002 08/22/2008
  3   MINIV0761  IL658     0   IL658(NEW 09/19/2008)
```

Example Overview

This example tracks the links between observations in a data set. It uses the value of a variable in one observation to find a subsequent observation with that value.

The following DATA step collects the registration history for the three vehicles in data set FLEET_REGISTRATION. Two vehicles have registration transfers and one has none. A vehicle is assigned a new registration ID when it is transferred. Variable ACTION indicates the type of registration transaction. For observations that record a vehicle transfer (i.e., ACTION= "XFER"), variable REGISTRATION stores the current registration ID, and variable NEW_REG stores the new registration ID.

The DATA step outputs one observation per vehicle with the vehicle registration history consolidated in two variables, NXFERS and HISTORY. Variable NXFERS records the number of times the vehicle was transferred. Character variable HISTORY concatenates all the registration IDs and registration transaction dates for a vehicle.

On its first iteration, the DATA step defines a hash table, loads data set FLEET_REGISTRATION into the hash table by using the ADD method, and defines hash keys on variables VEHICLE_ID and REGISTRATION. The data that are loaded into the hash table include variables from data set FLEET_REGISTRATION and new variable ALREADY_USED.

After loading the hash table, the DATA step processes the observations in FLEET_REGISTRATION sequentially and traverses the hash table for registration changes for each vehicle.

The DATA step has two DO UNTIL loops. The first reads each observation from FLEET_REGISTRATION. The second, which is nested in the first, looks for all the matches for a vehicle in the hash table. Observations are output in the second loop after all links between observations for a vehicle have been found.

Variable ALREADY_USED controls the processing of the first DO loop. It is defined to be a true/false (1/0) variable that tracks whether the DATA step already used the current observation as a link in the chain that connects observations. If an observation has already been used as a link in the chain, it is not processed again.

Variable ACTION can have one of three values that indicate the observation's transaction type. The DATA step examines the value of ACTION to determine how to process the observations. Only observations with type "XFER" have links to other observations in the data set. Here are the three values of ACTION:

❑ The value "XFER" indicates a registration transfer.

❑ The value "NEW" indicates a new fleet vehicle with no transfers.

❑ The value "TERM" indicates a fleet vehicle removed from service.

The DATA step code assumes that certain conditions of the input data set are met. Some of these assumptions are in the following list. When adapting this program, you might need to add code to handle different conditions in your data.

❑ The keys are unique.

❑ There are no breaks in the links between observations for a vehicle.

❑ The values for EFFECTIVE are in ascending order within the chain of links between observations for a vehicle.

❑ A value for NEW_REG is always present when ACTION= "XFER".

❑ NEW_REG is always missing when ACTION= "NEW" or ACTION= "TERM".

Program

Create data set FLEET_HISTORY.
Rename REGISTRATION to indicate
that its value is the current registration
ID.

```
data fleet_history(rename=(registration=current));
```

Assign attributes to variables. Define
new variable ALREADY_USED.

On the first iteration of the DATA step,
define and load a hash table.
Initialize ALREADY_USED.
Define hash table F.
Define key items on which to retrieve
data from F.

```
    keep vehicle_id registration history nxfers firstxfer
        lastxfer;
    length vehicle_id $ 9 registration $ 5 nxfers 3
            history $ 100 already_used 4;
    format firstxfer lastxfer mmddyy10.;
    if _n_=1 then do;

        already_used=0;
        declare hash f();
        f.definekey('vehicle_id','registration');
```

Specify the data items to store in F.
Include the key items and new variable
ALREADY_USED.
End the definition of F.
Load F with data from
FLEET_REGISTRATION and include
new variable ALREADY_USED in F
since it was defined as data.

Process a DO UNTIL loop until the
end of FLEET_REGISTRATION has
been reached.
Read the observations from
FLEET_REGISTRATION. Specify the
END= option so that code can test
when the last observation in
FLEET_REGISTRATION has been
read.
Look for a match in F for the current
observation's key values.
When a match is found and
ALREADY_USED is 1, do not process
the observation and return to the top of
the first DO UNTIL loop. A value of 1
for ALREADY_USED means that the
row in the hash table has already been
used as a link in the chain that connects
observations for the current vehicle.
Initialize NXFERS to 0 for each
observation that has not already been
used as a link between observations.
Process the block that performs the
lookups for links in the chain that
connects observations. In this example,
NEW_REG will be nonmissing only
when ACTION= "XFER".
Because the DATA step is currently
processing the first observation in the
chain of linked observations, initialize
the values of FIRSTXFER and
LASTXFER.
Initialize the value of HISTORY with
the first transfer data.
Increment NXFERS because a transfer
has occurred.
Copy the value of NEW_REG to
REGISTRATION because
REGISTRATION is one of the hash
table keys and the goal is to look for a
row in the hash table for this new
registration ID.
Process a DO UNTIL loop until no
more linked observations are found in
F.
Look for a match in F for the current
key values. On the first iteration of the
loop, the value of REGISTRATION is
the value that is copied from
NEW_REG in the statement preceding
the loop.

```
 f.definedata('vehicle_id', 'registration',
             'new_reg', 'action', 'effective',
             'already_used');
  f.definedone();
  do until(done);
    set fleet_registration end=done;
    rc=f.add();
  end;
end;
do until(done);


  set fleet_registration end=done;




  notfound=f.find();

  if notfound=0 and already_used=1 then continue;








  nxfers=0;


  if new_reg ne ' ' then do;




    firstxfer=effective;
    lastxfer=effective;



    history=catx('; ', registration,
      cats(new_reg,'(',put(effective,mmddyy10.),')'));
    nxfers+1;


    registration=new_reg;






    do until(rc ne 0);


      rc=f.find();
```

*Process this DO group when the
lookup in F is successful.*
*Process this DO group when the
lookup returns a row from the hash
table with a value for NEW_REG (i.e.,
a transfer).*
*Concatenate the registration change
data to HISTORY.*
*Change the value of LASTXFER,
which records the date of the last
transfer.*
*Increment NXFERS because a transfer
has occurred.*

*Flag the row returned from the hash
table as one that has already been used
as a link in the chain that connects
observations.*
*Replace the data in the row in F that is
associated with the current key values.*
This example changes only the value of
hash item ALREADY_USED.
*Copy the value of NEW_REG to
REGISTRATION because
REGISTRATION is one of the hash
table keys and the goal is to look for a
row in F for this new registration ID
when processing returns to the top of
the second DO UNTIL loop.*

*Process this DO group when the
lookup in the hash table does not find a
matching row for the current key
values.* This condition indicates that the
chain of links has ended.
*Assign specific text to HISTORY to
indicate that the vehicle was removed
from the fleet.*
*Output an observation when the end of
the chain of linked observations has
been reached.*

*Process this DO group when the
current observation from
FLEET_REGISTRATION does not
have a value of NEW_REG and its
value for ACTION is "NEW".*
*Because the block is processing a new
vehicle that has not yet been
transferred, initialize the values of
FIRSTXFER and LASTXFER to
missing.*
*When ACTION= "NEW", assign
specific text to HISTORY to indicate
that the vehicle is new to the fleet.*
Output the data for this new vehicle.
No further lookup in the hash table is
performed for this observation.

```
       if rc=0 then do;

          if new_reg ne ' ' then do;


             history=catx('; ', history,
      cats(new_reg,'(', put(effective,mmddyy10.), ')'));
             lastxfer=effective;


             nxfers+1;

          end;
          already_used=1;




             f.replace();




          registration=new_reg;









       end;
       else do;




          if action='TERM' then history=
      catx('; ', history, catx(' ', "REMOVED",
                         put(effective,mmddyy10.)));
          output;


       end;
    end;
  end;
  else if action="NEW" then do;




     firstxfer=.;
     lastxfer=.;



     history=cats(registration,
        catx(' ', "(NEW", put(effective,mmddyy10.)),')');

     output;


  end;
```

For unexpected errors, stop the program.

```
        else do;
          putlog "ERROR: Unexpected error. Program stopped
                                at " _all_;
          stop;
        end;
      end;
    run;
```

Related Technique

The following DATA step also tracks the links between observations in data set FLEET_REGISTRATION. It does this by processing the data set in BY groups that are defined by the values of VEHICLE_ID. Prior to the DATA step, the data set is sorted by variable VEHICLE_ID, and within each value of VEHICLE_ID, by the values of EFFECTIVE. This chronologically arranges each vehicle's group of observations.

The presence of a variable such as EFFECTIVE, which can arrange the observations in the same order as the way the links are made, enables the chaining process to be accomplished in a DATA step that processes the data in BY groups. Without such a variable, adapt the hash table approach that was presented in the main example.

Statements test the value of ACTION to determine what to add to variable HISTORY. Variable values are retained across iterations of the DATA step within each BY group, and observations are output only when processing the last observation in a BY group.

Sort the observations in the way they need to be processed by the DATA step.

```
proc sort data=fleet_registration;
  by vehicle_id effective;
run;
```

Create data set FLEET_HISTORY.
Read the observations from FLEET_REGISTRATION.
Process FLEET_REGISTRATION in BY groups that are defined by the values of VEHICLE_ID.

```
data fleet_history;
  set fleet_registration;

  by vehicle_id;


  keep vehicle_id current history nxfers firstxfer
      lastxfer;
  length vehicle_id $ 9 current $ 5 nxfers 3
        history $ 100;
  format firstxfer lastxfer mmddyy10.;
  retain history nxfers firstxfer lastxfer;
```

List the variables whose values should be retained across iterations of the DATA step.
Initialize several variables when processing the first observation in a BY group.
Because this is the first observation in a BY group and its only history at this point is its first registration, assign the value of REGISTRATION to HISTORY.

```
  if first.vehicle_id then do;

    history=registration;



    nxfers=0;
    firstxfer=.;
    lastxfer=.;
  end;
```

Process this block when NEW_REG has a nonmissing value.
Process this block for observations where the transaction is a registration transfer.
Concatenate the registration change data to HISTORY.
When the DATA step is processing the first observation in the BY group, which is when FIRSTXFER will be set to missing by the code several statements earlier, initialize the value

```
  if new_reg ne ' ' then do;

    if action='XFER' then do;


      history=catx('; ', history,
  cats(new_reg, '(', put(effective,mmddyy10.), ')'));
      if firstxfer=. then firstxfer=effective;
```

of FIRSTXFER.
Set the value of LASTXFER to
EFFECTIVE each time a transfer
transaction observation is processed.
Copy the value of NEW_REG to
CURRENT since this variable is
defined to contain the current
registration ID for the vehicle.
Increment NXFERS because a transfer
has occurred.

For unexpected errors, link to
ERRMSG, which stops the program.

Process this block for observations that
do not contain transfer information.
When ACTION= "NEW", assign
specific text to HISTORY to indicate
that the vehicle is new to the fleet.
Process this block for vehicles removed
from the fleet.
Set CURRENT to missing because the
vehicle has been removed from the
fleet and is no longer registered.
Assign specific text to indicate that the
vehicle was removed from the fleet.

For unexpected errors, link to
ERRMSG, which stops the program.

Output an observation at the end of the
BY group, which is when the end of the
chain of linked observations has been
reached.
Return to the top of the DATA step so
that the following block is not
executed.
Write an error message to the log and
stop the program.

```sas
      lastxfer=effective;

      current=new_reg;


      nxfers+1;

    end;
    else link errmsg;

  end;
  else do;

    if action='NEW' then
      history=cats(registration,
        catx(' ', "(NEW",put(effective,mmddyy10.)),')');
    else if action='TERM' then do;

      current=' ';


      history=catx('; ', history,
        catx(' ', "REMOVED", put(effective,mmddyy10.)));
    end;
    else link errmsg;

  end;
  if last.vehicle_id then output;



  return;


  errmsg:
    putlog "ERROR: Unexpected error. Program stopped at
                                " _all_;
    stop;
run;
```

CHAPTER 5

Combining Summary and Detail Data

The examples in this chapter show ways of adding summary information to your detail data sets. This is usually a two-step process. The first step obtains or calculates the summary information. The second step adds this information to detail observations. Often the goal is to compute new variables from the combined detail and summary information.

All examples include both DATA step and PROC SQL solutions.

Example 5.1   Adding Values to All Observations in a Data Set

Goal

Combine summary statistics that are saved in a single observation in one data set with all observations in another data set. Compute new variables based on the values of the summary and detail information.

Example Features

Featured Step	DATA step
Featured Step Options and Statements	IF _N_=1 statement
Related Technique	PROC SQL, Cartesian product
A Closer Look	Understanding How the DATA Step Adds Values from an Observation in One Data Set to All Observations in Another

Input Data Sets

The first 10 of 200 observations in STUDENTS are listed.

PROC MEANS created data set OVERALL by analyzing variable SCORE in data set STUDENTS. The 10th percentile and 25th percentile statistics for SCORE are saved in OVERALL.

```
STUDENTS (first 10 observations)                    OVERALL Data Set

         student_
  Obs    id        score          Obs    _TYPE_    _FREQ_    p10    p25
   1     101         74             1       0         200      70     74
   2     102         83
   3     103         76
   4     104         74
   5     105         84
   6     106         76
   7     107         79
   8     108         67
   9     109         70
  10     110         79
   . . .
```

Resulting Data Set
Output 5.1
First 10 Observations of PCSTUDENTS Data Set

```
            Example 5.1 PCSTUDENTS Data Set Created with DATA Step

                  student_
          Obs     id       score     top10pc     top25pc

           1      101        74         Y           Y
           2      102        83         Y           Y
           3      103        76         Y           Y
           4      104        74         Y           Y
           5      105        84         Y           Y
           6      106        76         Y           Y
           7      107        79         Y           Y
           8      108        67         N           N
           9      109        70         Y           N
          10      110        79         Y           Y
                        . . .
```

Example Overview

This example shows how to add one observation from one data set to all observations in a detail data set. The single observation contains summary statistics for the detail data set. By adding the summary statistics to each observation in the detail data set, you can then compare each detail observation to statistics for all observations.

The following DATA step reads the single observation in summary data set OVERALL only during the DATA step's first iteration. The values for P10 and P25 from OVERALL remain in the Program Data Vector (PDV) while the DATA step reads each observation in STUDENTS. Data set OVERALL does not have to be read more than once.

Data set STUDENTS contains the individual test scores for each student. The DATA step adds to each observation that is read from STUDENTS the same values for two variables P10 and P25, which are stored in data set OVERALL. The PROC MEANS step that precedes the DATA step analyzes variable SCORE and saves in data set OVERALL the 10th percentile and first quartile in variables P10 and P25.

On the DATA step's first iteration, which is when automatic variable _N_ equals 1, the DATA step places in the PDV the values for P10 and P25 from the single observation in OVERALL. The values remain in the PDV for the duration of the DATA step because the SET statement for OVERALL never executes again. Values that are read with a SET statement are automatically retained until another observation is read from the data set named in the SET statement.

Each iteration reads one observation from STUDENTS. The DATA step computes two new variables, TOP10PC and TOP25PC, based on variables P10 and P25 that were added from OVERALL. The DATA step assigns the value 'Y' to variable TOP10PC if the student's score is in the top 10%; otherwise, it assigns the value 'N'. A similar rule is applied when determining the values for the top quartile variable, TOP25PC.

Each iteration writes out an observation that contains all the data for each student, including the two ranking variables TOP10PC and TOP25PC.

Program

Save in data set OVERALL the 10th percentile and first quartile statistics for variable SCORE.

```
proc means data=students noprint;
   var score;
   output out=overall p10=p10 p25=p25;
run;
```

Create PCSTUDENTS.
Read an observation from OVERALL only on the first iteration and keep only the P10 and P25 variables.
Read each observation from STUDENTS.
Compute two new variables based on the values read from OVERALL that were retained in the PDV for P10 and P25.

```
data pcstudents(drop=p10 p25);
   if _n_=1 then set overall(keep=p10 p25);


   set students;


   top10pc='N';
   top25pc='N';
   if score ge p10 then top10pc='Y';
   if score ge p25 then top25pc='Y';

run;
```

Related Technique

The following PROC SQL step joins the two tables, OVERALL and STUDENTS. The program submits the same PROC MEANS step to create OVERALL that was shown in the main example. The join in the PROC SQL step produces a Cartesian product, which is a combination of each row from the first table with every row from the second table.

Generally, when joining larger data sets, you would want to avoid coding Cartesian product joins because of the large number of rows that would form the product. However, in this case, the size of the Cartesian product is manageable. With only one row in one of the tables (OVERALL) and 200 rows in the other table (STUDENTS), the number of rows in the product is 1 X 200=200.

When performing a Cartesian join, SAS generates a note in the SAS log about optimization of the join.

Save in data set OVERALL the 10th percentile and first quartile statistics for variable SCORE.

```
proc means data=students noprint;
   var score;
   output out=overall p10=p10 p25=p25;
run;
```

Create table PCSTUDENTS.
Select specific columns from each
table. Compute two new columns.

```
proc sql;
   create table pcstudents as
      select student_id, score,
               case when score ge p10 then 'Y'
                    else 'N'
               end as top10pc length=1,
               case when score ge p25 then 'Y'
                    else 'N'
               end as top25pc length=1
      from overall, students;
quit;
```

Specify a Cartesian product join.

A Closer Look

Understanding How the DATA Step Adds Values from an Observation in One Data Set to All Observations in Another

The program in the main example takes the one observation in OVERALL that was created by the PROC MEANS step and adds the values of the two variables, P10 and P25, to each observation in data set STUDENTS. The DATA step uses two SET statements. The following figures show how SAS processes the DATA step and adds P10 and P25 to each observation. The figures show only the first 10 of the 200 observations in STUDENTS.

Throughout execution of the DATA step, the two values that are contributed from OVERALL, P10 and P25, remain in the Program Data Vector (PDV). These values are also written to the data set PCSTUDENTS.

During the compilation phase, SAS reads the descriptor portions of the input data sets and creates the Program Data Vector (PDV).

The PDV contains the automatic variable, _N_, which keeps track of how many times the DATA step has iterated. (It does this by counting the number of times the DATA statement executes.) _N_ is a temporary variable and is not included in data set PCSTUDENTS.

OVERALL			
type	freq	p10	p25
0	200	70	74

STUDENTS	
id	score
101	74
102	83
103	76
104	74
105	84
106	76
107	79
108	67
109	70
110	79

The PDV also includes the two variables that were created by the DATA step, TOP10PC and TOP25PC.

Program Data Vector

n	p10	p25	id	score	top10pc	top25pc

Execution begins. On the first iteration of the DATA step, _N_ has a value of 1. The IF statement evaluates as true so the first SET statement executes. SAS reads the values of P10 and P25 from OVERALL and records the values in the PDV.

OVERALL			
type	freq	p10	p25
0	200	70	74

STUDENTS	
id	score
101	74
102	83
103	76
104	74
105	84
106	76
107	79
108	67
109	70
110	79

Program Data Vector

n	p10	p25	id	score	top10pc	top25pc
1	70	74				

The second SET statement executes and reads the first observation in STUDENTS. The DATA step stores the values of ID and SCORE for the first observation in the PDV.

OVERALL			
type	_freq_	p10	p25
0	200	70	74

STUDENTS	
id	score
101	74
102	83
103	76
104	74
105	84
106	76
107	79
108	67
109	70
110	79

Program Data Vector

n	p10	p25	id	score	top10pc	top25pc
1	70	74	101	74		

The DATA step calculates values for TOP10PC and TOP25PC and records the values in the PDV.

OVERALL			
type	_freq_	p10	p25
0	200	70	74

STUDENTS	
id	score
101	74
102	83
103	76
104	74
105	84
106	76
107	79
108	67
109	70
110	79

Program Data Vector

n	p10	p25	id	score	top10pc	top25pc
1	70	74	101	74	Y	Y

The first iteration of the DATA step concludes and variables ID, SCORE, TOP10PC, and TOP25PC are written to data set PCSTUDENTS. _N_ is a temporary variable. The DROP option on the DATA step prevents P10 and P25 from being saved in PCSTUDENTS.

OVERALL			
type	_freq_	p10	p25
0	200	70	74

STUDENTS	
id	score
101	74
102	83
103	76
104	74
105	84
106	76
107	79
108	67
109	70
110	79

Program Data Vector

n	p10	p25	id	score	top10pc	top25pc
1	70	74	101	74	Y	Y

PCSTUDENTS

id	score	top10pc	top25pc
101	74	Y	Y

SAS sets the value of _N_ to 2 at the beginning of the second iteration of the DATA step. The IF statement is false and so the first SET statement does not execute. However, the values of P10 and P25 remain in the PDV.

OVERALL			
type	freq	p10	p25
0	200	70	74

STUDENTS	
id	score
101	74
102	83
103	76
104	74
105	84
106	76
107	79
108	67
109	70
110	79

Program Data Vector

n	p10	p25	id	score	top10pc	top25pc
2	70	74	101	74		

The second SET statement executes. Values for ID and STUDENT from the second observation in STUDENTS are recorded in the PDV.

PCSTUDENTS

OVERALL			
type	freq	p10	p25
0	200	70	74

STUDENTS	
id	score
101	74
102	83
103	76
104	74
105	84
106	76
107	79
108	67
109	70
110	79

Program Data Vector

n	p10	p25	id	score	top10pc	top25pc
2	70	74	102	83		

PCSTUDENTS

id	score	top10pc	top25pc
101	74	Y	Y

The DATA steps computes values for TOP10PC and TOP25PC for the second observation and records them in the PDV. Lastly, it writes the contents of the PDV (except for _N_) to PCSTUDENTS.

OVERALL			
type	freq	p10	p25
0	200	70	74

STUDENTS	
id	score
101	74
102	83
103	76
104	74
105	84
106	76
107	79
108	67
109	70
110	79

Program Data Vector

n	p10	p25	id	score	top10pc	top25pc
2	70	74	102	83	Y	Y

PCSTUDENTS

id	score	top10pc	top25pc
101	74	Y	Y
102	83	Y	Y

The DATA step executes until all observations in STUDENTS are processed. The values for P10 and P25 remain in the PDV. Only the first 10 of the 200 observations in PCSTUDENTS are shown in this figure.

OVERALL

type	freq	p10	p25
0	200	70	74

STUDENTS

id	score
101	74
102	83
103	76
104	74
105	84
106	76
107	79
108	67
109	70
110	79

PCSTUDENTS

Id	score	top10pc	top25pc
101	74	Y	Y
102	83	Y	Y
103	76	Y	Y
104	74	Y	Y
105	84	Y	Y
106	76	Y	Y
107	79	Y	Y
108	67	N	N
109	70	Y	N
110	79	Y	Y

Example 5.2 Adding Values from the Last Observation in a Data Set to All Observations in a Data Set

Goal

Combine values from the last observation in one data set to all observations in another data set.

Example Features

Featured Step	DATA step
Featured Step Options and Statements	IF _N_=1 statement SET statement, POINT= and NOBS= options
Related Technique	PROC SQL, Cartesian product, subquery, MAX function

Input Data Sets

Data set MANAGERS contains a list of managers for a group over time.

Data set EMPLIST contains a list of employees in the group.

The observations in MANAGERS are arranged chronologically by MGRDATE, which is the date the manager was assigned to the group.

MANAGERS

Obs	mgrdate	manager
1	07/12/2005	Butler, RE
2	01/15/2006	Wright, MV
3	11/15/2006	Freeman, OG
4	06/10/2007	Jenkins, UI
5	12/03/2007	Phillips, OB
6	01/15/2008	Myers, SC
7	05/15/2008	Brown, HU

EMPLIST

Obs	empid	empname
1	827	Torres, Anthony T
2	887	Perry, Deborah C
3	660	Gray, Lisa U
4	111	White, Elizabeth Q
5	104	Mitchell, Edward Y
6	777	Evans, William I
7	127	Jones, Donald W
8	215	Anderson, Barbara V
9	345	Green, Daniel B
10	688	Butler, Sandra X
11	677	Lee, Mark I
12	323	Griffin, Linda K

Resulting Data Set
Output 5.2
EMPMGR Data Set

```
                  Example 5.2 EMPMGR Data Set Created with DATA Step

          Obs      mgrdate      manager      empid     empname

            1      05/15/2008   Brown, HU     827      Torres, Anthony T
            2      05/15/2008   Brown, HU     887      Perry, Deborah C
            3      05/15/2008   Brown, HU     660      Gray, Lisa U
            4      05/15/2008   Brown, HU     111      White, Elizabeth Q
            5      05/15/2008   Brown, HU     104      Mitchell, Edward Y
            6      05/15/2008   Brown, HU     777      Evans, William I
            7      05/15/2008   Brown, HU     127      Jones, Donald W
            8      05/15/2008   Brown, HU     215      Anderson, Barbara V
            9      05/15/2008   Brown, HU     345      Green, Daniel B
           10      05/15/2008   Brown, HU     688      323 Butler, Sandra X
           11      05/15/2008   Brown, HU     677      Lee, Mark I
           12      05/15/2008   Brown, HU     323      Griffin, Linda K
```

Example Overview

The following DATA step finds the last observation in a data set and adds values from that observation to all observations in another data set.

Data set MANAGERS contains a list of managers of a group over time. The observations are arranged chronologically by manager assignment date. Therefore, the last observation has data for the most recent manager assigned to the group. Data set EMPLIST contains a list of the employees in the group. The goal is to obtain the most recent manager assignment and add that manager's information to each observation in EMPLIST.

The following DATA step is similar to the DATA step in Example 5.1. It reads from a data set only once on the first iteration of the DATA step. The values that are read from this data set remain in the Program Data Vector (PDV) for the duration of the DATA step. The values are available to each observation in the second data set that is read.

The DATA step is different from the DATA step in Example 5.1 in that it reads once from a data set with multiple observations and specifies which observation to read. Example 5.1 was simpler. It read once from a data set with a single observation so no additional code was needed to specify which observation to read.

The IF-THEN statement with the _N_=1 specification causes the SET statement to read from MANAGERS only on the first iteration of the DATA step. The values for MGRDATE and MANAGER remain in the PDV for the duration of the DATA step.

The NOBS= option and POINT= option control which single observation to read from MANAGERS. The NOBS= option creates temporary variable, LAST, that contains the total number of observations in data set MANAGERS. The POINT= option specifies LAST, which is the temporary variable that the NOBS= option creates. The POINT= option causes the SET statement to directly access the observation that was specified by the value of LAST.

Program

Create data set EMPMGR.
Read the last observation from MANAGERS on the first iteration.
Specify temporary variable LAST on the NOBS= option to hold the total number of observations in MANAGERS. To directly access the last observation in MANAGERS, specify LAST on the POINT= option.
Read the observations from EMPLIST.

```
data empmgr;
  if _n_=1 then set managers nobs=last point=last;



  set emplist;
run;
```

Related Technique

The following PROC SQL step joins the two tables, MANAGERS and EMPLIST, to produce table EMPMGR, which is equivalent to the data set that was created in the main example.

You cannot directly specify in PROC SQL which row to select from a table the way you can use a DATA step to select an observation from a data set. PROC SQL does not contain features that work like the NOBS= and POINT= options on the DATA step's SET statement. The following PROC SQL step is then coded based on the requirement to select the most recent manager assignment. This assignment is determined by finding the row with the maximum value for MGRDATE.

The PROC SQL step executes a Cartesian product that is similar to the Related Technique in Example 5.1. It joins one row from MANAGERS to every row in EMPLIST. It finds the single row in MANAGERS by executing a single-value subquery that returns the maximum value of MGRDATE. A WHERE clause controls the row selection from MANAGERS in the join.

As with the Related Technique in Example 5.1, the Cartesian product in this example is manageable with only one row from MANAGERS and 12 rows from EMPLIST. The number of rows in the product is 12.

Create table EMPMGR.
Select all columns from MANAGERS
and EMPLIST.
Specify a Cartesian product join
restricted by the following WHERE
clause.
Specify a single-value subquery that
returns the most recent date value in
MGRDATE. Select the row from
MANAGERS where MGRDATE
equals the value that was returned by
the subquery.

```
proc sql;
  create table empmgr as
    select *

      from managers,emplist


      where mgrdate=(select max(mgrdate) from managers);




quit;
```

Example 5.3 Computing Summary Data and Combining Them with Detail Data

Goal

Summarize several variables in a data set. Add these summarizations to each observation in a data set. Compute new variables by combining summary and detail variables.

Example Features

Featured Step	DATA step
Featured Step Options and Statements	Multiple SET statements SET statement with END= option IF _N_=1 statement DO UNTIL loop
Related Technique	PROC SQL, remerging summary statistics
A Closer Look	Selecting a Method to Combine Summary and Detail Data

Input Data Set

Data set SESSIONS contains the number of attendees from four groups at each of three training sessions.

```
                         SESSIONS Data Set

Obs      session      group_a      group_b      group_c      group_d
 1       March           8           29           29           34
 2       June           19            3           27            8
 3       August          9           32            2           15
```

Resulting Data Set
Output 5.3
*ATTENDANCE_*
FIGURES Data Set

```
             Example 5.3 ATTENDANCE_FIGURES Data Set Created with DATA Step

                                                                    t      p
                                                                    o      c
                                                                    t      t
                                                                    _      _
        s    g  g  g  g  t  t  t  t                          o      s      s
        e    r  r  r  r  o  o  o  o                          v      e      e
        s    o  o  o  o  t  t  t  t   p   p   p   p          e      s      s
        s    u  u  u  u  a  a  a  a   c   c   c   c          r      s      s
  O     i    p  p  p  p  l  l  l  l   t   t   t   t          a      i      i
  b     o    _  _  _  _  _  _  _  _   _   _   _   _          l      o      o
  s     n    a  b  c  d  a  b  c  d   a   b   c   d          l      n      n

  1   March  8  29 29 34 36 64 58 57  22  45  50  60        215    100    47
  2   June  19   3 27  8 36 64 58 57  53   5  47  14        215     57    27
  3   August 9  32  2 15 36 64 58 57  25  50   3  26        215     58    27
```

Example Overview

Similar to Example 5.1, this program adds summary data to each observation in a data set. It computes summary data and adds them to each observation in a data set in the same DATA step. It does not start with a PROC MEANS step as in Example 5.1. Instead it reads the data set twice, first to calculate the summary statistics and second to add the summary data to each observation in the data set.

The DATA step accesses the same data set twice with two SET statements. A DO UNTIL loop at the top of the DATA step executes once on the first iteration of the DATA step. It reads every observation in the data set that is specified by the SET statement in the loop and computes summary statistics in this loop. The summary statistics that are computed in the DO UNTIL loop remain in the Program Data Vector (PDV) throughout execution of the DATA step.

The second SET statement reads the data set again. This time the DATA step computes the percentage statistics by using the observation's values and the summary values that are retained in the PDV throughout execution of the DATA step.

Data set SESSIONS tracks the number of attendees from four groups (A, B, C, and D) at a training session held in March, June, and August. The goal is to calculate attendance totals by group and monthly attendance percentages by group. The output variables TOTAL_A, TOTAL_B, TOTAL_C, and TOTAL_D record the total number of attendees in each group over the three months. These variables are used as the denominator for the calculation of the percentage variables, PCT_A, PCT_B, PCT_C, and PCT_D. The PCT variables are the percentage that a month's group session contributed to the total attendance of the group.

The statistics that are computed by the DATA step are relatively simple to code. If your data are more complicated or if you have more variables to analyze, you might want to use a procedure to compute the statistics for you. The "A Closer Look" section at the end of this example discusses the selection of methods to combine summary and detail data sets.

Program

Create data set
ATTENDANCE_FIGURES.
Specify variable attributes and arrays for the DATA step. Define the TOTALS array, which will contain the total number of participants in each group. Define the PCTS array, which will contain the percentage of total attendees for a group at a session.

Process a DO UNTIL loop only on the first iteration of the DATA step. Set the DO UNTIL condition to be the value of variable EOF, which is defined by the END= option in the following SET statement.
Read data set SESSIONS during the first iteration. Define EOF so that it can be determined when SAS reaches the end of SESSIONS.
During the first iteration of the DATA step, tally in array TOTALS the total number of attendees in each group and tally in variable OVERALL the total number of attendees in all groups.

Read data set SESSIONS again.
Initialize variable TOT_SESSION, which will contain the total number of attendees from all groups at one session.
Compute the percentage of total attendees by group at a session. Use as the denominator the totals for the groups that were computed in the DO UNTIL loop on the first iteration of the DATA step.

```
data attendance_figures;

   attrib session length=$8 label='Session Attended';

   array groups{*} group_a group_b group_c group_d;
   array totals{*} total_a total_b total_c total_d;
   array pcts{*} pct_a pct_b pct_c pct_d;


   drop i;
   if _n_=1 then do until(eof);




      set sessions end=eof;


      do i=1 to dim(totals);
         totals{i}+groups{i};
         overall+groups{i};
      end;

   end;
   set sessions;
   tot_session=0;


   do i=1 to dim(pcts);
      pcts{i}=round(100*groups{i}/totals{i},1);
```

Tally the number of attendees from all groups at one session.

```
     tot_session+groups{i};

   end;
   pct_session=round(100*tot_session/overall,1);
run;
```

Compute the percentage of total attendees for all groups at a session.

Related Technique

The following PROC SQL step creates a table equivalent to the data set that was created by the DATA step in the main example. The SELECT query combines the detail information from table SESSIONS with the summary statistics it produces by using the SUM aggregate function. This process is called remerging, and when a query remerges data, PROC SQL displays a note in the SAS log that this has occurred.

```
proc sql;
   create table attendance_figures as

     select *,
      round(group_a/sum(group_a)*100,1) as pct_a,
      round(group_b/sum(group_b)*100,1) as pct_b,
      round(group_c/sum(group_c)*100,1) as pct_c,
      round(group_d/sum(group_d)*100,1) as pct_d,


      group_a+group_b+group_c+group_d as tot_session,


      sum(group_a)+sum(group_b)+sum(group_c)+
                  sum(group_d) as overall,


      round( calculated tot_session/
              calculated overall*100,1) as pct_session


     from sessions;
quit;
```

Create table
ATTENDANCE_FIGURES.
Select all columns from SESSIONS.
Compute the percentage of total attendees for a group at each session.
Use the SUM aggregate function to obtain the total number of attendees in each group. Specify aliases for the four new columns.
Find the total number of attendees from all groups at one session. Specify an alias for the calculated column.
Use the SUM aggregate function to find the total number of attendees from all groups at all sessions. Specify an alias for the calculated column.
Compute the percentage of total attendees for all groups at each session. Place the CALCULATED keyword before each of the two column alias references, which were computed earlier in the SELECT query.

A Closer Look

Selecting a Method to Combine Summary and Detail Data

Having a general knowledge of the multiple methods for combining summary and detail data will help you select the method to combine your summary and detail data. In making this determination, you need to consider SAS coding requirements and have an understanding of your input data sets and the kind of output you need to produce.

The preceding example processed data set SESSIONS twice within a DATA step. It computed percentages for different cuts of the data and saved them in output data set ATTENDANCE_FIGURES. The DATA step included a simple tally of observations in the four different groups. This tally could have been computed instead by a PROC MEANS step similar to Example 5.1. The output data set could then have been combined with data set SESSIONS. Input data set SESSIONS is small, so either way the processing proceeds quickly. When your input data sets are large and your combinations are complex, you might want to select the method that reads your data set the fewest times or is the easiest to code.

The following program revises the main example to include the PROC MEANS step that was described in the previous paragraph.

```
proc means data=sessions;
  var group_a group_b group_c group_d;
  output out=groupsums sum=total_a total_b total_c total_d;
run;
data attendance_figures;
  attrib session length=$8 label='Session Attended';

  if _n_=1 then do;
    set groupsums(keep=total_a total_b total_c total_d);
    overall+total_a+total_b+total_c+total_d;
  end;

  array groups{*} group_a group_b group_c group_d;
  array totals{*} total_a total_b total_c total_d;
  array pcts{*} pct_a pct_b pct_c pct_d;

  drop i;

  set sessions;
  tot_session=0;
  do i=1 to dim(pcts);
    pcts{i}=round(100*groups{i}/totals{i},1);
    tot_session+groups{i};
  end;
  pct_session=round(100*tot_session/overall,1);
run;
```

The goal of this example and the others in this chapter is to produce an output data set. If your goal is to produce a report instead, most likely you will want to choose a procedure such as TABULATE or REPORT to compute and present the percentages.

Example 5.4 Subsetting a Table Based on the Calculated Average of a Group

Goal

Compute the average of a column for each group in a table. Select observations from each group based on the group's average.

Example Features

Featured Step	PROC SQL
Featured Step Options and Statements	AVG aggregate function GROUP BY clause HAVING clause
Related Technique	PROC MEANS, CLASS, OUTPUT, and TYPES statements DATA step, match-merging by value

Input Table

Table SOYBEANS contains the soybean yield and acres of soybeans planted for 30 farms in four regions.

SOYBEANS

Obs	region	farmid	yield	acres
1	NW	456	33	95
2	NW	269	38	346
3	NW	295	31	59
4	NW	689	22	373
5	NW	080	30	289
6	NW	319	28	83
7	NW	703	29	114
8	SW	700	36	122
9	SW	178	28	214
10	SW	358	31	817
11	SW	045	32	9
12	SW	741	24	66
13	SW	262	29	39
14	SE	983	44	370
15	SE	628	40	165
16	SE	042	43	576
17	SE	996	46	142
18	SE	257	40	168
19	SE	749	41	63
20	SE	869	43	965
21	SE	042	36	159
22	MID	894	42	151
23	MID	806	41	49
24	MID	848	44	114
25	MID	479	35	11
26	MID	959	33	831
27	MID	493	37	25
28	MID	939	43	691
29	MID	752	35	229
30	MID	077	48	316

Resulting Table
Output 5.4
AVGPLUS Table

```
                    Example 5.4 AVGPLUS Table Created with PROC SQL

                                                            region_
            Obs     region    farmid    yield    acres        avg
             1       MID       077       48       316        39.8
             2       MID       848       44       114        39.8
             3       MID       939       43       691        39.8
             4       MID       894       42       151        39.8
             5       MID       806       41        49        39.8
             6       NW        269       38       346        30.1
             7       NW        456       33        95        30.1
             8       NW        295       31        59        30.1
             9       SE        996       46       142        41.6
            10       SE        983       44       370        41.6
            11       SE        042       43       576        41.6
            12       SE        869       43       965        41.6
            13       SW        700       36       122        30.0
            14       SW        045       32         9        30.0
            15       SW        358       31       817        30.0
```

Example Overview

The PROC SQL step in this example computes a statistic for the groups that are defined by a column in a table, and it selects rows from the table based on the computed statistic. The SELECT statement adds a column that is the computed statistic. The GROUP BY clause defines the groups in which to compute the statistic. The HAVING clause returns rows from each group that meet a specific criterion based on each group's statistic.

The goal of this PROC SQL step is to find the farms in each region whose soybean yields are greater than the average for the region. The rows are grouped by REGION, which has four values. The mean value of YIELD is computed for each value of REGION and saved in column REGION_AVG. The HAVING clause returns rows with a value of YIELD greater than the average YIELD for the row's region.

Program

Create table AVGPLUS.
Select all columns from SOYBEANS.
Calculate the average of YIELD and save it in REGION_AVG.

Group the data by the values of REGION, which causes the AVG function to compute the mean soybean yield for each region.
Return only the rows for farms with yields greater than the region's average yield. Include the CALCULATED keyword because REGION_AVG is not a column, but instead the alias for the computation that the query performs.
Order the rows in AVGPLUS by REGION and within each value of REGION, order the rows in descending order of the values of YIELD.

```
proc sql;
  create table avgplus as
    select *,
           avg(yield) format=5.1 as region_avg

      from soybeans
      group by region



      having yield > calculated region_avg




      order by region, yield descending;

  quit;
```

Related Technique

The following program requires a PROC MEANS step, a PROC SORT step, and a DATA step to produce a data set equivalent to the table that was produced by PROC SQL earlier.

The program starts with a PROC MEANS step that computes the mean soybean yield per region and saves the means in output data set YIELDAVG. Next, the program sorts the input data set SOYBEANS by REGION and within REGION by descending values of YIELD. A DATA step follows that match-merges data sets SOYBEANS and YIELDAVG by REGION. It also selects observations where the value of YIELD is greater than the average yield for the observation's region.

Compute statistics on data set SOYBEANS. Do not print a report. Specify the variable whose values define the groups for which to compute the statistics.

Produce statistics only for the groups that are defined by variable REGION.
Specify the analysis variable.
Save the mean of YIELD for each value of REGION in data set YIELDAVG. Name this new variable REGION_AVG. Do not save the variables _TYPE_ and _FREQ_ that PROC MEANS automatically creates.

```
proc means data=soybeans noprint;

   class region;


   types region;


   var yield;
   output out=yieldavg(drop=_type_ _freq_)
            mean=region_avg;




run;
```

Sort the input data set by REGION so that it can be match-merged to YIELDAVG by REGION. Sort within REGION by descending values of YIELD.

Create data set AVGPLUS.
Merge the input data set and the data set with the soybean yield averages by the values of REGION.

Output the observations where the value of YIELD is greater than the average yield of the observation's region.

```
proc sort data=soybeans;
  by region descending yield;
run;


data avgplus;
  merge soybeans yieldavg;
    by region;

  format region_avg 5.1;
  if yield gt region_avg;



run;
```

Example 5.5 Calculating Totals across a BY Group to Produce Cumulative and Grand Totals

Goal

Create in one DATA step two data sets that summarize information found in one data set. Create one data set that contains cumulative totals for observations within a BY group. Create another data set that collapses each BY group into a single observation and produces grand totals for variables in each BY group.

Example Features

Featured Step	DATA step
Featured Step Options and Statements	BY-group processing Accumulator variables
Related Technique	PROC SQL, GROUP BY clause, CASE expression, MAX and SUM functions

Input Data Set

Data set TECHCERTIF contains certification-eligible events for five technologists.

```
                                  TECHCERTIF

                                                       event_
         Obs    techid    event_date     event_type    credits
          1      1756     08/22/2008     Seminar          5
          2      1756     09/12/2008     Practice       100
          3      1756     09/22/2008     Service         20
          4      1756     01/15/2009     Class          100
          5      1756     03/02/2009     Practice        75
          6      1756     05/23/2009     Practice       125
          7      1935     05/03/2008     Conference      75
          8      1935     08/22/2008     Seminar          5
          9      1935     09/12/2008     Practice       100
         10      1935     10/15/2008     Class           50
         11      1935     12/02/2008     Practice       125
         12      1935     03/12/2009     Seminar          5
         13      1935     06/12/2009     Conference     105
         14      2234     05/23/2009     Practice       125
         15      9185     01/15/2009     Class          100
         16      9186     04/22/2009     Seminar         10
         17      9186     05/23/2009     Practice       125
         18      9186     07/29/2009     Conference     150
```

Resulting Data Sets

Output 5.5a
CUMCREDITS Data Set

```
              Example 5.5 CUMCREDITS Data Set Created with DATA Step

                                                   event_      cum_
         Obs    techid    event_date    event_type  credits    credits

          1      1756     08/22/2008    Seminar         5          5
          2      1756     09/12/2008    Practice      100        105
          3      1756     09/22/2008    Service        20        125
          4      1756     01/15/2009    Class         100        225
          5      1756     03/02/2009    Practice       75        300
          6      1756     05/23/2009    Practice      125        425
          7      1935     05/03/2008    Conference     75         75
          8      1935     08/22/2008    Seminar         5         80
          9      1935     09/12/2008    Practice      100        180
         10      1935     10/15/2008    Class          50        230
         11      1935     12/02/2008    Practice      125        355
         12      1935     03/12/2009    Seminar         5        360
         13      1935     06/12/2009    Conference    105        465
         14      2234     05/23/2009    Practice      125        125
         15      9185     01/15/2009    Class         100        100
         16      9186     04/22/2009    Seminar        10         10
         17      9186     05/23/2009    Practice      125        135
         18      9186     07/29/2009    Conference    150        285
```

Output 5.5b
GRANDCREDITS
Data Set

```
            Example 5.5 GRANDCREDITS Data Set Created with DATA Step

                                                total_
                                      total_    practice_
         Obs    techid   last_event   credits   credits

          1     1756     05/23/2009     425       300
          2     1935     06/12/2009     465       225
          3     2234     05/23/2009     125       125
          4     9185     01/15/2009     100         0
          5     9186     07/29/2009     285       125
```

Example Overview

This example shows how to apply BY-group processing in a DATA step to produce cumulative and grand totals. It processes data set TECHCERTIF in BY groups defined by the values of variable TECHID. This data set contains certification-eligible events for five technologists identified by the values of TECHID.

The DATA step creates two data sets:

❑ CUMCREDITS, which contains cumulative credits over time for each technologist. Since these are cumulative totals, the number of observations in CUMCREDITS is the same as in TECHCERTIF.

❑ GRANDCREDITS, which contains the total certification-eligible credits and total practice-type credits for each technologist. Because these are overall totals for each technologist, the number of observations in GRANDCREDITS is equal to the number of technologists with data in TECHCERTIF, which is five.

Because the DATA step processes TECHCERTIF in BY groups defined by TECHID, it is sorted prior to the DATA step by TECHID. The observations are also sorted chronologically by LAST_EVENT within each value of TECHID because a running total of credits across time is needed.

The DATA step uses accumulator variables, CUM_CREDITS and TOTAL_PRACTICE_CREDITS, to tally the certification-eligible credits and practice-type credits.

The DATA statement renames and drops variables based on the type of content that each output data set contains.

Program

Create data set CUMCREDITS to contain the cumulative totals of credits across time. Do not keep the variable that has the cumulative total for practice credits.

```
data cumcredits(drop=total_practice_credits)
```

Create data set GRANDCREDITS to contain the grand totals of certification-eligible and practice credits. Rename variables to reflect that they are for the last event and credits grand total. Drop the variables that are pertinent only to the individual event attendance.

```
     grandcredits(rename=(event_date=last_event
                          cum_credits=total_credits)
                  drop=event_type event_credits);
```

Read the observations from TECHCERTIF.

```
set techcertif;
```

Process TECHCERTIF in BY groups that are defined by the values of TECHID.

```
by techid;
```

Initialize accumulator variables CUM_CREDITS and TOTAL_PRACTICE_CREDITS to 0 at the beginning of each BY group.

```
if first.techid then do;
  cum_credits=0;
  total_practice_credits=0;
end;
```

Add the current value of EVENT_CREDITS to the running total that is stored in accumulator variable CUM_CREDITS.

```
cum_credits+event_credits;
```

Add the current value of EVENT_CREDITS to the running total that is stored in accumulator variable TOTAL_PRACTICE_CREDITS. This pertains to "Practice" events only.

```
if event_type="Practice" then
        total_practice_credits +event_credits;
```

Output each observation from TECHCERTIF to CUMCREDITS.

```
output cumcredits;
```

Output the last observation in each BY group to GRANDCREDITS.

```
if last.techid then output grandcredits;

run;
```

Related Technique

The following PROC SQL step creates a grand total table equivalent to the GRANDCREDITS data set that was created in the main example. It does not create a cumulative total table equivalent to CUMCREDITS because the accumulator variable processing in the DATA step is not similarly available in PROC SQL.

Table GRANDCREDITS is not produced by combining summary and detail data, but it is presented here to illustrate another way to produce grand totals for BY groups.

The CREATE TABLE statement uses the MAX and SUM aggregate functions and the GROUP BY clause to summarize the EVENT_DATE and EVENT_CREDITS columns in TECHCERTIF in groups defined by the values of TECHID.

Computing the total practice credits requires testing the value of EVENT_TYPE. A CASE expression examines the values of EVENT_TYPE and assigns a value to EVENT_CREDITS during processing of the expression. When EVENT_TYPE is not 'Practice', the CASE expression assigns a value of 0. Otherwise, the CASE expression uses the value in EVENT_CREDITS. One technologist, 9185, does not have any practice credits. Therefore, the value for TOTAL_PRACTICE_CREDITS for 9185 is 0 in the GRANDCREDITS table.

Example 5.6 also uses aggregate functions and the GROUP BY clause.

```
proc sql;
  create table grandcredits as
    select techid
```

Create table GRANDCREDITS.
Specify the columns to select from GRANDCREDITS. Do not apply an aggregate function to TECHID since it is the GROUP BY column.
Determine the most recent event date for a technologist.

```
            max(event_date) as last_event
                            format=mmddyy10.
            sum(event_credits) as total_credits,
```

Determine the total number of credits.
Examine the value of EVENT_TYPE to determine the total practice credits. When it is 'Practice', use the value in EVENT_CREDITS. Otherwise, use 0.
Determine the total number of practice credits by applying the SUM function to the results of the CASE expression.

```
            sum(case when event_type='Practice' then
                            event_credits
                else 0
            end) as total_practice_credits
```

Read the rows in TECHCERTIF.
Group the rows by the values of TECHID.

```
        from techcertif
        group by techid;
quit;
```

Example 5.6 Calculating Percentages and Statistics That One Row Contributes to a BY Group

Goal

Calculate percentages that one row contributes to a BY group. Calculate statistics for the BY group, some of which are based on how the row contributes to the statistic for the BY group. Create columns to classify and contain the results of the calculations.

Example Features

Featured Step	PROC SQL
Featured Step Options and Statements	Aggregate functions CASE expression GROUP BY clause ORDER BY clause
Related Technique	PROC MEANS, CLASS, OUTPUT, and TYPES statements DATA step, match-merging by a value

Input Table

Table DISTRICTLEVY contains levy voting results for four towns and their precincts. Counts of voters voting for the levy are in the "YES" column. Counts of voters voting against the levy are in the "NO" column.

DISTRICTLEVY

Obs	town	precinct	yes	no
1	Blue Hills	1	335	264
2	Blue Hills	2	631	497
3	Blue Hills	3	529	375
4	Collegetown	1	909	1300
5	Collegetown	2	677	573
6	Collegetown	3	1314	1117
7	Collegetown	4	1135	1054
8	Collegetown	5	1153	1135
9	Fairview	1	721	906
10	Fairview	2	428	611
11	Fairview	3	788	962
12	Fairview	4	335	471
13	West Ridge	1	818	738
14	West Ridge	2	768	851
15	West Ridge	3	692	610
16	West Ridge	4	892	931
17	West Ridge	5	838	965
18	West Ridge	6	1533	1453

Resulting Table
Output 5.6
LEVYRESULTS Table

```
                      Example 5.6 LEVYRESULTS Table Created with PROC SQL

                                                total_
                                                voters_ pct_precinct_ pct_precinct_  most_
   Obs    town       precinct  yes   no nprecincts  town      town            yes    yes_pct

     1 Blue Hills        1     335   264     3       2631      22.8           55.9      No
     2 Blue Hills        2     631   497     3       2631      42.9           55.9      No
     3 Blue Hills        3     529   375     3       2631      34.4           58.5      Yes
     4 Collegetown       1     909  1300     5      10367      21.3           41.1      No
     5 Collegetown       2     677   573     5      10367      12.1           54.2      Yes
     6 Collegetown       3    1314  1117     5      10367      23.4           54.1      No
     7 Collegetown       4    1135  1054     5      10367      21.1           51.9      No
     8 Collegetown       5    1153  1135     5      10367      22.1           50.4      No
     9 Fairview          1     721   906     4       5222      31.2           44.3      No
    10 Fairview          2     428   611     4       5222      19.9           41.2      No
    11 Fairview          3     788   962     4       5222      33.5           45.0      Yes
    12 Fairview          4     335   471     4       5222      15.4           41.6      No
    13 West Ridge        1     818   738     6      11089      14.0           52.6      No
    14 West Ridge        2     768   851     6      11089      14.6           47.4      No
    15 West Ridge        3     692   610     6      11089      11.7           53.1      Yes
    16 West Ridge        4     892   931     6      11089      16.4           48.9      No
    17 West Ridge        5     838   965     6      11089      16.3           46.5      No
    18 West Ridge        6    1533  1453     6      11089      26.9           51.3      No
```

Example Overview

This example summarizes data by groups and computes new columns for each row in the input table by using the summary statistics. The PROC SQL step uses aggregate functions and the GROUP BY clause to compute percentages and statistics for groups of rows. The step creates new columns to hold the percentages and statistics and to classify some of the statistics. After computation, the summary statistics are merged back to each row in the input table. Therefore, the columns that hold the summary statistics are identical for all rows within a group. The output table has the same number of rows as the input table.

Aggregate functions summarize data in a table. Several functions are available that aggregate data. Not all of the statistics functions that are found in other procedures such as PROC MEANS and PROC TABULATE are available as aggregate functions. For a complete list of PROC SQL aggregate functions, see SAS documentation on PROC SQL.

Each row in table DISTRICTLEVY contains a precinct's YES or NO votes on a levy. The goal of the PROC SQL step is to analyze voting results per town. The number of precincts per town varies from three to six. The step computes five new columns:

❑ NPRECINCTS, which is computed by using the COUNT function to tally the number of precincts per town. The value of NPRECINCTS is the same for all rows within a BY group.

❑ TOTAL_VOTERS_TOWN, which is computed by using the SUM function to sum the number of YES votes and NO votes per town. The value of TOTAL_VOTERS_TOWN is the same for all rows within each BY value of TOWN.

❑ PCT_PRECINCT_TOWN, which is the percentage of voters that the precinct contributes to the town.

❑ PCT_PRECINCT_YES, which is the percentage of YES votes in the precinct.

❑ MOST_YES_PCT, which is a character column with possible values of 'Yes' or 'No'. It has a value of 'Yes' when the percentage of YES votes for the precinct is the highest precinct percentage within the town. Precincts where the percentage of YES votes is less than the maximum percentage of YES votes within the town have a value of 'No'. Computation of MOST_YES_PCT uses the MAX aggregate function and a CASE expression.

The step includes an ORDER BY clause that arranges the rows in LEVYRESULTS by TOWN and PRECINCT. Without the ORDER BY clause, the rows might not be output in the order in which they were input from LEVYRESULTS. This example merges the statistics back to the original table. The results of the remerge might not arrange the rows in the expected order so the ORDER BY clause is needed.

The Related Technique in Example 5.5 also uses the GROUP BY clause to compute statistics for groups. It is different from this example in that it produces a summary table with one row per group. This example maintains the same number of rows in the output table as was found in the input table.

Program

<table>
<tr>
<td>

Create table LEVYRESULTS.
Select all the columns from
DISTRICTLEVY.
Compute the number of precincts per
value of TOWN.
Compute the total number of voters per
value of TOWN.
Compute the percentage of voters that
the precinct contributes to the town.
Include the calculated keyword prior to
the reference to new column
PCT_VOTERS_PRECINCT since this
value is computed within the query.
Assign an alias and attribute to the
column.

Compute the percentage of YES votes
in the precinct. Do not use the SUM
aggregate function because the
percentage should be computed for
each row and not for all rows in the
group.
Compare the calculated column
PCT_PRECINCT_YES to the
maximum value of
PCT_PRECINCT_YES for the town.
Assign a value of "Yes" or "No" to
column MOST_YES_PCT depending
on whether the current row's value for
the calculated column
PCT_PRECINCT_YES is the
maximum of all precincts in the town.
Read the rows from DISTRICTLEVY.
Group the rows in DISTRICTLEVY by
the values of TOWN. When computing
aggregate statistics, compute them for
each value of TOWN.
Order the rows in LEVYRESULTS by
TOWN and PRECINCT.

</td>
<td>

```
proc sql;
  create table levyresults as
    select *,

            count(precinct) as nprecincts,

            sum(yes+no) as total_precinct,

            100*(yes+no)/calculated total_voters_town
                    as pct_voters_precinct format=5.1,




            100*yes/(yes+no) as pct_precinct_yes
                        format=5.1,



            case



                when max(calculated pct_precinct_yes)
                        = calculated pct_precinct_yes
                            then 'Yes'
                else 'No'
            end as most_yes_pct

    from districtlevy
    group by town


    order by town, precinct;
```

</td>
</tr>
</table>

Related Technique

The following program uses two PROC MEANS steps and two DATA steps to create a data set equivalent to table LEVYRESULTS that was produced by the PROC SQL step in the main example. The PROC MEANS steps compute the SUM, N, and MAX statistics, and the DATA steps merge the statistics with the observations in DISTRICTLEVY in order to compute and classify the BY group statistics.

The program in the main example is simpler because all computations are performed in one step. If you need to compute statistics that are not PROC SQL aggregate functions, or if you need to compute percentages of different combinations of the data, it might be more efficient to adapt the following program. With the CLASS and TYPES statements in PROC MEANS, you can compute statistics for different combinations of your classification variables in one PROC MEANS step.

So that the match-merges by TOWN complete successfully and the observations in LEVYRESULTS are arranged by TOWN and PRECINCT, assume data set DISTRICTLEVY is sorted by TOWN and PRECINCT prior to the program.

Compute statistics on the observations in DISTRICTLEVY. Suppress the default listing of the results.
```
proc means data=districtlevy noprint;
```
Specify the variable whose values define the groups for which to compute statistics.
```
  class town;
```
Produce statistics for the groups that are defined by the values of TOWN.
```
  types town;
```
Compute the statistics on the YES and NO votes.
```
  var yes no;
```
Save SUM and N statistics in data set SUMLEVY. Do not keep automatic variables _TYPE_ and _FREQ_ that PROC MEANS generates. Name the statistics.
```
  output out=sumlevy(drop=_type_ _freq_)
              sum=town_yes town_no n=nprecincts;
```
```
run;
```
Create an intermediate data set that merges input data set DISTRICTLEVY by TOWN to the statistics that are saved in SUMLEVY.
```
data levystep1;
  merge districtlevy sumlevy;
  by town;
```
```
  drop town_yes town_no;
```
Compute the total number of voters in the town by summing the SUM statistics for YES and NO votes that are produced by PROC MEANS.
```
  total_voters_town=sum(town_yes,town_no);
```
Compute the percentage of voters that the precinct contributes to the town. Use as the denominator the variable that was defined earlier.
```
  pct_precinct_town=100*(yes+no)/total_voters_town;
```
Compute the percentage of YES votes in the precinct.
```
  pct_precinct_yes=100*yes/(yes+no);
```
```
run;
```
Compute statistics on the intermediate data set so that the new variable PCT_PRECINCT_YES can be calculated.
```
proc means data=levystep1 noprint;
```
Repeat the CLASS and TYPES statement as in the first PROC MEANS step.
```
  class town;
  types town;
```
Compute statistics on new variable PCT_PRECINCT_YES.
```
  var pct_precinct_yes;
```
Save the MAX statistic in data set MAXLEVY.
```
  output out=maxlevy(drop=_type_ _freq_)
              max=max_pct_yes;
```
```
run;
```

Create data set LEVYRESULTS by merging intermediate data set LEVYSTEP1 to PCTLEVY by TOWN. Define new variable MOST_YES_PCT.

Assign a value of "Yes" to variable MOST_YES_PCT when the current observation's value of PCT_PRECINCT_YES is the maximum for all precincts in the town.

```
data levyresults;
  merge levystep1 pctlevy;
  by town;

  length most_yes_pct $ 3;
  format pct_voters_precinct pct_precinct_yes 5.1;
  drop max_pct_yes;
  if pct_precinct_yes=max_pct_yes then
              most_yes_pct='Yes';
  else most_yes_pct='No';


run;
```

CHAPTER 6

Updating Data Sets by Match-Merging by Value

The examples in this chapter illustrate how you can update a master data set with information from a transaction data set by match-merging the two data sets. All examples include both a DATA step and a PROC SQL solution. Some of the DATA steps use the UPDATE statement while others use the MERGE statement.

When you update one data set with transactions from another, you need to consider what to do when missing values exist in the transaction data set and duplicate values of the matching variables exist in the master or transaction data sets. This chapter's examples demonstrate how to use options, functions, and programming statements to handle these situations.

For a comparison of the MODIFY and UPDATE statements, see "Choosing between MODIFY and UPDATE" in Chapter 1. Chapter 7 includes examples that use the MODIFY statement.

Example 6.1   Updating a Data Set and Controlling Whether Common Variables Are Overwritten with Missing Values

Goal

Update a master data set with values from another data set. Do not replace a nonmissing value in the master data set with a missing value when the value for a common variable in the transaction data is missing. Also add a new variable to the updated master data set.

Examples 6.1, 6.2, 6.3, 6.4, and 6.5 illustrate ways to update common variables when combining data sets. The five examples apply the methods to the same master data set. Different transaction data sets are used in Examples 6.1, 6.2, and 6.3. Examples 6.4 and 6.5 use the same transaction data set and produce different resulting data sets.

Example Features

Featured Step	DATA step
Featured Step Options and Statements	UPDATE and BY statements
Related Technique	PROC SQL, full join using the ON clause, COALESCE function
A Closer Look	Allowing Missing Values to Replace Existing Values in the Master Data Set When Updating a Master Data Set
	Comparing the UPDATE and MERGE Statements
	Using UPDATE and MERGE When There Are Multiple Observations in a BY Group

Input Data Sets

Master data set BOOKLIST contains information about the chapters of three books. Transaction data set BOOKUPDATES contains updates of information that should be applied to BOOKLIST. It also has variable UPDATEDBY, which does not exist in BOOKLIST.

Both data sets have unique occurrences of the combinations of values of BOOKID and CHAPTER.

BOOKLIST

Obs	bookid	booktitle	chapter	author	duedate	editor
1	NF0586	Current Narratives	1	Smith, Rebecca	09/04/2010	Williams, Stephanie
2	NF0586	Current Narratives	2	Williams, Susan	09/04/2010	Williams, Stephanie
3	NF0586	Current Narratives	3	Torres, Christopher	09/11/2010	Williams, Stephanie
4	NF0586	Current Narratives	4	Torres, Christopher	09/11/2010	Williams, Stephanie
5	NF0586	Current Narratives	5	Powell, George	09/11/2010	Williams, Stephanie
6	NF0586	Current Narratives	6	Thompson, Tonya	09/11/2010	Williams, Stephanie
7	NF0586	Current Narratives	7	Allen, Linda	09/11/2010	Williams, Stephanie
8	NF0586	Current Narratives	8	Johnson, Tammy	09/11/2010	Williams, Stephanie
9	NF0586	Current Narratives	9	Kelly, Melissa	09/11/2010	Williams, Stephanie
10	NF0586	Current Narratives	10	Thompson, Tonya	09/11/2010	Williams, Stephanie
11	NF2413	Political Comments	1	Jones, Robin	07/31/2010	White, Michelle
12	NF2413	Political Comments	2	Sanchez, Brandon	08/07/2010	White, Michelle
13	NF2413	Political Comments	3	Jones, Robin	07/31/2010	White, Michelle
14	NF2413	Political Comments	4	Perez, Joshua	07/31/2010	White, Michelle
15	NF2413	Political Comments	5	Williams, Nicholas	07/31/2010	White, Michelle
16	NF2413	Political Comments	6	Patterson, Mary	08/14/2010	White, Michelle
17	NF2413	Political Comments	7	Torres, Christopher	08/07/2010	White, Michelle
18	NF2413	Political Comments	8	Robinson, Bonnie	08/07/2010	White, Michelle
19	NF2413	Political Comments	9	Brown, Patricia	08/07/2010	White, Michelle
20	NF8141	Favorite Essays	1	Clark, Todd	10/02/2010	Patterson, Daniel
21	NF8141	Favorite Essays	2	Barnes, David	10/02/2010	Patterson, Daniel
22	NF8141	Favorite Essays	3	Young, Richard	09/18/2010	Patterson, Daniel
23	NF8141	Favorite Essays	4	Barnes, David	10/02/2010	Patterson, Daniel
24	NF8141	Favorite Essays	5	Anderson, Daniel	09/18/2010	Patterson, Daniel
25	NF8141	Favorite Essays	6	Anderson, Daniel	09/18/2010	Patterson, Daniel
26	NF8141	Favorite Essays	7	Morris, Laura	09/18/2010	Patterson, Daniel
27	NF8141	Favorite Essays	8	Powell, George	09/18/2010	Patterson, Daniel

BOOKUPDATES

Obs	bookid	chapter	author	duedate	updatedby
1	NF0586	4	Banks, James	.	JWE
2	NF0586	9	King, Weston	09/18/2010	JWE
3	NF8141	6		10/02/2010	SAW

Resulting Data Set
Output 6.1a
REVISEDLIST
Data Set

```
                   Example 6.1 REVISEDLIST Data Set Created with DATA Step

Obs bookid    booktitle        chapter author              duedate    editor               updatedby
  1 NF0586 Current Narratives     1   Smith, Rebecca      09/04/2010 Williams, Stephanie
  2 NF0586 Current Narratives     2   Williams, Susan     09/04/2010 Williams, Stephanie
  3 NF0586 Current Narratives     3   Torres, Christopher 09/11/2010 Williams, Stephanie
  4 NF0586 Current Narratives     4   Banks, James        09/11/2010 Williams, Stephanie  JWE
  5 NF0586 Current Narratives     5   Powell, George      09/11/2010 Williams, Stephanie
  6 NF0586 Current Narratives     6   Thompson, Tonya     09/11/2010 Williams, Stephanie
  7 NF0586 Current Narratives     7   Allen, Linda        09/11/2010 Williams, Stephanie
  8 NF0586 Current Narratives     8   Johnson, Tammy      09/11/2010 Williams, Stephanie
  9 NF0586 Current Narratives     9   King, Weston        09/18/2010 Williams, Stephanie  JWE
 10 NF0586 Current Narratives    10   Thompson, Tonya     09/11/2010 Williams, Stephanie
 11 NF2413 Political Comments     1   Jones, Robin        07/31/2010 White, Michelle
 12 NF2413 Political Comments     2   Sanchez, Brandon    08/07/2010 White, Michelle
 13 NF2413 Political Comments     3   Jones, Robin        07/31/2010 White, Michelle
 14 NF2413 Political Comments     4   Perez, Joshua       07/31/2010 White, Michelle
 15 NF2413 Political Comments     5   Williams, Nicholas  07/31/2010 White, Michelle
 16 NF2413 Political Comments     6   Patterson, Mary     08/14/2010 White, Michelle
 17 NF2413 Political Comments     7   Torres, Christopher 08/07/2010 White, Michelle
 18 NF2413 Political Comments     8   Robinson, Bonnie    08/07/2010 White, Michelle
 19 NF2413 Political Comments     9   Brown, Patricia     08/07/2010 White, Michelle
 20 NF8141 Favorite Essays        1   Clark, Todd         10/02/2010 Patterson, Daniel
 21 NF8141 Favorite Essays        2   Barnes, David       10/02/2010 Patterson, Daniel
 22 NF8141 Favorite Essays        3   Young, Richard      09/18/2010 Patterson, Daniel
 23 NF8141 Favorite Essays        4   Barnes, David       10/02/2010 Patterson, Daniel
 24 NF8141 Favorite Essays        5   Anderson, Daniel    09/18/2010 Patterson, Daniel
 25 NF8141 Favorite Essays        6   Anderson, Daniel    10/02/2010 Patterson, Daniel    SAW
 26 NF8141 Favorite Essays        7   Morris, Laura       09/18/2010 Patterson, Daniel
 27 NF8141 Favorite Essays        8   Powell, George      09/18/2010 Patterson, Daniel
```

Example Overview

This example shows you how to update a master data set with only nonmissing values from observations in a transaction data set. The UPDATE and BY statements in the DATA step update the master data set for observations in the two data sets that match according to the values of the BY variables.

Data set BOOKLIST is the master data set, and it tracks information for the chapters of three books. The transaction data set BOOKUPDATES contains updated information about selected chapters in the books.

No duplicates are present in either the master data set or the transaction data set. Additional programming statements are required when duplicate BY values exist. The only variables that are present in the transaction data set besides the matching variables are the variables to be updated. This program also adds one new variable to the output data set that exists in the transaction data set.

The DATA step updates the two variables, AUTHOR and DUEDATE, in data set BOOKLIST with information from BOOKUPDATES when a variable value is not missing. It uses the default action of the UPDATE and BY statements to perform the updates. Observations are matched by two BY variables, BOOKID and CHAPTER.

Missing values are present in the first and third observations of the transaction data set BOOKUPDATES.

Assume both data sets were sorted or indexed by BOOKID and CHAPTER prior to the DATA step.

A MERGE statement could be used instead of the UPDATE statement. However, in this example, it is simpler to use the UPDATE statement. You can take advantage of its default action of not replacing a variable's nonmissing value in the master data set with a missing value when the variable value is missing in the matching observation in the transaction data set. For more information about when to choose UPDATE or MERGE, see "Comparing the UPDATE and MERGE Statements" in the following "A Closer Look" section and SAS documentation.

Program

Create data set REVISEDLIST.
Update data set BOOKLIST with
information in BOOKUPDATES. Place
the master data set first in the
UPDATE statement.
Specify how to match observations in
the two data sets.

```
data revisedlist;
   update booklist bookupdates;




   by bookid chapter;

run;
```

Related Technique

The following PROC SQL step creates a table equivalent to the data set that was created by the DATA step in the main example. A full join using the ON clause combines the two tables so that all matching and nonmatching rows in the two input tables are present in output table REVISEDBOOKLIST along with updates of specific rows that were contributed from BOOKUPDATES.

The COALESCE function performs the update of columns AUTHOR and DUEDATE in BOOKLIST. The first argument to each call to COALESCE is the column from BOOKUPDATES. The second argument is the column from BOOKLIST. The COALESCE function checks each of its arguments from left to right until it finds a nonmissing value. When the first argument is nonmissing, PROC SQL replaces the value in BOOKLIST with the value from BOOKUPDATES. When the first argument is missing, the value in BOOKLIST for the column remains the same.

The step also applies the COALESCE function to the matching columns, BOOKID and CHAPTER. In this example, you could select BOOKID and CHAPTER from the master table (B.BOOKID and B.CHAPTER) because all the transactions have a match in the master data set. However, if you have rows in your transaction table that do not have a match in your master table, the values of B.BOOKID are missing. Using the COALESCE function ensures that the unmatched values for the matching columns are copied to the output table.

Missing values are present in the first and third rows of table BOOKUPDATES. The missing values are not copied to REVISEDBOOKLIST.

The SELECT statement includes column UPDATEDBY, which is found only in the transaction table. Compared to the main example, you need to specify all columns you want to include in the output table when using PROC SQL. Unless you use the DROP or KEEP statements or options, the UPDATE statement in the main example copies all new variables in the transaction data set to the updated data set.

Create table REVISEDLIST.
Apply the COALESCE function to the
two matching columns so that if there
are nonmatches in the transaction
table, the nonmissing unmatched value
is copied to the output table.
Apply the COALESCE function to the
columns that are being updated. Put
the column contributed from the
transaction table BOOKUPDATES
first so that when it is nonmissing, it
replaces the value in BOOKLIST.

Combine the two tables with a full join
so that all matching and nonmatching

```
proc sql;
   create table revisedlist as
      select coalesce(u.bookid,b.bookid) as bookid,
             booktitle,
             coalesce(u.chapter,b.chapter) as chapter,


             coalesce(u.author,b.author) as author,
             coalesce(u.duedate,b.duedate) as duedate
                format=mmddyy10.,



             editor,
             updatedby
      from booklist b
         full join
      bookupdates u
```

rows are present in the output table.
Specify an alias for each table.
Specify the columns that match the two
tables.

```
              on b.bookid=u.bookid and b.chapter=u.chapter;

        quit;
```

A Closer Look

Allowing Missing Values to Replace Existing Values in the Master Data Set When Updating a Master Data Set

The DATA step in the preceding main example relies on the default action of the UPDATE statement that prevents missing values in the transaction data set from replacing existing values in the master data set. This action is controlled by UPDATE statement option UPDATEMODE=. This option can have one of two values: MISSINGCHECK or NOMISSINGCHECK. The default value for UPDATEMODE= is MISSINGCHECK. Because the default action is what this example requires, it was not necessary to add option UPDATEMODE= to the UPDATE statement.

If you want to allow missing values in the transaction data set to replace existing values in the master data set, add UPDATEMODE=NOMISSINGCHECK to the UPDATE statement. The DATA step in the main example is modified here to include this option:

```
        data revisedmissing;
          update booklist bookupdates updatemode=nomissingcheck;
          by bookid chapter;
        run;
```

Output 6.1b displays a PROC PRINT of the output data set REVISEDMISSING that was created by the preceding DATA step. Two missing values have replaced existing values in the updated data set. These correspond to the two missing values in the transaction data set:

❑ variable DUEDATE for BOOKID= "NF0586" CHAPTER=4

❑ variable AUTHOR for BOOKID= "NF8141" CHAPTER=6

Output 6.1b
REVISEDMISSING
Data Set

```
                   Example 6.1 REVISEDMISSING Data Set Created with DATA Step

      Obs  bookid     booktitle       chapter  author              duedate       editor             updatedby
        1  NF0586  Current Narratives     1     Smith, Rebecca      09/04/2010  Williams, Stephanie
        2  NF0586  Current Narratives     2     Williams, Susan     09/04/2010  Williams, Stephanie
        3  NF0586  Current Narratives     3     Torres, Christopher 09/11/2010  Williams, Stephanie
        4  NF0586  Current Narratives     4     Banks, James               .    Williams, Stephanie    JWE
        5  NF0586  Current Narratives     5     Powell, George      09/11/2010  Williams, Stephanie
        6  NF0586  Current Narratives     6     Thompson, Tonya     09/11/2010  Williams, Stephanie
        7  NF0586  Current Narratives     7     Allen, Linda        09/11/2010  Williams, Stephanie
        8  NF0586  Current Narratives     8     Johnson, Tammy      09/11/2010  Williams, Stephanie
        9  NF0586  Current Narratives     9     King, Weston        09/18/2010  Williams, Stephanie    JWE
       10  NF0586  Current Narratives    10     Thompson, Tonya     09/11/2010  Williams, Stephanie
       11  NF2413  Political Comments     1     Jones, Robin        07/31/2010  White, Michelle
       12  NF2413  Political Comments     2     Sanchez, Brandon    08/07/2010  White, Michelle
       13  NF2413  Political Comments     3     Jones, Robin        07/31/2010  White, Michelle
       14  NF2413  Political Comments     4     Perez, Joshua       07/31/2010  White, Michelle
       15  NF2413  Political Comments     5     Williams, Nicholas  07/31/2010  White, Michelle
       16  NF2413  Political Comments     6     Patterson, Mary     08/14/2010  White, Michelle
       17  NF2413  Political Comments     7     Torres, Christopher 08/07/2010  White, Michelle
       18  NF2413  Political Comments     8     Robinson, Bonnie    08/07/2010  White, Michelle
       19  NF2413  Political Comments     9     Brown, Patricia     08/07/2010  White, Michelle
       20  NF8141  Favorite Essays        1     Clark, Todd         10/02/2010  Patterson, Daniel
       21  NF8141  Favorite Essays        2     Barnes, David       10/02/2010  Patterson, Daniel
       22  NF8141  Favorite Essays        3     Young, Richard      09/18/2010  Patterson, Daniel
       23  NF8141  Favorite Essays        4     Barnes, David       10/02/2010  Patterson, Daniel
       24  NF8141  Favorite Essays        5     Anderson, Daniel    09/18/2010  Patterson, Daniel
       25  NF8141  Favorite Essays        6                         10/02/2010  Patterson, Daniel      SAW
       26  NF8141  Favorite Essays        7     Morris, Laura       09/18/2010  Patterson, Daniel
       27  NF8141  Favorite Essays        8     Powell, George      09/18/2010  Patterson, Daniel
```

Comparing the UPDATE and MERGE Statements

The UPDATE and MERGE statements can perform the similar task of updating a master data set with information that is supplied in a transaction data set. It is important to understand their usage differences so that you choose the better tool for your application. Table 6.1 presents an abridged comparison of the two statements. For detailed information about these statements, see SAS documentation.

Table 6.1 Comparing the UPDATE and MERGE Statements

UPDATE Statement	MERGE Statement
Can process only two data sets at a time	Can process an unlimited number of data sets
Can update and add observations to the master data set	Can update and add observations to the output data set
Can add and delete variables in the master data set	Can add and delete variables in the output data set
Must list master data set first	Usually list master data set first, but not required
Requires a BY statement	Updating usually uses a BY statement, but not required
Requires the master and transaction data sets be sorted or indexed by the matching variables in the BY statement	Updating usually expects the input data sets to be sorted or indexed by the matching variables in the BY statement, but not required
Must be no more than one observation in the BY group in the master data set (the DATA step will execute but with warnings, and SAS sets the _ERROR_ variable to 1)	Updating usually expects no more than one observation in the BY group in the master data set, but not required (this condition does not set the _ERROR_ variable to 1)
Outputs observation at the end of the BY group	Outputs each observation at the bottom of the DATA step or by explicit OUTPUT statement
Does not replace missing values in the master data set with missing values found in the matched observations in the transaction data set unless the UPDATE statement option UPDATEMODE= is set to NOMISSINGCHECK or if using special missing values	Replaces existing values in the first data set with missing values found in the matched observations in the second data set if the variables have the same names

The next section describes with examples how the UPDATE and MERGE statements process your master and transaction data sets when they have multiple observations in a BY group.

Using UPDATE and MERGE When There Are Multiple Observations in a BY Group

The UPDATE and MERGE statements differ in how they combine data sets when either the master or transaction data set contains multiple observations per BY group. The next code samples contrast how the two statements handle these duplicates.

Transaction data set with multiple observations in a BY group: When you use the UPDATE statement and have more than one observation in the transaction data set in a BY group, only the last in the series of multiple observations updates the matching observation in the master data set. When you use the MERGE statement and have more than one observation in the transaction data set in a BY group, all transaction observations in that BY group are added to the master data set.

For example, the following DATA step creates the transaction data set DUPDATES and it has three observations in the BY group of BOOKID= "NF8141" and CHAPTER=6.

```
data dupdates;
   input bookid $ 1-6 chapter duedate : mmddyy10.;
   format duedate mmddyy10.;
datalines;
NF8141 6  10/02/2010
NF8141 6  10/22/2010
NF8141 6  11/01/2010
;;;;
```

A DATA step that uses the UPDATE statement and a DATA step that uses the MERGE statement follow. Both DATA steps apply the transactions in DUPDATES to the original BOOKLIST data set that was created in the main example, and the two DATA steps produce different output data sets.

Using the UPDATE Statement	Using the MERGE Statement
| ```
data upddups;
   update booklist dupdates;
   by bookid chapter;
run;
``` | ```
data mrgdups;
   merge booklist dupdates;
   by bookid chapter;
run;
``` |

PROC PRINTs of UPDDUPS and MRGDUPS show the differences in the results. Data set UPDDUPS has only one observation for BOOKID= "NF8141" CHAPTER=6, and this observation has the value for DUEDATE equal to the value of DUEDATE in the last observation in DUPDATES (11/01/2010). Data set MRGDUPS has three observations for BOOKID= "NF8141" CHAPTER=6, one for each of the three observations in MRGDUPS.

The output lists only variables BOOKID, CHAPTER, and DUEDATE for the observations where BOOKID= "NF8141". The rows for CHAPTER=6 in each output display are highlighted.

Using the UPDATE Statement				Using the MERGE Statement			
UPDDUPS				MRGDUPS			
Obs	bookid	chapter	duedate	Obs	bookid	chapter	duedate
20	NF8141	1	10/02/2010	20	NF8141	1	10/02/2010
21	NF8141	2	10/02/2010	21	NF8141	2	10/02/2010
22	NF8141	3	09/18/2010	22	NF8141	3	09/18/2010
23	NF8141	4	10/02/2010	23	NF8141	4	10/02/2010
24	NF8141	5	09/18/2010	24	NF8141	5	09/18/2010
25	**NF8141**	**6**	**11/01/2010**	**25**	**NF8141**	**6**	**10/02/2010**
26	NF8141	7	09/18/2010	**26**	**NF8141**	**6**	**10/22/2010**
27	NF8141	8	09/18/2010	**27**	**NF8141**	**6**	**11/01/2010**
				28	NF8141	7	09/18/2010
				29	NF8141	7	09/18/2010

Master data set with multiple observations in a BY group: When you use the UPDATE statement and have more than one observation in the master data set in a BY group, the variables in common between the master and transaction data sets on the first matching observation in the BY group are updated. The variables in common between the master and transaction data sets in subsequent matching observations in that BY group of multiple observations are not updated. Additionally, values for any new variables that are present in the transaction data set are copied only to the first matching observation in a BY group with multiple observations. Missing values are assigned to these new variables for all subsequent matching observations in that BY group.

SAS issues a WARNING and sets the automatic variable _ERROR_ to 1 when your master data set contains more than one observation in a BY group. The DATA step can execute, but this is a process you should program carefully because the design of the UPDATE statement is to process only one observation per BY group in the master data set. Here is the WARNING message that SAS displays in the situation of multiple observations per BY group:

```
WARNING: The MASTER data set contains more than one
         observation for a BY group.
```

When you use the MERGE statement and have more than one observation in the master data set in a BY group, only the variables in common between the master and transaction data sets in the first matching observation in the BY group are updated. This part of the MERGE statement process is identical to that of the UPDATE statement.

The process of adding new variables when using the MERGE statement differs from that of the UPDATE statement. With the MERGE statement, the values for any new variables that are present in the transaction data set are copied to all matching observations in the series of duplicates, not just the first observation as is done with the UPDATE statement. The DATA step loads the observation in the transaction data set into the Program Data Vector (PDV). With new variables found only in the transaction data set, the values for those variables remain in the PDV until the next observation in the transaction data set is processed (unless you change them with SAS language statements in the DATA step).

Unlike the UPDATE statement, the MERGE statement does not consider multiple observations in a BY group to be an error, and it does not write a message to the SAS log. However, SAS does write a warning if more than one of the data sets in your MERGE statement has multiple observations in a BY group.

For example, the following DATA step creates the transaction data set NEWTITLES, and it has one observation with the BY-variable value of BOOKID= "NF8141." The variable VERSION in NEWTITLES is not present in the master data set BOOKLIST.

```
data newtitles;
   input bookid $ 1-6 booktitle $ 8-25 version;
datalines;
NF8141 Popular Essays 2
;;;;
```

The master data set BOOKLIST has eight observations with the BY-variable value of BOOKID= "NF8141".

A DATA step that uses the UPDATE statement and a DATA step that uses the MERGE statement follow. Both DATA steps apply the transactions in NEWTITLES to the original BOOKLIST data set that was created in the main example, and they produce different output data sets. Note that these DATA steps have only one BY variable (BOOKID) compared to the two BY variables, BOOKID and CHAPTER, in the preceding DATA steps.

Using the UPDATE Statement	Using the MERGE Statement
| ```
data updtitles;
  update booklist newtitles;
  by bookid;
run;
``` | ```
data mrgtitles;
  merge booklist newtitles;
  by bookid;
run;
``` |

PROC PRINTs of UPDTITLES and MRGTITLES show the similarities and differences in the results. Both data sets have an updated value for BOOKTITLE in only the first of the eight observations for BOOKID= "NF8141". A nonmissing value for VERSION is found only on the first of the eight observations for BOOKID= "NF8141" in data set UPDTITLES, while all eight observations for BOOKID= "NF8141" in data set MRGTITLES have a value for VERSION.

The following output lists only variables BOOKID, BOOKTITLE, CHAPTER, and VERSION for the observations where BOOKID= "NF8141".

Remember that using the UPDATE statement when there are multiple observations in a BY group in the master data set causes SAS to write warnings to the SAS log and to set the automatic variable _ERROR_ to 1.

Using the UPDATE Statement	Using the MERGE Statement
UPDTITLES	MRGTITLES
Obs bookid booktitle chapter version	Obs bookid booktitle chapter version
20 NF8141 Popular Essays 1 2	20 NF8141 Popular Essays 1 2
21 NF8141 Favorite Essays 2 .	21 NF8141 Favorite Essays 2 2
22 NF8141 Favorite Essays 3 .	22 NF8141 Favorite Essays 3 2
23 NF8141 Favorite Essays 4 .	23 NF8141 Favorite Essays 4 2
24 NF8141 Favorite Essays 5 .	24 NF8141 Favorite Essays 5 2
25 NF8141 Favorite Essays 6 .	25 NF8141 Favorite Essays 6 2
26 NF8141 Favorite Essays 7 .	26 NF8141 Favorite Essays 7 2
27 NF8141 Favorite Essays 8 .	27 NF8141 Favorite Essays 8 2

See Example 6.4 for how to write a DATA step that uses the MERGE statement to update a master data set that has multiple observations in a BY group.

<u>Master and transaction data sets with multiple observations in a BY group:</u> Updating or merging data sets when both master and transaction data sets have multiple observations in a BY group can be problematic. You should understand your data well before programming a DATA step where this situation exists.

The concepts that were illustrated in the previous two sections apply. When using the UPDATE statement, only the last observation in a BY group of multiple observations updates the first observation in the matching BY group of multiple observations. When using the MERGE statement, one-to-one matching occurs between observations in the master and transaction data sets within the matching BY group of multiple observations.

For example, the following DATA step creates the transaction data set MULTTITLES, and it has two observations with the BY-variable value of BOOKID= "NF8141". The variable VERSION in MULTTITLES is not present in the master data set BOOKLIST.

```
data multtitles;
   input bookid $ 1-6 booktitle $ 8-25 version;
datalines;
NF8141 Popular Essays    2
NF8141 Essays for All    3
;;;;
```

The master data set BOOKLIST has eight observations with the BY-variable value of BOOKID= "NF8141".

A DATA step that uses the UPDATE statement and a DATA step that uses the MERGE statement follow. Both DATA steps apply the transactions in MULTTITLES to the original BOOKLIST data set that was created in the main example, and they produce different output data sets. Note that these DATA steps have only one BY variable (BOOKID) compared to the two BY variables, BOOKID and CHAPTER, in some of the preceding DATA steps.

Using the UPDATE Statement	**Using the MERGE Statement**

`data updmult;`
`  update booklist multtitles;`
`  by bookid;`
`run;`
	`data mrgmult;`
	`  merge booklist multtitles;`
	`  by bookid;`
	`run;`

The following output for data set UPDMULT shows that only the first of the eight observations for BOOKID= "NF8141" has an updated value for BOOKTITLE and that this value comes from the second observation in MULTTITLES. The value of VERSION on the first observation also comes from the second observation in MULTTITLES.

The output for MRGMULT shows for BY group BOOKID= "NF8141" one-to-one matching of the two observations in MULTTITLES to the first two observations in BOOKLIST. The first observation in the BY group has values for BOOKTITLE and VERSION that were copied from the first observation in MULTTITLES. The second observation in the BY group has values for BOOKTITLE and VERSION copied from the second observation in MULTTITLES. The remaining six observations also have a value of VERSION from the second observation in MULTTITLES. Similar to the previous MERGE statement example, the value of VERSION from the second observation in MULTITLES is moved to the PDV and remains there until the next BY group is processed.

The following output lists only variables BOOKID, BOOKTITLE, CHAPTER, and VERSION for the observations where BOOKID= "NF8141".

Use of the UPDATE statement when there are multiple observations in the master data set BY group causes SAS to write warnings to the SAS log and to set the automatic variable _ERROR_ to 1.

When there are multiple observations in more than one of the data sets in the MERGE statement, SAS writes the following note to the SAS log and does not flag this as a warning or error.

```
NOTE: MERGE statement has more than one data set with
      repeats of BY values.
```

Using the UPDATE Statement				Using the MERGE Statement			
UPDMULT				MRGMULT			
Obs	bookid booktitle	chapter	version	Obs	bookid booktitle	chapter	version
20	NF8141 Essays for All	1	3	20	NF8141 Popular Essays	1	2
21	NF8141 Favorite Essays	2	.	21	NF8141 Essays for All	2	3
22	NF8141 Favorite Essays	3	.	22	NF8141 Favorite Essays	3	3
23	NF8141 Favorite Essays	4	.	23	NF8141 Favorite Essays	4	3
24	NF8141 Favorite Essays	5	.	24	NF8141 Favorite Essays	5	3
25	NF8141 Favorite Essays	6	.	25	NF8141 Favorite Essays	6	3
26	NF8141 Favorite Essays	7	.	26	NF8141 Favorite Essays	7	3
27	NF8141 Favorite Essays	8	.	27	NF8141 Favorite Essays	8	3

Example 6.2   Updating a Data Set and Allowing Some Values to Be Updated with Missing Values

Goal

Update a master data set with values from another data set. The second data set contains missing values. Control which missing values in the second data set can overwrite existing values in the master data set.

Examples 6.1, 6.2, 6.3, 6.4, and 6.5 illustrate ways to update common variables when combining data sets. The five examples apply the methods to the same master data set. Different transaction data sets are used in Examples 6.1, 6.2, and 6.3. Examples 6.4 and 6.5 use the same transaction data set and produce different resulting data sets.

Example Features

Featured Step	DATA step
Featured Step Options and Statements	MISSING statement UPDATE and BY statements Special missing values
Related Technique	PROC SQL, full join, CASE expression, COALESCE function, special missing values

Input Data Sets

Master data set BOOKLIST contains information about the chapters of three books. Transaction data set BOOKMISS contains updates of information that should be applied to BOOKLIST. Some of the values for DUEDATE are missing, and some values are coded with the special missing value, "_" (underscore).

Both data sets have unique occurrences of the combinations of values of BOOKID and CHAPTER.

BOOKLIST

Obs	bookid	booktitle	chapter	author	duedate	editor
1	NF0586	Current Narratives	1	Smith, Rebecca	09/04/2010	Williams, Stephanie
2	NF0586	Current Narratives	2	Williams, Susan	09/04/2010	Williams, Stephanie
3	NF0586	Current Narratives	3	Torres, Christopher	09/11/2010	Williams, Stephanie
4	NF0586	Current Narratives	4	Torres, Christopher	09/11/2010	Williams, Stephanie
5	NF0586	Current Narratives	5	Powell, George	09/11/2010	Williams, Stephanie
6	NF0586	Current Narratives	6	Thompson, Tonya	09/11/2010	Williams, Stephanie
7	NF0586	Current Narratives	7	Allen, Linda	09/11/2010	Williams, Stephanie
8	NF0586	Current Narratives	8	Johnson, Tammy	09/11/2010	Williams, Stephanie
9	NF0586	Current Narratives	9	Kelly, Melissa	09/11/2010	Williams, Stephanie
10	NF0586	Current Narratives	10	Thompson, Tonya	09/11/2010	Williams, Stephanie
11	NF2413	Political Comments	1	Jones, Robin	07/31/2010	White, Michelle
12	NF2413	Political Comments	2	Sanchez, Brandon	08/07/2010	White, Michelle
13	NF2413	Political Comments	3	Jones, Robin	07/31/2010	White, Michelle
14	NF2413	Political Comments	4	Perez, Joshua	07/31/2010	White, Michelle
15	NF2413	Political Comments	5	Williams, Nicholas	07/31/2010	White, Michelle
16	NF2413	Political Comments	6	Patterson, Mary	08/14/2010	White, Michelle
17	NF2413	Political Comments	7	Torres, Christopher	08/07/2010	White, Michelle
18	NF2413	Political Comments	8	Robinson, Bonnie	08/07/2010	White, Michelle
19	NF2413	Political Comments	9	Brown, Patricia	08/07/2010	White, Michelle
20	NF8141	Favorite Essays	1	Clark, Todd	10/02/2010	Patterson, Daniel
21	NF8141	Favorite Essays	2	Barnes, David	10/02/2010	Patterson, Daniel
22	NF8141	Favorite Essays	3	Young, Richard	09/18/2010	Patterson, Daniel
23	NF8141	Favorite Essays	4	Barnes, David	10/02/2010	Patterson, Daniel
24	NF8141	Favorite Essays	5	Anderson, Daniel	09/18/2010	Patterson, Daniel
25	NF8141	Favorite Essays	6	Anderson, Daniel	09/18/2010	Patterson, Daniel
26	NF8141	Favorite Essays	7	Morris, Laura	09/18/2010	Patterson, Daniel
27	NF8141	Favorite Essays	8	Powell, George	09/18/2010	Patterson, Daniel

BOOKMISS

Obs	bookid	chapter	author	duedate
1	NF0586	3		
2	NF0586	4		_
3	NF2413	4	Loren, Marie	_
4	NF2413	7		.
5	NF8141	5		10/03/2010
6	NF8141	6		10/03/2010

Resulting Data Set
Output 6.2
REVISEDMISS
Data Set

```
                   Example 6.2 REVISEDMISS Data Set Created with DATA Step

    Obs   bookid     booktitle      chapter   author                duedate      editor

      1   NF0586   Current Narratives     1    Smith, Rebecca        09/04/2010  Williams, Stephanie
      2   NF0586   Current Narratives     2    Williams, Susan       09/04/2010  Williams, Stephanie
      3   NF0586   Current Narratives     3    Torres, Christopher        .      Williams, Stephanie
      4   NF0586   Current Narratives     4    Torres, Christopher        .      Williams, Stephanie
      5   NF0586   Current Narratives     5    Powell, George        09/11/2010  Williams, Stephanie
      6   NF0586   Current Narratives     6    Thompson, Tonya       09/11/2010  Williams, Stephanie
      7   NF0586   Current Narratives     7    Allen, Linda          09/11/2010  Williams, Stephanie
      8   NF0586   Current Narratives     8    Johnson, Tammy        09/11/2010  Williams, Stephanie
      9   NF0586   Current Narratives     9    Kelly, Melissa        09/11/2010  Williams, Stephanie
     10   NF0586   Current Narratives    10    Thompson, Tonya       09/11/2010  Williams, Stephanie
     11   NF2413   Political Comments     1    Jones, Robin          07/31/2010  White, Michelle
     12   NF2413   Political Comments     2    Sanchez, Brandon      08/07/2010  White, Michelle
     13   NF2413   Political Comments     3    Jones, Robin          07/31/2010  White, Michelle
     14   NF2413   Political Comments     4    Loren, Marie          07/31/2010  White, Michelle
     15   NF2413   Political Comments     5    Williams, Nicholas    07/31/2010  White, Michelle
     16   NF2413   Political Comments     6    Patterson, Mary       08/14/2010  White, Michelle
     17   NF2413   Political Comments     7    Torres, Christopher        .      White, Michelle
     18   NF2413   Political Comments     8    Robinson, Bonnie      08/07/2010  White, Michelle
     19   NF2413   Political Comments     9    Brown, Patricia       08/07/2010  White, Michelle
     20   NF8141   Favorite Essays        1    Clark, Todd           10/02/2010  Patterson, Daniel
     21   NF8141   Favorite Essays        2    Barnes, David         10/02/2010  Patterson, Daniel
     22   NF8141   Favorite Essays        3    Young, Richard        09/18/2010  Patterson, Daniel
     23   NF8141   Favorite Essays        4    Barnes, David         10/02/2010  Patterson, Daniel
     24   NF8141   Favorite Essays        5    Anderson, Daniel      10/03/2010  Patterson, Daniel
     25   NF8141   Favorite Essays        6    Anderson, Daniel      10/03/2010  Patterson, Daniel
     26   NF8141   Favorite Essays        7    Morris, Laura         09/18/2010  Patterson, Daniel
     27   NF8141   Favorite Essays        8    Powell, George        09/18/2010  Patterson, Daniel
```

Example Overview

This example shows you how to allow some missing values to replace existing values
when updating a master data set. The UPDATE and BY statements update the
information in the master data set for observations that are matched by the values of the
BY variables. By default, the UPDATE statement does not replace existing values with
missing values. Example 6.1 discussed in the "A Closer Look" section the use of
UPDATE statement option UPDATEMODE= to control this replacement action.

This example does not use the UPDATEMODE= option to selectively replace existing
values in the master data set with missing values. Instead it maintains the default value of
MISSINGCHECK for option UPDATEMODE=, and it uses special missing values and
regular missing values to replace some existing values with missing values.

Data set BOOKLIST is the master data set, and it tracks information about the chapters of
three books.

The transaction data set BOOKMISS contains values for DUEDATE that have regular
missing values and values that have the underscore character (_) assigned as a special
missing value. Special missing values apply to numeric variables. The design of the
UPDATE statement with UPDATEMODE=MISSINGCHECK in effect causes an
existing value for a variable in the master data set to be overwritten with a regular
missing value. This occurs if a special missing value has been assigned to the variable in
its matched observation in the transaction data set. In this example, a regular missing
value in the transaction data set still does not overwrite an existing value in the master
data set.

The DATA step updates two variables, AUTHOR and DUEDATE, in data set
BOOKLIST with information from BOOKMISS. Observations are matched by two BY
variables, BOOKID and CHAPTER.

Missing values for DUEDATE are present in the first four observations of transaction
data set BOOKMISS. Special missing values are found in observations 1, 2, and 4.
Observations 5 and 6 have regular missing values for variable AUTHOR and new values

for variable DUEDATE. Observation 3 has a new value for variable AUTHOR and a regular missing value for DUEDATE.

Assume both data sets were sorted or indexed by BOOKID and CHAPTER prior to the DATA step.

The DATA step in this example is identical to the one in Example 6.1. The difference between the two examples is the assignment of the special missing value prior to the DATA step.

Program

Precede the DATA step that creates BOOKMISS with the MISSING statement. Assign the underscore (_) character as a special missing value.

Create data set BOOKMISS. Note the underscores in the DUEDATE fields in rows 1, 2, and 4. Note the regular missing value for DUEDATE in row 3.

```
missing _;
```

```
data bookmiss;
   input bookid $ 1-6 chapter author $ 11-30
         duedate : mmddyy10.;
   format duedate mmddyy10.;
datalines;
NF0586 3                          _
NF0586 4                          _
NF2413 4  Loren, Marie            .
NF2413 7                          _
NF8141 5                          10/03/2010
NF8141 6                          10/03/2010
;;;;
```

Create data set REVISEDMISS. Update data set BOOKLIST with information in BOOKMISS. Place the master data set first in the UPDATE statement.
Specify how to match observations in the two data sets.

```
data revisedmiss;
   update booklist bookmiss;



   by bookid chapter;

run;
```

Related Technique

The PROC SQL step that follows creates a table equivalent to the REVISEDMISS data set that was created by the DATA step in the main example. It uses CASE expressions and the COALESCE function to determine how to update the BOOKLIST table. The COALESCE function returns the first nonmissing value in the arguments that are supplied to it.

The two input tables are combined with a full join. All matching and nonmatching rows in both tables are present in REVISEDMISS along with the updates to specific rows and columns as specified in BOOKMISS.

As in the preceding DATA step, the following PROC SQL step distinguishes between regular and special missing values so that some missing values can replace existing values in the master data set when updating the master data set. The code is written so that a column with a special missing value in the transaction data set is assigned a regular missing value in the output table. A regular missing value in a column in the transaction data set does not replace an existing value in the master data set.

The CASE expression tests when the value for DUEDATE in the transaction table has the special missing value of underscore. When testing a numeric variable, the value is written as the regular missing value of period followed by the special missing value. When a value for DUEDATE is the special missing value of underscore, PROC SQL assigns a regular missing value to the value of DUEDATE in the output table. Otherwise, PROC SQL applies the COALESCE function to the two values of DUEDATE from the two input tables BOOKMISS and BOOKLIST in that order. When the value of DUEDATE in BOOKMISS is a regular missing value, the COALESCE function returns the value for DUEDATE from BOOKLIST if it is nonmissing. If both are missing, the result is missing.

Create table REVISEDMISS.
Apply the COALESCE function to the two matching columns so that if there are nonmatches in the transaction table, the nonmissing unmatched value is copied to the output table.

If the value for DUEDATE in the transaction table is the special missing value of underscore (_), assign a regular missing value to DUEDATE. Otherwise, assign it the first nonmissing value of the two arguments.
End the CASE expression. Format the values of DUEDATE in the output table.

Combine the two tables with a full join so that all matching and nonmatching rows are present in the output table. Specify an alias for each of the two tables.
Specify the columns that match the two tables.

```
proc sql;
   create table revisedmiss as
      select coalesce(m.bookid,b.bookid) as bookid,
             booktitle,
             coalesce(m.chapter,b.chapter) as chapter,
             coalesce(m.author,b.author) as author,

             case when m.duedate=._ then .
                  else coalesce(m.duedate,b.duedate)

             end as duedate format=mmddyy10.,

             editor
      from booklist b
         full join
      bookmiss m

      on b.bookid=m.bookid and b.chapter=m.chapter;
quit;
```

Example 6.3 Merging Data Sets and Conditionally Overwriting Common Variables

Goal

Merge two data sets so that the values of common variables in the master data set are updated with the values of the common variables in another data set for all matching observations. When an observation in the master data set does not have a match in the second data set, do not overwrite values for the common variables with missing values.

Examples 6.1, 6.2, 6.3, 6.4, and 6.5 illustrate ways to update common variables when combining data sets. The five examples apply the methods to the same master data set. Different transaction data sets are used in Examples 6.1, 6.2, and 6.3. Examples 6.4 and 6.5 use the same transaction data set and produce different resulting data sets.

Example Features

Featured Step	DATA step
Featured Step Options and Statements	Match-merge with MERGE and BY statements
Related Technique	PROC SQL, full join, COALESCE function
A Closer Look	Understanding Why the UPDATE Statement Would Not Produce the Required Output Data Set in This Example
	Illustrating How SAS Merges Data Sets and Conditionally Overwrites Common Variables

Input Data Sets

Master data set BOOKLIST contains information about the chapters of three books. Transaction data set BOOKCHANGES contains updates of information to apply to BOOKLIST.

Data set BOOKLIST has multiple occurrences for each of the three values of BOOKID. One of the three values of BOOKID in BOOKLIST does not have a match in BOOKCHANGES.

The data sets must be sorted or indexed by the values of BOOKID because this is the variable that will match the two data sets.

```
                                   BOOKLIST

Obs bookid    booktitle      chapter author            duedate    editor
  1 NF0586 Current Narratives     1  Smith, Rebecca     09/04/2010 Williams, Stephanie
  2 NF0586 Current Narratives     2  Williams, Susan    09/04/2010 Williams, Stephanie
  3 NF0586 Current Narratives     3  Torres, Christopher 09/11/2010 Williams, Stephanie
  4 NF0586 Current Narratives     4  Torres, Christopher 09/11/2010 Williams, Stephanie
  5 NF0586 Current Narratives     5  Powell, George     09/11/2010 Williams, Stephanie
  6 NF0586 Current Narratives     6  Thompson, Tonya    09/11/2010 Williams, Stephanie
  7 NF0586 Current Narratives     7  Allen, Linda       09/11/2010 Williams, Stephanie
  8 NF0586 Current Narratives     8  Johnson, Tammy     09/11/2010 Williams, Stephanie
  9 NF0586 Current Narratives     9  Kelly, Melissa     09/11/2010 Williams, Stephanie
 10 NF0586 Current Narratives    10  Thompson, Tonya    09/11/2010 Williams, Stephanie
 11 NF2413 Political Comments     1  Jones, Robin       07/31/2010 White, Michelle
 12 NF2413 Political Comments     2  Sanchez, Brandon   08/07/2010 White, Michelle
 13 NF2413 Political Comments     3  Jones, Robin       07/31/2010 White, Michelle
 14 NF2413 Political Comments     4  Perez, Joshua      07/31/2010 White, Michelle
 15 NF2413 Political Comments     5  Williams, Nicholas 07/31/2010 White, Michelle
 16 NF2413 Political Comments     6  Patterson, Mary    08/14/2010 White, Michelle
 17 NF2413 Political Comments     7  Torres, Christopher 08/07/2010 White, Michelle
 18 NF2413 Political Comments     8  Robinson, Bonnie   08/07/2010 White, Michelle
 19 NF2413 Political Comments     9  Brown, Patricia    08/07/2010 White, Michelle
 20 NF8141 Favorite Essays        1  Clark, Todd        10/02/2010 Patterson, Daniel
 21 NF8141 Favorite Essays        2  Barnes, David      10/02/2010 Patterson, Daniel
 22 NF8141 Favorite Essays        3  Young, Richard     09/18/2010 Patterson, Daniel
 23 NF8141 Favorite Essays        4  Barnes, David      10/02/2010 Patterson, Daniel
 24 NF8141 Favorite Essays        5  Anderson, Daniel   09/18/2010 Patterson, Daniel
 25 NF8141 Favorite Essays        6  Anderson, Daniel   09/18/2010 Patterson, Daniel
 26 NF8141 Favorite Essays        7  Morris, Laura      09/18/2010 Patterson, Daniel
 27 NF8141 Favorite Essays        8  Powell, George     09/18/2010 Patterson, Daniel
```

```
                 BOOKCHANGES

Obs   bookid    duedate      editor
  1   NF2413 09/18/2010   Zhang, Amy
  2   NF8141 10/02/2010   McHale, Andrew
```

Resulting Data Set
Output 6.3
NEWBOOKLIST
Data Set

```
                  Example 6.3 NEWBOOKLIST Data Set Created with DATA Step

   Obs bookid     booktitle        chapter author              duedate    editor

     1 NF0586 Current Narratives      1   Smith, Rebecca       09/04/2010 Williams, Stephanie
     2 NF0586 Current Narratives      2   Williams, Susan      09/04/2010 Williams, Stephanie
     3 NF0586 Current Narratives      3   Torres, Christopher  09/11/2010 Williams, Stephanie
     4 NF0586 Current Narratives      4   Torres, Christopher  09/11/2010 Williams, Stephanie
     5 NF0586 Current Narratives      5   Powell, George       09/11/2010 Williams, Stephanie
     6 NF0586 Current Narratives      6   Thompson, Tonya      09/11/2010 Williams, Stephanie
     7 NF0586 Current Narratives      7   Allen, Linda         09/11/2010 Williams, Stephanie
     8 NF0586 Current Narratives      8   Johnson, Tammy       09/11/2010 Williams, Stephanie
     9 NF0586 Current Narratives      9   Kelly, Melissa       09/11/2010 Williams, Stephanie
    10 NF0586 Current Narratives     10   Thompson, Tonya      09/11/2010 Williams, Stephanie
    11 NF2413 Political Comments      1   Jones, Robin         09/18/2010 Zhang, Amy
    12 NF2413 Political Comments      2   Sanchez, Brandon     09/18/2010 Zhang, Amy
    13 NF2413 Political Comments      3   Jones, Robin         09/18/2010 Zhang, Amy
    14 NF2413 Political Comments      4   Perez, Joshua        09/18/2010 Zhang, Amy
    15 NF2413 Political Comments      5   Williams, Nicholas   09/18/2010 Zhang, Amy
    16 NF2413 Political Comments      6   Patterson, Mary      09/18/2010 Zhang, Amy
    17 NF2413 Political Comments      7   Torres, Christopher  09/18/2010 Zhang, Amy
    18 NF2413 Political Comments      8   Robinson, Bonnie     09/18/2010 Zhang, Amy
    19 NF2413 Political Comments      9   Brown, Patricia      09/18/2010 Zhang, Amy
    20 NF8141 Favorite Essays         1   Clark, Todd          10/02/2010 McHale, Andrew
    21 NF8141 Favorite Essays         2   Barnes, David        10/02/2010 McHale, Andrew
    22 NF8141 Favorite Essays         3   Young, Richard       10/02/2010 McHale, Andrew
    23 NF8141 Favorite Essays         4   Barnes, David        10/02/2010 McHale, Andrew
    24 NF8141 Favorite Essays         5   Anderson, Daniel     10/02/2010 McHale, Andrew
    25 NF8141 Favorite Essays         6   Anderson, Daniel     10/02/2010 McHale, Andrew
    26 NF8141 Favorite Essays         7   Morris, Laura        10/02/2010 McHale, Andrew
    27 NF8141 Favorite Essays         8   Powell, George       10/02/2010 McHale, Andrew
```

Example Overview

This example shows you how to update selected variables in common when match-merging a master data set and another data set. The master data set can have duplicate occurrences of the matching variable while the second data set has only unique occurrences of the matching variable. This example illustrates how SAS updates the Program Data Vector (PDV) during match-merges and how you can control the process with your code.

Data set BOOKLIST is the master data set, and it tracks information about the chapters of three books. Data set BOOKCHANGES contains updates of information to apply to BOOKLIST.

The DATA step uses the MERGE and BY statements to update variables DUEDATE and EDITOR in BOOKLIST with values from BOOKCHANGES. The two data sets are matched by the values of variable BOOKID. The DATA step accomplishes two tasks:

❑ For matches by BOOKID when there are multiple occurrences of BOOKID, the values for DUEDATE and EDITOR in BOOKCHANGES are assigned to all matching observations in BOOKLIST.

❑ For nonmatches by BOOKID, the original values of DUEDATE and EDITOR in BOOKLIST are preserved.

Before the DATA step executes, the RENAME= option applied to master data set BOOKLIST renames the common variables DUEDATE and EDITOR to HOLDDATE and HOLDEDITOR, respectively. This action and the subsequent IF-THEN block prevent the replacement of existing values for DUEDATE and EDITOR in BOOKLIST with missing values when there are nonmatches. The renaming also causes all matching observations to be updated with new values for DUEDATE and EDITOR. Without the renaming and the IF-THEN block later in the DATA step, only the first observation in a BY group would be updated with the new values.

For diagrams of the processing steps of this program, see the "A Closer Look" section.

Because variables BOOKTITLE, CHAPTER, and AUTHOR are found only in BOOKLIST, you do not need to include any additional programming to save their original values.

Assume both data sets were sorted or indexed by BOOKID prior to the DATA step.

Program

Create NEWBOOKLIST.
Combine BOOKLIST and
BOOKCHANGES. Rename the two
common variables, DUEDATE and
EDITOR, in BOOKLIST to preserve
their original values in BOOKLIST.
Define temporary variable INUPD so
that statements can test whether
BOOKCHANGES contributes to the
current observation.
Match the data sets by BOOKID.
Drop the variables that came from
BOOKLIST because they are needed
only during execution of the DATA
step to preserve the original values of
DUEDATE and EDITOR in
BOOKLIST.
When BOOKCHANGES does not
contribute to the current observation,
reset the values of DUEDATE and
EDITOR with their original values,
which were preserved in HOLDDATE
and HOLDEDITOR.

```
data newbooklist;
   merge booklist(rename=(duedate=holddate
                          editor=holdeditor))
         bookchanges(in=inupd);




   by bookid;
   drop holddate holdeditor;




   if not inupd then do;
      duedate=holddate;
      editor=holdeditor;
   end;


run;
```

Related Technique

The following PROC SQL step creates a table equivalent to the data set that was created by the DATA step in the main example. A full join combines the two tables so that all matching and nonmatching rows from BOOKLIST and NEWBOOKLIST are in the output table along with updates of specific rows that were contributed from BOOKCHANGES.

The COALESCE function performs the update of DUEDATE and EDITOR. The first argument to each COALESCE function call is the column from BOOKCHANGES. The second argument is the column from BOOKLIST. The COALESCE function checks each of its arguments from left to right until it finds a nonmissing value. When it finds a match on BOOKID in BOOKCHANGES, the values that were contributed from BOOKCHANGES are stored in NEWBOOKLIST. When it does not find a match for BOOKID in BOOKCHANGES, the first argument to each COALESCE function is missing so it checks whether the second argument is nonmissing. In this example, the second arguments for those rows without a match in BOOKCHANGES are all nonmissing so PROC SQL saves the values from master table BOOKLIST in NEWBOOKLIST.

Create table NEWBOOKLIST.
Specify the columns to save in table
NEWBOOKLIST. Precede the column
names with the alias of the table from
which they're selected. Apply the
COALESCE function to the columns
that will be updated. Specify as the first
argument to each COALESCE
function call the column that was

```
proc sql;
   create table newbooklist as
      select coalesce(u.bookid,b.bookid) as bookid,
             booktitle, chapter, author,
             coalesce(u.duedate,b.duedate) as duedate
                               format=mmddyy10.,
             coalesce(u.editor,b.editor) as editor
```

contributed from BOOKCHANGES.
Name the columns that result from
COALESCE the same as that in
BOOKLIST.
Combine the two tables with a full join
so that all matching and nonmatching
rows are present in the output table.
Specify an alias for each of the two
tables.
Specify the column that matches the
two tables.

```
from booklist b
  full join
bookchanges u


on b.bookid=u.bookid;

quit;
```

A Closer Look

Understanding Why the UPDATE Statement Would Not Produce the Required Output Data Set in This Example

Example 6.1 used the UPDATE statement to perform an updating action that was similar to the main program in this example. The difference is that the master data set in the main DATA step in Example 6.1 did not have multiple observations per BY group while this example does. You would not produce the same output data set if you used the UPDATE statement in this example instead of the MERGE statement. The UPDATE statement is not designed to process multiple observations per BY group in the master data set.

Example 6.1 compares similar features of the MERGE and UPDATE statements in "Comparing the UPDATE and MERGE Statements" in the "A Closer Look" section. The section also discusses the differences in using the MERGE and UPDATE statements when processing data sets that have multiple observations in a BY group. For more information, see "Using UPDATE and MERGE When There Are Multiple Observations in a BY Group" in the "A Closer Look" section for Example 6.1.

Illustrating How SAS Merges Data Sets and Conditionally Overwrites Common Variables

This section shows how the DATA step in the main example match-merges data sets BOOKLIST and BOOKCHANGES to update the information in BOOKLIST.

During the compilation phase, SAS reads the descriptor portions of the input data sets and creates the Program Data Vector (PDV). Also, SAS determines the BY groups in each input data set for the variables that are listed in the BY statement. The three unique BOOKID values define three BY groups.

The PDV in this example has allocated space for variables HOLDDATE and HOLDEDITOR, which are the renamed versions of DUEDATE and EDITOR from data set BOOKLIST. It also has allocated space for variables DUEDATE and EDITOR from data set BOOKCHANGES.

SAS looks at the first BY group in each input data set to determine whether the BY values match. In this example, the first BY group, which is BOOKID= "NF0586", is found only in BOOKLIST. Its row is highlighted in the following display. The second and third BY groups, BOOKID= "NF2413" and BOOKID= "NF8141", are found in both input data sets.

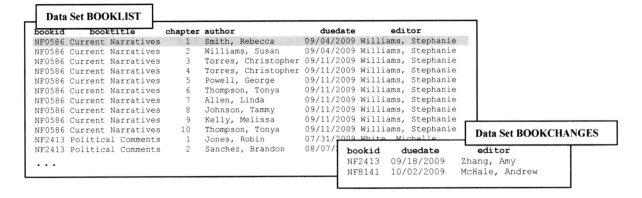

Data Set BOOKLIST

bookid	booktitle	chapter	author	duedate	editor
NF0586	Current Narratives	1	Smith, Rebecca	09/04/2009	Williams, Stephanie
NF0586	Current Narratives	2	Williams, Susan	09/04/2009	Williams, Stephanie
NF0586	Current Narratives	3	Torres, Christopher	09/11/2009	Williams, Stephanie
NF0586	Current Narratives	4	Torres, Christopher	09/11/2009	Williams, Stephanie
NF0586	Current Narratives	5	Powell, George	09/11/2009	Williams, Stephanie
NF0586	Current Narratives	6	Thompson, Tonya	09/11/2009	Williams, Stephanie
NF0586	Current Narratives	7	Allen, Linda	09/11/2009	Williams, Stephanie
NF0586	Current Narratives	8	Johnson, Tammy	09/11/2009	Williams, Stephanie
NF0586	Current Narratives	9	Kelly, Melissa	09/11/2009	Williams, Stephanie
NF0586	Current Narratives	10	Thompson, Tonya	09/11/2009	Williams, Stephanie
NF2413	Political Comments	1	Jones, Robin	07/31/2009	White, Michelle
NF2413	Political Comments	2	Sanchez, Brandon	08/07/	

. . .

Data Set BOOKCHANGES

bookid	duedate	editor
NF2413	09/18/2009	Zhang, Amy
NF8141	10/02/2009	McHale, Andrew

The BY group for BOOKID= "NF0586" in BOOKLIST does not have a match in BOOKCHANGES. Therefore, no values are moved from BOOKCHANGES into variables DUEDATE and EDITOR and their values are missing in the PDV.

Program Data Vector (PDV)								
INUPD	BOOKID	BOOKTITLE	CHAPTER	AUTHOR	HOLDDATE	HOLDEDITOR	DUEDATE	EDITOR
0	NF0586	Current Narratives	1	Smith, Rebecca	09/04/2009	Williams, Stephanie	.	

The value of INUPD is 0 (not true) so the IF-THEN block executes and moves the values from HOLDDATE and HOLDEDITOR into variables DUEDATE and EDITOR, respectively. This process continues for all 10 observations in the first BY group. Variables HOLDDATE and HOLDEDITOR are not saved in the output data set NEWBOOKLIST. Variable INUPD is also not saved in NEWBOOKLIST because it is a temporary variable defined with the IN= data set option in the MERGE statement.

The observations for this first BY group remain the same.

The DATA step now processes the second BY group, BOOKID= "NF2413". This BY group is found in both input data sets. The rows that SAS loads into the PDV at the beginning of this second BY group are highlighted in the following display.

Data Set BOOKLIST

```
bookid     booktitle        chapter author              duedate     editor
NF0586 Current Narratives       1    Smith, Rebecca      09/04/2009 Williams, Stephanie
NF0586 Current Narratives       2    Williams, Susan     09/04/2009 Williams, Stephanie
NF0586 Current Narratives       3    Torres, Christopher 09/11/2009 Williams, Stephanie
NF0586 Current Narratives       4    Torres, Christopher 09/11/2009 Williams, Stephanie
NF0586 Current Narratives       5    Powell, George      09/11/2009 Williams, Stephanie
NF0586 Current Narratives       6    Thompson, Tonya     09/11/2009 Williams, Stephanie
NF0586 Current Narratives       7    Allen, Linda        09/11/2009 Williams, Stephanie
NF0586 Current Narratives       8    Johnson, Tammy      09/11/2009 Williams, Stephanie
NF0586 Current Narratives       9    Kelly, Melissa      09/11/2009 Williams, Stepha
NF0586 Current Narratives      10    Thompson, Tonya     09/11/2009 Williams, Stepha
NF2413 Political Comments       1    Jones, Robin        07/31/2009 White, Michelle
NF2413 Political Comments       2    Sanchez, Brandon    08/07/
. . .
```

Data Set BOOKCHANGES

```
bookid     duedate       editor
NF2413 09/18/2009    Zhang, Amy
NF8141 10/02/2009    McHale, Andrew
```

The DATA step moves the values of DUEDATE and EDITOR found in BOOKCHANGES into the PDV.

Program Data Vector (PDV)								
INUPD	BOOKID	BOOKTITLE	CHAPTER	AUTHOR	HOLDDATE	HOLDEDITOR	DUEDATE	EDITOR
1	NF2413	Political Comments	1	Jones, Robin	07/31/2009	White, Michelle	09/18/2009	Zhang, Amy

The IF-THEN block does not execute because the value of INUPD is 1(true). Because variables HOLDDATE and HOLDEDITOR are dropped from the output data set, the original values for DUEDATE and EDITOR for this BY group are not saved in the output data set NEWBOOKLIST. Instead the values for DUEDATE and EDITOR for BOOKID= "NF2413" in the output data set are the values for DUEDATE and EDITOR from the transaction data set.

The DATA step moves to the second observation in the BOOKID= "NF2413" BY group in data set BOOKCHANGES. Because there is only one observation in the BOOKID= "NF2413" BY group in BOOKCHANGES, the values for DUEDATE and EDITOR that were contributed from that data set remain in the PDV.

Program Data Vector (PDV)								
INUPD	BOOKID	BOOKTITLE	CHAPTER	AUTHOR	HOLDDATE	HOLDEDITOR	DUEDATE	EDITOR
1	NF2413	Political Comments	2	Sanchez, Brandon	08/07/2009	White, Michelle	09/18/2009	Zhang, Amy

The same process is repeated for the remaining seven observations in BY group BOOKID= "NF2413". All nine observations found in BOOKLIST now have the same new values for DUEDATE and EDITOR in NEWBOOKLIST.

Lastly, the DATA step processes the third BY group for BOOKID. It saves the new information found for BOOKID= "NF8141" for DUEDATE and EDITOR in output data set NEWBOOKLIST.

Example 6.4 | Adding Observations and Variables to the Master Data Set When Duplicate Matching Variable Values Exist in the Transaction Data Set

Goal

Match a master data set and transaction data set where the master data set has only unique combinations of the values of the matching variables and the transaction data set can have duplicate combinations. Keep the multiple observations for the duplicate combinations of the matching variables in the output data set. Only keep information from the transaction data set for observations with a match in the master data set.

Examples 6.1, 6.2, 6.3, 6.4, and 6.5 illustrate ways to update common variables when combining data sets. The five examples apply the methods to the same master data set. Different transaction data sets are used in Examples 6.1, 6.2, and 6.3. Examples 6.4 and 6.5 use the same transaction data set and produce different resulting data sets.

Example Features

Featured Step	DATA step
Featured Step Options and Statements	Match-merge with MERGE and BY statements IN= data set option
Related Technique	PROC SQL, left join

Input Data Sets

Master data set BOOKLIST contains information about the chapters of three books. Transaction data set SUBMISSIONS contains updates of information to apply to BOOKLIST.

Data set BOOKLIST has unique occurrences of the combinations of BOOKID and CHAPTER. Data set SUBMISSIONS contains multiple occurrences for two combinations of BOOKID and CHAPTER.

BOOKLIST

Obs	bookid	booktitle	chapter	author	duedate	editor
1	NF0586	Current Narratives	1	Smith, Rebecca	09/04/2010	Williams, Stephanie
2	NF0586	Current Narratives	2	Williams, Susan	09/04/2010	Williams, Stephanie
3	NF0586	Current Narratives	3	Torres, Christopher	09/11/2010	Williams, Stephanie
4	NF0586	Current Narratives	4	Torres, Christopher	09/11/2010	Williams, Stephanie
5	NF0586	Current Narratives	5	Powell, George	09/11/2010	Williams, Stephanie
6	NF0586	Current Narratives	6	Thompson, Tonya	09/11/2010	Williams, Stephanie
7	NF0586	Current Narratives	7	Allen, Linda	09/11/2010	Williams, Stephanie
8	NF0586	Current Narratives	8	Johnson, Tammy	09/11/2010	Williams, Stephanie
9	NF0586	Current Narratives	9	Kelly, Melissa	09/11/2010	Williams, Stephanie
10	NF0586	Current Narratives	10	Thompson, Tonya	09/11/2010	Williams, Stephanie
11	NF2413	Political Comments	1	Jones, Robin	07/31/2010	White, Michelle
12	NF2413	Political Comments	2	Sanchez, Brandon	08/07/2010	White, Michelle
13	NF2413	Political Comments	3	Jones, Robin	07/31/2010	White, Michelle
14	NF2413	Political Comments	4	Perez, Joshua	07/31/2010	White, Michelle
15	NF2413	Political Comments	5	Williams, Nicholas	07/31/2010	White, Michelle
16	NF2413	Political Comments	6	Patterson, Mary	08/14/2010	White, Michelle
17	NF2413	Political Comments	7	Torres, Christopher	08/07/2010	White, Michelle
18	NF2413	Political Comments	8	Robinson, Bonnie	08/07/2010	White, Michelle
19	NF2413	Political Comments	9	Brown, Patricia	08/07/2010	White, Michelle
20	NF8141	Favorite Essays	1	Clark, Todd	10/02/2010	Patterson, Daniel
21	NF8141	Favorite Essays	2	Barnes, David	10/02/2010	Patterson, Daniel
22	NF8141	Favorite Essays	3	Young, Richard	09/18/2010	Patterson, Daniel
23	NF8141	Favorite Essays	4	Barnes, David	10/02/2010	Patterson, Daniel
24	NF8141	Favorite Essays	5	Anderson, Daniel	09/18/2010	Patterson, Daniel
25	NF8141	Favorite Essays	6	Anderson, Daniel	09/18/2010	Patterson, Daniel
26	NF8141	Favorite Essays	7	Morris, Laura	09/18/2010	Patterson, Daniel
27	NF8141	Favorite Essays	8	Powell, George	09/18/2010	Patterson, Daniel

SUBMISSIONS

Obs	bookid	chapter	author	draftdate
1	NF0586	3	Torres, Christopher	05/13/2010
2	NF0586	3	Torres, Christopher	06/17/2010
3	NF0586	3	Torres, Christopher	06/30/2010
4	NF2413	2	Sanchez, Brandon	04/22/2010
5	NF2413	2	Sanchez, Brandon	06/02/2010
6	NF2413	8	Robinson, Bonnie	04/01/2010
7	NF8141	5	Anderson, Daniel	05/26/2010
8	NF8141	6	Anderson, Daniel	07/01/2010

Resulting Data Set
Output 6.4
ALLDRAFTS Data Set

```
                   Example 6.4 ALLDRAFTS Data Set Created with DATA Step

Obs bookid      booktitle      chapter author              duedate      editor             draftdate

  1 NF0586 Current Narratives     1  Smith, Rebecca     09/04/2010 Williams, Stephanie        .
  2 NF0586 Current Narratives     2  Williams, Susan    09/04/2010 Williams, Stephanie        .
  3 NF0586 Current Narratives     3  Torres, Christopher 09/11/2010 Williams, Stephanie 05/13/2010
  4 NF0586 Current Narratives     3  Torres, Christopher 09/11/2010 Williams, Stephanie 06/17/2010
  5 NF0586 Current Narratives     3  Torres, Christopher 09/11/2010 Williams, Stephanie 06/30/2010
  6 NF0586 Current Narratives     4  Torres, Christopher 09/11/2010 Williams, Stephanie        .
  7 NF0586 Current Narratives     5  Powell, George     09/11/2010 Williams, Stephanie        .
  8 NF0586 Current Narratives     6  Thompson, Tonya    09/11/2010 Williams, Stephanie        .
  9 NF0586 Current Narratives     7  Allen, Linda       09/11/2010 Williams, Stephanie        .
 10 NF0586 Current Narratives     8  Johnson, Tammy     09/11/2010 Williams, Stephanie        .
 11 NF0586 Current Narratives     9  Kelly, Melissa     09/11/2010 Williams, Stephanie        .
 12 NF0586 Current Narratives    10  Thompson, Tonya    09/11/2010 Williams, Stephanie        .
 13 NF2413 Political Comments     1  Jones, Robin       07/31/2010 White, Michelle            .
 14 NF2413 Political Comments     2  Sanchez, Brandon   08/07/2010 White, Michelle     04/22/2010
 15 NF2413 Political Comments     2  Sanchez, Brandon   08/07/2010 White, Michelle     06/02/2010
 16 NF2413 Political Comments     3  Jones, Robin       07/31/2010 White, Michelle
 17 NF2413 Political Comments     4  Perez, Joshua      07/31/2010 White, Michelle            .
 18 NF2413 Political Comments     5  Williams, Nicholas 07/31/2010 White, Michelle
 19 NF2413 Political Comments     6  Patterson, Mary    08/14/2010 White, Michelle
 20 NF2413 Political Comments     7  Torres, Christopher 08/07/2010 White, Michelle           .
 21 NF2413 Political Comments     8  Robinson, Bonnie   08/07/2010 White, Michelle     04/01/2010
 22 NF2413 Political Comments     9  Brown, Patricia    08/07/2010 White, Michelle            .
 23 NF8141 Favorite Essays        1  Clark, Todd        10/02/2010 Patterson, Daniel          .
 24 NF8141 Favorite Essays        2  Barnes, David      10/02/2010 Patterson, Daniel          .
 25 NF8141 Favorite Essays        3  Young, Richard     09/18/2010 Patterson, Daniel          .
 26 NF8141 Favorite Essays        4  Barnes, David      10/02/2010 Patterson, Daniel          .
 27 NF8141 Favorite Essays        5  Anderson, Daniel   09/18/2010 Patterson, Daniel   05/26/2010
 28 NF8141 Favorite Essays        6  Anderson, Daniel   09/18/2010 Patterson, Daniel   07/01/2010
 29 NF8141 Favorite Essays        7  Morris, Laura      09/18/2010 Patterson, Daniel          .
 30 NF8141 Favorite Essays        8  Powell, George     09/18/2010 Patterson, Daniel
```

Example Overview

This example illustrates match-merge processing when your transaction data set contains multiple values of matching variables. The DATA step is written so that all observations found in the master data set are copied to the output data set whether or not they have a match in the transaction data set.

The transaction data set contributes to the output data set only when a transaction observation matches an observation in the master data set. Multiple observations with the same matching variable values in the transaction data set form the same number of multiple observations in the output data set. Also, the DATA step adds to the output data set all variables that are unique to the transaction data set. Missing values are assigned to these variables for observations in the master data set without matches in the transaction data set.

At the beginning of each BY group, the values of the variables from the master data set are loaded into the Program Data Vector (PDV). The values of the variables that are unique to the master data set remain in the PDV during the processing of the matches in the transaction data set. Unless otherwise changed by statements in the DATA step, they are copied to the output data set.

Each match in the transaction data set, along with the information from the master data set already in the PDV, is written to the output data set as one observation.

Data set BOOKLIST is the master data set, and it tracks information for the chapters of three books. Data set SUBMISSIONS contains updates of information to apply to BOOKLIST.

The DATA step uses the MERGE and BY statements to combine the two data sets. The IN= data set option that is applied to BOOKLIST defines the temporary variable INLIST, which the program tests to determine whether data set BOOKLIST contributes to the current observation. The subsetting IF statement tests INLIST and writes out observations only if they are found in BOOKLIST. This means that the DATA step does not output an observation in SUBMISSIONS that has a combination of BOOKID and CHAPTER not found in BOOKLIST.

Example 6.4 and Example 6.5 use the same transaction data set, SUBMISSIONS, and produce different resulting data sets. The resulting data set for Example 6.4 has an observation for each matching observation from SUBMISSIONS. Thus, the data set has more observations than in BOOKLIST because of multiple observations for two combinations of BOOKID and CHAPTER values found in SUBMISSIONS. The resulting data set for Example 6.5 has only one observation from each of the two combinations of BOOKID and CHAPTER values found in SUBMISSIONS that have multiple observations. Therefore, the resulting data set in Example 6.5 has the same number of observations as found in BOOKLIST.

Before processing the DATA step, both data sets BOOKLIST and SUBMISSIONS must either be sorted or indexed by BOOKID and CHAPTER.

Program

Create data set ALLDRAFTS. Combine the two data sets. Place the master data set first in the MERGE statement. Define temporary variable INLIST so that the IF statement can test its value to determine whether the current observation has information contributed from BOOKLIST.
Match the two data sets by BOOKID and CHAPTER.
Keep all observations from BOOKLIST.

```
data alldrafts;
  merge booklist(in=inlist)
        submissions;




  by bookid chapter;

  if inlist;

run;
```

Related Technique

The following PROC SQL step creates a table equivalent to the data set that was created by the DATA step in the main example. A left join combines the two tables because the goal is to save all rows from BOOKLIST in ALLDRAFTS along with the matches of specific rows that were contributed from SUBMISSIONS. The program does not write to the output table the rows that are found only in SUBMISSIONS.

The table alias that is attached to the three columns in common is for table BOOKLIST. Because the step saves all rows present in BOOKLIST and only those rows from SUBMISSIONS that have a match in BOOKLIST, the values for the columns in common should come from BOOKLIST.

Create table ALLDRAFTS.
Specify the columns to save in the output table. Specify the origin of the three columns in common between the two tables being joined by preceding the column name with the table alias.
Combine the two tables with a left join.
Specify an alias for each of the two tables.
Specify the columns that match the two tables.

```
proc sql;
  create table alldrafts as
    select b.bookid, booktitle, b.chapter,
           b.author, duedate, editor,
           draftdate


      from booklist b
           left join
           submissions s

      on b.bookid=s.bookid and b.chapter=s.chapter;

quit;
```

Example 6.5

Saving Observations from Only the Master Data Set When the Transaction Data Set Contains Duplicates

Goal

Match a master data set and transaction data set where the master data set has only unique combinations of the values of the matching variables and the transaction data set can have multiple combinations. Keep only the observations from the master data set in the output data set. Order the observations in the transaction data set so that a specific observation from the transaction data set is kept in the output data set when there are multiple matches for a combination of the values of the matching variables.

Examples 6.1, 6.2, 6.3, 6.4, and 6.5 illustrate ways to update common variables when combining data sets. The five examples apply the methods to the same master data set. Different transaction data sets are used in Examples 6.1, 6.2, and 6.3. Examples 6.4 and 6.5 use the same transaction data set and produce different resulting data sets.

Example Features

Featured Step	DATA step
Featured Step Options and Statements	Match-merge with MERGE and BY statements IN= data set option
Related Technique	PROC SQL, left join, COALESCE function, subquery

Input Data Sets

Master data set BOOKLIST contains information about the chapters of three books. Transaction data set SUBMISSIONS contains updates of information to apply to BOOKLIST.

Data set BOOKLIST has unique occurrences of the combinations of BOOKID and CHAPTER. Data set SUBMISSIONS contains multiple occurrences for two combinations of BOOKID and CHAPTER.

BOOKLIST

Obs	bookid	booktitle	chapter	author	duedate	editor
1	NF0586	Current Narratives	1	Smith, Rebecca	09/04/2010	Williams, Stephanie
2	NF0586	Current Narratives	2	Williams, Susan	09/04/2010	Williams, Stephanie
3	NF0586	Current Narratives	3	Torres, Christopher	09/11/2010	Williams, Stephanie
4	NF0586	Current Narratives	4	Torres, Christopher	09/11/2010	Williams, Stephanie
5	NF0586	Current Narratives	5	Powell, George	09/11/2010	Williams, Stephanie
6	NF0586	Current Narratives	6	Thompson, Tonya	09/11/2010	Williams, Stephanie
7	NF0586	Current Narratives	7	Allen, Linda	09/11/2010	Williams, Stephanie
8	NF0586	Current Narratives	8	Johnson, Tammy	09/11/2010	Williams, Stephanie
9	NF0586	Current Narratives	9	Kelly, Melissa	09/11/2010	Williams, Stephanie
10	NF0586	Current Narratives	10	Thompson, Tonya	09/11/2010	Williams, Stephanie
11	NF2413	Political Comments	1	Jones, Robin	07/31/2010	White, Michelle
12	NF2413	Political Comments	2	Sanchez, Brandon	08/07/2010	White, Michelle
13	NF2413	Political Comments	3	Jones, Robin	07/31/2010	White, Michelle
14	NF2413	Political Comments	4	Perez, Joshua	07/31/2010	White, Michelle
15	NF2413	Political Comments	5	Williams, Nicholas	07/31/2010	White, Michelle
16	NF2413	Political Comments	6	Patterson, Mary	08/14/2010	White, Michelle
17	NF2413	Political Comments	7	Torres, Christopher	08/07/2010	White, Michelle
18	NF2413	Political Comments	8	Robinson, Bonnie	08/07/2010	White, Michelle
19	NF2413	Political Comments	9	Brown, Patricia	08/07/2010	White, Michelle
20	NF8141	Favorite Essays	1	Clark, Todd	10/02/2010	Patterson, Daniel
21	NF8141	Favorite Essays	2	Barnes, David	10/02/2010	Patterson, Daniel
22	NF8141	Favorite Essays	3	Young, Richard	09/18/2010	Patterson, Daniel
23	NF8141	Favorite Essays	4	Barnes, David	10/02/2010	Patterson, Daniel
24	NF8141	Favorite Essays	5	Anderson, Daniel	09/18/2010	Patterson, Daniel
25	NF8141	Favorite Essays	6	Anderson, Daniel	09/18/2010	Patterson, Daniel
26	NF8141	Favorite Essays	7	Morris, Laura	09/18/2010	Patterson, Daniel
27	NF8141	Favorite Essays	8	Powell, George	09/18/2010	Patterson, Daniel

SUBMISSIONS

Obs	bookid	chapter	author	draftdate
1	NF0586	3	Torres, Christopher	05/13/2010
2	NF0586	3	Torres, Christopher	06/17/2010
3	NF0586	3	Torres, Christopher	06/30/2010
4	NF2413	2	Sanchez, Brandon	04/22/2010
5	NF2413	2	Sanchez, Brandon	06/02/2010
6	NF2413	8	Robinson, Bonnie	04/01/2010
7	NF8141	5	Anderson, Daniel	05/26/2010
8	NF8141	6	Anderson, Daniel	07/01/2010

Resulting Data Set
Output 6.5
LASTDRAFT Data Set

```
                   Example 6.5 LASTDRAFT Data Set Created with DATA Step

Obs bookid    booktitle       chapter author              duedate    editor              draftdate

  1 NF0586 Current Narratives     1  Smith, Rebecca      09/04/2010 Williams, Stephanie      .
  2 NF0586 Current Narratives     2  Williams, Susan     09/04/2010 Williams, Stephanie      .
  3 NF0586 Current Narratives     3  Torres, Christopher 09/11/2010 Williams, Stephanie 06/30/2010
  4 NF0586 Current Narratives     4  Torres, Christopher 09/11/2010 Williams, Stephanie      .
  5 NF0586 Current Narratives     5  Powell, George      09/11/2010 Williams, Stephanie      .
  6 NF0586 Current Narratives     6  Thompson, Tonya     09/11/2010 Williams, Stephanie      .
  7 NF0586 Current Narratives     7  Allen, Linda        09/11/2010 Williams, Stephanie      .
  8 NF0586 Current Narratives     8  Johnson, Tammy      09/11/2010 Williams, Stephanie      .
  9 NF0586 Current Narratives     9  Kelly, Melissa      09/11/2010 Williams, Stephanie      .
 10 NF0586 Current Narratives    10  Thompson, Tonya     09/11/2010 Williams, Stephanie      .
 11 NF2413 Political Comments     1  Jones, Robin        07/31/2010 White, Michelle          .
 12 NF2413 Political Comments     2  Sanchez, Brandon    08/07/2010 White, Michelle     06/02/2010
 13 NF2413 Political Comments     3  Jones, Robin        07/31/2010 White, Michelle          .
 14 NF2413 Political Comments     4  Perez, Joshua       07/31/2010 White, Michelle          .
 15 NF2413 Political Comments     5  Williams, Nicholas  07/31/2010 White, Michelle          .
 16 NF2413 Political Comments     6  Patterson, Mary     08/14/2010 White, Michelle          .
 17 NF2413 Political Comments     7  Torres, Christopher 08/07/2010 White, Michelle          .
 18 NF2413 Political Comments     8  Robinson, Bonnie    08/07/2010 White, Michelle     04/01/2010
 19 NF2413 Political Comments     9  Brown, Patricia     08/07/2010 White, Michelle          .
 20 NF8141 Favorite Essays        1  Clark, Todd         10/02/2010 Patterson, Daniel        .
 21 NF8141 Favorite Essays        2  Barnes, David       10/02/2010 Patterson, Daniel        .
 22 NF8141 Favorite Essays        3  Young, Richard      09/18/2010 Patterson, Daniel        .
 23 NF8141 Favorite Essays        4  Barnes, David       10/02/2010 Patterson, Daniel        .
 24 NF8141 Favorite Essays        5  Anderson, Daniel    09/18/2010 Patterson, Daniel   05/26/2010
 25 NF8141 Favorite Essays        6  Anderson, Daniel    09/18/2010 Patterson, Daniel   07/01/2010
 26 NF8141 Favorite Essays        7  Morris, Laura       09/18/2010 Patterson, Daniel        .
 27 NF8141 Favorite Essays        8  Powell, George      09/18/2010 Patterson, Daniel        .
```

Example Overview

This example illustrates match-merge processing when your transaction data set contains multiple observations with the same matching variable values and you want to update one observation in the master data set. When there are multiple observations in the transaction data set for a combination of matching variable values, only one observation from the group updates the master data set. The DATA step is written so that all observations found in the master data set are copied to the output data set whether or not they have a match in the transaction data set.

The transaction data set contributes values to the output data set only for matched observations in the transaction data set. When a BY group has multiple observations in the transaction data set, only the values from the first observation in the BY group in the transaction data set update the matching observation in the master data set. Prior to the DATA step, PROC SORT arranges the observations in the transaction data set so that a specific observation is placed first in the BY group when there are multiple observations with the same combination of values of the matching variables.

The DATA step also adds to the output data set all variables that are unique to the transaction data set. Missing values are assigned to these variables for observations in the master data set without matches in the transaction data set.

Data set BOOKLIST is the master data set, and it tracks information for the chapters of three books. Data set SUBMISSIONS contains updates of information to apply to BOOKLIST.

The DATA step uses the MERGE and BY statements to combine the two data sets. The IN= data set option that is applied to BOOKLIST defines the temporary variable INLIST, which the program tests to determine whether data set BOOKLIST contributes to the current observation. The subsetting IF statement tests INLIST and writes out observations only if they are found in BOOKLIST. This means that the DATA step does not output an observation in SUBMISSIONS that has a combination of BOOKID and CHAPTER not found in BOOKLIST.

Compared to Example 6.4, this DATA step adds a statement to reset INLIST to zero with each iteration of the DATA step. Example 6.4 demonstrated that by default the value of INLIST is set at the start of each BY group and remains constant during processing of the BY group. This example instead forces INLIST to be reset to zero with each iteration of the DATA step. This action causes only the first observation in the BY group to be matched to the observation in BOOKLIST because the INLIST variable has a value of 1 only when processing the first occurrence of the combination of BOOKID and CHAPTER in BOOKLIST.

Before processing the DATA step, both data sets BOOKLIST and SUBMISSIONS must either be sorted or indexed by BOOKID and CHAPTER. Data set SUBMISSIONS adds a third BY variable, DRAFTDATE, to the PROC SORT step. Observations are arranged in descending order of DRAFTDATE within each combination of BOOKID and CHAPTER. Because each BY group is sorted in reverse chronological order by DRAFTDATE, the most recent DRAFTDATE value is the one that is saved in LASTDRAFT when there are multiple observations in a BY group in SUBMISSIONS.

Example 6.4 and Example 6.5 use the same transaction data set SUBMISSIONS, and produce different resulting data sets. The resulting data set for Example 6.4 has an observation for each matching observation from SUBMISSIONS. Thus, the data set has more observations than in BOOKLIST because of multiple observations for two combinations of BOOKID and CHAPTER values found in SUBMISSIONS. However, the resulting data set for Example 6.5, has only one observation from each of the two specific combinations of BOOKID and CHAPTER values found in SUBMISSIONS that have multiple observations. Therefore, the resulting data set in Example 6.5 has the same number of observations as found in BOOKLIST.

Program

Sort the observations in SUBMISSIONS by the matching variables BOOKID and CHAPTER. Sort the observations within each combination of BOOKID and CHAPTER in reverse chronological order by DRAFTDATE.

```
proc sort data=submissions;
  by bookid chapter descending draftdate;
run;
```

Create data set LASTDRAFT. Reset INLIST to 0 at the top of the DATA step so that a previous value of 1 is not retained throughout the processing of a BY group.

```
data lastdraft;
  inlist=0;
```

Combine the two data sets. Place the master data set first in the MERGE statement. Define temporary variable INLIST so that the IF statement can tests its value to determine whether the current observation has information contributed from BOOKLIST.

```
  merge booklist(in=inlist)
        submissions;
```

Match the two data sets by BOOKID and CHAPTER.

```
  by bookid chapter;
```

Keep all observations from BOOKLIST.

```
  if inlist;
```

```
run;
```

Related Technique

The following PROC SQL step creates a table equivalent to the data set that was created by the DATA step in the main example. A left join combines table BOOKLIST with the results of a query applied to SUBMISSIONS. This subquery selects rows from SUBMISSIONS with the most recent value for DRAFTDATE from each combination of BOOKID and CHAPTER values. The MAX aggregate function finds the most recent value of DRAFTDATE.

As with Example 6.4, the table alias that is attached to the three columns in common is for table BOOKLIST. Because the step saves all rows present in BOOKLIST and only those rows from the query applied to SUBMISSIONS that have a match in BOOKLIST, the values for the columns in common should come from BOOKLIST.

Create table LASTDRAFT.
Specify the columns to save in the output table. Specify the origin of the three columns in common between the two tables being joined by preceding the column name with the table alias.

Combine table BOOKLIST with the results of a query applied to SUBMISSIONS. Specify an alias for BOOKLIST.

Specify the subquery. Select rows from SUBMISSIONS with the most recent value of DRAFTDATE for unique combinations of BOOKID and CHAPTER.

Group the rows in SUBMISSIONS by the values of BOOKID and CHAPTER.
Specify an alias for the subquery.
Specify the columns that match the table and results of the subquery.

```
proc sql;
  create table lastdraft as
    select b.bookid, booktitle, b.chapter,
           b.author, duedate, editor,
           draftdate



      from booklist b
        left join



      (select bookid, chapter,
          max(draftdate) as draftdate format=mmddyy10.
        from submissions



        group by bookid,chapter)


              c
      on b.bookid=c.bookid and b.chapter=c.chapter;

quit;
```

Modifying Data Sets in Place

The examples in this chapter show you how to change the contents of a data set in place without making a copy of it. The DATA steps use the MODIFY statement rather than the SET or MERGE statement, which each makes a copy of the data set.

You use the MODIFY statement when you want to change, add, or delete observations and you do not need to add variables to the data set. This technique is useful when you need to conserve resources or when you have a very large master data set compared to a small number of changes to be made to the master data set.

Although you can create new variables in a DATA step that uses the MODIFY statement, these new variables are not output to the data set it is modifying. The MODIFY statement does not allow changes to the data set descriptor portion of the data set it is modifying.

Example 7.1 includes a PROC SQL solution as well as a DATA step solution. The UPDATE clause in PROC SQL allows you to modify a table in place, but it does not have the features that the MODIFY statement in the DATA step has to modify a master data set with transactions from another data set. In PROC SQL, you would need to join the master and transaction tables. In this process, PROC SQL would make a new copy of the table and modify the master table in place.

Because the MODIFY statement changes a data set in place, you are at risk of damaging or losing your data set if your system terminates abnormally during the processing of your DATA step. Make sure you can re-create your original data set if necessary or that you maintain backups.

For a comparison of the MODIFY and UPDATE statements, see "Choosing between MODIFY and UPDATE" in Chapter 1. Chapter 6 includes examples that use the UPDATE statement.

Example 7.1 Modifying All Observations in a Data Set in Place

Goal

Modify the values of existing variables in a data set without creating a new copy of the data set.

Example Features

Featured Step	DATA step
Featured Step Options and Statements	MODIFY statement
Related Technique	PROC SQL, UPDATE clause
A Closer Look	Reviewing the CONTENTS Output for a Data Set Modified with the MODIFY Statement

Input Data Set

Data set DATACONFERENCE stores the schedule for one day of a conference. This data set is also the master data set in Example 7.2.

DATACONFERENCE

Obs	section	starttime	talktime	speaker	topic
1	Applications	8:00 AM	50	Brooks, Jason	Customer Service
2	Data Mining	8:00 AM	50	Jones, Janet	Direct Marketing
3	Statistics	8:00 AM	50	Thomas, Linda	New Analytic Features
4	Tutorials	8:00 AM	50	Evans, Matthew	Graphics
5	Applications	9:00 AM	50	Washington, Debra	TBD
6	Data Mining	9:00 AM	50	Edwards, Andrew	Text Mining Overview
7	Statistics	9:00 AM	50	Cox, David	Mixed Models
8	Tutorials	9:00 AM	50	Mitchell, Jeremy	Writing Functions
9	Applications	10:30 AM	50	Robinson, Catherine	Clinical Trials
10	Data Mining	10:30 AM	50	Wilson, Joshua	Retail Industry
11	Statistics	10:30 AM	50	Anderson, James	TBD
12	Tutorials	10:30 AM	50	Nelson, Stephen	Reporting
13	Applications	1:30 PM	50	Moore, Patrick	Energy Industry
14	Data Mining	1:30 PM	50	Harris, Michael	Credit Risk
15	Statistics	1:30 PM	50	Brown, Brandon	Cluster Analysis
16	Tutorials	1:30 PM	50	White, Elizabeth	External Files
17	Applications	3:00 PM	50	TBD	TBD
18	Data Mining	3:00 PM	50	Johnson, Joshua	Fraud Detection
19	Statistics	3:00 PM	50	Cox, Mary	Predictive Modeling
20	Tutorials	3:00 PM	50	Torres, Tara	Efficient Programming
21	Applications	4:00 PM	50	Sanders, Joyce	Healthcare
22	Data Mining	4:00 PM	50	White, Kimberly	Decision Making
23	Statistics	4:00 PM	50	Richardson, Lisa	Bayesian Basics
24	Tutorials	4:00 PM	50	Morris, Nicole	Customized Output

Resulting Data Set
Output 7.1a
DATACONFERENCE
Data Set

```
         Example 7.1 DATACONFERENCE Data Set Modified with DATA Step

  Obs    section    starttime talktime speaker              topic

    1 Applications  8:00 AM      40     Brooks, Jason        Customer Service
    2 Data Mining   8:00 AM      40     Jones, Janet         Direct Marketing
    3 Statistics    8:00 AM      40     Thomas, Linda        New Analytic Features
    4 Tutorials     8:00 AM      40     Evans, Matthew       Graphics
    5 Applications  9:00 AM      40     Washington, Debra    TBD
    6 Data Mining   9:00 AM      40     Edwards, Andrew      Text Mining Overview
    7 Statistics    9:00 AM      40     Cox, David           Mixed Models
    8 Tutorials     9:00 AM      40     Mitchell, Jeremy     Writing Functions
    9 Applications 10:30 AM      40     Robinson, Catherine  Clinical Trials
```

```
10 Data Mining  10:30 AM    40    Wilson, Joshua      Retail Industry
11 Statistics   10:30 AM    40    Anderson, James     TBD
12 Tutorials    10:30 AM    40    Nelson, Stephen     Reporting
13 Applications  1:30 PM    45    Moore, Patrick      Energy Industry
14 Data Mining   1:30 PM    45    Harris, Michael     Credit Risk
15 Statistics    1:30 PM    45    Brown, Brandon      Cluster Analysis
16 Tutorials     1:30 PM    45    White, Elizabeth    External Files
17 Applications  3:00 PM    45    TBD                 TBD
18 Data Mining   3:00 PM    45    Johnson, Joshua     Fraud Detection
19 Statistics    3:00 PM    45    Cox, Mary           Predictive Modeling
20 Tutorials     3:00 PM    45    Torres, Tara        Efficient Programming
21 Applications  4:00 PM    45    Sanders, Joyce      Healthcare
22 Data Mining   4:00 PM    45    White, Kimberly     Decision Making
23 Statistics    4:00 PM    45    Richardson, Lisa    Bayesian Basics
24 Tutorials     4:00 PM    45    Morris, Nicole      Customized Output
```

Example Overview

This example presents a simple application of the MODIFY statement. The DATA step changes the value of a variable for all observations. Because it is not necessary to change the data set by adding variables, deleting variables, or modifying the descriptor portion of the data set, the MODIFY statement can be used to modify the data set in place. A DATA step that uses the MODIFY statement does not make a copy of the data set as it would if it used the SET statement or the UPDATE statement.

Data set DATACONFERENCE stores the schedule for one day of a conference. The goal of the program is to modify variable TALKTIME based on the value of STARTTIME. It reads one observation from DATACONFERENCE on each iteration of the DATA step. The program changes the value of TALKTIME from 50 to 40 for morning presentations and from 50 to 45 for afternoon presentations. An implicit REPLACE statement at the end of the DATA step writes each observation to its previous location in DATACONFERENCE.

Program

Specify the same name of the data set that the DATA step will modify in place.

Modify data set DATACONFERENCE.
Modify the values of TALKTIME.

```
data dataconference;

  modify dataconference;
    if starttime le '12:00'T then talktime=40;
    else talktime=45;
run;
```

Related Technique

The PROC SQL step in this related technique updates table DATACONFERENCE in place as was done in the DATA step in the main example. The UPDATE statement in PROC SQL allows you to modify values in a table, but not add columns to the table.

Modify data values in table DATACONFERENCE.
Modify the values of TALKTIME based on the value of STARTTIME.

```
proc sql;
  update dataconference

    set talktime= case
                    when starttime le '12:00'T then 40
                    else 45
                  end;
quit;
```

A Closer Look

Reviewing the CONTENTS Output for a Data Set Modified with the MODIFY Statement

When you modify a data set in place by using the MODIFY statement, or when you update a table in place by using the PROC SQL UPDATE clause, SAS changes only the modification date and time in the descriptor portion of the data set or table and does not change the creation date and time.

For example, if you submit the following code before and after executing the DATA step with the MODIFY statement, your CONTENTS output shows that the creation date and time remain the same while the modification date and time value change.

```
proc datasets library=work nolist;
   title "DATACONFERENCE";
   contents data=dataconference;
run;
quit;
```

Output 7.1b presents the attribute part of the CONTENTS output before executing the DATA step with the MODIFY statement.

Output 7.1b
CONTENTS of
DATACONFERENCE
Data Set Prior to
Modifying

```
                            DATACONFERENCE

                        The DATASETS Procedure

Data Set Name         WORK.DATACONFERENCE            Observations          24
Member Type           DATA                           Variables             5
Engine                V9                             Indexes               0
Created               Fri, Apr 16, 2009 04:06:42 PM  Observation Length    68
Last Modified         Fri, Apr 16, 2009 04:06:42 PM  Deleted Observations  0
Protection                                           Compressed            CHAR
Data Set Type                                        Reuse Space           NO
Label                                                Point to Observations YES
Data Representation   WINDOWS_32                      Sorted                NO
Encoding              wlatin1  Western (Windows)
```

Output 7.1c presents the attribute part of the CONTENTS output after executing the DATA step with the MODIFY statement about two minutes after creating the data set.

Output 7.1c
CONTENTS of
DATACONFERENCE
Data Set After
Modifying

```
                            DATACONFERENCE

                        The DATASETS Procedure

Data Set Name         WORK.DATACONFERENCE            Observations          24
Member Type           DATA                           Variables             5
Engine                V9                             Indexes               0
Created               Fri, Apr 16, 2009 04:06:42 PM  Observation Length    68
Last Modified         Fri, Apr 16, 2009 04:09:02 PM  Deleted Observations  0
Protection                                           Compressed            CHAR
Data Set Type                                        Reuse Space           NO
Label                                                Point to Observations YES
Data Representation   WINDOWS_32                      Sorted                NO
Encoding              wlatin1  Western (Windows)
```

Example 7.2 Modifying a Non-Indexed Data Set in Place by Matching by a Common Variable

Goal

Modify a non-indexed master data set in place with transactions supplied in a second data set. Add and delete observations from the master data set. Match the two data sets by variables in common that uniquely identify the observations. The transaction data set can contain duplicate BY values of the variables in common while the master data set does not.

Example Features

Featured Step	DATA step
Featured Step Options and Statements	MODIFY and BY statements _IORC_ automatic variable Macro function %SYSRC
A Closer Look	Controlling When the MODIFY Statement Outputs an Observation Handling Missing Values When Using the MODIFY and BY Statements

Input Data Sets

Data set DATACONFERENCE stores the schedule for one day of a conference. This data set is also used in Example 7.1.

Data set CONFERENCECHANGES contains the updates to apply to DATACONFERENCE. Observations 4, 5, and 6 are not in DATACONFERENCE. Observations 3 and 7 have the same values for SECTION and STARTTIME.

DATACONFERENCE

Obs	section	starttime	talktime	speaker	topic
1	Applications	8:00 AM	50	Brooks, Jason	Customer Service
2	Data Mining	8:00 AM	50	Jones, Janet	Direct Marketing
3	Statistics	8:00 AM	50	Thomas, Linda	New Analytic Features
4	Tutorials	8:00 AM	50	Evans, Matthew	Graphics
5	Applications	9:00 AM	50	Washington, Debra	TBD
6	Data Mining	9:00 AM	50	Edwards, Andrew	Text Mining Overview
7	Statistics	9:00 AM	50	Cox, David	Mixed Models
8	Tutorials	9:00 AM	50	Mitchell, Jeremy	Writing Functions
9	Applications	10:30 AM	50	Robinson, Catherine	Clinical Trials
10	Data Mining	10:30 AM	50	Wilson, Joshua	Retail Industry
11	Statistics	10:30 AM	50	Anderson, James	TBD
12	Tutorials	10:30 AM	50	Nelson, Stephen	Reporting
13	Applications	1:30 PM	50	Moore, Patrick	Energy Industry
14	Data Mining	1:30 PM	50	Harris, Michael	Credit Risk
15	Statistics	1:30 PM	50	Brown, Brandon	Cluster Analysis
16	Tutorials	1:30 PM	50	White, Elizabeth	External Files
17	Applications	3:00 PM	50	TBD	TBD
18	Data Mining	3:00 PM	50	Johnson, Joshua	Fraud Detection
19	Statistics	3:00 PM	50	Cox, Mary	Predictive Modeling
20	Tutorials	3:00 PM	50	Torres, Tara	Efficient Programming
21	Applications	4:00 PM	50	Sanders, Joyce	Healthcare
22	Data Mining	4:00 PM	50	White, Kimberly	Decision Making
23	Statistics	4:00 PM	50	Richardson, Lisa	Bayesian Basics
24	Tutorials	4:00 PM	50	Morris, Nicole	Customized Output

CONFERENCECHANGES

Obs	section	starttime	talktime	speaker	topic
1	Applications	9:00	.		Interfaces
2	Statistics	10:30	.		Statistical Graphics
3	Applications	15:00	.	Brown, Cynthia	
4	Tutorials	17:00	30	Richardson, Lisa	Basic Statistics
5	Break	10:15	15	(none)	(none)
6	Break	14:45	15	(none)	(none)
7	Applications	15:00	.		Quality Control
8	Data Mining	16:00	.	REMOVE	

Resulting Data Set
Output 7.2
DATACONFERENCE
Data Set

```
                      Example 7.2 DATACONFERENCE Data Set Modified with DATA Step

       Obs section       starttime talktime speaker              topic

         1 Applications  8:00 AM     50     Brooks, Jason        Customer Service
         2 Data Mining   8:00 AM     50     Jones, Janet         Direct Marketing
         3 Statistics    8:00 AM     50     Thomas, Linda        New Analytic Features
         4 Tutorials     8:00 AM     50     Evans, Matthew       Graphics
         5 Applications  9:00 AM     50     Washington, Debra    Interfaces
         6 Data Mining   9:00 AM     50     Edwards, Andrew      Text Mining Overview
         7 Statistics    9:00 AM     50     Cox, David           Mixed Models
         8 Tutorials     9:00 AM     50     Mitchell, Jeremy     Writing Functions
         9 Applications 10:30 AM     50     Robinson, Catherine  Clinical Trials
        10 Data Mining  10:30 AM     50     Wilson, Joshua       Retail Industry
        11 Statistics   10:30 AM     50     Anderson, James      Statistical Graphics
        12 Tutorials    10:30 AM     50     Nelson, Stephen      Reporting
        13 Applications  1:30 PM     50     Moore, Patrick       Energy Industry
        14 Data Mining   1:30 PM     50     Harris, Michael      Credit Risk
        15 Statistics    1:30 PM     50     Brown, Brandon       Cluster Analysis
        16 Tutorials     1:30 PM     50     White, Elizabeth     External Files
        17 Applications  3:00 PM     50     Brown, Cynthia       Quality Control
        18 Data Mining   3:00 PM     50     Johnson, Joshua      Fraud Detection
        19 Statistics    3:00 PM     50     Cox, Mary            Predictive Modeling
        20 Tutorials     3:00 PM     50     Torres, Tara         Efficient Programming
        21 Applications  4:00 PM     50     Sanders, Joyce       Healthcare
        23 Statistics    4:00 PM     50     Richardson, Lisa     Bayesian Basics
        24 Tutorials     4:00 PM     50     Morris, Nicole       Customized Output
        25 Tutorials     5:00 PM     30     Richardson, Lisa     Basic Statistics
        26 Break        10:15 AM     15     (none)               (none)
        27 Break         2:45 PM     15     (none)               (none)
```

Example Overview

This example shows how to update a master data set in place with transactions that are matched to the master data set by the values of variables in common. The transactions in this example cause values in the master data set to be updated. They also add and delete observations.

Because it is not necessary to change the data set by adding variables, deleting variables, or modifying the descriptor portion of the data set, the data set can be modified in place and the MODIFY statement can be used. A DATA step that uses the MODIFY statement does not make a copy of the data set as it would if it used the SET statement or the UPDATE statement.

A BY statement matches the two data sets by the values of variables SECTION and STARTTIME. When you use a MODIFY statement, unlike when you match-merge with the SET statement, you do not have to sort or index your master and transaction data sets by the BY variables. However, sorting or indexing your data sets prior to the step does make the step process more efficiently.

The reason you do not have to sort or index your data sets is because the MODIFY statement completes the modifications by using dynamic WHERE processing. The only observations it processes in the master data set are the ones that match to an observation in the transaction data set. Every observation in the transaction data set is processed one at a time, and the MODIFY statement issues a dynamic WHERE statement on the master data set for the BY variable values in the observation in the transaction data set that is currently being processed.

Data set DATACONFERENCE stores the schedule for one day of a conference. The transactions in CONFERENCECHANGES that are identified in the following list by observation number result in these updates of data set DATACONFERENCE:

❏ overlay of values in DATACONFERENCE with values from
CONFERENCECHANGES for matched observations (observations 1, 2, 3, and 7)
where the value in CONFERENCECHANGES is not missing.

❏ addition of new observations (observations 4, 5, and 6 in
CONFERENCECHANGES) to DATACONFERENCE.

❏ removal of one observation (observation 8) from DATACONFERENCE. The special
variable value of "REMOVE" for SPEAKER indicates in the DATA step code when
an observation should be removed.

Note that the PROC PRINT report in Output 7.2 shows the three new observations
appended to the end of DATACONFERENCE in the order in which they were read from
CONFERENCECHANGES. The modified version of DATACONFERENCE after
executing the DATA step has 26 observations. The observation for the "Data Mining"
talk at 4:00 PM is marked for deletion, but not physically removed from the data set.
Therefore, SAS does not list observation 22 in Output 7.2.

Data set CONFERENCECHANGES has two observations with the same BY values for
SECTION and STARTTIME. The DATA step applies the transactions from both
observations one after the other to the matching observation in the maser data set.

The DATA step processes each observation in CONFERENCECHANGES and attempts
to link it to an observation in DATACONFERENCE. A numeric return code value is
assigned to automatic variable _IORC_ to indicate the success of the match. This variable
is created automatically when you use the MODIFY statement.

The values of the _IORC_ automatic variable are internal and subject to change. Instead
of hardcoding the values in your SAS statements, you use the autocall macro program
%SYSRC that SAS has supplied to enable you to test the values of _IORC_ while
protecting your code from future changes in _IORC_ values. For more information about
IORC and %SYSRC, see "Checking for Errors When Using the MODIFY Statement
or the SET Statement with the KEY= Option" in Example 3.11 in the "A Closer Look"
section.

Program

*Specify the name of the data set that
the DATA step will modify.*

```
data dataconference;
```

*Modify data set DATACONFERENCE
by applying the transactions in
CONFERENCECHANGES.*

```
  modify dataconference conferencechanges;
```

*Match the two data sets by the values
of SECTION and STARTTIME.*

```
  by section starttime;
```

*Test the values of automatic variable
IORC that indicate the status of the
search in the master data set for the
current value of BY variables supplied
by the transaction data set.*

```
  select (_iorc_);
```

*Test if _IORC_ indicates that the
search was successful.*

```
    when (%sysrc(_sok)) do;
```

*Replace data values in the
DATACONFERENCE observation
that is matched to an observation in
CONFERENCECHANGES. Replace a
value only if the value from
CONFERENCECHANGES is not
missing. Remove observations from
DATACONFERENCE when
SPEAKER= "REMOVE".*

```
      if speaker ne 'REMOVE' then replace;
      else remove;
```

```
    end;
    when (%sysrc(_dsenmr)) do;
```

*Test if _IORC_ indicates that the
search did not find a match.*

*Prevent writing an error message to the
SAS log when no match is found.*

```
      _error_=0;
```

| ***Add this new observation to the end of the master data set.*** | ```
      output;

    end;
``` |
| ***Stop the program for all other values of _IORC_, which indicate an unexpected error. Write messages to the SAS log about the error.*** | ```
    otherwise do;
      putlog 'ERROR: Program stopped at record ' _n_ '
                          of POLICY_UPDATES';
      stop;
    end;
  end;
run;
``` |

A Closer Look

Controlling When the MODIFY Statement Outputs an Observation

As a DATA step with a MODIFY statement processes a data set, each observation's variable values are moved into the Program Data Vector (PDV). By default, when the DATA step finishes processing the observation, it writes the observation back to the same physical position in the data set from where it was retrieved.

Using the REPLACE, OUTPUT, and REMOVE statements in conjunction with the MODIFY statement can control how the MODIFY statement handles the observations it is processing. The default action of a DATA step that uses the MODIFY statement and does not include at least one of these three statements is the same as if the REPLACE statement was placed as the last statement executed by the DATA step.

If you use any one of these three statements in a DATA step, you must explicitly program each action that you want to take.

❑ The REPLACE statement rewrites the current observation in the data set to the same location from where it was retrieved. Any values you change during processing of the observation replace existing values in the data set. You would use this statement when you want to modify an observation. The REPLACE statement executes at the point it is processed in the DATA step.

❑ The OUTPUT statement writes the current observation to the end of the data set. You would use this statement when you want to add an observation to the data set you are modifying. The OUTPUT statement executes at the point it is processed in the DATA step.

❑ The REMOVE statement deletes the current observation in the data set. This might be either a physical or logical deletion. Output 7.2 shows how PROC PRINT lists a data set where a logical deletion has been made. Observation 22 is missing from the report.

If you modify variable values in an observation and use OUTPUT instead of REPLACE, you will have two occurrences of the observation in the data set. The original observation will remain as it was when read in. The modified version of the observation will be added to the end of the data set because of the OUTPUT statement.

Handling Missing Values When Using the MODIFY and BY Statements

The transaction data set in this example has several missing values, but these missing values do not replace nonmissing values in the master data set. The default action when using the MODIFY and BY statements is to not replace values in the master data set with missing values from the transaction data set. If the missing values are special missing values, then the MODIFY and BY statements do replace the existing values in the master data set with regular missing values.

Similar to the UPDATE statement that was used in Chapter 6, the MODIFY statement has the UPDATEMODE= option. This option can have one of two values: MISSINGCHECK or NOMISSINGCHECK. The default value for UPDATEMODE= is MISSINGCHECK. Because the default action is what this example requires, it was not necessary to add option UPDATEMODE= to the MODIFY statement.

If you want to allow missing values in the transaction data set to replace existing values in the master data set, add UPDATEMODE=NOMISSINGCHECK to the MODIFY statement.

For more information about the UPDATEMODE= option, see "Allowing Missing Values to Replace Existing Values in the Master Data Set When Updating a Master Data Set" in Example 6.1 in the "A Closer Look" section. This topic is discussed in the context of the UPDATE statement, but the uses and results are similar to that of the MODIFY statement.

Example 7.3   Modifying an Indexed Master Data Set in Place

Goal

Modify a master data set in place based on information supplied by a transaction data set. Observations can be added to, modified in, or deleted from the master data set. The master data set and transaction data set do not contain any multiple occurrences of the key variables.

Example Features

Featured Step	DATA step
Featured Step Options and Statements	MODIFY statement in conjunction with the OUTPUT, REPLACE, and REMOVE statements KEY= option in the MODIFY statement _IORC_ automatic variable Macro function %SYSRC

Input Data Sets

Data set POLICIES contains data for 12 policy holders. Assume it has a simple index on variable ID. The POLICIES data set is also used in Example 4.5.

The ACTION variable in POLICY_UPDATES determines how the observation should be processed by the program that updates POLICIES.

Neither data set has duplicate values of matching variable ID.

```
                           POLICIES
                              policy_
  Obs       id       lname    type    lastpayment
    1   6PP97SYCJ6MR  Aamodt     A     01/10/2009
    2   3K3JWQ1WWCY0  Ababa      A     01/15/2009
    3   70QAL1JLV1FF  Abad       A     10/04/2008
    4   JL80SHJ0981I  Abate      B     03/22/2009
    5   B4ZAM563BAN6  Abbas      B     06/12/2008
    6   WEFSBW6US11T  Abbey      C     07/31/2008
    7   3EB21R22VMPZ  Abbott     A     02/27/2009
    8   CNT2MDT1LP9K  Abbott     B     12/06/2008
    9   6VIKYDYXMC8I  Abel       A     11/01/2008
   10   9XUIQK04MHO8  Abell      A     07/12/2008
   11   E1U1T182R2J9  Abraham    B     02/15/2009
   12   9VOEB36I3F2D  Abraham    C     09/12/2008
```

```
                      POLICY_UPDATES
                                 newpolicy_
  Obs  action       id      newlname   type    newlastpayment
    1    M     CNT2MDT1LP9K  Abbot                      .
    2    D     WEFSBW6US11T                             .
    3    M     6VIKYDYXMC8I                         05/02/2009
    4    A     BS2EHK465VJ8  Aasen        B         06/15/2009
    5    M     43PG0RNFJ43E               A               .
```

Resulting Data Set
Output 7.3 **Modified POLICIES Data Set and New Data Set PROBLEMS**

```
            Example 7.3 Modified POLICIES Data Set Modified with DATA Step

                                              policy_
                 Obs        id      lname      type     lastpayment
                  1    6PP97SYCJ6MR  Aamodt      A      01/10/2009
                  2    3K3JWQ1WWCY0  Ababa       A      01/15/2009
                  3    70QAL1JLV1FF  Abad        A      10/04/2008
                  4    JL80SHJ0981I  Abate       B      03/22/2009
                  5    B4ZAM563BAN6  Abbas       B      06/12/2008
                  7    3EB21R22VMPZ  Abbott      A      02/27/2009
                  8    CNT2MDT1LP9K  Abbot       B      12/06/2008
                  9    6VIKYDYXMC8I  Abel        A      05/02/2009
                 10    9XUIQK04MHO8  Abell       A      07/12/2008
                 11    E1U1T182R2J9  Abraham     B      02/15/2009
                 12    9VOEB36I3F2D  Abraham     C      09/12/2008
                 13    BS2EHK465VJ8  Aasen       B      06/15/2009

              Example 7.3 PROBLEMS Data Set Created with DATA Step
                    Observations Rejected from Update Process

                                            newpolicy_
        Obs   action       id      newlname    type    newlastpayment
         1      M     43PG0RNFJ43E              A            .
```

Example Overview

This example highlights how you can modify an indexed data set. The MODIFY statement in the DATA step updates the data set in place. The KEY= option that is added to the MODIFY statement directly accesses the observations in the master data set. This process can save resources, especially when the master data set is large and the transaction data set is small, because the master data set is not completely rewritten as it would be if a SET statement was used. Furthermore, when you directly access observations, the entire data set does not have to be read.

This example is simpler than you would likely encounter in your programming. Duplicate key values do not exist in either the master data set or in the transaction data set. Special programming considerations are required for duplicates, and Example 7.4 shows how you can process duplicates.

One of the changes this program makes to POLICIES is to delete the observation with key value "WEFSBW6US11T". Because the data set is modified in place and not rewritten, SAS does not remove the space allocated to this observation. Instead the observation is marked for deletion. Therefore, in the PROC PRINT output for the resulting data set, you will see that value 6 in the OBS column is omitted from the list. This corresponds to observation 6 in POLICIES, which is the observation marked for deletion. Once POLICIES is rewritten, the same PROC PRINT step would list the same 12 observations with the value of OBS ranging from 1 to 12 with no gaps.

The DATA step outputs observations to two data sets. The first, POLICIES, is the master data set that is modified by the DATA step. The second, PROBLEMS, is a new data set that contains observations from POLICY_UPDATES for which no action could be successfully completed.

The DATA step starts with a SET statement that names the transaction data set, POLICY_UPDATES. The SET statement causes sequential processing of the observations in POLICY_UPDATE. The MODIFY statement that follows specifies the master data set POLICIES. The KEY= option in the MODIFY statement identifies the indexed variable, ID, in the master data set that links the master and transaction data sets. For each observation in POLICY_UPDATES, the MODIFY statement searches in POLICIES for an observation with the current value of ID from POLICY_UPDATES.

The KEY= option in this DATA step specifies variable ID. The KEY= option is not limited to simple indexes; a composite index of multiple variables can be specified.

When you use the KEY= option with either the SET statement or MODIFY statement, SAS creates an automatic variable named _IORC_ whose numeric values indicate the success of the search. This DATA step checks two specific values of _IORC_ in the SELECT block and executes specific sections of code based on the results. Because the values of _IORC_ are internal and subject to change, the %SYSRC macro program was created by SAS to test for specific conditions while protecting your code from future changes in _IORC_ values. For more information about _IORC_ and %SYSRC, see "Checking for Errors When Using the MODIFY Statement or the SET Statement with the KEY= Option" in Example 3.11 in the "A Closer Look" section.

Variable ACTION in data set POLICY_UPDATES specifies the action to take for each observation in POLICY_UPDATES. IF-THEN statements test the value of ACTION in the SELECT block. Here are the valid values of ACTION:

❑ "M" directs a modification of existing information in POLICIES.

❑ "D" directs deletion of the observation from POLICIES.

❑ "A" directs addition of the observation to POLICIES.

Action values "M" or "D" imply that an observation with that ID value already exists in POLICIES. Action value "A" implies that an observation with that ID value does not exist in POLICIES. Table 7.1 describes how the DATA step processes each of the five observations in POLICY_UPDATES.

Table 7.1 Actions Taken for Each Observation in POLICY_UPDATES

Observation and ID Value	Value of ACTION	Match Found in POLICIES?	Action Taken in POLICIES Data Set
1: CNT2MDT1LP9K	M	Yes	Value of LNAME changed from "Abbott" to "Abbot".
2: WEFSBW6US11T	D	Yes	Observation marked for deletion.
3: 6VIKYDYXMC8I	M	Yes	Value of LASTPAYMENT changed from 11/01/2008 to 05/02/2009.
4: BS2EHK465VJ8	A	No	Observation added.
5: 43PG0RNFJ43E	M	No	No modification to POLICIES. Observation output to data set PROBLEMS.

Program

Modify data set POLICIES.
Create data set PROBLEMS to contain observations from POLICY_UPDATES for which no updating action could be taken.

Specify the transaction data set.
Specify the master data set and the indexed variable on which to search for matches in the master data set.

Evaluate the results of the search in the master data set for the current value of the index variable that is supplied by the transaction data set.

Test if the value of _IORC_ indicates that the search was successful.
Test the values of ACTION to determine how to process the observation from POLICY_UPDATES.
Delete observations from POLICIES when the value of ACTION is "D".

```
data policies
     problems(keep=action id newlname newpolicy_type
                   newlastpayment);


set policy_updates;
modify policies key=id;


select (_iorc_);



  when (%sysrc(_sok)) do;

     if action='D' then remove policies;
```

Update variables in POLICIES by using nonmissing values from POLICY_UPDATES. Replace current values with those found in the transaction data set. Assigning values to the variables in POLICIES is necessary when using MODIFY with the KEY= option. An automatic overlay of nonmissing transaction values does not occur as it would if you were using the MODIFY statement with the BY statement and not the KEY= option.

Do not update POLICIES when a match is found and the value of ACTION is "A", which indicates the observation should be added. Instead write this observation to data set PROBLEMS.

Test if the value of _IORC_ indicates that the search did not find a match. Prevent writing an error message to the SAS log when no match is found.

Add the current observation from POLICY_UPDATES to POLICIES.

Copy the values from the variables in POLICY_UPDATES to the variables in POLICIES.

Do not add this unmatched observation from POLICY_UPDATES to POLICIES. Instead write this observation to data set PROBLEMS.

Stop the program for all other values of _IORC_, which indicate an unexpected error. Write messages to the SAS log about the error.

```
   else if action='M' then do;
     if newlname ne ' ' then lname=newlname;
     if newpolicy_type ne ' ' then
          policy_type=newpolicy_type;
     if newlastpayment ne . then
          lastpayment=newlastpayment;
     replace policies;
   end;




   else if action='A' then output problems;
end;




when (%sysrc(_dsenom)) do;

  _error_=0;

  if action='A' then do;
    lname=newlname;
    policy_type=newpolicy_type;
    lastpayment=newlastpayment;
    output policies;
  end;
  else output problems;
end;


otherwise do;
  putlog 'ERROR: Program stopped at record ' _n_
  ' of POLICY_UPDATES';
  stop;

end;
    end;
   end;
run;
```

Example 7.4 Modifying an Indexed Master Data Set in Place When Both the Master and Transaction Data Sets Contain Duplicate Key Values

Goal

Modify in place a master data set with information from a second data set. The master data set is indexed. Both data sets can contain duplicates of the key variables. Update an observation in the master data set with information from all matching observations in the transaction data set. No variables will be added or removed from the master data set and no changes will be made to the descriptor portion of the master data set.

Example Features

Featured Step	DATA step
Featured Step Options and Statements	MODIFY statement with KEY= option in conjunction with the REPLACE statement _IORC_ automatic variable Macro function %SYSRC
A Closer Look	Processing Duplicate Key Values in the Master and Transaction Data Sets When Using the MODIFY Statement

Input Data Sets

Data set TEAMS identifies members of two teams. It is indexed by variable TEAM. There are multiple observations per value of TEAM.

Data set TEAMBONUSES contains bonus information for each of the two teams. There are multiple observations per value of TEAM.

```
                      TEAMS

        Obs     team     member     points
         1      Blue     Mason       275
         2      Blue     Brady       350
         3      Blue     Stone       395
         4      Blue     Amos        280
         5      Gray     Taylor      300
         6      Gray     Ross        325
         7      Gray     Jordan      425


                    TEAMBONUSES

   Obs     team     bonusdate     factor    bonus
    1      Gray     04/30/2010     1.00      100
    2      Blue     04/30/2010     1.25       25
    3      Gray     05/15/2010     1.00       50
    4      Blue     05/31/2010     2.00       75
    5      Gray     05/31/2010     2.00       50
```

Resulting Data Set
Output 7.4
Modified TEAMS Data Set

```
              Example 7.4 TEAMS Data Set Modified with DATA Step

                     Obs     team     member     points

                      1      Blue     Mason       457
                      2      Blue     Brady       532
                      3      Blue     Stone       577
                      4      Blue     Amos        462
                      5      Gray     Taylor      550
                      6      Gray     Ross        575
                      7      Gray     Jordan      675
```

Example Overview

This example updates a master data set in place with information from a transaction data set. The master data set is indexed. Both data sets can contain duplicate values of the key variables.

The master data set, TEAMS, identifies members of two teams. The transaction data set, TEAMBONUSES, contains bonus information for the two teams. Variable TEAM links the two data sets, and there are multiple observations per value of TEAM in both data sets. Data set TEAMS is indexed by variable TEAM. Data set TEAMBONUSES is sorted by variable TEAM to allow for BY-group processing in the DATA step.

The DATA step starts with a SET statement that processes each observation in transaction data set TEAMBONUSES. For each observation in TEAMBONUSES, the program executes a DO UNTIL loop to locate all matching observations in TEAMS and to add points to variable POINTS in TEAMS.

The return code of the search after the last matching observation in TEAMS is located indicates that there are no more matches. In order to return to the top of TEAMS for the next observation in the same BY group, one assignment statement assigns 1 to the DATA step variable DUPTEAM, and another resets the _IORC_ variable to 0.

When this tracking variable DUPTEAM equals 1, the DATA step assigns a missing value to TEAM prior to the search with the MODIFY statement. By assigning a value to TEAM, you force the index pointer to return to the beginning of the index so that the process of finding several matches in TEAMS with the same value of TEAM can be repeated.

Resetting _IORC_ to 0 allows the searching to continue.

Because the TEAMS data set is modified in place and not rewritten, the DATA step does not add variable DUPTEAM to TEAMS.

Program

Specify the same name of the data set that the DATA step will modify in place.	```data teams;```
Specify the transaction data set that will be processed sequentially.	```set teambonuses;```
Define BY-group processing of data set TEAMBONUSES.	```by team;```
Initialize a flag variable to zero to track when processing a duplicate BY value in data set TEAMBONUSES.	```dupteam=0;```
Execute a DO UNTIL loop to find all matching observations in TEAMS for each observation in TEAMBONUSES. Stop the loop when the return code of the search indicates that no more matches are found in TEAMS.	```do until (_iorc_=%sysrc(_dsenom));```
Assign a value to TEAM when DUPTEAM is true (equal to 1) to force the index pointer back to the top of the index so that the process of finding all matching observations in TEAMS can be repeated for the next observation in the same BY group from TEAMBONUSES.	``` if dupteam then team=' ';```
Modify data set TEAMS. Locate observations in TEAMS for the current value of TEAM from TEAMBONUSES by the indexed key variable TEAM.	``` modify teams key=team;```

Branch to different code blocks based on the return code from the keyed search in TEAMS.

When a match is found, compute the bonus points by using the variables from the current observation in TEAMBONUSES. Replace the existing value of POINTS in TEAMS with the new value.

Execute this block when no match is found in TEAMS for the observation from TEAMBONUSES currently being processed.

Reset automatic variable _ERROR_ to 0 to prevent an error condition that would write the contents of the PDV to the SAS log.

Execute this block if the observation from TEAMBONUSES currently being processed is not the last one in the BY group and if variable DUPTEAM has not been set to 1.

Set DUPTEAM to 1 to indicate that there are more observations to process in the current BY group from TEAMBONUSES.

Reset _IORC_ to 0 to remove the condition that there are no more observations to examine for a match.

For all other return codes, write an error message to the SAS log.

```
   select (_iorc_);


   when (%sysrc(_sok)) do;
     points=points + ceil(factor*bonus);
     replace;
   end;



   when (%sysrc(_dsenom)) do;



     _error_=0;



     if not last.team and dupteam=0 then do;



       dupteam=1;



       _iorc_=0;


     end;
   end;

   otherwise do;
     putlog "ERROR: Unexpected error for " team=
                            factor= bonuspoints=;
   end;
   end;
  end;
 run;
```

A Closer Look

Processing Duplicate Key Values in the Master and Transaction Data Sets When Using the MODIFY Statement

When your master or transaction data sets have duplicate key values, you need to carefully understand how you want your master data set updated so that you write your code correctly. The presence of duplicate key values in either of the two data sets and the consecutive arrangement of the duplicates in the data sets can make the modification process more complicated to understand.

For each transaction data set observation in the preceding example, the code found multiple matching observations in the master data set. A DO UNTIL loop was required to find all the key value matches in the master data set. Without the loop, only the first matching observation in the master data set would have been updated.

After completion of processing of the first transaction data set observation, it was necessary to reset conditions so that the master data set could be completely read again from start to finish for each subsequent transaction data set observation with the same key value.

Code altered the value of the return code from the MODIFY statement after the last observation in the master data set was found for one observation in the transaction data set. Changing the return code from the end-of-file condition to not end-of-file allows the master data set to be searched again for subsequent transaction data set observations with the same key value. However, the index pointer remains at the end of the file. To force the index pointer back to the beginning of the index, the value of the key variable was changed before the MODIFY statement executed again to find matches for the new transaction data set observation.

In general, the MODIFY statement uses two different access methods:

❑ matching observations by value using the BY statement, as shown in Example 7.2

❑ finding matching observations directly by values of a KEY= variable, as shown in Examples 7.3 and 7.4

The following paragraphs describe how MODIFY processes your data when you use either of the two access methods and either your master or transaction data set contains duplicates.

<u>When matching observations by value and the master data set has duplicates</u>: When matching a master and transaction data set with a MODIFY and BY statement and the master data set contains duplicates, only the first occurrence of the BY value is updated because the implied WHERE statement that the MODIFY statement applies always starts with the first occurrence of the key value in the master data set no matter how many times it is applied.

<u>When matching observations by value and the transaction data set has duplicates</u>: When matching a master and transaction data set with a MODIFY and BY statement and the transaction data set contains duplicates, the duplicates are applied one on top of another unless you write an accumulation statement to add all of them to the master observation. Without the accumulation statement, the values in the duplicates overwrite each other one after the other so that only the value in the last transaction observation is saved in the master observation.

<u>When finding a matching observation directly and the master data set has duplicates</u>: When matching a master and transaction data set with the MODIFY statement and KEY= option, and both an index on the KEY=variables exists and the master data set contains duplicates, only the first occurrence in the master data set is accessed. To access all occurrences in the master data set, modify the return codes and set condition flags as in this example.

<u>When finding a matching observation directly and the transaction data set has duplicates</u>: When matching a master and transaction data set with the MODIFY statement and KEY= option and an index on the KEY=variables exists, and the transaction data set contains duplicates, the duplicates are applied one on top of another unless you write an accumulation statement to add all of them to the master observation. Without the accumulation statement, the values in the duplicates overwrite each other one after the other so that only the value in the last transaction observation is saved in the master observation. This example used an accumulation statement to accumulate the points from the several point awards per team in the transaction data set.

CHAPTER 8

Manipulating Data from a Single Source

The examples in this chapter work with a single data set or table. They show several techniques of rearranging the contents of your data set by using DATA step statements, SAS procedures, and PROC SQL features. The last example shows how to work with generation data sets.

The examples include techniques for transposing observations into variables and variables into observations, finding duplicate and unique observations in a data set, adding observations at specific locations to a data set, and obtaining variable values from preceding or succeeding observations.

Some of the examples are similar to ones already presented in that the program performs a merge or join, but in this chapter a single data set is merged or joined with itself.

Example 8.1   Performing a Simple Subset

Goal

Create a subset of a SAS data set efficiently by selecting for processing only observations that meet a particular condition.

Example Features

Featured Step	DATA step
Featured Step Options and Statements	WHERE statement
Related Technique	PROC SQL, WHERE clause
A Closer Look	Comparing the WHERE Statement in the DATA Step and the Subsetting IF Statement

Input Data Set

Data set CELLPHONES contains the support records for one day. Only the first 25 of 10,000 observations are shown.

CELLPHONES

Obs	callhour	calllength	status	reason
1	00	10	Resolved	Text Msg Help
2	00	2	Transferred	Other Feature Help
3	01	3	Resolved	Start Service
4	01	2	Resolved	Other
5	01	4	Resolved	Voice Mail Help
6	01	4	Resolved	Billing Change
7	01	3	Resolved	Other Feature Help
8	02	3	Resolved	Start Service
9	02	6	Transferred	Other
10	02	3	Resolved	Account Status
11	02	8	Resolved	Account Status
12	02	5	Transferred	Other
13	02	6	Transferred	Ringtones Help
14	02	2	Transferred	Other Feature Help
15	02	7	Resolved	Account Status
16	02	1	Resolved	Password Question
17	02	5	Resolved	Other Feature Help
18	02	5	Resolved	Address Change
19	02	4	Resolved	Text Msg Help
20	03	7	Resolved	Password Question
21	03	8	Resolved	Start Service
22	03	12	Resolved	Start Service
23	03	2	Resolved	Start Service
24	03	5	Transferred	Other
25	03	3	Resolved	Other Feature Help

. . .

Resulting Data Set
Output 8.1
FEATUREQUESTIONS Data Set

Example 8.1 FEATUREQUESTIONS Data Set Created with DATA Step

Obs	callhour	calllength	status	reason
1	00	10	Resolved	Text Msg Help
2	00	2	Transferred	Other Feature Help
3	01	4	Resolved	Voice Mail Help
4	01	3	Resolved	Other Feature Help
5	02	6	Transferred	Ringtones Help
6	02	2	Transferred	Other Feature Help
7	02	5	Resolved	Other Feature Help
8	02	4	Resolved	Text Msg Help
9	03	3	Resolved	Other Feature Help
10	03	1	Resolved	Other Feature Help
11	03	2	Resolved	Voice Mail Help
12	03	4	Resolved	Other Feature Help
13	03	5	Resolved	Ringtones Help

```
        14      03         8       Transferred    Text Msg Help
        15      03         2       Resolved       Other Feature Help
        16      03         2       Resolved       Ringtones Help
        17      04         3       Resolved       Text Msg Help
        18      04         1       Transferred    Other Feature Help
        19      04         5       Transferred    Other Feature Help
        20      04         3       Transferred    Text Msg Help
        21      04         3       Resolved       Text Msg Help
        22      04        10       Resolved       Text Msg Help
        23      04         1       Resolved       Other Feature Help
        24      04         4       Resolved       Voice Mail Help
        25      04         5       Resolved       Voice Mail Help
    . . .
```

Example Overview

This example demonstrates how to efficiently create a subset of a data set by using the WHERE statement. This technique is efficient because a WHERE statement evaluates observations before the SET statement executes. Only those observations that satisfy the conditions in the WHERE statement are moved into the Program Data Vector (PDV).

Data set CELLPHONES contains 10,000 cell phone support records. The goal is to select all observations where the reason entered for the technical support call contains the text "Help".

Note that variations on the specification of the text, such as all lowercase, are not checked by this example's WHERE statement. It is common to uppercase a character variable when specifying a condition so that all possible spellings can be found. However, if you add functions to your WHERE statement, you will slow down the processing of the DATA step and reduce the advantage of using WHERE processing.

Program

Create data set
FEATUREQUESTIONS.
Read observations from
CELLPHONES.
Specify that the SET statement read
only those observations that satisfy the
condition in the WHERE statement.

```
data featurequestions;

  set cellphones;

  where reason contains "Help";

run;
```

Related Technique

The PROC SQL step in this related technique creates a table equivalent to the data set that was created by the DATA step in the main example. This example selects all columns from CELLPHONES, including the column REASON that is specified on the WHERE clause.

Although not demonstrated in this example, you can specify columns on your WHERE clause that are not in the columns specified on the SELECT clause.

Create table FEATUREQUESTIONS.
Select all columns from table
CELLPHONES.
Read only those rows that satisfy the
condition in the WHERE statement.

```
proc sql;
  create table featurequestions as
    select * from cellphones

      where reason contains "Help";

quit;
```

A Closer Look

Comparing the WHERE Statement in the DATA Step and the Subsetting IF Statement

You can create subsets of your data sets in the DATA step with either the WHERE statement or the subsetting IF statement. While they both test a condition to determine whether SAS should process an observation, only the WHERE statement can prevent observations from being read into the Program Data Vector (PDV), thereby potentially yielding significant savings in processing time.

WHERE Statement in the DATA Step: A WHERE statement tests the condition *before* an observation is read into the PDV. If the condition is true, SAS reads the observation into the PDV and processes it. If the condition is false, SAS does not read the observation into the PDV and moves on to evaluating the next observation. Preventing unneeded observations from being read into the PDV and then processed in the DATA step can save processing time. Other advantages of the WHERE statement over the subsetting IF statement include that it can be optimized with indexes on the variables that define the subsets and that more operators, such as LIKE and CONTAINS, can be used with the WHERE statement.

Subsetting IF Statement: A subsetting IF statement tests the condition *after* an observation is read into the PDV. If the condition is true, SAS continues processing this observation. If the condition is false, SAS discards the observation, ends the current iteration of the DATA step, and continues processing with the next observation. The subsetting IF statement does not use indexes even if they exist on the subsetting variables. A reason to use the subsetting IF statement instead of the WHERE statement is if you have complex conditions to test or complex calculations to perform that would make it difficult to write the WHERE statement.

Generally it is more efficient to use the WHERE statement, but if your data set is small (variables, or observations, or both), or if the subset is a large proportion of your data set, or both, it might not make much difference in processing time to use the subsetting IF statement. Also, if you need to use functions in your WHERE expression, the advantage of using WHERE might also diminish.

Example 8.2 — Separating Unique Observations from Duplicate Observations Based on BY Values

Goal

According to their BY-group values, identify unique and duplicate observations in a data set.

Example Features

Featured Step	DATA step
Featured Step Options and Statements	FIRST.*variable* and LAST.*variable* temporary variables

Input Data Set

Data set COMPSCISTUDENTS contains enrollment information about four students. Note that three students have duplicate observations: two each for Fred Lopez and Martyn Ross and three for Janie Nguyen.

COMPSCISTUDENTS

Obs	studentid	studentname	department	classid	credits
1	91838	Nguyen, Janie	Computer Science	520	2
2	91838	Nguyen, Janie	Speech	476	3
3	91838	Nguyen, Janie	Speech	476	3
4	91838	Nguyen, Janie	Speech	476	3
5	103722	Lopez, Fred	Computer Science	210	3
6	103722	Lopez, Fred	Computer Science	210	3
7	137193	Ross, Martyn	Computer Science	201	3
8	137193	Ross, Martyn	Computer Science	220	2
9	137193	Ross, Martyn	Technical Communication	201	4
10	137193	Ross, Martyn	Technical Communication	201	4
11	987175	Young, Kaitlyn	Design	301	4
12	987175	Young, Kaitlyn	Electrical Engineering	301	3

Resulting Data Sets

Output 8.2a
OKCLASSES Data Set

Example 8.2 OKCLASSES Data Set Created with DATA Step

Obs	studentid	studentname	department	classid	credits
1	91838	Nguyen, Janie	Computer Science	520	2
2	137193	Ross, Martyn	Computer Science	201	3
3	137193	Ross, Martyn	Computer Science	220	2
4	987175	Young, Kaitlyn	Design	301	4
5	987175	Young, Kaitlyn	Electrical Engineering	301	3

Output 8.2b
DUPCLASSES Data Set

Example 8.2 DUPCLASSES Data Set Created with DATA Step

Obs	studentid	studentname	department	classid	credits
1	91838	Nguyen, Janie	Speech	476	3
2	91838	Nguyen, Janie	Speech	476	3
3	91838	Nguyen, Janie	Speech	476	3
4	103722	Lopez, Fred	Computer Science	210	3
5	103722	Lopez, Fred	Computer Science	210	3
6	137193	Ross, Martyn	Technical Communication	201	4
7	137193	Ross, Martyn	Technical Communication	201	4

Example Overview

This example shows how to determine when there is more than one observation in a BY group and to separate the BY groups with multiple observations from BY groups with only one observation.

The DATA step requires BY-group processing. When you process your data in BY groups, SAS automatically creates the FIRST. and LAST. temporary variables for the variables named in the BY statement, which are used in this example. These variables are not saved to the output data sets.

Data set COMPSCISTUDENTS contains enrollment information about four computer science students. Two of the four have two identical observations each. One of the four has three identical observations. The goal is to separate the observations that are represented only once in a BY group from those represented more than once.

Assume that data set COMPSCISTUDENTS is sorted by the three variables, STUDENTID, DEPARTMENT, and CLASSID prior to the DATA step. The BY statement in the DATA step lists these three variables.

The third variable in the BY statement is CLASSID. The DATA step tests the temporary variables FIRST.CLASSID and LAST.CLASSID to determine when an observation is the only one in the BY group. It outputs observations to the appropriate data set based on the values of these temporary variables.

With data set COMPSCISTUDENTS sorted, the FIRST.CLASSID and LAST.CLASSID temporary variables will both equal 1 (true) when processing a single occurrence of a BY group. If either or both of the two variables are 0 (false), the DATA step is processing an observation from a BY group that has more than one observation with the same BY values.

Note that the DATA step determines duplicates only by the values of the variables in the BY statement. To make a more complete check of duplicate information in all variables in an observation, you would need to add code to test the values. This can be done by defining variables with a RETAIN statement that hold values across the observation that can be tested, or by using the LAG function.

Example 8.3 and Example 8.4 are similar to this example in that they also separate unique observations from duplicate observations. Both examples use PROC SORT, the DUPOUT= option, and either the NODUPRECS or NUPKEY option. They differ from this example in that they keep the first observation in a BY group that has multiple observations rather than separating it from BY groups with only one observation.

Program

Sort by the variables that define the BY groups.

```
proc sort data=compscistudents;
  by studentid department classid;
run;
```

Create two data sets, OKCLASSES and DUPCLASSES.
Read each observation from COMPSCISTUDENTS.
Define BY-group processing for COMPSCISTUDENTS.
Test the values of the FIRST. and LAST. temporary variables defined for the third BY variable, CLASSID.
Output an observation to OKCLASSES if it is the only one in the BY group.
Output an observation to DUPCLASSES when either or both FIRST.CLASSID and LAST.CLASSID are 0 (false), which is when there is more than one observation in the BY group.

```
data okclasses dupclasses;

  set compscistudents;

  by studentid department classid;

  if first.classid and last.classid then
            output okclasses;



  else output dupclasses;



run;
```

Example 8.3 Separating Completely Duplicate Observations from Unique Observations

Goal

Identify observations that are a complete copy of another observation. Write the unique observations to one data set and write the duplicate observations to another data set.

Example Features

Featured Step	PROC SORT
Featured Step Options and Statements	DUPOUT=, NODUPRECS, and OUT= options
Related Technique	DATA step, BY statement and LAG function

Input Data Set

Data set PMTEMPS records the hourly afternoon weather data for three locations. Note that the 17:00 Rooftop measurement is recorded identically three times. The 18:00 Rooftop, 16:00 Beach, and 16:00 Downtown measurements are recorded twice. The 14:00 and 15:00 Downtown measurements are identical except for the time of the measurement.

PMTEMPS

Obs	location	temptime	tempf	dewpoint	relhum
1	Rooftop	13:00	73	50	44
2	Rooftop	14:00	72	52	49
3	Rooftop	15:00	72	53	51
4	Rooftop	16:00	74	51	45
5	Rooftop	17:00	75	51	43
6	Rooftop	17:00	75	51	43
7	Rooftop	17:00	75	51	43
8	Rooftop	18:00	74	50	43
9	Rooftop	18:00	74	50	43
10	Beach	13:00	67	56	68
11	Beach	14:00	71	58	63
12	Beach	15:00	74	59	60
13	Beach	16:00	76	58	54
14	Beach	16:00	76	58	54
15	Beach	17:00	79	58	48
16	Beach	18:00	81	59	47
17	Downtown	13:00	68	62	81
18	Downtown	14:00	69	62	78
19	Downtown	15:00	69	62	78
20	Downtown	16:00	71	63	76
21	Downtown	16:00	71	63	76
22	Downtown	17:00	70	64	81
23	Downtown	18:00	73	64	73

Resulting Data Sets
Output 8.3a
UNIQUETEMPS
Data Set

```
          Example 8.3 UNIQUETEMPS Data Set Created with PROC SORT

     Obs   location   temptime   tempf   dewpoint   relhum
      1    Beach        13:00      67       56         68
      2    Beach        14:00      71       58         63
      3    Beach        15:00      74       59         60
      4    Beach        16:00      76       58         54
      5    Beach        17:00      79       58         48
      6    Beach        18:00      81       59         47
      7    Downtown     13:00      68       62         81
      8    Downtown     14:00      69       62         78
      9    Downtown     15:00      69       62         78
     10    Downtown     16:00      71       63         76
     11    Downtown     17:00      70       64         81
     12    Downtown     18:00      73       64         73
     13    Rooftop      13:00      73       50         44
     14    Rooftop      14:00      72       52         49
     15    Rooftop      15:00      72       53         51
     16    Rooftop      16:00      74       51         45
     17    Rooftop      17:00      75       51         43
     18    Rooftop      18:00      74       50         43
```

Output 8.3b
DUPTEMPS Data Set

```
                    Example 8.3 DUPTEMPS Data Set Created with PROC SORT

          Obs    location    temptime    tempf    dewpoint    relhum
           1     Beach        16:00        76         58         54
           2     Downtown     16:00        71         63         76
           3     Rooftop      17:00        75         51         43
           4     Rooftop      17:00        75         51         43
           5     Rooftop      18:00        74         50         43
```

Example Overview

This example demonstrates how to separate unique observations from duplicate observations. With the DUPOUT=, NODUPRECS, and OUT= options, PROC SORT can write unique observations to one data set and duplicate observations to another. The NODUPRECS option finds multiple copies of an observation by comparing an observation to the previous observation. The first observation in a group of identical observations is written to the OUT= data set. Subsequent copies are written to the DUPOUT= data set.

The identification of duplicate observations does depend on how you specify the BY statement. Because PROC SORT identifies a duplicate observation by comparing an observation to the previous observation, it is possible that the input data set might be in such an order that the sort specified in the BY statement does not arrange the duplicates consecutively. In this situation, you could end up with a data set that still had complete duplicate observations.

Usually you sort a data set by its key identifier variables when using NODUPRECS. This will usually make it more likely that PROC SORT finds and removes all duplicate observations from the input data set.

Data set PMTEMPS has hourly weather observations for one afternoon for three locations. The goal is to clean the data set by removing duplicate observations. The key variables in PMTEMPS are LOCATION and TEMPTIME.

The EQUALS/NOEQUALS PROC SORT option can also affect the results of the NODUPRECS option. It specifies the order of the observations in the output data set and is not used in this example. Its default setting is EQUALS. For observations with identical BY-variable values, EQUALS maintains the relative order of the observations within the input data set in the output data set. The NOEQUALS option does not necessarily preserve this order in the output data set. For information about this option, see SAS documentation on PROC SORT.

Program

Sort data set PMTEMPS.
Write unique observations in a BY group or observations that are first in a group of identical observations to the OUT= data set.
Write the observations that are duplicate copies of the first in a group of identical observations to the DUPOUT= data set.
Specify the BY variables. Write the BY statement so that identical observations will be arranged consecutively.

```
proc sort data=pmtemps
          noduprecs
          out=uniquetemps



          dupout=duptemps;




   by location temptime;

run;
```

Related Technique

The following DATA step produces two data sets equivalent to the data sets that were produced by PROC SORT in the preceding main example. It performs a similar process as PROC SORT with the NODUPRECS option by comparing an observation to the previous observation. As with PROC SORT, it is possible that your code might not find all duplicate observations because of the arrangement of the observations. Ensure that you sort your data set in a way that the duplicates would be arranged consecutively. Typically, you would order your data by its key identifiers. The key identifiers in data set PMTEMPS are LOCATION and TEMPTIME.

PROC SORT sorts data set PMTEMPS by LOCATION and TEMPTIME prior to the DATA step so that observations recorded at the same place and time are consecutive.

Assignment statements apply the LAG*n* function to each of the five variables. Because no numeric suffix is specified, the calls to the LAG*n* function retrieve values from the previous observation. An IF statement in the DATA step compares the variables that contain the lagged values to the variables in the observation that is currently being processed.

A queue of lagged values is initialized with the first call to a LAG function. Each iteration of the DATA step must execute the LAG function so that the queue is populated correctly.

If the values of all variables in an observation are equal to the values in the previous observation, the observation is output to DUPTEMPS. The first observation in a group of consecutive identical observations is always output to UNIQUETEMPS. This happens because when compared to the previous observation, the current observation's values are not identical because the previous observation is in a different group.

Note that the DATA step does not include a BY statement. The observations are arranged by LOCATION and TEMPTIME prior to the DATA step, but they are not processed in BY groups by the DATA step.

The PROC SORT step is easier to code than the multiple comparisons in the IF statement in the DATA step. However, you might need to use a DATA step because of additional processing you need to include.

Arrange the observations so that identical observations for a location and time of measurement are arranged consecutively.

```
proc sort data=pmtemps;
  by location temptime;
run;
```

Create data sets UNIQUETEMPS and DUPTEMPS.

Read each observation in PMTEMPS.

Drop the variables that hold the lagged variables because they are needed only during execution of the DATA step.

Retrieve variable values from the previous observation.

```
data uniquetemps duptemps;

  set pmtemps;
  drop lagloc lagtemptime lagtempf lagdewpoint
       lagrelhum;

  lagloc=lag(location);
  lagtemptime=lag(temptime);
  lagtempf=lag(tempf);
  lagdewpoint=lag(dewpoint);
  lagrelhum=lag(relhum);
```

Test the values of all variable values in the observation that is currently being processed to their lagged values.

Output an observation to DUPTEMPS if all comparisons show that the values are equal.

```
  if lagloc=location and lagtemptime=temptime and
     lagtempf=tempf and lagdewpoint=dewpoint and
     lagrelhum=relhum then output duptemps;
```

Output an observation to UNIQUETEMPS if any of the comparison tests show that a value is unequal.

```
  else output uniquetemps;

run;
```

Example 8.4 Separating the First Observation in a BY Group from the Other Observations in the BY Group

Goal

Write the first observation in a BY group to one data set. Write the other observations in the BY group to a second data set.

Example Features

Featured Step	DATA step
Featured Step Options and Statements	FIRST.*variable* and LAST.*variable* temporary variables
Related Technique	PROC SORT, DUPOUT=, NODUPKEY, and OUT= options

Input Data Set

Data set TRADE_ASSN contains membership records for four members of a trade association. Each observation stores the membership information for one company for one year. Note that three of the four companies have more than one observation and that one company, Surname Associates, has only one observation.

```
                            TRADE_ASSN

Obs          company          membershipyear nemployees   revenue
 1 Always Ready Fix-it             2008           4         103929
 2 Always Ready Fix-it             2009           5         198482
 3 Always Ready Fix-it             2010           3         154105
 4 Fairlakes Manufacturing         2006          50         763120
 5 Fairlakes Manufacturing         2007          25        5301903
 6 Fairlakes Manufacturing         2008          31        7928185
 7 Fairlakes Manufacturing         2009          28        8391869
 8 Fairlakes Manufacturing         2010          27        8678291
 9 Surname Associates              2010          22       10682910
10 Wise Wizards Consulting         2005          10        3918593
11 Wise Wizards Consulting         2006           5         645120
12 Wise Wizards Consulting         2008           2          38371
```

Resulting Data Sets

Output 8.4a
JOINED_ASSN
Data Set

```
          Example 8.4 JOINED_ASSN Data Set Created with DATA Step

   Obs          company          membershipyear nemployees   revenue

    1  Always Ready Fix-it             2008           4        103929
    2  Fairlakes Manufacturing         2006          50        763120
    3  Surname Associates              2010          22      10682910
    4  Wise Wizards Consulting         2005          10       3918593
```

Output 8.4b
RENEWED_ASSN
Data Set

```
          Example 8.4 RENEWED_ASSN Data Set Created with DATA Step

   Obs          company          membershipyear nemployees revenue

    1  Always Ready Fix-it             2009           5        198482
    2  Always Ready Fix-it             2010           3        154105
    3  Fairlakes Manufacturing         2007          25       5301903
    4  Fairlakes Manufacturing         2008          31       7928185
    5  Fairlakes Manufacturing         2009          28       8391869
    6  Fairlakes Manufacturing         2010          27       8678291
    7  Wise Wizards Consulting         2006           5        645120
    8  Wise Wizards Consulting         2008           2         38371
```

Example Overview

This example shows how you can determine when an observation is the first observation in a BY group so that you can separate it from the other observations in its BY group.

The DATA step requires a BY statement that lists the BY-group variables. When you process your data in BY groups, SAS automatically creates the FIRST. and LAST. temporary variables for the variables that are named in the BY statement. The DATA step does not write these variables to the output data sets.

Data set TRADE_ASSN maintains membership records for four members of a trade association starting in 2005. The goal is to find the record when the member joined the association and to find all of the member's subsequent renewal records.

Assume that the observations in data set TRADE_ASSN have already been sorted or indexed by the two variables, COMPANY and MEMBERSHIPYEAR. The BY statement names only one variable, COMPANY. The data are sorted by MEMBERSHIPYEAR within each value of COMPANY so that the first observation in a BY group will be the first year the company was in the trade association. (Your program will not generate an error if you keep MEMBERSHIPYEAR in the BY statement.)

The DATA step tests the value of the temporary variable FIRST.COMPANY to determine when an observation is the first one in the BY group. It outputs observations to the appropriate data set based on the value of this temporary variable.

With data set TRADE_ASSN sorted by COMPANY and within each value of COMPANY by MEMBERSHIPYEAR, the FIRST.COMPANY temporary variable is 1 (true) only when processing the first observation in a BY group. This condition exists when the company joined the trade association. If it is not the first observation in the BY group, the value of FIRST.COMPANY is 0 (false). This condition exists for membership renewal observations.

Create data sets JOINED_ASSN and
RENEWED_ASSN.
Read each observation from
TRADE_ASSN.
Define BY-group processing for
TRADE_ASSN.
Output observations that are first in
their BY group to JOINED_ASSN.
Output observations that are not first in
their BY group to RENEWED_ASSN.

```
data joined_assn renewed_assn;

   set trade_assn;

   by company;

   if first.company then output joined_assn;

   else output renewed_assn;

run;
```

Related Technique

The following PROC SORT step creates two data sets identical to the data sets JOINED_ASSN and RENEWED_ASSN that were created by the preceding DATA step. A combination of PROC SORT options can achieve the same results as a DATA step in this example.

Because this technique sorts and separates the observations in one step, it is more efficient than sorting the data set and executing the DATA step in the main example. When you do not need to add additional programming statements and your data set has not already been sorted or indexed prior to executing the DATA step, consider the PROC SORT technique.

The step uses the NODUPKEY option to separate the observations that are first in a BY group from the remaining observations in the BY group. The OUT= option specifies the data set that will hold these first observations. Using the OUT= option will prevent PROC SORT from overwriting TRADE_ASSN. The DUPOUT= option specifies the data set that will contain the observations removed from TRADE_ASSN because of the NODUPKEY option.

Sort data set TRADE_ASSN.
Write only the first observation in a BY
group to the OUT= data set.
Save the observations that are not the
first ones in each BY group in the
DUPOUT= data set.
Specify the BY variables.

```
proc sort data=trade_assn
          nodupkey
          out=joined_assn
          dupout=renewed_assn;

  by company membershipyear;
run;
```

Example 8.5 Accessing a Specific Number of Observations from the Beginning and End of a Data Set

Goal

Process a specific number of observations at the beginning and end of a data set. Efficiently access the observations by not reading the entire data set. If the total number of observations in the data set is less than the sum of observations to access, process the entire data set.

Example Features

Featured Step	DATA step
Featured Step Options and Statements	Direct access, SET statement, NOBS= and POINT= options

Input Data Set

Data set BLOODPRESSURE contains 20 blood pressure measurements.

BLOODPRESSURE

Obs	bptime	systolic	diastolic	pulse
1	8:20	160	90	99
2	8:22	171	92	103
3	8:24	158	88	102
4	8:30	155	90	93
5	8:43	144	88	90
6	8:51	145	82	88
7	8:59	140	80	86
8	9:02	138	82	84
9	9:06	130	80	78
10	9:09	130	76	75
11	9:13	128	77	78
12	9:18	126	75	73
13	9:25	125	75	72
14	9:31	122	73	74
15	9:42	124	75	70
16	9:45	123	73	68
17	9:50	120	73	67
18	9:52	115	70	67
19	9:55	116	73	66
20	9:59	115	68	65

Resulting Data Set
Output 8.5
FIRSTLAST4BP
Data Set

Example 8.5 FIRSTLAST4BP Data Set Created with DATA Step

Obs	measurement	bptime	systolic	diastolic	pulse
1	1	8:20	160	90	99
2	2	8:22	171	92	103
3	3	8:24	158	88	102
4	4	8:30	155	90	93
5	17	9:50	120	73	67
6	18	9:52	115	70	67
7	19	9:55	116	73	66
8	20	9:59	115	68	65

Example Overview

This example shows you how to write a DATA step that can select a specific number of observations from the beginning and the end of a data set. The DATA step accesses the observations directly by observation number by using the POINT= option in the SET statement; it does not process the data set sequentially.

Data set BLOODPRESSURE contains 20 blood pressure measurements for a person over a period of time.

The following DATA step selects the first four observations and last four observations from BLOODPRESSURE. The NOBS= option in the SET statement assigns to variable TOTALOBS the number of observations in BLOODPRESSURE.

The value of TOTALOBS is assigned during compilation before the DATA step executes. Therefore, the value of TOTALOBS is available at the top of the DATA step when execution commences.

The IF-THEN block executes when there are more observations in BLOODPRESSURE than the sum of the total number of observations to read from the beginning and end of the data set. It contains a DO loop with two sets of ranges of index values: the first specifies the range of observations to access at the beginning of the data set, and the second specifies the range of observations to access at the end of the data set. The DO loop in this example reads observations 1 through 4 and 17 through 20.

If the check on the number of observations did not exist, and the first DO loop executed unconditionally when the sum of TOTAL1 and TOTAL2 was greater than TOTALOBS, your output data set would contain duplicates of some observations because of the overlap of the two ranges of observations. Additionally, the ranges that were specified might attempt to access observations that don't exist, which would result in errors.

The ELSE-DO block executes when the total number of observations in the data set is less than the sum of the number of observations to access from the beginning and the end of the data set. The DO loop in this block simply reads each observation in the data set causing the output data set to have the same number of observations as the input data set.

The DATA step iterates only once. The DO loops iterate the number of times equal to the number of observations they read. Therefore, assignment statements assign the constant values to the variables that specify the DO loop index values. Usually when a DATA step executes for every observation in a data set, it is more efficient to assign the constant values with a RETAIN statement that executes only once.

Program

Create data set FIRSTLAST4BP.

Assign constant values to the two variables that define how many observations to read from the beginning of the data set (TOTAL1) and from the end of the data set (TOTAL2).

Execute this block if the total number of observations in BLOODPRESSURE is greater than the sum of the total number of observations to access from BLOODPRESSURE.

Specify the lower index value of the range of observations to select from the beginning of the data set.

Compute the upper index value of the range of observations to select from the beginning of the data set.

Compute the lower index value of the range of observations to select from the end of the data set.

Specify the upper index value of the range of observations to select from the end of the data set.

Specify a DO loop with two sets of ranges, the first for the observations to access from the beginning of the data

```
data firstlast4bp;
  keep measurement bptime systolic diastolic pulse;
  total1=4;
  total2=4;




  if totalobs ge (total1+total2) then do;




    start1=1;



    end1=start1+total1-1;



    start2=totalobs-total2+1;



    end2=totalobs;



    do i=start1 to end1,start2 to end2;
```

set and the second for the observations to access from the end of the data set. Assign the observation number that is currently being accessed to variable MEASUREMENT. With I designated as the POINT= variable, SAS considers it a temporary variable. Therefore, to save its value in the output data set, it must be assigned to a data set variable.	`measurement=i;`
Read the ith observation from BLOODPRESSURE.	`set bloodpressure point=i`
Assign the total number of observations in BLOODPRESSURE to variable TOTALOBS.	`    nobs=totalobs;`
Output each observation that is accessed directly.	`output;`
	`   end;`
	`end;`
Execute this block when the total number of observations in BLOODPRESSURE is less than the sum of the total number of observations to access from BLOODPRESSURE.	`else do;`
Execute this loop once for each observation in BLOODPRESSURE.	`do i=1 to totalobs;`
Assign the observation number that is currently being accessed to variable MEASUREMENT.	`   measurement=i;`
Read the ith observation from data set BLOODPRESSURE.	`set bloodpressure point=i`
Assign the total number of observations in BLOODPRESSURE to variable TOTALOBS.	`    nobs=totablobs;`
Output each observation that is accessed directly, which in this loop is every observation in BLOODPRESSURE.	`output;`
	`   end;`
	`end;`
Use a STOP statement to prevent the DATA step from continuous looping because there is no end-of-file condition when SAS reads data with direct access.	`stop;`
	`run;`

Example 8.6   Creating a Customized Sort Order without Adding a New Column to the Table

Goal

Sort the rows in a table in a customized, complex order. Define a new column temporarily to hold the sort order and do not save it in the output table.

Example Features

Featured Step	PROC SQL
Featured Step Options and Statements	Subquery CASE and ORDER expressions

Input Table

Table EMP_ROSTER contains recent on-call hours for an employee group. Variable HOURS_WEEK is the number of hours the employee has been on-call in the past week. Variable HOURS_4WEEKS is the number of hours the employee has been on-call in the past four weeks.

EMP_ROSTER

Obs	id	hours_ week	hours_ 4weeks	level
1	4GJBU	0	130	Staff
2	7SFWY	5	43	Staff
3	AT4S3	28	102	Staff
4	BGPP9	18	25	Staff
5	BXPQM	38	152	Staff
6	EYFYX	29	123	Staff
7	GSSMJ	14	56	Staff
8	IRFVM	8	62	Staff
9	L15GM	41	142	Staff
10	XCU73	32	115	Staff
11	Z86ZR	20	40	Staff
12	62EFL	5	105	Lead
13	6EI4N	21	87	Lead
14	7TZ7T	12	31	Lead
15	E2C61	27	54	Lead
16	MVZ8P	14	36	Lead
17	XLFLN	2	28	Lead
18	YELJB	29	44	Lead
19	2G8JY	3	21	Senior
20	63337	14	55	Senior
21	IHLJF	8	25	Senior
22	J4V0J	29	71	Senior
23	URAOV	18	41	Senior
24	IM76W	3	10	Manager
25	KULNC	12	20	Manager

Resulting Table
Output 8.6
ONCALL_ROSTER
Table

Example 8.6 ONCALL_ROSTER Table Created with PROC SQL

Obs	id	hours_ week	hours_ 4weeks	level
1	7SFWY	5	43	Staff
2	IRFVM	8	62	Staff
3	GSSMJ	14	56	Staff
4	BGPP9	18	25	Staff
5	Z86ZR	20	40	Staff
6	XLFLN	2	28	Lead
7	2G8JY	3	21	Senior
8	62EFL	5	105	Lead
9	IHLJF	8	25	Senior
10	7TZ7T	12	31	Lead
11	63337	14	55	Senior
12	MVZ8P	14	36	Lead

13	AT4S3	28	102	Staff
14	URAOV	18	41	Senior
15	6EI4N	21	87	Lead
16	E2C61	27	54	Lead
17	J4V0J	29	71	Senior
18	YELJB	29	44	Lead
19	XCU73	32	115	Staff
20	4GJBU	0	130	Staff
21	IM76W	3	10	Manager
22	KULNC	12	20	Manager
23	EYFYX	29	123	Staff
24	BXPQM	38	152	Staff
25	L15GM	41	142	Staff

Example Overview

This example shows you how to rearrange the rows in a table in a customized, complex order with PROC SQL.

The goal of the program is to determine the on-call order for the group of employees in EMP_ROSTER. Complex rules based on the employee's level, hours worked in the past week, and hours worked in the past four weeks determine where to place the employee on the call list. The rules are expressed as the WHEN conditions in a CASE clause that is assigned the alias SORTCOLUMN. The lower the value assigned to SORTCOLUMN, the higher the employee is placed on the call list. In general, employees with level="STAFF" are higher on the list, while employees with level="MANAGER" are lower on the list.

The SORTCOLUMN column is used only to sort the rows in the input table EMP_ROSTER and is not saved in the output table ONCALL_ROSTER.

The step performs a subquery of EMP_ROSTER that defines SORTCOLUMN and returns the sorted rows, including the new column SORTCOLUMN to the outer query. The outer query selects only the columns found in EMP_ROSTER, and it does not select SORTCOLUMN.

This process can be easily accomplished in the DATA step by writing a series of IF-THEN statements to define new variable SORTCOLUMN, and then sorting the observations and not saving SORTCOLUMN in the output data set from PROC SORT. A reason to use PROC SQL is that the creation of the new column, ordering the rows, and saving specific columns can be done in one step.

Program

Create table ONCALL_ROSTER.
Specify the outer query. Select only the columns found in EMP_ROSTER.
Begin the subquery. Select the columns found in EMP_ROSTER and a new column defined by the following CASE expression.
Specify the complex rules to determine the order of the call list. When the combination of LEVEL, HOURS_WEEK, and HOURS_4WEEKS is not present in the WHEN conditions, assign a value of 9 to SORTCOLUMN to put these observations at the bottom of the list.

```
proc sql;
  create table oncall_roster as
    select emp.* from

      (select emp.*,


        case
          when hours_week gt 35 or hours_4weeks gt 120
                              then 5
          when level='Manager' then 5
          when (level='Lead' or level='Senior') and
                hours_week le 16 then 2
          when (level='Lead' or level='Senior') and
                hours_week between 17 and 24 then 3
          when (level='Lead' or level='Senior') and
                hours_week gt 24 then 4
          when level='Staff' and hours_week gt 30 and
                hours_4weeks gt 40 then 4
          when level='Staff' and hours_week gt 30 and
                hours_4weeks le 40 then 3
          when level='Staff' and hours_week le 20 then 1
          when level='Staff' and (hours_week between 21
                and 30) and
                hours_4weeks le 40 then 1
```

```
                                    when level='Staff' and (hours_week between 21
                                             and 30) and
                                             hours_4weeks gt 40 then 2
                                        else 9
                                      end as sortcolumn
                                 from emp_roster as emp)
```

Select rows from EMP_ROSTER.
Assign an alias to EMP_ROSTER.
Terminate the subquery.
Order the rows in the output table.

```
                                 order by sortcolumn, hours_week;
                            quit;
```

Example 8.7 — Adding New Observations to the End of a Data Set

Goal

Add new observations to the end of a data set, while retaining the original name of the data set.

Example Features

Featured Step	DATA step
Featured Step Options and Statements	SET statement END= option, OUTPUT statement

Input Data Set

Data set FINALSALES contains nine years of final sales results for five categories of books.

```
                           FINALSALES

Obs  year  internet  networks      os     apps  training
 1   2001  $62,529   $49,070   $34,506  $45,055  $79,316
 2   2002  $66,068   $50,325   $33,711  $45,640  $75,248
 3   2003  $69,785   $46,015   $33,092  $45,841  $77,029
 4   2004  $64,115   $46,068   $35,185  $44,273  $76,394
 5   2005  $60,832   $51,456   $34,757  $45,015  $79,474
 6   2006  $66,635   $46,017   $34,121  $46,006  $78,829
 7   2007  $69,696   $50,846   $33,560  $45,468  $77,847
 8   2008  $65,127   $49,995   $35,899  $46,874  $79,364
 9   2009  $63,073   $48,654   $33,237  $44,064  $75,760
```

Resulting Data Set
Output 8.7
**PROJ_FINALSALES
Data Set**

```
         Example 8.7 PROJ_FINALSALES Data Set Created with DATA Step

 Obs  year  internet  networks      os     apps  training type

  1  2001   $62,529   $49,070   $34,506  $45,055  $79,316 Final
  2  2002   $66,068   $50,325   $33,711  $45,640  $75,248 Final
  3  2003   $69,785   $46,015   $33,092  $45,841  $77,029 Final
  4  2004   $64,115   $46,068   $35,185  $44,273  $76,394 Final
  5  2005   $60,832   $51,456   $34,757  $45,015  $79,474 Final
  6  2006   $66,635   $46,017   $34,121  $46,006  $78,829 Final
  7  2007   $69,696   $50,846   $33,560  $45,468  $77,847 Final
  8  2008   $65,127   $49,995   $35,899  $46,874  $79,364 Final
  9  2009   $63,073   $48,654   $33,237  $44,064  $75,760 Final
 10  2010   $64,650   $48,800   $33,071  $44,108  $79,548 Projected
 11  2011   $66,266   $48,946   $32,906  $44,152  $83,525 Projected
 12  2012   $67,923   $49,093   $32,741  $44,196  $87,701 Projected
```

Example Overview

The following DATA step shows you how to use options in the SET statement to add observations to the end of a data set.

The data in input data set FINALSALES contain final book sales figures for five categories for the nine years from 2001 to 2009.

The goal of the DATA step is to create a new data set that contains all the observations in FINALSALES plus the projected sales figures for 2010 to 2012. Variable TYPE is defined to classify the observations as final sales figures or projected sales figures.

The END= option in the SET statement detects when the end of the data set has been reached. A DO loop executes when processing the last observation. The DO loop outputs three new observations by using information from the last observation in the input data set.

The loop that executes when processing the last observation in input data set FINALSALES projects the sales for the next three years, 2010 to 2012. An array of percentage change values for the five categories is used to project the change from one year to the next. The projected sales for 2010 are based on the actual sales for 2009. The projected sales for 2011 are based on the projected sales for 2010, and the projected sales for 2012 are based on the projected sales for 2011.

Program

Create data set PROJ_FINALSALES.
Process each observation in
FINALSALES. Define EOF so that it
can be detected when processing the
last observation in FINALSALES.
Define array DEPT to hold the sales
results for the five categories.
Define temporary array GROWTH.
Initialize the five elements of
GROWTH with the annual projected
percentage change in sales for the five
categories.

Assign a value to TYPE for
observations with final sales figures.
Include an OUTPUT statement so that
the DATA step writes out all
observations in the input data set. This
statement is needed here because one is
required in the following IF-THEN
block that outputs the new observations.
Execute this block when processing the
last observation in FINALSALES.
Assign a value to TYPE for the new
observations.
Project values for the three years from
2010 to 2012.
Project values for the five categories.
Compute the projected result for a
category based on the prior year's
value and round to the nearest dollar.

Output each new observation.

```
data proj_finalsales;
  set finalsales end=eof;



  array dept{*} internet networks os apps training;

  array growth{5} _temporary_ (2.5,0.3,-.5,.1,5);




  drop i;
  retain type 'Final';

  output;




  if eof then do;

    type='Projected';

    do year=2010 to 2012;

      do i=1 to dim(dept);
        dept{i}=round((dept{i} +
                growth{i}*dept{i}/100),1);

      end;
      output;
    end;
  end;
run;
```

Example 8.8 Adding Observations to a Data Set Based on the Value of a Variable

Goal

Add a specific number of observations to a data set based on the value of one of its variables.

Example Features

Featured Step	DATA step
Featured Step Options and Statements	OUTPUT statement

Input Data Set

Data set NEWSOFTWARE contains the project steps and step duration for a new software installation.

```
              NEWSOFTWARE

    Obs    task          totaldays
    1      install           1
    2      benchmarks        2
    3      review 1          2
    4      parallel          5
    5      review 2          3
    6      complete          1
```

Resulting Data Set
Output 8.8
NEWSOFTWAREDAILY
Data Set

```
      Example 8.8 NEWSOFTWAREDAILY Data Set Created with DATA Step

      Obs              workdate    task         totaldays   taskday

       1       Monday, Mar  1, 2010   install        1         1
       2       Tuesday, Mar  2, 2010  benchmarks     2         1
       3       Wednesday, Mar  3, 2010 benchmarks    2         2
       4       Thursday, Mar  4, 2010 review 1       2         1
       5       Friday, Mar  5, 2010   review 1       2         2
       6       Monday, Mar  8, 2010   parallel       5         1
       7       Tuesday, Mar  9, 2010  parallel       5         2
       8       Wednesday, Mar 10, 2010 parallel      5         3
       9       Thursday, Mar 11, 2010 parallel       5         4
      10       Friday, Mar 12, 2010   parallel       5         5
      11       Monday, Mar 15, 2010   review 2       3         1
      12       Tuesday, Mar 16, 2010  review 2       3         2
      13       Wednesday, Mar 17, 2010 review 2      3         3
      14       Thursday, Mar 18, 2010 complete       1         1
```

Example Overview

The DATA step in this example uses the value of an existing variable in an input data set to determine how many observations to output for each observation in the input data set.

The sequence of tasks in installing some new software is stored in data set NEWSOFTWARE. Each observation has the title of one task and the number of days to complete the task. The goal of the DATA step is to output one observation for each day of the project.

The DATA step executes a DO loop for every observation in data set NEWSOFTWARE. The upper index of the DO loop is the value of TOTALDAYS for the observation that is currently being processed. The DO loop outputs an observation for each day that the task will be performed.

The beginning date of the installation process is set by the RETAIN statement for WORKDATE at the beginning of the DATA step. The value of WORKDATE is incremented by 1 with each iteration of the DO loop unless the date of the task would fall on a Saturday or Sunday. When the task would fall on the weekend, the value of WORKDATE is incremented by an additional one or two days to move the task work to the following Monday.

Program

Create data set NEWSOFTWAREDAILY.
Assign attributes to new variable WORKDATE.
Read each observation from NEWSOFTWARE.
Initialize variable WORKDATE and retain its value across iterations of the DATA step.

Define a variable to track the day within the task.
Execute a DO loop the number of times equal to the value of TOTALDAYS.
Increment the variable that tracks the day within the task.
Determine the day of the week of the current value of WORKDATE.
For Saturdays, increment WORKDATE two days to the following Monday.
For Sundays, increment WORKDATE one day to the following Monday.
Output one observation for each day of a task.
Increment WORKDATE by 1 to move to the next day in the installation process.

```
data newsoftwaredaily;

   format workdate weekdate25.;

   set newsoftware;

   retain workdate '01mar2010'd;


   drop dayofweek i;
   taskday=0;

   do i=1 to totaldays;

      taskday+1;

      dayofweek=weekday(workdate);

      if dayofweek=7 then workdate+2;


      else if dayofweek=1 then workdate+1;

      output;

      workdate+1;

   end;
run;
```

Example 8.9   Adding Observations to a SAS Data Set So the Values of a Variable Are Consecutive throughout the BY Group

Goal

Add observations to a data set to fill out each BY group so that the value of a specified variable consistently increments for every observation in the BY group.

Example 8.10 is similar to Example 8.9 except that the data are more complex in Example 8.10 and require different programming steps.

The example uses the same input data set as Example 8.12.

Example Features

Featured Step	DATA step
Featured Step Options and Statements	BY-group processing, FIRST.*variable* and LAST.*variable* temporary variables, RETAIN statement
Related Technique	PROC MEANS, COMPLETETYPES, NOPRINT and NWAY options, ID and OUTPUT statements
A Closer Look	Examining the Processing of Data Set WEIGHT_BMI by the DATA Step

Input Data Set

Data set WEIGHT_BMI contains weight, BMI, and session information for four study participants over a four-week period. Only ID S003 had data recorded for all four weeks.

```
                          WEIGHT_BMI

        Obs     id      week     weight     bmi     session
         1      S001      1        231      29.7      AM1
         2      S001      2        223      28.6      AM2
         3      S002      1        187      28.4      AM1
         4      S002      3        176      26.8      AM2
         5      S003      1        154      27.3      PM1
         6      S003      2        151      26.7      AM1
         7      S003      3        148      26.2      PM1
         8      S003      4        142      25.2      PM1
         9      S004      1        134      25.3      PM3
        10      S004      2        133      25.1      PM3
        11      S004      4        129      24.4      PM3
```

Resulting Data Set
Output 8.9
WEIGHT_BMI_4WEEKS Data Set

```
        Example 8.9 WEIGHT_BMI_4WEEKS Data Set Created with DATA Step

              Obs     id      week     weight     bmi     session

               1      S001      1        231      29.7      AM1
               2      S001      2        223      28.6      AM2
               3      S001      3         .        .
               4      S001      4         .        .
               5      S002      1        187      28.4      AM1
               6      S002      2         .        .
               7      S002      3        176      26.8      AM2
               8      S002      4         .        .
               9      S003      1        154      27.3      PM1
              10      S003      2        151      26.7      AM1
              11      S003      3        148      26.2      PM1
              12      S003      4        142      25.2      PM1
              13      S004      1        134      25.3      PM3
              14      S004      2        133      25.1      PM3
              15      S004      3         .        .
              16      S004      4        129      24.4      PM3
```

Example Overview

This example shows you how to add observations to fill out BY groups in a data set so that each BY group has the same number of observations. The observations it adds fill specific positions in the BY group based on the requirement that a specific variable's values be sequentially represented.

Data set WEIGHT_BMI has weights and BMIs for four study participants over a four-week period. Only one of the participants, S003, has information recorded for all four weeks. The goal is to add observations for the other three participants so that they each also have four observations. The variable WEEK records the week of the measurement and its values are 1, 2, 3, and 4. The program examines the observations for each participant and adds an observation for missing weeks. The values for WEIGHT, BMI, and SESSION for that inserted week are set to missing.

The DATA step processes WEIGHT_BMI in BY groups that are defined by the values of variable ID. It starts by renaming variables WEIGHT, BMI, and SESSION so that the processing in the DATA step does not overwrite existing values.

The DATA step tests when it is at the beginning of the BY group and assigns a value of 1 to WEEK in case the BY group is missing an observation for WEEK=1. Next it tests whether the current observation is the last in the BY group.

The results of testing whether the current observation is the first or last in the BY group determine the bounds of a DO loop. Each iteration of the DO loop outputs one observation. When an observation is not the last in the BY group, the loop executes between the current value of WEEK and the current value of HOLDWEEK, which is the name of the renamed WEEK variable. When an observation is the last in the BY group, it executes between the current value of WEEK and the value 4, which is the maximum number of observations per BY group. This upper bound value is assigned to variable UPPER.

Table 8.1 in "Examining the Processing of Data Set WEIGHT_BMI by the DATA Step" in the "A Closer Look" section lists the bounds of the DO loop on each iteration of the DATA step.

Example 8.10 is similar in that it fills out BY groups. It is more complex because the BY variables include character variables whose values are not numerically sequential as they are in this example.

Program

Create data set
WEIGHT_BMI_4WEEKS.
Read the observations from
WEIGHT_BMI. Rename all variables
except for the BY variable ID so that
the values of these variables are
available in the DATA step and do not
get overwritten.

```
data weight_bmi_4weeks;

   set weight_bmi(rename=(week=holdweek weight=holdweight
                          bmi=holdbmi
                          session=holdsession));
```

Process the data set in groups defined
by the values of ID.

```
   by id;
```

Retain the values of WEEK across
iterations of the DATA step.

```
   retain week;
```

Drop the renamed variables since their
values are assigned to new variables
later in the DATA step.

```
   drop holdweek holdweight holdbmi holdsession upper;
```

Initialize WEEK to 1 at the beginning
of each BY group.

```
   if first.id then week=1;
```

When processing the last observation
in the BY group, set the value of the
upper bound of the DO loop to the
maximum number of observations per
BY group.

```
   if last.id then upper=4;
```

When not processing the last observation in the BY group, assign to the upper bound of the DO loop the renamed value of WEEK. This causes the DO loop to possibly iterate more than once because the value of WEEK might be less than HOLDWEEK. This allows for observations with missing data for the intervening weeks to be added to the output data set.

```
                                  else upper=holdweek;
```

Process a DO loop between the bounds that are defined by the preceding code. Assign missing values to variables WEIGHT, BMI, and SESSION when WEEK is not equal to HOLDWEEK because an observation for the current value of WEEK is not present in the BY group.

```
                          do week=week to upper;

                            if week ne holdweek then do;
                              weight=.;
                              bmi=.;
                              session='   ';
                            end;
```

Assign values to WEIGHT, BMI, and SESSION from the renamed variables when WEEK is equal to HOLDWEEK because an observation for the current value of WEEK is present in the BY group.

```
                            else do;
                              weight=holdweight;
                              bmi=holdbmi;
                              session=holdsession;
                            end;
```

Output an observation on each iteration of the DO loop. The DO loop iterates in increments of 1 so that even when a value of WEEK has no observation for the BY group in WEIGHT_BMI, it writes an observation to WEIGHT_BMI_4WEEKS.

```
                            output;



                          end;
                       run
```

Related Technique

The following program uses PROC MEANS to create a data set equivalent to the data set that was created in the main example. By adding the COMPLETETYPES and NWAY options to the PROC MEANS statement, the PROC MEANS step creates a data set that has all possible combinations of ID and WEEK.

The COMPLETEYPES option creates all possible combinations of the classification variables even if the combination does not occur in the input data set. The NWAY option causes PROC MEANS to save only the combinations of the two variables and not the classifications of ID alone and WEEK alone as well as an observation for the entire data set.

The combinations of ID and WEEK are saved in an output data set along with the participant's values of WEIGHT, BMI, and SESSION. The VAR statement specifies the two numeric variables, WEIGHT and BMI.

The ID statement specifies the character variable, SESSION. When there is more than one observation in a combination of the CLASS variables, PROC MEANS saves in the output data set the maximum value of the variable that is specified in the ID statement. If the variable is a character variable, PROC MEANS determines the maximum value by the sort order of the characters.

The OUTPUT statement requests that the MIN statistic be saved in an output data set. Because there is only one observation per combination of ID and WEEK in WEIGHT_BMI, the MIN statistic equals the actual data value.

The following program is a good choice if you don't need to add programming statements to a DATA step. Also, when the increments between your values are not sequential or if you are using character variables, the programming of the bounds of the

DO loop in the main example can be complicated. PROC MEANS would handle the complexity of defining the combinations without additional programming.

PROC FREQ and the SPARSE option in the TABLES statement can provide a similar solution. This method is used in the Related Technique in Example 8.10.

Analyze data set WEIGHT_BMI.
Create all possible combinations of the variables listed in the CLASS statement even if a combination does not occur in the input data set.

Suppress the output report.
Specify that PROC MEANS compute statistics only for the groups that are defined by the combinations of ID and WEEK.

Specify the classification variables whose values define the combinations for which to compute statistics.

Include SESSION in the output data set. Because each combination of ID and WEEK has at most one observation, the actual value of SESSION is saved in the output data set.

Specify the two numeric variables whose values will be saved in the output data set.

Save the results in WEIGHT_BMI_4WEEKS. Do not keep the automatic variables that PROC MEANS creates.

Compute the MIN statistic on WEIGHT and BMI. Name the statistics WEIGHT and BMI. Because each combination of ID and WEEK has at most one observation, the MIN statistics for WEIGHT and BMI equal their actual values.

```
proc means data=weight_bmi
                          completetypes




                          noprint
                          nway;

     class id week;


     id session;




     var weight bmi;



     output out=weight_bmi_4weeks(drop=_freq_ _type_)



                 min=;





run;
```

A Closer Look

Examining the Processing of Data Set WEIGHT_BMI by the DATA Step

Table 8.1 shows how the DO loop bounds are set on each iteration of the DATA step in the main example. Because the value of new variable WEEK is retained across iterations of the DATA step, the DATA step starts out its next iteration with the value it had when the DO loop ended in the previous iteration. For example, when the DO loop ends on the first iteration of the DATA step, the value of WEEK is 2. The second iteration starts out with WEEK=2, which is the lower bound of the DO loop.

Table 8.1 DO Loop Bounds on Each Iteration of the DATA Step

| Observation ID | DATA Step Iteration (_N_) | DO Loop | | Times DO loop iterates |
		Lower bound (new variable WEEK)	Upper bound (variable UPPER)	
S001	1	1	1	1
S001	2	2	4	3
S002	3	1	1	1
S002	4	2	4	3
S003	5	1	1	1
S003	6	2	2	1
S003	7	3	3	1
S003	8	4	4	1
S004	9	1	1	1
S004	10	2	2	1
S004	11	3	4	2

Example 8.10   Adding Rows to a Table So That All Possible Values of Specific Columns Are Present in Each BY Group

Goal

Add rows to a table so that all possible combinations of specific columns are present in each BY group in the output table. The columns that are not used to define the combinations will have missing values.

This example is similar to Example 8.9 in that it fills out BY groups so that there is the same number of rows in each BY group and each BY group has the same combinations of specific variables. It differs from Example 8.9 in that the columns that define the combinations are character columns and not columns with sequential numeric values. Sequential numeric values as in Example 8.9 are straightforward to program with arrays and the DATA step while working with character values adds some complexity to the coding.

Example Features

Featured Step	PROC FREQ and PROC SQL
Featured Step Options and Statements	PROC FREQ: TABLES statement with NOPRINT, OUT=, and SPARSE options PROC SQL: Left join

Input Table

Table WOODPECKERS records the presence of six species of woodpeckers at four tract locations on seven dates. Only tract MV28 was visited on all seven dates.

Value "H" means the bird was heard. Value "N" means the bird was not seen or heard. Value "S" means the bird was observed.

WOODPECKERS

Obs	visit_date	tract	red_bellied	sapsucker	downy	hairy	flicker	pileated
1	03/15/2009	JN72	H	N	S	S	N	N
2	03/15/2009	MV28	N	N	S	N	N	N
3	03/20/2009	JN72	S	N	S	H	N	H
4	03/20/2009	KT05	N	S	S	N	N	N
5	03/20/2009	MV28	S	N	H	H	N	S
6	03/25/2009	JN72	N	H	S	S	N	N
7	03/25/2009	MV28	N	S	S	S	N	H
8	03/30/2009	JN72	H	S	N	H	N	N
9	03/30/2009	KT05	N	N	H	S	N	H
10	03/30/2009	LT83	H	S	S	S	N	H
11	03/30/2009	MV28	S	N	S	N	N	S
12	04/04/2009	LT83	N	N	S	S	H	N
13	04/09/2009	JN72	S	N	S	S	N	S
14	04/09/2009	LT83	N	N	S	H	N	N
15	04/09/2009	MV28	S	S	S	S	N	H
16	04/14/2009	LT83	N	N	S	S	S	H
17	04/14/2009	MV28	H	N	S	S	H	S

Resulting Table
Output 8.10
FULLBIRDSURVEY
Table

```
             Example 8.10 FULLBIRDSURVEY Table Created with PROC SQL

                        red_
    Obs visit_date tract bellied sapsucker downy hairy flicker pileated

     1 03/15/2009 JN72    H        N        S     S      N        N
     2 03/15/2009 KT05
     3 03/15/2009 LT83
     4 03/15/2009 MV28    N        N        S     N      N        N
     5 03/20/2009 JN72    S        N        S     H      N        H
     6 03/20/2009 KT05    N        S        S     N      N        N
     7 03/20/2009 LT83
     8 03/20/2009 MV28    S        N        H     H      N        S
     9 03/25/2009 JN72    N        H        S     S      N        N
    10 03/25/2009 KT05
    11 03/25/2009 LT83
    12 03/25/2009 MV28    N        S        S     S      N        H
    13 03/30/2009 JN72    H        S        N     H      N        N
    14 03/30/2009 KT05    N        N        H     S      N        H
    15 03/30/2009 LT83    H        S        S     S      N        H
    16 03/30/2009 MV28    S        N        S     N      N        S
    17 04/04/2009 JN72
    18 04/04/2009 KT05
    19 04/04/2009 LT83    N        N        S     S      H        N
    20 04/04/2009 MV28
    21 04/09/2009 JN72    S        N        S     S      N        S
    22 04/09/2009 KT05
    23 04/09/2009 LT83    N        N        S     H      N        N
    24 04/09/2009 MV28    S        S        S     S      N        H
    25 04/14/2009 JN72
    26 04/14/2009 KT05
    27 04/14/2009 LT83    N        N        S     S      S        H
    28 04/14/2009 MV28    H        N        S     S      H        S
```

Example Overview

The following program uses PROC FREQ to determine all the possible combinations of specific variables, and then combine the data set that contains the combinations with the input data set by using PROC SQL. The resulting output table has the same number of observations in each BY group.

Table WOODPECKERS records observations on the presence of six species of woodpeckers in four tracts on seven dates. Observations were made in tract MV28 for all seven dates while observations were made on five of the seven dates in tract JN72, two of the seven dates in tract KT05, and four of the seven dates in tract LT83.

The goal of the PROC SQL step is to add rows to the table so that each tract has seven rows, one for each of the seven observation dates.

By adding the SPARSE option to the TABLES statement, the PROC FREQ step creates a data set that has all possible combinations of VISIT_DATE and TRACT even when the combination does not exist in the input data set. With seven values of VISIT_DATE and the four values of TRACT in the data set, PROC FREQ creates an output data set with 28 observations.

Observations that are unique to ALLVISITS have missing values in output table FULLBIRDSUVEY for columns found only in WOODPECKERS.

Program

Create a table of all possible combinations of VISIT_DATE and TRACT.
Suppress printing the table.
Save the table in data set ALLVISITS.
Keep only the variables that are needed to define all the possible combinations.
Include all possible combinations of VISIT_DATE and TRACT even when a combination does not occur in the input data set.

```
proc freq data=woodpeckers;
  tables visit_date*tract

              / noprint
                out=allvisits(keep=visit_date tract)

              sparse;

run;
```

Create table FULLBIRDSURVEY.
Perform a left join of ALLVISITS and WOODPECKERS. Put ALLVISITS on the left side of the join so that all rows from ALLVISITS are present in FULLBIRDSURVEY whether or not a row has a match in WOODPECKERS.
Assign aliases to both tables.
Specify how to match the rows.

```
proc sql;
  create table fullbirdsurvey as
    select *
      from allvisits v left join woodpeckers w

        on v.visit_date=w.visit_date and v.tract=w.tract;
quit;
```

Example 8.11 Expanding Single Observations into Multiple Observations

Goal

Reshape data by creating multiple observations from a single observation in the input data set and by assigning variable names as values in the output data set.

Example Features

Featured Step	DATA step
Featured Step Options and Statements	OUTPUT statement VNAME variable information call routine
Related Technique	PROC TRANSPOSE, NAME= option, BY statement

Input Data Set

Data set CUSTRESP contains survey results for 25 customers on the number of visits to three sites that resulted in sales.

CUSTRESP

Obs	customer	website	store	event
1	1	0	1	1
2	2	0	8	.
3	3	0	4	0
4	4	10	3	2
5	5	1	.	0
6	6	3	0	0
7	7	0	6	1
8	8	0	2	3
9	9	0	1	0
10	10	0	4	0
11	11	6	4	1
12	12	4	4	2
13	13	9	3	5
14	14	0	3	0
15	15	1	0	0
16	16	0	2	0
17	17	0	5	1
18	18	6	1	2
19	19	0	7	4
20	20	5	3	0
21	21	0	1	0
22	22	5	1	3
23	23	1	0	0
24	24	0	2	0
25	25	1	1	1

Resulting Data Set
Output 8.11
SALESVISITS
Data Set

```
              Example 8.11 SALESVISITS Data Set Created with DATA Step (first 21 observations)

                         Obs      customer      salessite      visits

                          1          1           website          0
                          2          1           store            1
                          3          1           event            1
                          4          2           website          0
                          5          2           store            8
                          6          2           event            .
                          7          3           website          0
                          8          3           store            4
                          9          3           event            0
                         10          4           website         10
                         11          4           store            3
                         12          4           event            2
                         13          5           website          1
                         14          5           store            .
                         15          5           event            0
                         16          6           website          3
                         17          6           store            0
                         18          6           event            0
                         19          7           website          0
                         20          7           store            6
                         21          7           event            1
```

Example Overview

This example shows you how to turn variables into observations with the DATA step. The names of the variables become values for a new variable. The values of these input variables are assigned to a second new variable.

Data set CUSTRESP stores the responses of 25 customers to a survey about the number of visits they made to three sales sites that resulted in sales. Each observation in CUSTRESP has the counts for one customer for the number of visits he or she made to the website, store, and event. The counts are stored in three numeric variables, WEBSITE, STORE, and EVENT.

The goal of the program is to create a new data set in which three observations are created from each input observation. Each new observation stores the number of visits to one of three sites in new variable VISITS. A second new variable, SALESSITE, retains the sales site location. The program assigns to variable SALESSITE the name of the variable from which the value of VISITS was derived.

Variable names WEBSITE, STORE, and EVENT in input data set CUSTRESP become the three character values for the new variable SALESSITE. The numeric values of WEBSITE, STORE, and EVENT are written to the new numeric variable VISITS.

The SITENAME temporary array is initialized on the first iteration of the DATA step with the names of the three variables by using the CALL VNAME routine. The values remain in the Program Data Vector (PDV) throughout execution of the DATA step and are accessed in the DO loop.

Program

Create data set SALESVISITS.
Read observations from CUSTRESP.
Define the array SITE to hold the three
variables that correspond to the three
sales locations.
Define temporary array SITENAME
whose elements will store the names of
the elements in array SITE. The values
that are saved in SITENAME are
assigned to SALESSITE.
Define new variable SALESSITE
whose values will be one of the three
variable names that are saved in the
SITENAME array.
Keep only the two new variables and
the observation identifier, which is
variable CUSTOMER. Do not keep
WEBSITE, STORE, and EVENT,
which are used to assign values to
SALESSITE and VISITS.
Initialize the elements of the
SITENAME array on the first iteration
of the DATA step.

Return the name of each element in the
SITE array and assign it to its
corresponding element in SITENAME.

Iterate a DO loop the number of times
equal to the number of elements in the
SITE array.
Assign to SALESSITE the name of the
SITE array element that is currently
being processed by the DO loop.
Move the value of the SITE array
element that is currently being
processed to VISITS.
Output an observation on each
iteration of the DO loop, which is once
for each element of the SITE array.

```
data salesvisits;
  set custresp;
  array site{*} website store event;


  array sitename{3} $25 _temporary_ ;




  length salessite $ 7;




  keep customer salessite visits;






  if _n_=1 then do;


    do i=1 to 3;

      call vname(site{i},sitename{i});



    end;
  end;
  do i=1 to dim(site);


    salessite=sitename{i};



    visits=site{i};



    output;


  end;
run;
```

Related Technique

The following PROC TRANSPOSE step creates a data set equivalent to the data set that was produced by the DATA step in the main example. Using PROC TRANSPOSE to reshape CUSTRESP is an easy solution in this example because no additional programming is needed in a DATA step; the variables to be transposed are all numeric, and there is only one observation per value of CUSTOMER. When you want to modify the observations that are written to the output data set, for example, or if you need to transpose both character and numeric variables, the DATA step is a better choice than PROC TRANSPOSE. If you need to compute new variables, you will have to use the DATA step.

The program starts by sorting CUSTRESP by CUSTOMER. The PROC TRANSPOSE step that follows transposes the observations in CUSTRESP by the values of CUSTOMER. For each BY group, PROC TRANSPOSE creates one observation for each variable that it transposes. Because this step transposes three numeric variables, PROC TRANSPOSE outputs three observations for each CUSTOMER BY group.

The Related Technique in Example 8.12 also uses PROC TRANSPOSE to reshape a data set.

Sort CUSTRESP by the variable that defines the BY groups for which to transpose the data set.

```
proc sort data=custresp;
  by customer;
run;
```

Transpose data set CUSTRESP. Identify the variable in the output data set that contains the name of the variable that is being transposed, which will have one of three values: "website", "store", or "event".

Name the output data set. Specify a more meaningful name for the variable that is automatically defined by PROC TRANSPOSE. Because there is only one observation per value of CUSTOMER in CUSTRESP, PROC TRANSPOSE will create only one new variable, COL1, with the values of the three transposed variables.

```
proc transpose data=custresp
               name=salessite




               out=salesvisits(rename=(col1=visits));
```

Specify the variable that defines the BY groups. This variable will not be transposed, and one observation will be created for each transposed variable within each BY group.

```
  by customer;
```

Name the variables whose variable names will become values and whose values will be moved to new variable COL1, which is renamed to VISITS.

```
  var website store event;



run;
```

Example 8.12 Collapsing Observations within a BY Group into a Single Observation

Goal

Rearrange a data set by changing selected variables in a group of observations to a group of variables in one observation. Reshape data by collapsing observations within a BY group into a single observation in order to simplify data analysis and report generation.

The example uses the same input data set as Example 8.9.

Example Features

Featured Step	DATA step
Featured Step Options and Statements	BY statement FIRST.*variable* and LAST.*variable* temporary variables OUTPUT statement
Related Technique	PROC TRANSPOSE, PREFIX= option, BY, ID, RETAIN, and VAR statements DATA step, match-merging by value and merging a data set with itself

Input Data Set

Data set WEIGHT_BMI contains weight, BMI, and session information for four study participants over a four-week period. Only ID S003 had data recorded for all four weeks.

```
                              WEIGHT_BMI

          Obs    id     week    weight    bmi    session
           1    S001      1       231     29.7    AM1
           2    S001      2       223     28.6    AM2
           3    S002      1       187     28.4    AM1
           4    S002      3       176     26.8    AM2
           5    S003      1       154     27.3    PM1
           6    S003      2       151     26.7    AM1
           7    S003      3       148     26.2    PM1
           8    S003      4       142     25.2    PM1
           9    S004      1       134     25.3    PM3
          10    S004      2       133     25.1    PM3
          11    S004      4       129     24.4    PM3
```

Resulting Data Set
Output 8.12a
WTRESULTS
Data Set

```
            Example 8.12 WTRESULTS Data Set Created with PROC TRANSPOSE and DATA Step

                                             bmi_   bmi_   bmi_   bmi_   session_  session_  session_  session_
  Obs   id  wt_week1 wt_week2 wt_week3 wt_week4 week1 week2 week3 week4  week1     week2     week3     week4

   1  S001    231      223       .        .    29.7  28.6    .      .     AM1       AM2
   2  S002    187       .       176       .    28.4    .   26.8     .     AM1                 AM2
   3  S003    154      151      148      142   27.3  26.7  26.2   25.2    PM1       AM1       PM1       PM1
   4  S004    134      133       .       129   25.3  25.1    .    24.4    PM3       PM3                 PM3
```

Example Features

This example takes a data set with multiple observations per BY group and collapses each BY group's observations into one observation. The DATA step changes the shape of the input data from "long and narrow" to "short and wide." The output data set will have fewer observations and more variables.

The DATA step copies the values for several variables to arrays of new variables where each element of the array is a specific variable's value in one observation in the BY group.

The DATA step uses FIRST. and LAST. temporary variables to determine when it is processing the first observation and last observation in a BY group. When processing the first observation in a BY group, the DATA step initializes to missing all the elements in the arrays of new variables. A RETAIN statement retains the values of these new variables across observations. The DATA step outputs an observation to the data set only when processing the last observation in the BY group. When processing reaches the last observation in a BY group, all rearrangement of variables within a BY group is completed.

Data set WEIGHT_BMI contains up to four observations for each of four study participants over a four-week period. Each observation records weight, BMI, and session attendance for a subject for one week.

The goal of the DATA step is to rearrange the observations in WEIGHT_BMI so that there is only one observation per study participant. The values for weight, BMI, and session attendance are defined in data set WEIGHT_BMI as the three variables WEIGHT, BMI, and SESSION. The values of these three variables are to be moved to new variables. Variable WEEK tracks the week in the period for which the measurements were obtained for the study participant.

The DATA step defines an array for each of the three variables, WEIGHT, BMI, and SESSION. Their input data set values will be moved to new output data set variables that are defined by these arrays. Because it is known that measurements are recorded a maximum of four times per participant, the ARRAY statements specify four variables with each element's position identifying the week for which a measurement was obtained. The DATA step points to the correct array element by using variable WEEK as the array index value.

Because it is necessary to process WEIGHT_BMI in BY groups that are defined by the values of ID, data set WEIGHT_BMI is sorted by ID prior to the DATA step.

Program

Sort the observations in WEIGHT_BMI by the variable that defines the BY groups.
Create data set WTRESULTS.
Read the observations in WEIGHT_BMI.
Process WEIGHT_BMI in BY groups.
Define three arrays to hold the weekly measurements for each participant.
Define the elements as serial variables from 1 to 4.
Drop WEIGHT, BMI, and SESSION because their values are moved to the elements of the three arrays that were defined earlier. Drop WEEK because the suffix on the new variables identifies the week.
Retain the values of the new variables across observations.
When processing the first observation in a BY group, initialize all the new variables to missing.

When the value of week is inclusively between the expected values of 1 and 4, copy the current values of WEIGHT, BMI, and SESSION to the array elements that are pointed to by the value of WEEK.

```
proc sort data=weight_bmi;
  by id;
run;

data wtresults;
  set weight_bmi;

  by id;
  array wts{*} wt_week1-wt_week4;
  array bmis{*} bmi_week1-bmi_week4;
  array sessions{*} $ 3 session_week1-session_week4;

  drop i week weight bmi session;




retain wt_week1-wt_week4 bmi_week1-bmi_week4
       session_week1-session_week4;
if first.id then do;
  do i=1 to 4;
    wts{i}=.;
    bmis{i}=.;
    sessions{i}=' ';
  end;
end;
if 1 le week le 4 then do;
  wts{week}=weight;
  bmis{week}=bmi;
  sessions{week}=session;
end;
```

When the value of WEEK is outside its expected range, write an error message. Output an observation only when processing the last observation in a BY group, which is after all rearrangement of the values of input variables WEIGHT, BMI, and SESSION.

```
else putlog "ERROR: Week value " week
            "out of range from 1 to 4 for id=" id;

if last.id then output;



run;
```

Related Technique

The following program uses PROC TRANSPOSE and the DATA step to produce a data set equivalent to the one that was produced by the DATA step in the main example. It uses one PROC TRANSPOSE step to transpose the two numeric variables, WEIGHT and BMI, and a second PROC TRANSPOSE step to transpose the character variable, SESSION.

If you transpose both character and numeric variables in the same PROC TRANSPOSE step, SAS converts the numeric variable values to character values. By submitting one step for the numeric variables and a second for the character variable, the transposed values of WEIGHT and BMI remain numeric.

PROC TRANSPOSE uses variable WEEK to determine how to name the transposed variables. However, if you had missing data for all observations for one week for one of the variables, a variable would not be created for that missing week. You should understand the limitations of your data and possibly specify ATTRIB, LENGTH, or ARRAY statements in the final DATA step to make sure all elements are defined.

For more information about creating variables with PROC TRANSPOSE, see "Naming the Variables in the Transposed Data Set" in Example 3.12 in the "A Closer Look" section.

The first PROC TRANSPOSE step saves two observations per value of the BY variable ID. One observation contains the transposed values of WEIGHT and the other observation contains the transposed values of BMI. These values are saved in the same four variables. To distinguish between the two observations for each ID, the variable _NAME_ that was created by PROC TRANSPOSE saves the name of the variable that created the transposed variables.

A DATA step match-merges the two data sets that PROC TRANSPOSE produced by ID. The MERGE statement lists data set TRANSWTBMI twice and data set TRANSSESSION once. The two occurrences of TRANSWTBMI in the MERGE statement cause the data set to be merged with itself. Its first placement in the MERGE statement applies a WHERE statement to select observations where the value of the _NAME_ variable is "WEIGHT". Its second placement applies a WHERE statement to select observations where the value of the _NAME_ variable is "BMI".

When you use PROC TRANSPOSE as in this example, you do not need to know how many occurrences of observations there are per BY group. This is an advantage over using the DATA step in the main example. However, when running the DATA step that match-merges the PROC TRANSPOSE data sets, you do need to know the maximum number of measurements made because it is necessary to rename the numeric transposed variables. A way around the renaming requirement is to execute PROC TRANSPOSE once for each variable, ensuring that the PREFIX= values are unique.

Output 8.12b shows intermediate data set TRANSWTBMI. Note the two observations per value of ID, each with a different value for _NAME_.

Output 8.12b
TRANSWTBMI
Data Set

			TRANSWTBMI			
Obs	id	_NAME_	week1	week2	week3	week4
1	S001	weight	231.0	223.0	.	.
2	S001	bmi	29.7	28.6	.	.
3	S002	weight	187.0	.	176.0	.
4	S002	bmi	28.4	.	26.8	.
5	S003	weight	154.0	151.0	148.0	142.0
6	S003	bmi	27.3	26.7	26.2	25.2
7	S004	weight	134.0	133.0	.	129.0
8	S004	bmi	25.3	25.1	.	24.4

Output 8.12c shows intermediate data set TRANSSESSION.

Output 8.12c
TRANSSESSION
Data Set

		TRANSSESSION			
Obs	id	session_ week1	session_ week2	session_ week3	session_ week4
1	S001	AM1	AM2		
2	S002	AM1		AM2	
3	S003	PM1	AM1	PM1	PM1
4	S004	PM3	PM3		PM3

Transpose data set WEIGHT_BMI. Save the transposed observations in TRANSWTBMI.
Specify a prefix to use in constructing names for transposed variables in the output data set.
Create one observation per BY value for each variable that is transposed.
Transpose two variables.
Specify that the values of WEEK name the transposed variables in TRANSWTBMI.

```
proc transpose data=weight_bmi out=transwtbmi


                      prefix=week;

  by id;

  var weight bmi;
  id week;

run;
```

Transpose the character variable. Save the transposed data in TRANSSESSION. Specify a different PREFIX= value than in the previous PROC TRANSPOSE step.

```
proc transpose data=weight_bmi out=transsession
                 prefix=session_week;
  by id;
  var session;
  id week;
run;
```

Create data set WTRESULTS. Merge data set TRANSWTBMI with itself and with TRANSSESSION. On the first placement of TRANSWTBMI, select observations where the uppercased value of _NAME_ is "WEIGHT" and rename the four WEEK variables to reflect the source of the four values.

```
data wtresults;
  merge transwtbmi(where=(upcase(_name_)='WEIGHT')
               rename=(week1=wt_week1 week2=wt_week2
                       week3=wt_week3
                       week4=wt_week4))
```

**Select observations where the
uppercased value of _NAME_ is
"BMI" and rename the four WEEK
variables to reflect the source of the
four values.**

```
             transwtbmi(where=(upcase(_name_)='BMI')
                   rename=(week1=bmi_week1
                           week2=bmi_week2
                           week3=bmi_week3
                           week4=bmi_week4))

        transsession;
```

Match-merge the three data sets.

```
    by id;
```

**Drop variable _NAME_ since it is no
longer needed to identify the source of
any of the variable values.**

```
  drop _name_;

run;
```

Example 8.13 Obtaining the Previous Value of a Variable within a BY Group

Goal

Create variables that have the values of a variable from previous observations. Process the data set in BY groups so that the process of obtaining lagged values starts over with each new BY group.

This example uses the same input data set as Example 8.14.

Example Features

Featured Step	DATA step
Featured Step Options and Statements	LAG*n* function
Related Technique	DATA step, BY and RETAIN statements, FIRST. and LAST. automatic variables
A Closer Look	More on the DATA Step in This Example

Input Data Set

Data set PRODUCTION records the number of units of an item made on several days at four plant locations.

PRODUCTION

Obs	plant	proddate	units_ made
1	Aux Plant	03/02/2009	76
2	Main Plant	02/27/2009	393
3	Main Plant	03/03/2009	501
4	Main Plant	03/04/2009	492
5	Main Plant	03/05/2009	719
6	Main Plant	03/06/2009	111
7	Main Plant	03/09/2009	268
8	Main Plant	03/10/2009	350
9	Port Park	02/20/2009	791
10	Port Park	02/27/2009	658
11	Port Park	03/10/2009	981
12	Port Park	03/11/2009	612
13	Port Park	03/13/2009	664
14	West Side	02/23/2009	629
15	West Side	02/24/2009	543

Resulting Data Set
Output 8.13
PRODLAST3
Data Set

			Example 8.13 PRODLAST3 Data Set Created with DATA Step					
Obs	plant	proddate	units_ made	too_few_ days	run_avg_ units	units_ made1	units_ made2	units_ made3
1	Aux Plant	03/02/2009	76	***	76	.	.	.
2	Main Plant	03/05/2009	719		526	492	501	393
3	Main Plant	03/06/2009	111		456	719	492	501
4	Main Plant	03/09/2009	268		398	111	719	492
5	Main Plant	03/10/2009	350		362	268	111	719
6	Port Park	03/11/2009	612		761	981	658	791
7	Port Park	03/13/2009	664		729	612	981	658
8	West Side	02/24/2009	543	***	586	629	.	.

Example Overview

This DATA step uses the LAG*n* function in conjunction with BY-group processing to obtain lagged values for a variable within each BY group. The goal of the program is for each observation read, find variable values in the three observations previous to it within the BY group. The DATA step includes code to handle the situation when a BY group does not have sufficient observations to look back three observations.

Data set PRODUCTION records the number of units of an item made on several days at four plant locations. One plant has only one production day, one has two production days, one has four production days, and the fourth has seven production days.

The goal of the DATA step is to find the three most recent production counts in the plant for the observation that is currently being processed. Variable UNITS_MADE stores the counts. Prior to the DATA step, PRODUCTION is sorted by PLANT, and within each value of PLANT, observations are sorted by PRODDATE. This sort arranges the observations in chronological order within each value of PLANT so that the lagged values are obtained in reverse chronological order: UNITS_MADE1 is the lagged value of UNITS_MADE for the most recent previous observation; UNITS_MADE2 is the lagged value of UNITS_MADE for the second most recent previous observation; and UNITS_MADE3 is the lagged value of UNITS_MADE for the third most recent previous observation.

Because it is required that the program must retrieve previous values within the BY group, the DATA step includes code to reset the variables that retain the lagged values at the beginning of each BY group. If you did not reset the lag variables at the beginning of the BY group, you would end up obtaining lagged values from a different BY group.

The program writes out observations under one of two conditions:

❑ For BY groups with four or more production dates, all observations starting with the fourth production date. These observations will have values for all three lagged value variables (UNITS_MADE1, UNITS_MADE2, and UNITS_MADE3).

❑ For BY groups with fewer than four production dates, one observation with as many lagged values as available. This corresponds to the last observation in the BY group.

The DATA step also computes an average of the current value of UNITS_MADE and the three lagged values. When a BY group has fewer than four production dates, the average is computed and variable TOO_FEW_DAYS is assigned a value of "***" to flag observations that do not have the full four days of production values to evaluate.

For a description of the processing of this DATA step, see the following "A Closer Look" section and Table 8.2.

Program

Create data set PRODLAST3.
Read the observations from data set PRODUCTION.
Process the data in BY groups.

Define new variable TOO_FEW_DAYS to flag observations with fewer than four production values to evaluate.

Define an array of the three lagged value variables.
Obtain the three lagged values of UNITS_MADE for the current observation.
When the first observation in each BY group is processed, reset COUNT to 1.
Accumulator variable COUNT is used by the following DO loop to set appropriate elements of array UNITS to

```
data prodlast3;
  set production;

  by plant;
  drop count i;
  length too_few_days $ 3;


  format run_avg_units 5.;
  array units{3} units_made1-units_made3;

  units_made1=lag1(units_made);
  units_made2=lag2(units_made);
  units_made3=lag3(units_made);

  if first.plant then count=1;
```

missing.

On each iteration of the DO loop, set to missing the array elements that have not yet received a lagged value for the current BY group. This action prevents the observation from having values from previous BY groups.

```
do i=count to dim(units);
  units{i}=.;
end;
```

Execute this DO group when processing at least the fourth observation in a BY group of at least four observations, or when processing the last observation in a BY group of fewer than four observations.

```
if count ge 4 or (last.plant and count lt 4) then do;
```

Compute the running average of the current value of UNITS_MADE and the three lagged values of UNITS_MADE.

```
  run_avg_units=mean(units_made, units_made1,
                     units_made2, units_made3);
```

Flag observations from BY groups that have fewer than four observations in the BY group.

```
  if n(units_made, units_made, units_made2,
     units_made3) lt 4 then too_few_days='***';
```

Output the observations that are processed by the IF-THEN-DO group.

```
  output;
```

```
end;
count+1;
```

Increase COUNT by 1 so that on the next iteration of the DATA step, if it is still the same BY group, the appropriate elements of UNITS will be set to missing when the DO loop executes.

```
run;
```

Related Technique

The following DATA step creates a data set equivalent to the one that was created by the DATA step in the main example. Instead of using the LAG*n* function, this DATA step simulates the action of the LAG*n* function by retaining the values of the three lagged variables—UNITS_MADE1, UNITS_MADE2, and UNITS_MADE3—across iterations of the DATA step. The variables' names are listed in a RETAIN statement.

Prior to the DATA step, PRODUCTION is sorted by PLANT, and within each value of PLANT, observations are sorted by PRODDATE. This sort arranges the observations in chronological order within each value of PLANT so that the lagged values are obtained in reverse chronological order as they are in the DATA step in the main example.

An IF-THEN-DO block executes when processing the first observation in a BY group. The statement in the DO loop inside the block initializes the three lagged variables to missing at the beginning of each BY group. Another statement in the block initializes the variable COUNT to 1. The use of variable COUNT in this DATA step is similar to its use in the DATA step in the main example.

A DO loop near the end of the DATA step shifts the values of UNITS_MADE and the three lagged variables down one element in the UNITS array.

As in the main example, this DATA step computes a running average of the UNITS_MADE series of variables, and it assigns a value to TOO_FEW_DAYS when there are fewer than four observations in a BY group. This DATA step also writes out observations under the same two conditions as the main DATA step.

Neither of the two DATA steps that are presented in this example has a distinct advantage over the other.

Create data set PRODLAST3.	`data prodlast3;`
Read the observations from data set	`  set production;`
PRODUCTION.	
Process the data in BY groups that are	`by plant;`
defined by the values of PLANT.	
	`drop count i;`
	`length too_few_days $ 3;`
	`format run_avg_units 5.;`
Define an array of UNITS_MADE and	`array units{4} units_made units_made1-units_made3;`
the three retained variables.	
Specify the three variables whose	`retain units_made1-units_made3;`
values should be retained across	
iterations of the DATA step.	
At the beginning of each BY group,	`if first.plant then do;`
initialize the variables whose values	`  do i=2 to 4;`
contain the lagged values of	`    units{i}=.;`
UNITS_MADE. Initialize COUNT to	`  end;`
indicate the first observation in the BY	`  count=1;`
group.	`end;`
Execute this DO group when	`if (1 le count lt 4) and last.plant then do;`
processing the first three observations	
in a BY group and one of them is the	
last observation in the BY group.	
Flag observations from BY groups that	`  too_few_days='***';`
have fewer than four observations in	
the BY group.	
Compute the running average of	`  run_avg_units=mean(units_made, units_made1,`
UNITS_MADE and the three lagged	`                   units_made2, units_made3);`
values of UNITS_MADE.	
Output the observations that are	`  output;`
processed by the IF-THEN-DO block.	
	`end;`
Execute this block when processing the	`else if count ge 4 then do;`
fourth or greater observation in a BY	
group.	
	`  run_avg_units=mean(units_made, units_made1,`
	`                   units_made2, units_made3);`
Output the observations that are	`  output;`
processed by the ELSE-THEN-DO	
block.	
	`end;`
Increase COUNT by 1 to track the	`count+1;`
position of the next observation in the	
BY group.	
	`run;`

A Closer Look

More on the DATA Step in This Example

Each call to the LAG*n* function stores a value in a queue and returns a value that was stored previously in that queue. Each occurrence of a LAG*n* function in a DATA step generates its own queue of values. The DATA step in the main example has three assignment statements that each invoke a different LAG*n* function: LAG1, LAG2, and LAG3. Therefore, this DATA step creates three queues of values that are independent of each other.

The DATA step invokes the LAG*n* functions on each iteration of the DATA step, even if the LAG*n* function retrieves values from a different BY group. Conditionally invoking the LAG*n* functions based on BY values would not produce the required data set. This is because storing values at the bottom of the LAG*n* queue and returning values from the top of the queue occurs *only* when the LAG*n* function executes. Conditional calls to

LAG*n* would store and return values only from the observations for which the condition is satisfied.

Table 8.2 shows the values of selected variables at two places in the DATA step during execution. The "Top" position is immediately after the first IF statement executes. This is the IF statement that assigns a value to COUNT at the beginning of a BY group. The "Bottom" position is at the end of the DATA step following the COUNT+1 statement. The eight highlighted rows are the observations that the DATA step writes to data set PRODLAST3.

Table 8.2 Variable Values at Different Places during the Processing of the DATA Step in This Example

DATA Step Position	_N_	LAST. PLANT	PLANT	PRODDATE	UNITS_ MADE	UNITS_ MADE1	UNITS_ MADE2	UNITS_ MADE3	COUNT
Top	1	1	Aux Plant	03/02/2009	76	.	.	.	1
Bottom	1	1	Aux Plant	03/02/2009	76	.	.	.	1
Top	2	0	Main Plant	02/27/2009	393	76	.	.	1
Bottom	2	0	Main Plant	02/27/2009	393	.	.	.	2
Top	3	0	Main Plant	03/03/2009	501	393	.	.	2
Bottom	3	0	Main Plant	03/03/2009	501	.	.	.	3
Top	4	0	Main Plant	03/04/2009	492	501	393	.	3
Bottom	4	0	Main Plant	03/04/2009	492	501	393	.	4
Top	5	0	Main Plant	03/05/2009	719	492	501	393	4
Bottom	5	0	Main Plant	03/05/2009	719	492	501	393	5
Top	6	0	Main Plant	03/06/2009	111	719	492	501	5
Bottom	6	0	Main Plant	03/06/2009	111	719	492	501	6
Top	7	0	Main Plant	03/09/2009	268	111	719	492	6
Bottom	7	0	Main Plant	03/09/2009	268	111	719	492	7
Top	8	1	Main Plant	03/10/2009	350	268	111	719	7
Bottom	8	1	Main Plant	03/10/2009	350	268	111	719	8
Top	9	0	Port Park	02/20/2009	791	350	268	111	1
Bottom	9	0	Port Park	02/20/2009	791	.	.	.	2
Top	10	0	Port Park	02/27/2009	658	791	350	268	2
Bottom	10	0	Port Park	02/27/2009	658	791	.	.	3
Top	11	0	Port Park	03/10/2009	981	658	791	350	3
Bottom	11	0	Port Park	03/10/2009	981	658	791	.	4
Top	12	0	Port Park	03/11/2009	612	981	658	791	4
Bottom	12	0	Port Park	03/11/2009	612	981	658	791	5
Top	13	1	Port Park	03/13/2009	664	612	981	658	5
Bottom	13	1	Port Park	03/13/2009	664	612	981	658	6
Top	14	0	West Side	02/23/2009	629	664	612	981	1
Bottom	14	0	West Side	02/23/2009	629	.	.	.	2
Top	15	1	West Side	02/24/2009	543	629	.	.	2
Bottom	15	1	West Side	02/24/2009	543	629	.	.	3

Example 8.14 Comparing the Value of a Variable to Its Value in the Next Observation

Goal

Within the same data set, look ahead from a variable value in one observation to return the value of the same variable in the observation that immediately follows it. Then compare the returned value with the current observation or use it in a calculation on the current observation.

This example uses the same input data set as Example 8.13.

Example Features

Featured Step	DATA step
Featured Step Options and Statements	MERGE statement, FIRSTOBS= data set option

Input Data Set

Data set PRODUCTION records the number of units of an item made on several days at four plant locations.

PRODUCTION

Obs	plant	proddate	units_ made
1	Aux Plant	03/02/2009	76
2	Main Plant	02/27/2009	393
3	Main Plant	03/03/2009	501
4	Main Plant	03/04/2009	492
5	Main Plant	03/05/2009	719
6	Main Plant	03/06/2009	111
7	Main Plant	03/09/2009	268
8	Main Plant	03/10/2009	350
9	Port Park	02/20/2009	791
10	Port Park	02/27/2009	658
11	Port Park	03/10/2009	981
12	Port Park	03/11/2009	612
13	Port Park	03/13/2009	664
14	West Side	02/23/2009	629
15	West Side	02/24/2009	543

Resulting Data Set
Output 8.14
PRODNEXT Data Set

Example 8.14 PRODNEXT Data Set Created with DATA Step

Obs	plant	proddate	units_ made	next_ proddate	next_ units_ made	days_ btwn
1	Aux Plant	03/02/2009	76	.	.	.
2	Main Plant	02/27/2009	393	03/03/2009	501	4
3	Main Plant	03/03/2009	501	03/04/2009	492	1
4	Main Plant	03/04/2009	492	03/05/2009	719	1
5	Main Plant	03/05/2009	719	03/06/2009	111	1
6	Main Plant	03/06/2009	111	03/09/2009	268	3
7	Main Plant	03/09/2009	268	03/10/2009	350	1
8	Main Plant	03/10/2009	350	.	.	.
9	Port Park	02/20/2009	791	02/27/2009	658	7
10	Port Park	02/27/2009	658	03/10/2009	981	11
11	Port Park	03/10/2009	981	03/11/2009	612	1
12	Port Park	03/11/2009	612	03/13/2009	664	2
13	Port Park	03/13/2009	664	.	.	.
14	West Side	02/23/2009	629	02/24/2009	543	1
15	West Side	02/24/2009	543	.	.	.

Example Overview

This example demonstrates how you can perform a one-to-one merge of a data set with itself. This technique staggers the alignment of the observations so that you can look ahead from the observation that is currently being processed to the next one within the same data set.

Data set PRODUCTION records the number of units of an item made on several days at four plant locations. One plant has only one production day, one has two production days, one has four production days, and the fourth has seven production days.

The goal of the program is to examine each plant's production schedule and align in one observation one day's production information with the information from the next production date.

Prior to the DATA step, PRODUCTION is sorted by PLANT, and within each value of PLANT, observations are sorted by PRODDATE. This sort arranges the observations in chronological order within each value of PLANT so that the look-ahead values are obtained in chronological order.

To accomplish the one-to-one merge of the data set with itself, the data set name is specified twice in the MERGE statement. The FIRSTOBS= data set option is assigned to the second data set with a value of 2. This means that the first observation that was contributed from the first reference to data set PRODUCTION is lined up with the second observation from the second reference to data set PRODUCTION. This action achieves the look-ahead to the next observation.

The merge of the data set with itself is not a match-merge. Therefore, the data set is not processed in BY groups and a BY statement is omitted.

The second reference to data set PRODUCTION renames the variables. Renaming the variables in common prevents the look-ahead values from overwriting the values read from the first reference. Code in the DATA step checks to see whether the next observation has a value of PLANT different from the value in the observation that is currently being processed. If the value is different, the renamed variables from the second reference to the data set are set to missing.

The DATA step computes a new variable, DAYS_BTWN, which is the number of days between the production date (PRODDATE) in the observation that is currently being processed and the production date (NEXT_PRODDATE) for the next observation.

Program

Sort data set PRODUCTION so that the observations are in chronological order within each plant location.
Create data set PRODNEXT.
Merge data set PRODUCTION with itself. Start reading the second reference to PRODUCTION with the second observation.

Rename the variables in common that are contributed from the second reference to PRODUCTION to prevent overwriting the values that are read from the first reference.

Process this DO group when the merge aligns observations from different plants.
Set the values of the variables that are contributed from the second reference to missing because they pertain to a different plant.
When the merge aligns observations from the same plant, compute DAYS_BTWN, which is the number of days between production at the plant.

```
proc sort data=production;
  by plant proddate;
run;
data prodnext;
  merge production
        production(firstobs=2

                        rename=(plant=plant_next
                                proddate=next_proddate
                                units_made=next_units_made));

  drop plant_next;
  if plant ne plant_next then do;

    plant_next=' ';
    next_proddate=.;
    next_units_made=.;
  end;
  else days_btwn=next_proddate-proddate;

run;
```

Example 8.15   Applying the Same Operation to a Group of Variables

Goal

Apply operations to selected numeric and character variables in a data set by using arrays without explicitly listing all the variables' names.

Example Features

Featured Step	DATA step
Featured Step Options and Statements	ARRAY statement, _NUMERIC_ and _CHARACTER_ lists

Input Data Set

Data set GLUCOSE records several glucose measurements at different times for four patients. The data set has allocated four variables to hold the evaluations of the four glucose results. When this data set is created, the evaluations are not completed and are coded with question marks (?).

```
                                            GLUCOSE

      patient_  glucose_  eval_  glucose_           glucose_           glucose_
Obs     id       fast     fast     1hr    eval_1hr    2hr    eval_2hr    4hr    eval_4hr
 1    ARD123      101       ?       135       ?        98       ?         .        ?
 2    DKJ891       75       ?        88       ?       103       ?        79        ?
 3    EWP006        .       ?         .       ?         .       ?         .        ?
 4    TAB234       79       ?        94       ?       126       ?       133        ?
```

Resulting Data Set
Output 8.15
EVAL_GLUCOSE Data Set

```
              Example 8.15 EVAL_GLUCOSE Data Set Created with DATA Step

        patient_  glucose_  result_  glucose_  result_  glucose_  result_  glucose_  result_
Obs       id       fast     fast      1hr       1hr       2hr      2hr       4hr      4hr

 1      ARD123      101       P        135       H         98       N         .        -
 2      DKJ891       75       N         88       N        103       P        79        N
 3      EWP006        .       -          .       -          .       -         .        -
 4      TAB234       79       N         94       N        126       H       133        H
```

Example Overview

This DATA step shows how you can specify lists of variables according to type by using the _NUMERIC_ and _CHARACTER_ keywords.

The DATA step evaluates data set GLUCOSE, which contains four glucose results for four patients. The results are saved in numeric variables. The evaluations are saved in character variables. The ordering of the variables is such that each result is followed by its evaluation. Because of this structure and because an array must have variables of only one type, you cannot specify the array elements by writing beginning and ending variables separated with double dashes (e.g., A- - B). Additionally, the variables that store the results and evaluations do not end in sequential numeric suffixes so you cannot list the elements with the beginning and ending elements separated with a single dash (e.g., X1-X12).

The DATA step defines two arrays: numeric array GLUCOSE with the results and character array EVALS with the evaluations. The only numeric variables in the data set are the results so the list in the ARRAY statement can be specified simply with the _NUMERIC_ keyword. Variable PATIENT_ID is a character variable so you cannot specify the list of array elements for EVALS with just the _CHARACTER_ keyword. Instead you can specify the beginning and ending elements of the array and separate them with the _CHARACTER_ keyword. This structure indicates that the elements of the array are all the character variables inclusively between the beginning and ending elements.

You must know the order in which your variables are saved in the Program Data Vector (PDV) when specifying a list of variables that includes either the _NUMERIC_ or _CHARACTER_ keyword. You must also know the characteristics of all the numeric or character variables if you use just the _NUMERIC_ or _CHARACTER_ keyword. Without understanding the structure and contents of your data set, you could inadvertently modify variable values when you use these keywords. Run PROC CONTENTS or PROC DATASETS to examine your data set.

See also the "A Closer Look" section "Specifying Variable Lists" in Example 9.3 for more applications of the _CHARACTER_ and _NUMERIC_ keywords.

Program

Create data set EVAL_GLUCOSE.
Read the observations from data set GLUCOSE.
Define the array of numeric variables. Because the only numeric variables in GLUCOSE are the ones that belong in the ARRAY statement, use the _NUMERIC_ keyword to specify them.
Define the array of character variables. Because PATIENT_ID is a character variable, do not write the list as "_CHARACTER_". Instead specify the list of EVALS elements with the beginning and ending evaluation variables separated with the CHARACTER keyword.

Assign an evaluation code to each glucose result.

```
data eval_glucose;
  set glucose;

  array glucose{*} _numeric_;




  array evals{*} eval_fast-character-eval_4hr;









  drop i;
  do i=1 to dim(glucose);
    if glucose{i}=. then eval{i}='-';
    else if glucose{i} lt 100 then eval{i}='N';
    else if 100 le glucose{i} le 125 then eval{i}='P';
    else if glucose{i} gt 125 then eval{i}='H';
  end;
run;
```

Example 8.16 Obtaining Hierarchical Data from a Table and Matching Them to the Rows in the Same Table

Goal

Identify hierarchically related rows in a table. For each group of hierarchically related rows, extract data from the row that is at the higher level of the hierarchy and join these values to all rows in the group.

Example Features

Featured Step	PROC SQL
Featured Step Options and Statements	Self-join, WHERE clause
Related Technique	DATA step, match-merging a data set with itself

Input Table

Table PERSONS records survey information about persons in households. It has data for four households. The respondent to the survey has a value of "reference" for column RELATIONSHIP. These rows are considered at the higher level of the hierarchy within each household's set of rows.

PERSONS

Obs	household	person	relationship	gender	dob	education	work_status
1	1001	1	reference	F	09/13/1972	AA	PT
2	1001	2	spouse	M	10/25/1970	MS	FT
3	1001	3	child	F	02/12/2002	00	NA
4	1001	4	child	F	02/12/2002	00	NA
5	1001	5	child	M	06/21/2005	00	NA
6	1011	1	reference	F	07/12/1985	BA	FT
7	1012	1	reference	F	01/30/1946	HS	RT
8	1012	2	spouse	M	02/04/1940	HS	RT
9	1012	3	other relative	F	12/22/1921	BA	RT
10	1015	1	reference	M	06/28/1990	HS	SC
11	1015	2	other	M	05/25/1990	HS	SC
12	1015	3	other	M	07/16/1989	HS	SC
13	1015	4	other	M	11/02/1988	BS	SC

Resulting Table
Output 8.16
FAMILY_SURVEY Table

Example 8.16 FAMILY_SURVEY Table Created with PROC SQL

Obs	household	person	relationship	gender	dob	education	work_status	age	reference_educ	reference_work	reference_gender	reference_age
1	1001	1	reference	F	09/13/1972	AA	PT	36	AA	PT	F	36
2	1001	2	spouse	M	10/25/1970	MS	FT	38	AA	PT	F	36
3	1001	3	child	F	02/12/2002	00	NA	7	AA	PT	F	36
4	1001	4	child	F	02/12/2002	00	NA	7	AA	PT	F	36
5	1001	5	child	M	06/21/2005	00	NA	3	AA	PT	F	36
6	1011	1	reference	F	07/12/1985	BA	FT	23	BA	FT	F	23
7	1012	1	reference	F	01/30/1946	HS	RT	63	HS	RT	F	63
8	1012	2	spouse	M	02/04/1940	HS	RT	69	HS	RT	F	63
9	1012	3	other relative	F	12/22/1921	BA	RT	87	HS	RT	F	63
10	1015	1	reference	M	06/28/1990	HS	SC	18	HS	SC	M	18
11	1015	2	other	M	05/25/1990	HS	SC	19	HS	SC	M	18
12	1015	3	other	M	07/16/1989	HS	SC	19	HS	SC	M	18
13	1015	4	other	M	11/02/1988	BS	SC	20	HS	SC	M	18

Example Overview

This example shows how to extract hierarchically related data from a table and join them back to rows in the same table by a matching column.

The table in this example has two levels of hierarchy. Table PERSONS records survey information about the members of a household with one person in the household serving as the reference person. This person's information is considered to be at the higher level of the hierarchy. Column RELATIONSHIP identifies the roles of the members of the household.

The goal of the program is to extract the reference person's information and join it to each row in the reference person's household.

The PROC SQL step performs a self-join, also called a reflexive join. It lists table PERSONS twice on the FROM clause. A different alias, P or REF, is assigned to each reference to PERSONS.

The SELECT clause specifies the columns to retrieve from the join. It assigns new column names to the columns that are retrieved from the second reference to PERSONS so that PROC SQL does not overwrite the person's unique values. It also computes the age of each person in the household and the age of the reference person. The age of the reference person is computed using the reference person's value of DOB. The new column's value is the same for all rows within a household.

A WHERE clause joins table PERSONS to itself by values of column FAMILY, and it selects rows only from the second reference to PERSONS where the value of RELATIONSHIP is "reference".

Note that the code does not check if a household is missing a row for the reference person. When adapting the code for your use, you might need to add code for situations of missing data.

Program

Create table HOUSEHOLD_SURVEY.
Select all columns from the first reference to PERSONS, as specified by alias P.
Compute the age of each member in the household. Use the formula that is discussed in Example 9.13.
Retrieve values for three columns from the second reference to PERSONS, as specified by alias REF. Specify new names for the columns so that their values do not replace the same-named columns that were retrieved from the first reference to PERSONS.
Using the date of birth for the reference person, which is retrieved from the second reference to PERSONS, compute the age of the reference person so that this constant value within the household is added to each row.
Specify a self-join of table PERSONS. Assign an alias to each reference to table PERSONS.
Join the rows by the values of HOUSEHOLD. Select from the second reference to PERSONS only the rows for the household member at the higher level in the hierarchy.
Order the rows in table HOUSEHOLD_SURVEY.

```
proc sql;
  create table household_survey as
    select p.*,


          floor((intck('month',p.dob,'15jun2010'd) -
          (day('15jun2010'd) < day(p.dob)))/12) as age,


          ref.education as reference_educ,
          ref.work_status as reference_work,
          ref.gender as reference_gender,




          floor((intck('month',ref.dob,'15jun2010'd) -
            (day('15jun2010'd) < day(ref.dob)))/12) as
                        reference_age



      from persons p, persons ref


      where p.household=ref.household and
            ref.relationship='reference'



      order by p.household,p.person;
  quit;
```

Related Technique

The DATA step that follows creates a data set equivalent to the table that was produced by PROC SQL in the main example. It merges data set PERSONS with itself by the values of HOUSEHOLD. The second reference to PERSONS in the MERGE statement specifies that only rows where the value of RELATIONSHIP is "reference" be merged to the observations that were retrieved by the first reference to PERSONS. It also renames several variables so that the values from the second reference do not overwrite the unique values for each person in the household that were retrieved by the first reference to PERSONS.

There can be multiple observations per value of HOUSEHOLD in the data set. At the beginning of each BY group, the second reference to PERSONS in the MERGE statement causes the DATA step to load into the Program Data Vector (PDV) the single observation in PERSONS that corresponds to the reference person. The values of the variables that are contributed from the second reference to PERSONS remain in the PDV throughout the remainder of processing for the BY group. These values for the person higher in the hierarchy are output with each observation in the BY group.

For a description of how SAS retains a variable value across iterations of a DATA step, see "Understanding How the DATA Step Adds Values from an Observation in One Data Set to All Observations in Another" in Example 5.1 in the "A Closer Look" section.

Assume prior to the DATA step, data set PERSONS is sorted by HOUSEHOLD, and within the values of HOUSEHOLD, by the values of PERSON. It is necessary to sort or index PERSONS by HOUSEHOLD so that the match-merging can be performed. Additionally, sorting by PERSON causes the observations to be in the same order as the rows in the table that was created by PROC SQL in the main example.

Create data set
HOUSEHOLD_SURVEY.
Merge PERSONS with itself. From the second reference to PERSONS, select only the rows for the reference person. Rename variables that were extracted from the second reference to PERSONS so that they do not overwrite the unique values for each person as extracted from the first reference to PERSONS.
Drop this unneeded variable so that its values do not replace the values that were extracted from the first reference to PERSONS.
Match data set PERSONS to itself by the values of HOUSEHOLD.

Compute the age of each member in the household.
Using the date of birth for the reference person, which is retrieved from the second reference to PERSONS, compute the age of the reference person so that this constant value within the household is added to each observation.

```
data household_survey;

   merge persons
         persons(where=(relationship='reference')

                 rename=(education=reference_educ
                         work_status=reference_work
                         dob=reference_dob
                         gender=reference_gender)


                 drop=person);



   by household;

drop reference_dob;
age=floor((intck('month',dob,'15jun2010'd) -
       (day('15jun2010'd) < day(dob)))/12);
reference_age= floor(
       (intck('month',reference_dob,'15jun2010'd) -
       (day('15jun2010'd) <  day(reference_dob)))/12);

run;
```

Example 8.17   Combining Generation Data Sets

Goal

Concatenate specific data sets in a generation group of data sets.

Example Features

Featured Step	PROC APPEND DATA step PROC SQL
Featured Step Options and Statements	GENNUM= option

Input Data Sets

A library system maintains daily circulation records for the main library. The system maintains copies of the daily records for three days. It adds the daily records to a monthly data set daily after closing.

Assume the display of data set CITYLIB. MAINLIB_DAILY was produced after the library closed on March 8, 2010. Two versions back correspond to March 6, 2010. The first list shows the observations in the daily data set for March 6, 2010. The second list shows the observations in the daily data set for March 7, 2010. The third list shows the observations in the daily data set for March 8, 2010.

The daily data sets have the same variables. Each daily data set has 14 observations, one for each category of material circulated. These categories are maintained in all data sets. The monthly data set has an observation for each category on each day in the month.

```
             CITYLIB.MAINLIB_DAILY  (GENNUM=-2)

Obs    circdate  type                 adult  juvenile  youngpeople
  1  03/06/2010  Audiocassettes          16       7           5
  2  03/06/2010  CompactDiscs           111      78          11
  3  03/06/2010  HardcoverFiction        31       4           1
  4  03/06/2010  HardcoverNonfiction    236      87          18
  5  03/06/2010  LargeTypeFiction        10       0           0
  6  03/06/2010  LargeTypeNonfiction     16       0           0
  7  03/06/2010  PaperbackFiction       213     159         134
  8  03/06/2010  PaperbackNonfiction     44      24          15
  9  03/06/2010  PeriodicalsLargeType     0       0           0
 10  03/06/2010  Periodicals            161      33           5
 11  03/06/2010  AudioBooksFiction       40      21           3
 12  03/06/2010  AudioBooksNonfiction    43       4           4
 13  03/06/2010  DVDFiction               6       3          12
 14  03/06/2010  DVDNonfiction           51       6           1


             CITYLIB.MAINLIB_DAILY  (GENNUM=-1)

Obs    circdate  type                 adult  juvenile  youngpeople
  1  03/07/2010  Audiocassettes          20       7           5
  2  03/07/2010  CompactDiscs           117      81          11
  3  03/07/2010  HardcoverFiction        28       6           2
  4  03/07/2010  HardcoverNonfiction    216      76          18
  5  03/07/2010  LargeTypeFiction        11       0           0
  6  03/07/2010  LargeTypeNonfiction     15       0           0
  7  03/07/2010  PaperbackFiction       216     166         140
  8  03/07/2010  PaperbackNonfiction     47      33          14
  9  03/07/2010  PeriodicalsLargeType     0       0           0
 10  03/07/2010  Periodicals            178      35           6
 11  03/07/2010  AudioBooksFiction       40      22           3
 12  03/07/2010  AudioBooksNonfiction    44       4           3
 13  03/07/2010  DVDFiction              16      15           8
 14  03/07/2010  DVDNonfiction           52       6           1


             CITYLIB.MAINLIB_DAILY  (GENNUM=0)

Obs    circdate  type                 adult  juvenile  youngpeople
  1  03/08/2010  Audiocassettes          18       7           5
  2  03/08/2010  CompactDiscs           110      72          10
  3  03/08/2010  HardcoverFiction        35       3           2
  4  03/08/2010  HardcoverNonfiction    206      86          17
  5  03/08/2010  LargeTypeFiction        11       0           0
  6  03/08/2010  LargeTypeNonfiction     16       0           0
  7  03/08/2010  PaperbackFiction       231     162         142
  8  03/08/2010  PaperbackNonfiction     41      34          12
  9  03/08/2010  PeriodicalsLargeType     0       0           0
 10  03/08/2010  Periodicals            177      35           5
 11  03/08/2010  AudioBooksFiction       44      19           3
 12  03/08/2010  AudioBooksNonfiction    39       4           3
 13  03/08/2010  DVDFiction              13      13           6
 14  03/08/2010  DVDNonfiction           55       6           1
```

SAS Log
Output 8.17
**SAS Log with PROC
DATASETS Report
Produced after
Library Closing
March 8, 2010**

```
1001   proc datasets library=cmds;
                               Directory

                   Libref          CITYLIB
                   Engine          V9
                   Physical Name   q:\citylib\circulation\datasets
                   File Name       q: \citylib\circulation\datasets


                          Gen  Member    File
       #  Name            Num  Type      Size  Last Modified

       1  MAINLIB_2010         DATA     46080  01Mar10:02:03:50
       2  MAINLIB_2010      1  DATA     46080  01Feb10:01:49:40
       3  MAINLIB_DAILY        DATA      9216  08Mar10:21:43:52
       4  MAINLIB_DAILY     65  DATA      9216  06Mar10:21:59:03
       5  MAINLIB_DAILY     66  DATA      9216  07Mar10:21:13:25
       6  MAINLIB_FEB2010      DATA     25600  28Feb10:23:04:52
       7  MAINLIB_FEB2010   21  DATA     25600  22Feb10:23:18:11
       8  MAINLIB_FEB2010   22  DATA     25600  23Feb10:23:59:25
       9  MAINLIB_FEB2010   23  DATA     25600  24Feb10:23:43:52
      10  MAINLIB_FEB2010   24  DATA     25600  25Feb10:23:31:10
      11  MAINLIB_FEB2010   25  DATA     25600  26Feb10:23:29:04
      12  MAINLIB_FEB2010   26  DATA     25600  27Feb10:23:21:27
      13  MAINLIB_JAN2010      DATA     25600  31Jan10:23:10:19
      14  MAINLIB_JAN2010   24  DATA     25600  25Jan10:23:14:55
      15  MAINLIB_JAN2010   25  DATA     25600  26Jan10:23:26:46
      16  MAINLIB_JAN2010   26  DATA     25600  27Jan10:23:52:33
      17  MAINLIB_JAN2010   27  DATA     25600  28Jan10:23:49:24
      18  MAINLIB_JAN2010   28  DATA     25600  29Jan10:23:43:08
      19  MAINLIB_JAN2010   29  DATA     25600  30Jan10:23:43:12
      20  MAINLIB_MAR2010      DATA     13312  09Mar10:23:51:24
      21  MAINLIB_MAR2010    2  DATA      9216  03Mar10:23:23:19
      22  MAINLIB_MAR2010    3  DATA      9216  04Mar10:23:38:55
      23  MAINLIB_MAR2010    4  DATA      9216  05Mar10:23:21:48
      24  MAINLIB_MAR2010    5  DATA     13312  06Mar10:23:43:30
      25  MAINLIB_MAR2010    6  DATA     13312  07Mar10:23:48:26
      26  MAINLIB_MAR2010    7  DATA     13312  08Mar10:23:21:52
1002   quit;
```

Example Overview

The code in this example shows how to reference specific versions of generation data sets. Data set MAINLIB_DAILY is a generation data set that was defined to have three generations (GENMAX=3). It maintains the daily circulation records for a library.

This data set is started on January 2 of the year and is updated every day the library is open. Assume that the list of data sets in the CITYLIB library is made after closing on March 8, 2010. The base version of MAINLIB_DAILY is for that day's circulation records. The most recent historical version is for March 7, and the next most recent historical version is for March 6.

The code that follows combines the three MAINLIB_DAILY generation data sets into one data set MOSTRECENT3. It shows first how you can reference the data sets by their absolute version number, which is the version that is listed in the PROC DATASETS output in Output 8.17. Secondly, it shows how to reference the data sets by their relative version number.

The data sets are combined three ways: by PROC APPEND, by the DATA step, and by PROC SQL.

Programs

The following code samples concatenate the three data sets in the MAINLIB_DAILY generation group in chronological order. The oldest of the three data sets contains records for March 6, the second oldest contains records for March 7, and the third contains records for March 8.

The code in the left column for each code section references the data sets relatively where 0 means the current version, -1 means the next most recent version (one generation back), and -2 means the second most recent version (two generations back).

The code in the right column references the data sets by using the version number that is assigned to the data set. The version numbers can be found by referring to the list in Output 8.17.

When referencing the base version of the data set, you can omit the GENNUM= option. By default, when you omit a generation number, SAS interprets that you mean the most recent generation data set. The relative generation number for the base data set is 0 while the absolute generation number depends on how many previous versions have been created. In this example, the data for March 8th are stored in the 67th version of MAINLIB_DAILY.

The code samples in Table 8.3 use PROC APPEND to concatenate the three data sets in chronological order. It starts by deleting the output data set MOSTRECENT3 in library CITYLIB. If that data set already existed, the PROC APPEND steps would add to this existing data set.

Use PROC APPEND when you have the same variables in the group of data sets you're appending, which is the situation in this example. If you have different variables or same-named variables with different attributes, the steps might not execute as expected, and you might receive errors or warnings. For more information about restrictions in using PROC APPEND, see SAS documentation.

Table 8.3 Using PROC APPEND to Combine Generation Data Sets

```
Relative Generation Number                Absolute Generation Number
proc datasets library=citylib nolist;    proc datasets library=work nolist;
  delete mostrecent3;                       delete mostrecent3;
run;                                       run;
quit;                                      quit;
proc append base=mostrecent3             proc append base=mostrecent3
        data=citylib.mainlib_daily               data=citylib.mainlib_daily
            (gennum=-2);                             (gennum=65);
run;                                       run;
proc append base=mostrecent3             proc append base=mostrecent3
        data=citylib.mainlib_daily               data=citylib.mainlib_daily
            (gennum=-1);                             (gennum=66);
run;                                       run;
proc append base=mostrecent3             proc append base=mostrecent3
        data=citylib.mainlib_daily               data=citylib.mainlib_daily
            (gennum=0);                              (gennum=67);
run;                                       run;
```

The code samples in Table 8.4 use the DATA step to concatenate the three generation data sets in generation group MAINLIB_DAILY in chronological order.

Table 8.4 Using the DATA Step to Combine Generation Data Sets

```
Relative Generation Number                Absolute Generation Number
data mostrecent3;                         data mostrecent3;
  set citylib.mainlib_daily(gennum=-2)      set citylib.mainlib_daily(gennum=65)
      citylib.mainlib_daily(gennum=-1)          citylib.mainlib_daily(gennum=66)
      citylib.mainlib_daily(gennum=0);          citylib.mainlib_daily(gennum=67);
run;                                       run;
```

The code samples in Table 8.5 use the UNION operator in PROC SQL to combine the three generation tables in generation group MAINLIB_DAILY in chronological order.

Table 8.5 Using PROC SQL to Combine Generation Data Sets

Relative Generation Number

```
proc sql;
  create table mostrecent3 as
      select *
    from citylib.mainlib_daily (gennum=-2)
        union
      select *
    from citylib.mainlib_daily (gennum=-1)
        union
      select *
    from citylib.mainlib_daily (gennum=0);
quit;
```

Absolute Generation Number

```
proc sql;
  create table mostrecent3 as
      select *
    from citylib.mainlib_daily (gennum=65)
        union
      select *
    from citylib.mainlib_daily (gennum=66)
        union
      select *
    from citylib.mainlib_daily (gennum=67);
quit;
```

CHAPTER 9
Manipulating Data with Utilities and Functions

This chapter presents examples of programs that solve common programming tasks. They use functions and CALL routines in DATA steps and PROC SQL steps to manipulate data in single data sets.

The general topics these examples cover include the following:

❑ converting variable types from character to numeric and vice versa

❑ working dynamically with formats

❑ sorting data within an observation as opposed to across observations

❑ generating random numbers and samples

❑ computing date and time intervals

❑ working with and cleaning character data

Example 9.1 Converting Variable Types from Character to Numeric and Vice Versa

Goal

Read the value of a character variable and write its value to a numeric variable, and vice versa.

Example Features

Featured Step	DATA step
Featured Step Options and Statements	INPUT and PUT functions

Input Data Set

Data set PRELIM_RESULTS contains preliminary test results for five test takers. TESTDATE and TEST_VERSION are numeric variables. SCORE is a character variable.

```
                    PRELIM_RESULTS

                                          test_
     Obs     id      testdate    score    version
     1      3205      41509       9        40012
     2      3019      30109       20       103
     3      4310        .                  20101
     4      4817        .         0          .
     5      4182     11032009     18       251
```

Resulting Data Set
Output 9.1
RECODED_RESULTS
Data Set

```
                    Example 9.1 RECODED_RESULTS

                                            test_
          Obs     id      testdate    score  version

          1      3205   04/15/2009      9    40012
          2      3019   03/01/2009     20    10300
          3      4310        .          .    20101
          4      4817        .          0    00000
          5      4182   11/03/2009     18    25100
```

Example Overview

You cannot directly change the type of a variable from character to numeric or vice versa. One way of changing the type is to rename the variable whose type you want to change with the RENAME= option in the SET statement in a DATA step. An assignment statement that uses the INPUT or PUT function can convert the renamed variable's type and save it in a variable that has the name of the original variable.

The INPUT function can convert a character variable to numeric. The PUT function can convert a numeric variable to character.

Data set PRELIM_RESULTS contains test results for five test takers. Variable TESTDATE looks like a date, but it is not stored as a SAS date. Variable SCORE looks like a number, but it is stored as a character variable. Variable TEST_VERSION is numeric and is displayed with different widths.

The following DATA step converts the value of TESTDATE temporarily from numeric to character in order to put its value in a format that can be converted to a SAS date. It also converts SCORE from character to numeric and TEST_VERSION from numeric to character.

❑ An assignment statement converts the numeric value of TESTDATE to character with the PUT function and the Z8 format. The temporary character value of TESTDATE is padded with leading zeros. Then this character value is converted to a numeric SAS date value by applying the INPUT function and the MMDDYY8 informat.

❑ An assignment statement applies the INPUT function to convert the character value of CSCORE to numeric and save the result in SCORE. Because it is known that the maximum width of the value of CSCORE is 2, an informat of 2 is sufficient to convert the value.

❑ An assignment statement applies the PUT function to convert the numeric value of NVERSION to character. The –L modifier in the format shifts the result to the left, and the TRANSLATE function pads the value that is five bytes in length with trailing zeros. The TRANSLATE function converts blanks and periods to zeros. When the value of NVERSION is missing, the numeric missing value representation of a period is returned by the PUT function. The TRANSLATE function then converts the period to a zero.

The SET statement includes the RENAME= option that renames SCORE to CSCORE and TEST_VERSION to NVERSION. The DROP= option in the DATA statement drops variables CSCORE and NVERSION.

Program

Create data set RECODED_RESULTS. Do not keep the two variables that are the renamed versions of the input variables SCORE and TEST_VERSION.
Read data set PRELIM_RESULTS. Rename the two variables whose types need to be converted.
Define the variables with new types to prevent the DATA step from maintaining the same variable types if they were first encountered in the assignment statements.

Modify the values of TESTDATE so they can be converted to a SAS date.
Convert CSCORE from character to numeric.
Convert the numeric value of NVERSION to fill five bytes of a character value. Shift the returned character value to the left. Change blanks and periods in the returned character value to zeros.

```
data recoded_results(drop=cscore nversion);



   set prelim_results(rename=(score=cscore
                              test_version=nversion));

   length score 4 test_version $ 5;




   format testdate mmddyy10.;
   testdate=input(put(testdate,z8.),mmddyy8.);

   score=input(cscore,2.);

   test_version=translate(put(nversion,5.-l),
                          '0',' ',
                          '0','.');




run;
```

Example 9.2   Determining the Type of a Variable's Content

Goal

Determine whether a character variable's value contains numeric data, alphabetic text, missing data, or nonalphanumeric characters. Save the values that are determined to be numeric in a numeric variable.

Example Features

Featured Step	DATA step
Featured Step Options and Statements	COMPRESS, INPUT with ?? format modifier, NOTALPHA, REVERSE, STRIP, SUBSTR, and UPCASE functions
A Closer Look	Understanding Functions That Evaluate the Content of Variable Values

Input Data Set

Data set CHEMTEST contains preliminary results of 14 lab samples in character variable CHEM_PPB. The values of CHEM_PPB contain a mix of alphanumeric and other characters.

```
                  CHEMTEST

     Obs    sample    chem_ppb

      1     57175     1250.3
      2     71309     2.53E3
      3     28009     40 ppb
      4     40035     -81
      5     55128     3,900
      6     41930     ~1000
      7     21558     4?23
      8     46801     <1%
      9     18322
     10     11287     <1000
     11     37175     >5000
     12     22195     Sample lost
     13     81675     Invalid: GHK
     14     88810     N/A
```

Resulting Data Set

Output 9.2
CHEMEVAL
Data Set

```
                  Example 9.2 CHEMEVAL Data Set

     Obs    sample    chem_ppb       eval          result

      1     57175     1250.3         Numeric       1250.3
      2     71309     2.53E3         Numeric       2530.0
      3     28009     40 ppb         Numeric         40.0
      4     40035     -81            Error            .
      5     55128     3,900          Error            .
      6     41930     ~1000          Error            .
      7     21558     4?23           Error            .
      8     46801     <1%            Error            .
      9     18322                    Undefined        .
     10     11287     <1000          Below Range      .
     11     37175     >5000          Above Range      .
     12     22195     Sample lost    Text             .
     13     81675     Invalid: GHK   Text             .
     14     88810     N/A            Text             .
```

Example Overview

This example examines a character variable's values. It uses the information that is returned by several SAS functions to determine the content of a variable value. The values of the character variable are categorized based on the results that are returned by the SAS functions. The category assignments are saved in a new character variable. Values that the DATA step determines to be numeric are saved in a numeric variable.

Data set CHEMTEST contains preliminary results of 12 lab samples in character variable CHEM_PPB. The values of CHEM_PPB contain a mix of alphanumeric and other characters.

The goal of the DATA step is to examine and categorize the values of CHEM_PPB. Variable CHEM_PPB holds the chemical concentration in parts per billion of a sample. The values of CHEM_PPB vary widely from numbers to text. A series of IF statements applies several SAS functions to determine the content of CHEM_PPB. Only the values that are evaluated to be numeric are saved as numeric data in new variable RESULT. Each value of CHEM_PPB is categorized into one of the following six categories. The character category value is saved in variable EVAL:

❑ Numeric: The value of CHEM_PPB can be read in as numeric. This includes numbers that are written in exponential notation and numbers that include decimal points. It also includes values that are specified as numbers followed by the PPB label in uppercase or lowercase. Values that contain commas or negative signs are considered errors in data entry.

❑ Below range: The value of CHEM_PPB is below the lowest detectable value. The value starts with a less than sign and the remaining value can be read in as numeric.

❑ Above range: The value of CHEM_PPB is above the highest detectable value. The value starts with a greater than sign and the remaining value can be read in as numeric.

❑ Undefined: CHEM_PPB is missing.

❑ Text: The value of CHEM_PPB contains alphabetic characters and no numbers and no special characters other than blanks, or the value contains the text "N/A".

❑ Error: The value of CHEM_PPB does not fit into any of the other five categories.

Note that the CHEM_PPB value for sample 55128 was a number specified with a comma: 3,900. The program determined this value was an error. You could use the COMMA*w.d* informat instead of the BEST12. informat to read this value as a number. However, if you do that, the COMMA*w.d* informat would remove the percent sign from sample 46801. This might or might not be acceptable in your application. A way around this would be to remove the commas from the values of CHEM_PPB before reading them with the INPUT function. This would successfully convert the character value of '3900' to a numeric value.

Program

Create data set CHEMEVAL.
Read the observations in CHEMTEST.
Define a new character variable and a
new numeric variable.
When the value of CHEM_PPB is
missing, assign the text "Undefined" to
variable EVAL.
Execute this DO group when
CHEM_PPB is not missing.
Attempt to read CHEM_PPB as a
numeric value. Include the '??' format
modifier in the INPUT function to
suppress error messages and prevent
automatic variable _ERROR_ from

```
data chemeval;
  set chemtest;
  length eval $ 12 result 8;

  if chem_ppb=' ' then eval='Undefined';


  else do;

    result=input(chem_ppb,?? best12.);
```

being set to 1 that would result if
CHEM_PPB cannot be read in as a
number. Use the BEST12. informat to
allow for various types of numeric
value representation.
Evaluate numeric values that are
successfully returned by the INPUT
function.
Assign an evaluation of "Numeric"
when the value that is returned is
greater than or equal to 0.
For negative or missing values, classify
the observation as an error and reset
RESULT to missing.

Execute this DO group when the value
that is returned by the INPUT function
is missing, which means the BEST12.
informat could not be successfully
applied to CHEM_PPB.
Check if the value of CHEM_PPB ends
with the uppercase or lowercase text
"PPB". Reverse the text of
CHEM_PPB, strip leading and trailing
blanks from the reversed string, and
convert it to uppercase before checking
for the "PPB" text.
Attempt to read the value of
CHEM_PPB with the "PPB" text at the
end removed to see if the beginning
part of CHEM_PPB is numeric.
Evaluate numeric values that are
successfully returned by the INPUT
function.
Assign an evaluation of "Numeric"
when the value that is returned is
greater than or equal to 0.
For negative or missing values, classify
the observation as an error and reset
RESULT to missing.

Test if the value of CHEM_PPB is a
mix of letters and specific punctuation
or if its uppercased value is 'N/A'.
Remove acceptable nonalphabetic
characters from CHEM_PPB with
COMPRESS so that the NOTALPHA
function does not find them. Use
NOTALPHA to determine whether any
of the remaining characters are not
uppercase or lowercase alphabetic
letters.
Execute this DO group when the value
of CHEM_PPB has not been
categorized as text only.

```
if result ne . then do;

  if result ge 0 then eval='Numeric';


  else do;
    result=.;
    eval='Error';
  end;
end;
else do;



  if upcase(strip(reverse(chem_ppb)))=:'BPP'
        then do;




    result=input(
substr(chem_ppb,1,length(chem_ppb)-3),?? best12.);


    if result ne . then do;


      if result ge 0 then eval='Numeric';


      else do;
        result=.;
        eval='Error';
      end;
    end;
  end;
  if notalpha(compress(chem_ppb,' ().,-&:'))=0
      or upcase(chem_ppb)='N/A' then eval='Text';






  else do;
```

Determine whether the value of CHEM_PPB is structured to indicate the sample was below the limit of detection. If the first byte of the CHEM_PPB value starts with a less than sign and the remainder can be read in as a numeric value, conclude that the value is for a sample below the limit of detection.

```
if char(chem_ppb)='<' and
    input(substr(chem_ppb,2),?? best12.) ne .
        then eval='Below Range';
```

Follow a similar process as in the preceding IF statement to determine whether the sample was above the limit of detection.

```
else if char(chem_ppb)='>' and
    input(substr(chem_ppb,2),? ? best12.)
        then eval='Above Range';
```

For all values that remain unclassified, assign a value of 'Error' to EVAL.

```
else eval='Error';
```

```
            end;
          end;
        end;
      run;
```

A Closer Look

Understanding Functions That Evaluate the Content of Variable Values

The SAS language contains many functions that can test the content of variable values. With functions FIND, FINDC, INDEX, INDEXC, INDEXW, and VERIFY, you can specify complex arguments to search for sets of specific values. The two series of functions—one that starts with ANY and the other that starts with NOT—look for specific types of values within a character string. The preceding DATA step used one of these, NOTALPHA, to look for nonalphabetic characters in a string where specific characters had been removed by the COMPRESS function. These specific characters were allowed in the value when categorizing the value as text.

The ANY- and NOT- functions are simple to use because they look for specific sets of predefined characters. The first argument to these functions is your character variable. The second optional argument to these functions is the position in which to start the examination of the value. The direction of the search can be specified. For left to right, specify the column position. For right to left, precede the column position with a minus sign (-).

The ANY- series of functions returns the first column position where a character of the type being searched for is found. It returns a value of 0 when its argument does not contain any characters of the type being searched for.

The NOT- series of functions returns the first column position where a character is found that is not of the type being searched for. It returns a value of 0 when all the characters in the argument are of the type being searched for.

Table 9.1 lists the ANY- and NOT- series of functions that can examine the content of a variable value. For more information about the other six functions listed at the beginning of this section, see SAS documentation.

Table 9.1 ANY- and NOT- Series of SAS Functions

Searches for This Type of Character	ANY Version	NOT Version
Alphanumeric: digits 0–9, uppercase letter, lowercase letter	ANYALNUM	NOTALNUM
Alphabetic: uppercase letter, lowercase letter	ANYALPHA	NOTALPHA
Control: line feeds, page ejects, etc.	ANYCNTRL	NOTCNTRL
Digit: digits 0–9	ANYDIGIT	NOTDIGIT
Character that is valid as the first character in a SAS variable name under VALIDVARNAME=V7: uppercase letter, lowercase letter, underscore	ANYFIRST	NOTFIRST
Graphical: any printable character other than white space	ANYGRAPH	NOTGRAPH
Alphabetic: lowercase letter	ANYLOWER	NOTLOWER
Character that is valid in a SAS variable name under the rules for SAS system option VALIDVARNAME=V7	ANYNAME	NOTNAME
Printable character	ANYPRINT	NOTPRINT
Punctuation	ANYPUNCT	NOTPUNCT
White-space character: blank, horizontal, and vertical tab, carriage return, line feed, form feed	ANYSPACE	NOTSPACE
Alphabetic: uppercase letter	ANYUPPER	NOTUPPER
Hexadecimal character that represents a digit	ANYXDIGIT	NOTXDIGIT

Example 9.3 Determining Whether a Variable Is Character or Numeric

Goal

Determine whether a variable is character or numeric to ensure that you have the right type of data for your application.

Example Features

Featured Step	DATA step
Featured Step Options and Statements	ATTRN, CLOSE, INDEX, OPEN, UPCASE, VARNAME, and VARTYPE functions CALL SYMPUTX routine Open code macro variables
Related Technique	PROC SQL, DICTIONARY.COLUMNS table, INTO clause to create a macro variable, INDEX and UPCASE functions
A Closer Look	Using the SAS File I/O Functions Specifying Variable Lists

Input Data Set

Data set ENTRANCE_EXAM stores exam results for 15 applicants to an academic program. The results are saved in a mix of character and numeric variables.

ENTRANCE_EXAM

Obs	id	examversion	examdate	essay	speech	mathematics	physics	vocabulary	logic	spatial	athletics
1	MXMI	V4.1	07/02/2010	Meets	Below	19	17	14	Exceeds	14	Below
2	URQU	V4.3	07/31/2010	Meets	Meets	2	14	2	Meets	14	Meets
3	JOPE	V4.2	07/13/2010	Exceeds	Exceeds	5	8	4	Below	17	Exceeds
4	TYJP	V4.3	07/21/2010	Meets	Exceeds	14	6	10	Meets	18	Meets
5	YPDF	V4.3	07/30/2010	Exceeds	Exceeds	6	2	7	Meets	17	Meets
6	PRGH	V4.3	07/01/2010	Below	Below	12	7	15	Below	9	Meets
7	AYPX	V4.3	07/06/2010	Below	Below	20	5	6	Meets	12	Exceeds
8	DKEG	V4.1	07/23/2010	Meets	Exceeds	4	4	1	Meets	14	Exceeds
9	UPYM	V4.1	07/03/2010	Below	Meets	2	17	9	Below	16	Below
10	THCL	V4.1	07/23/2010	Meets	Exceeds	7	19	8	Meets	19	Below
11	SSPN	V4.2	07/20/2010	Exceeds	Meets	6	2	8	Exceeds	14	Exceeds
12	YRNJ	V4.2	07/25/2010	Exceeds	Meets	2	14	17	Below	12	Exceeds
13	MHVT	V4.1	07/22/2010	Meets	Meets	10	18	4	Exceeds	6	Below
14	TVKT	V4.2	07/19/2010	Meets	Exceeds	7	13	10	Exceeds	9	Below
15	HXRV	V4.1	07/27/2010	Below	Exceeds	10	6	13	Meets	15	Below

Resulting Output
Output 9.3a
Frequencies of Specific Character Variables in ENTRANCE_EXAM

```
                            Example 9.3 ENTRANCE_EXAM

                               The FREQ Procedure

                                                 Cumulative    Cumulative
        examversion    Frequency      Percent     Frequency      Percent
        ---------------------------------------------------------------------
        V4.1               6           40.00           6          40.00
        V4.2               4           26.67          10          66.67
        V4.3               5           33.33          15         100.00


                                                 Cumulative    Cumulative
        essay          Frequency      Percent     Frequency      Percent
        ---------------------------------------------------------------------
        Below              4           26.67           4          26.67
        Exceeds            4           26.67           8          53.33
        Meets              7           46.67          15         100.00


                                                 Cumulative    Cumulative
        speech         Frequency      Percent     Frequency      Percent
        ---------------------------------------------------------------------
        Below              3           20.00           3          20.00
        Exceeds            7           46.67          10          66.67
        Meets              5           33.33          15         100.00


                                                 Cumulative    Cumulative
        logic          Frequency      Percent     Frequency      Percent
        ---------------------------------------------------------------------
        Below              4           26.67           4          26.67
        Exceeds            4           26.67           8          53.33
        Meets              7           46.67          15         100.00


                                                 Cumulative    Cumulative
        athletics      Frequency      Percent     Frequency      Percent
        ---------------------------------------------------------------------
        Below              6           40.00           6          40.00
        Exceeds            5           33.33          11          73.33
        Meets              4           26.67          15         100.00
```

Output 9.3b
PROC MEANS of Specific Numeric Variables in ENTRANCE_EXAM

```
                            Example 9.3 ENTRANCE_EXAM

                              The MEANS Procedure

        Variable      N        Mean        Std Dev      Minimum       Maximum
        -----------------------------------------------------------------------
        mathematics   15    8.4000000     5.7669006    2.0000000    20.0000000
        physics       15   10.1333333     6.0811966    2.0000000    19.0000000
        vocabulary    15    8.5333333     4.7639519    1.0000000    17.0000000
        spatial       15   13.7333333     3.6344909    6.0000000    19.0000000
        -----------------------------------------------------------------------
```

Example Overview

The DATA step in this example examines the names and type attribute of variables in a data set in order to select character variables to analyze with PROC FREQ and to select numeric variables to analyze with PROC MEANS.

Data set ENTRANCE_EXAM contains exam results for 15 applicants to an academic program. The results are a mix of character and numeric variables. The goal is to produce a frequency table for each character exam result variable and to compute descriptive statistics for each numeric exam result variable.

The DATA step applies several data set metadata functions that access data set ENTRANCE_EXAM and evaluate its variable attributes. It does not read the observations in ENTRANCE_EXAM, and it does not create an output data set. The DATA step instead iterates only once and applies the following functions to read descriptive information about the data set and select the analysis variables:

- ❑ open the data set with OPEN

- ❑ determine the number of variables with ATTRN

- ❑ determine the variable name with VARNAME

- ❑ determine the variable type with VARTYPE

- ❑ close the data set with CLOSE

An IF statement excludes from the lists variable names that contain specific text. At the end of the DATA step after all variables have been examined, CALL SYMPUTX saves the names of the selected character variables in global macro variable CHARLIST and the names of the selected numeric variables in global macro variable NUMLIST.

The TABLES statement in PROC FREQ specifies macro variable CHARLIST, which resolves so that PROC FREQ produces a one-way frequency table for each selected character variable. The VAR statement in PROC MEANS specifies macro variable NUMLIST, which resolves so that PROC MEANS produces descriptive statistics for each selected numeric variable.

Program

Start a DATA step. Do not create an output data set.
```
data _null_;
```

Open data set ENTRANCE_EXAM for input only. Save in DSID the unique data set identifier that OPEN assigns.
```
  dsid=open('work.entrance_exam','i');
```

Write an error message to the SAS log and stop the DATA step when the DSID value indicates that the data set could not be opened.
```
  if dsid=0 then do;
    putlog
      'ERROR: Data set ENTRANCE_EXAM could not be opened.';
    stop;
  end;
```

Define CHARVARS and NUMVARS to be long enough to hold all of the names of the character variables (CHARVARS) and the names of the numeric variables (NUMVARS).
```
  length examvarname $ 32 charvars $ 200 numvars $ 200;
```

Determine the total number of variables in ENTRANCE_EXAM.
```
  totalvars=attrn(dsid,'nvars');
```

Execute a DO loop the number of times equal to the number of variables in ENTRANCE_EXAM. Examine the attributes of a variable on each iteration of the loop.
```
  do i=1 to totalvars;
```

Obtain the name of the variable in ENTRANCE_EXAM in the position in the data set data vector that corresponds to the current value of I.
```
    examvarname=varname(dsid,i);
```

Reject variables whose names contain the text string 'ID' or 'DATE'. Return to the top of the DO loop.

```
if index(upcase(examvarname),'ID') gt 0 or
   index(upcase(examvarname),'DATE') gt 0 then
              continue;
```

If the ith variable in the data set data vector is character, add its name to the list of variables that are saved in CHARVARS. Separate the names with spaces.

```
if vartype(dsid,i)='C' then charvars=
              catx(' ',charvars,examvarname);
```

If the ith variable in the data set data vector is numeric, add its name to the list of variables that are saved in NUMVARS. Separate the names with spaces.

```
else if vartype(dsid,i)='N' then numvars=
              catx(' ',numvars,examvarname);
```

Close data set ENTRANCE_EXAM. If the data set does not close successfully, as evidenced by a non-zero return code, write an error message to the SAS log.

```
end;
rc=close(dsid);
if rc ne 0 then
      putlog 'ERROR: Problem in closing ENTRANCE_EXAM';
```

Copy the list of character variables that are stored in CHARVARS to macro variable CHARLIST.

```
call symputx('CHARLIST',charvars);
```

Copy the list of numeric variables that are stored in NUMVARS to macro variable NUMLIST.

```
call symputx('NUMLIST',numvars);
```

Compute one-way frequency tables for the character variables whose names are saved in macro variable CHARLIST.

Compute descriptive statistics for the numeric variables whose names are saved in macro variable NUMLIST.

```
run;
proc freq data=entrance_exam;
   title "Example 9.3 ENTRANCE_EXAM";
   tables &charlist;
run;
proc means data=entrance_exam;
   title "Example 9.3 ENTRANCE_EXAM";
   var &numlist;
run;
```

Related Technique

The following PROC SQL step selects the same character and numeric analysis columns as the DATA step in the main example. It also stores the lists of columns in the same macro variables, CHARLIST and NUMLIST.

The PROC SQL step extracts column names and column type from the COLUMNS dictionary table. A dictionary table is a read-only PROC SQL table that is supplied by SAS. The COLUMNS dictionary table contains data about the columns in tables. The data that are available include library name, member name, column name, column type, and column label.

Accessible directly through PROC SQL programming or through views in the SASHELP library, these tables can provide you with information about tables, options, external files, and many other objects in your current SAS session. SAS automatically defines the DICTIONARY libref for you when your SAS session starts.

The following PROC SQL step has two SELECT statements: one to select the character columns and save their names in macro variable CHARLIST, and a second to select the numeric columns and save their names in macro variable NUMLIST. A WHERE clause added to each SELECT statement specifies the table from which to select the column data, the type of variable to select, and text that the variable name must not contain.

Example 9.5 also accesses dictionary tables and includes details about the tables in the "A Closer Look" section.

Suppress printed output.
Select NAME, which is the column (or variable) name in the table. Store

```
proc sql noprint;
   select name into :numlist separated by ' '
```

the column name values in macro variable NUMLIST and separate them with a space.

Select rows from the COLUMNS dictionary table.

Specify that the rows selected from DICTIONARY.COLUMNS must be for the WORK.ENTRANCE_EXAM table, that the column type is numeric, and that the column name must not contain the text "DATE" or "ID". Columns LIBNAME, MEMNAME, and TYPE are columns in DICTIONARY.COLUMNS.

Specify that the rows selected from DICTIONARY.COLUMNS must be for the WORK.ENTRANCE_EXAM table, that the column type is character, and that the column name must not contain the text "DATE" or "ID".

Compute one-way frequency tables for the character variables whose names are saved in macro variable CHARLIST.

Compute descriptive statistics for the numeric variables whose names are saved in macro variable NUMLIST.

```
from dictionary.columns

where libname='WORK' and memname='ENTRANCE_EXAM'
      and type='num' and index(upcase(name),'DATE')=0
      and index(upcase(name),'ID')=0;
```

```
select name into :charlist separated by ' '
from dictionary.columns
where libname='WORK' and memname='ENTRANCE_EXAM' and
      type='char' and index(upcase(name),'DATE')=0
      and index(upcase(name),'ID')=0;
```

```
quit;
proc freq data=entrance_exam;
   title "Example 9.3 ENTRANCE_EXAM";
   tables &charlist;
run;

proc means data=entrance_exam;
   title "Example 9.3 ENTRANCE_EXAM";
   var &numlist;
run;
```

A Closer Look

Using the SAS File I/O Functions

The DATA step in the main example uses several SAS file input/output functions. As demonstrated, you can programmatically work with metadata about your SAS data sets in a DATA step without reading the SAS data set.

Typically, you start by opening the SAS file with the OPEN function in the DATA step. This function assigns an identifier to your data set that you can reference later in calls to other functions that extract information about the data set. When the DATA step ends, SAS automatically closes the data set. You can also close it yourself with the CLOSE function before the DATA step ends as shown in the example.

The two functions ATTRN and ATTRC return information about the attributes of a SAS data set. The ATTRN returns attributes that are numeric in value while ATTRC returns attributes that are character in value.

Other useful functions include EXIST, which tests whether a SAS library member exists; PATHNAME, which returns the physical name of an external file or SAS library; and a series of variables that obtain metadata about the variables in a data set. These functions include VARFMT, VARINFMT, VARLABEL, VARLEN, VARNAME, VARNUM, and VARTYPE.

Similar to the SAS file input/output functions is the set of functions that work with external files. These functions can return information about external files, and they can add to and delete data from external files.

For more information about these functions, see SAS documentation.

Specifying Variable Lists

It is possible to skip the DATA step or PROC SQL step that evaluates variable attributes and names and instead specify the lists of variables in PROC FREQ and PROC MEANS by using a combination of techniques to specify groups of variables:

❑ DROP or KEEP data set options. The following PROC FREQ step does not compute one-way frequency tables for numeric variables or for any variable whose name starts with the text "ID".

```
proc freq data=entrance_exam(drop=_numeric_ id:);
run;
```

❑ _CHARACTER_ and _NUMERIC_ keywords. The following PROC FREQ step computes one-way frequency tables for all character variables.

```
proc freq data=entrance_exam;
  tables _character_;
run;
```

❑ Variable range lists that use the _CHARACTER_ and _NUMERIC_ keywords. The following PROC MEANS step computes descriptive statistics on the numeric variables between ESSAY and ATHLETICS in the data set data vector. Even though it is implicit that PROC MEANS can compute descriptive statistics only on numeric variables, SAS generates an error if a character variable is in the list of variables. Character variables ESSAY, SPEECH, LOGIC, and ATHLETICS are within the list and cause the PROC MEANS step to stop when the _NUMERIC_ keyword is omitted.

```
proc means data=entrance_exam;
  var essay-numeric-athletics;
run;
```

However, depending on the complexities of including and excluding specific variables using lists, it might be easier to specify the lists by using a process that is similar to the one demonstrated in the DATA step or PROC SQL step.

See also Example 8.15 for its usage of the _CHARACTER_ and _NUMERIC_ keywords in ARRAY statements in a DATA step.

Example 9.4 Specifying a Numeric or Character Format at Run Time

Goal

Format the value of a variable in each observation with a format based on the value of another variable.

Example Features

Featured Step	PROC FORMAT and DATA step
Featured Step Options and Statements	CATX, PUT, and PUTN functions

Input Data Set

Data set GLOBAL_REVENUE contains annual revenue results from several countries. Values from the USA and Canada are dollars. Values from Belgium, France, and Germany are euros. Values from Japan are yen.

GLOBAL_REVENUE

Obs	country	year	revenue
1	USA	2008	3819501.03
2	USA	2009	-19391.88
3	USA	2010	1033.65
4	Canada	2008	471868.81
5	Canada	2009	297654.01
6	Canada	2010	111123.09
7	Belgium	2008	-1201.30
8	Belgium	2009	404019.87
9	Belgium	2010	-55414.86
10	France	2008	917378.02
11	France	2009	891785.31
12	France	2010	953919.07
13	Germany	2008	1860.03
14	Germany	2009	-61545.32
15	Germany	2010	777541.26
16	Japan	2008	549871.03
17	Japan	2009	391830.68
18	Japan	2010	-140001.78

Resulting Data Set

Output 9.4
GLOBAL_TEXT
Data Set

```
            Example 9.4 GLOBAL_TEXT

     Obs              revenue_text

      1    USA 2008 Revenue: US$3,819,501.03
      2    USA 2009 Revenue: US$-19,391.88
      3    USA 2010 Revenue: US$1,033.65
      4    Canada 2008 Revenue: C$471,868.81
      5    Canada 2009 Revenue: C$297,654.01
      6    Canada 2010 Revenue: C$111,123.09
      7    Belgium 2008 Revenue: €-1.201,30
      8    Belgium 2009 Revenue: €404.019,87
      9    Belgium 2010 Revenue: €-55.414,86
     10    France 2008 Revenue: €917.378,02
     11    France 2009 Revenue: €891.785,31
     12    France 2010 Revenue: €953.919,07
     13    Germany 2008 Revenue: €1.860,03
     14    Germany 2009 Revenue: €-61.545,32
     15    Germany 2010 Revenue: €777.541,26
     16    Japan 2008 Revenue: \549,871.03
     17    Japan 2009 Revenue: \391,830.68
     18    Japan 2010 Revenue: \-140,001.78
```

Example Overview

The DATA step in this example uses the value of one variable to determine the format to apply to another variable. The PROC FORMAT step that precedes the DATA step creates a user-defined format whose values specify a SAS format as their label.

As the DATA step processes each observation, it looks up the SAS format to apply to the current observation. The labels of a user-defined format are these SAS formats. The DATA step applies the user-defined format to the variable whose values determine which SAS format to use. An assignment statement in the DATA step then formats the variable of interest with the selected SAS format.

Data set GLOBAL_REVENUE contains annual revenue results from several countries. Values from the USA and Canada are dollars. Values from Belgium, France, and Germany are euros. Values from Japan are yen.

The goal of this example is to create a text string from the three variables COUNTRY, YEAR, and REVENUE in data set GLOBAL_REVENUE. The values of REVENUE should be written with the currency sign and style of the nation. The three SAS formats, DOLLAR, EUROX, and YEN specify the currency style for the countries in GLOBAL_REVENUE.

A PROC FORMAT step that precedes the DATA step defines format $MONEY. Its values are the countries present in data set GLOBAL_REVENUE. The labels in $MONEY are the SAS formats to apply to variable REVENUE.

The PUT function in the first assignment statement in the DATA step applies format $MONEY to variable REVENUE. It returns the selected format name to variable FMT.

The remaining assignment statements use the CATX function to combine the three variables into one variable GLOBAL_TEXT. The DATA step applies the PUTN function to variable REVENUE. The PUTN function allows for a format to be specified at run time. When an observation is processed is when PUTN applies the specified format.

The program tests if the country value is USA or Canada. Both of those select the dollar format. To distinguish between U.S. dollars and Canadian dollars, the "US" and "C" prefixes are concatenated with the CATS function to the value that is returned by the PUTN function.

Program

Define format $MONEY. Specify the values of COUNTRY as the values of $MONEY. Assign a SAS format to the countries.
Create data set GLOBAL_TEXT.
Read the observations in GLOBAL_REVENUE.

Find the name of the format to apply to variable REVENUE based on the values of COUNTRY. Save the format name in variable FMT.
Concatenate the elements in REVENUE_TEXT based on whether the country is a "non-dollar" country.

Convert the numeric value of YEAR to character so that it can be concatenated without generating notes in the SAS log.

```
proc format;
  value $money 'USA','Canada'='dollar'
               'Belgium','France','Germany'='eurox'
               'Japan'='yen';

data global_text;
  set global_revenue;

  length revenue_text $ 50 fmt $ 12;
  keep revenue_text;
  fmt=put(country,$money.);



  if upcase(country) not in ('CANADA','USA') then
      revenue_text=
                   putn(revenue,fmt,14,2));

                 catx(' ',country,
                      put(year,4.),
```

Specify a text string to include in the value of REVENUE_TEXT.

Apply the format that is specified by the value of FMT to the current observation's value of REVENUE. Write the value with a maximum width of 14 and two decimal points. Separate the third and fourth arguments with a comma.

```
                             'Revenue:',

                 putn(revenue,fmt,14,2));
```

Concatenate the elements of REVENUE_TEXT for the two "dollar" countries.

```
    else if upcase(country)='CANADA' then revenue_text=
           catx(' ',country,put(year,4.),'Revenue: ',
           cats('C',putn(revenue,fmt,14,2)));
    else if upcase(country)='USA' then revenue_text=
           catx(' ',country,put(year,4.),'Revenue: ',
           cats('US',putn(revenue,fmt,14,2)));
run;
```

Example 9.5   Creating Columns That Contain the Attributes of Other Columns

Goal

Create a table that has metadata for columns in specific tables. Determine the name, type, length, label, and format of the columns and designate these as columns in the new table.

Example Features

Featured Step	PROC SQL
Featured Step Options and Statements	DICTIONARY tables COLUMNS and TABLES Subqueries
A Closer Look	Accessing SAS System Information Using Dictionary Tables

Input Tables

Tables TRIAL3_WEEK01, TRIAL3_WEEK02, TRIAL3_WEEK04, and TRIAL3_WEEK08 contain medical information for two patients in a clinical trial. The tables have a combination of variables that are in common and that are unique among the four tables. Assume the tables are saved in a library that has a libref of TESTCODE.

```
                             TRIAL3_WEEK01

Obs   id    age gender ht_cm wt_kg systol diastol ekg          init_bmi
 1  AW37BD 52   Male    173   88    131    077    Normal         29.4
 2  23GM02 53   Male    180   83    144    090    Abnormal-LVH   25.6


                             TRIAL3_WEEK02

Obs      id        systol     diastol     gluc     chol     tri     hdl
 1     AW37BD        132         084        100      224     122      45
 2     23GM02        136         083         86      188     100      51


                             TRIAL3_WEEK04

 Obs       id      wt_kg      systol    diastol     gluc     tri
  1      AW37BD      86        128        085        104      99
  2      23GM02      85        130        079         92     124


                             TRIAL3_WEEK08

Obs      id      wt_kg   systol    diastol    gluc    chol    tri    hdl
 1     AW37BD      85     125        080        98     210     100     48
 2     23GM02      82     126        083        90     193     118     53
```

SAS Log

The PROC DATASETS step lists the data members in libref TESTCODE. The four input tables of interest are in this library. Their names are highlighted.

```
    1  proc datasets library=testcode memtype=data;
                        Directory

               Libref        TESTCODE
               Engine        V9
               Physical Name  c:\trials\datasets
               Filename       c:\trials\datasets
               Gen  Member    File
    #  Name     Num  Type     Size  Last Modified

    1  TRIAL1_WEEK01      DATA   9216  11Jan09:08:42:23
    2  TRIAL1_WEEK02      DATA   5120  18Jan09:10:05:52
    3  TRIAL1_WEEK04      DATA   5120  10Feb09:14:22:08
    4  TRIAL1_WEEK08      DATA   5120  12Mar09:16:02:49
    5  TRIAL2_WEEK01      DATA   9216  01Feb09:13:03:39
```

```
    6   TRIAL2_WEEK02           DATA      5120   09Feb09:09:23:01
    7   TRIAL2_WEEK04           DATA      5120   25Feb09:16:03:18
    8   TRIAL2_WEEK08           DATA      5120   31Mar09:15:29:41
    9   TRIAL3_WEEK01           DATA      9216   01May09:10:49:19
   10   TRIAL3_WEEK02           DATA      5120   16May09:08:32:08
   11   TRIAL3_WEEK04           DATA      5120   01Jun09:12:07:48
   12   TRIAL3_WEEK08           DATA      5120   28Jun09:17:08:20
   13   TRIAL4_WEEK01           DATA      9216   01Jul09:11:41:22
   14   TRIAL4_WEEK02           DATA      9216   15Jul09:12:33:42
   15   TRIAL4_WEEK04           DATA      9216   01Aug09:08:59:12
   16   TRIAL4_WEEK08           DATA      9216   06Sep09:11:32:50

    2   quit;

NOTE: PROCEDURE DATASETS used (Total process time):
          real time            0.01 seconds
          cpu time             0.01 seconds
```

Resulting Tables
Output 9.5
NUM_STUDYVARS
and
CHAR_STUDYVARS
Tables

```
                          Example 9.5 NUM_STUDYVARS

     Obs    name      type    length    label                     format

      1     age       num        3      Age                       2.
      2     chol      num        4      Cholesterol Result        4.
      3     diastol   num        4      Diastolic Blood Pressure  Z3.
      4     gluc      num        4      Glucose Result            4.
      5     hdl       num        4      HDL Result                4.
      6     ht_cm     num        4      Height(cm)                3.
      7     init_bmi  num        8      Initial BMI (computed)    4.1
      8     systol    num        4      Systolic Blood Pressure   Z3.
      9     tri       num        4      Triglycerides Result      4.
     10     wt_kg     num        4      Weight(kg)                2.




                          Example 9.5 CHAR_STUDYVARS

      Obs    name      type    length    label         format

       1     ekg       char      25      EKG Result
       2     gender    char       2      Gender        $GENDER.
       3     id        char       6      Study ID
```

Example Overview

The following example demonstrates how you can access two of the dictionary tables that SAS provides to collect information about tables and columns. The goal of the program is to make a table of the character column names and a table of the numeric column names in a group of tables in a library.

The program uses the read-only PROC SQL dictionary tables that are supplied by SAS. Accessible directly through PROC SQL programming or through views in the SASHELP library, these tables and views can provide you with information about tables, options, external files, and many other objects in your current SAS session. SAS automatically defines the DICTIONARY libref for you when your SAS session starts.

Here are the two dictionary tables that are used in this example:

❑ The TABLES dictionary table. This table contains data about tables. The data that are available include library name, member name, creation date, number of observations, number of variables, and table label.

❑ The COLUMNS dictionary table. This table contains data about the columns in tables. The data that are available include library name, member name, column name, column type, and column label.

The following PROC SQL step uses the TABLES dictionary table to find the set of tables that were created between May 1, 2009, and June 30, 2009. It then uses the COLUMNS dictionary table to make a table of the numeric column names and a table of the character column names in that set of tables.

The program has two CREATE TABLE statements: one to obtain the numeric columns and a second to obtain the character columns. A subquery finds the set of table names that were created between May 1, 2009, and June 30, 2009. The main query then extracts the column type information for the table names that were returned by the subquery.

The DISTINCT keyword on each SELECT clause causes duplicate rows to be removed from the results so that each column name is represented only once. For example, character column ID exists in all four tables while EKG exists only in TRIAL3_WEEK01. Without the DISTINCT keyword, four rows for column ID are output to table CHAR_STUDYVARS. The other attributes that were specified by the SELECT clauses have all been assigned identically for each column name.

Program

Create table NUM_STUDYVARS.
Select specific columns from
DICTIONARY.COLUMNS. Do not
save duplicate rows in the output table.
Select information for columns whose
type is numeric.
Select column information for tables in
the TESTCODE library.
Select column information from
members in the TESTCODE library
that were created between May 1, 2009,
and June 30, 2009, by examining the
creation date of the tables.
Order by the column name.

Create table CHAR_STUDYVARS.
Select specific columns from
DICTIONARY.COLUMNS. Do not
save duplicate rows in the output table.
Select information for columns whose
type is character.

```
proc sql ;
  create table num_studyvars as
    select distinct name,type,length,label,format
              from dictionary.columns

      where type='num' and

          libname='TESTCODE' and

          memname in
            (select memname from dictionary.tables
                where libname='TESTCODE' and
                      memtype='DATA' and
            datepart(crdate) between
                  '01may2009'd and '30jun2009'd)
          order by name;

  create table char_studyvars as
    select distinct name,type,length,label,format
       from dictionary.columns

      where type='char' and

          libname='TESTCODE' and memname in
            (select memname from dictionary.tables
                where libname='TESTCODE' and
                      memtype='DATA' and
            datepart(crdate) between
                  '01may2009'd and '30jun2009'd)
          order by name;
quit;
```

A Closer Look

Accessing SAS System Information Using Dictionary Tables
SAS supplies the read-only PROC SQL dictionary tables and associated views in the SASHELP library from which you can extract metadata about tables, options, external files, and many other objects in your current SAS session. SAS automatically defines the DICTIONARY libref for you when your SAS session starts.

Each time you reference a dictionary table, SAS collects and returns the pertinent information. When you use PROC SQL to obtain data from a dictionary table, PROC SQL optimizes the query that could potentially search libraries, open tables, and execute views. Although you can also obtain the same data by using the SASHELP view in a

DATA step or PROC step, it might be more efficient to use PROC SQL to create a table that contains the information you need. After creating a table that contains only the data you need, you could then process that table with a DATA step or PROC step.

The specification of DICTIONARY.*table-name* is valid only in a PROC SQL step. You cannot place the specification as the object of the DATA= option in a PROC statement and you cannot place it in a SET statement in a DATA step.

The specification of SASHELP.*view-name* is used when you want to reference the view that is associated with a dictionary table. The views are stored in the SASHELP library and their names start with the letter "V". The remainder of each view's name is identical to or similar to the dictionary table name from which it is derived. A table in SAS documentation lists the dictionary table name and its associated view name.

The following PROC PRINT step shows how to reference a dictionary table view. It prints the variable information for ENTRANCE_EXAM by using PROC PRINT. View VCOLUMN is the view that is derived from the DICTIONARY.COLUMNS table.

```
proc print data=sashelp.vcolumn;
  where libname='WORK' and memname='ENTRANCE_EXAM';
run;
```

Here is the equivalent PROC SQL step:

```
proc sql;
  select * from dictionary.columns
  where libname='WORK' and memname='ENTRANCE_EXAM';
quit;
```

The preceding main example extracted data from two of the tables, COLUMNS and TABLES. In SAS 9.2 under Windows, many dictionary tables are available. One table, DICTIONARY.DICTIONARIES, contains metadata about all the dictionary tables. Each row in this table contains data for one column in one of the dictionary tables. Table LIBNAMES contains 11 columns of information about the libnames that are defined in your current SAS session. Therefore, in DICTIONARY.DICTIONARIES, there are 11 rows of information for the LIBNAMES dictionary table.

If you want to list the names of the dictionary tables that are available to your SAS session, submit the following step:

```
proc sql;
  select unique(memname) from dictionary.dictionaries;
quit;
```

In this step, MEMNAME is the column in DICTIONARY.DICTIONARIES that contains the dictionary name.

If you want to find out how SAS defines a specific dictionary table, use the DESCRIBE TABLE statement in a PROC SQL step. The following step writes the description of DICTIONARY.LIBNAMES to the SAS log:

```
proc sql;
  describe table dictionary.libnames;
quit;
```

For more information about dictionary tables, see SAS documentation.

Example 9.6   Sorting Variable Values within an Observation

Goal

Sort a series of character variable values and a series of numeric variable values within an observation.

Example Features

Featured Step	DATA step
Featured Step Options and Statements	CALL SORTC and CALL SORTN CALL routines LARGEST, ORDINAL, and SMALLEST functions
Related Technique	DATA step and ORDINAL function: ORDINAL sort in descending order

Input Data Set

Data set ADSURVEY contains responses from five partipants in a survey for a store. The three character variables NOTICED1, NOTICED2, and NOTICED3 list where the respondent saw an ad. The three numeric variables AMOUNT1, AMOUNT2, and AMOUNT3 are the amounts spent (if positive) or refunded (if negative) as recalled by the respondent on recent visits to the store. The NOTICED and the AMOUNT series are stored in no specific order.

ADSURVEY

Obs	surveyid	noticed1	noticed2	noticed3	amount1	amount2	amount3
1	106	website	flyer	MAIL	300	0	0
2	153	website	newspaper	email	-55	.	.
3	192	email	?	email	0	.	.
4	145	Online	n/a	website	75	95	250
5	162	insert	on-line		-45	.	10

Resulting Data Set

Output 9.6a
SURVEYSORTED
Data Set

```
                           Example 9.6 SURVEYSORTED Data Set


        Obs    surveyid     noticed1      noticed2      noticed3     amount1
         1       106         MAIL          flyer         website        0
         2       153         email         newspaper     website        .
         3       192         ?             email         email          .
         4       145         Online        n/a           website       75
         5       162                       insert        on-line        .


        Obs    amount2     amount3     ord_amt1     ord_amt2     ord_amt3
         1        0          300          0            0            300
         2        .         -55           .            .           -55
         3        .           0           .            .             0
         4       95          250         75           95           250
         5      -45          10           .          -45            10

                 small_      small_      small_      large_      large_      large_
        Obs      amt1        amt2        amt3        amt1        amt2        amt3
         1         0           0          300         300          0           0
         2       -55           .            .        -55           .           .
         3         0           .            .          0           .           .
         4        75          95          250         250         95          75
         5       -45          10            .         10         -45           .
```

Example Overview

This example demonstrates how you can use CALL routines and SAS language functions in a DATA step to sort character values and numeric values *within* an observation. When you use PROC SORT, you sort the values of variables *across* observations, not within.

The following DATA step sorts a series of character variable values with CALL SORTC. It sorts a series of numeric variable values with CALL SORTN and the functions LARGEST, ORDINAL, and SMALLEST.

Data set ADSURVEY has responses from five participants in a store survey. A series of character variables NOTICED1, NOTICED2, and NOTICED3 lists the places that the respondent had seen a recent advertisement. The responses are not in any specific order nor are the text values formatted uniformly. A series of numeric variables AMOUNT1, AMOUNT2, and AMOUNT3 shows the respondents' recalled amounts spent (if positive) or amount refunded (if negative) on three visits to the store. The responses are not in any specific order.

The DATA step sorts the values of the NOTICED series of character variables in ascending order by using CALL SORTC. The three variables are not elements of an array.

The DATA step sorts the AMOUNT series of numeric variables four times by using the four tools: CALL SORTN CALL routine and the LARGEST, ORDINAL, and SMALLEST functions. The three AMOUNT variables are defined as elements in the AMOUNT array.

The DATA step places calls to the three functions within an iterative DO loop. The upper bound of the DO loop is the total number of elements in the numeric array AMOUNT whose elements are the variables that are being sorted. The first argument that is supplied to each of the functions is the DO loop index variable I.

On each iteration of the DO loop, the ORDINAL and SMALLEST functions find the ith *smallest* value in the AMOUNT array. The ORDINAL function includes any missing values in the selection and places missing values lowest in the ordering while SMALLEST ignores any missing values. The LARGEST function finds the ith *largest* value in the AMOUNT array ignoring missing values.

The three functions do not overwrite the original values of the variables with the same set of values in sorted order. Instead the DATA step creates three new arrays of variables, one for each of the functions.

❑ The results of applying the ORDINAL function are stored in the ORD_AMT array.

❑ The results of applying the SMALLEST function are stored in the SMALL_AMT array.

❑ The results of applying the LARGEST function in the LARGE_AMT array.

The two CALL routines sort their arguments within the series of variables that are specified as their arguments. They overwrite the original values of the variables with the same set of values in sorted order. The CALL routines sort only in ascending order, placing missing values lowest in the sort order.

Note that the values of the NOTICED variables are mixed-case alphabetic and nonalphabetic characters and that NOTICED3 is missing for SURVEYID=162. Uppercase letters sort before lowercase letters. For example, for SURVEYID=106, the value 'MAIL' is lower in order than the value 'flyer'.

Note that several of the AMOUNT variable values are missing and a few are negative.

Program

Create data set SURVEYSORTED.
Read the observations in ADSURVEY.
Define the array of numeric values that the three functions will sort.
Save the results from applying the three functions, ORDINAL, SMALLEST, and LARGEST, in these arrays.

```
data surveysorted;
  set adsurvey;
  array amount{3} amount1-amount3;

  array ord_amt{3} ord_amt1-ord_amt3;
  array small_amt{3} small_amt1-small_amt3;
  array large_amt{3} large_amt1-large_amt3;
  drop i;
  do i=1 to dim(amount);
    ord_amt{i}=ordinal(i, of amount{*});
```

Sort AMOUNT in ascending order.
Find the ith element in ascending order on each iteration of the DO loop.
Include missing values in the sorting process.

Sort AMOUNT in ascending order.
Find the ith element in ascending order on each iteration of the DO loop, ignoring any missing values that are present in the list.

```
    small_amt{i}=smallest(i, of amount{*});
```

Sort AMOUNT in descending order.
Find the ith element in descending order on each iteration of the DO loop, ignoring any missing values that are present in the list.

```
    large_amt{i}=largest(i, of amount{*});
```

Sort character variables NOTICED1, NOTICED2, and NOTICED3.
Overwrite the original values with the sorted values.
Sort the AMOUNT array. Overwrite the original values with the sorted values.

```
  end;
  call sortc(of noticed1-noticed3);


  call sortn(of amount{*});

run;
```

Related Technique

You can achieve a descending sort with the ORDINAL function by modifying the index specification on the array element that is receiving the result. The following program applies the ORDINAL function to the AMOUNT array. The results are saved in array REV_AMT. The index value specification for REV_AMT is modified so the elements are arranged in descending order. Output 9.6b shows the elements of the REV_AMT array.

```
data revsorted;
  set adsurvey;

  array amount{3} amount1-amount3;
  array rev_amt{3} rev_amt1-rev_amt3;

  drop i;

  do i=1 to dim(amount);
      rev_amt{dim(amount)-i+1}=
               ordinal(i, of amount{*});
```

Specify the index value for REV_AMT so that its elements are arranged in descending order.

```
  end;
run;
```

Output 9.6b
REVSORTED
Data Set

```
                            Example 9.6 REVSORTED Data Set

 Obs  surveyid  noticed1  noticed2   noticed3  amount1 amount2 amount3 rev_amt1 rev_amt2 rev_amt3

  1     106      website   flyer      MAIL       300      0       0      300       0        0
  2     153      website   newspaper  email      -55      .       .      -55       .        .
  3     192      email     ?          email        0      .       .        0       .        .
  4     145      Online    n/a        website      75     95     250      250      95       75
  5     162      insert    on-line              -45       .      10       10     -45        .
```

Example 9.7   Shifting Nonmissing Values Left in an Observation

Goal

Shift to the left the nonmissing values in a list of values that are stored in an array.

Example Features

Featured Step	DATA step
Featured Step Options and Statements	Array processing MAX, N, WHICHN functions
Related Technique	DATA step: Array processing, MAX, N, WHICHN functions

Input Data Set

Data set TEST_MONTHS contains the admission test scores for five applicants over a six-month period.

TEST_MONTHS

Obs	applicant	sept09	oct09	nov09	jan10	feb10	mar10
1	BN0Q6B	387	.	.	.	381	.
2	ENAD1C	297	327	.	354	.	.
3	EM5OBF	252	.	301	.	.	276
4	HVPGZH	.	.	.	.	.	398
5	2V1E4D	365	.	.	.	.	.

Resulting Data Set
Output 9.7
ADMISSION_TESTS
Data Set

Example 9.7 ADMISSION_TESTS

Obs	applicant	score1	score2	score3	ntimes	besttest	besttry
1	BN0Q6B	387	381	.	2	387	1
2	ENAD1C	297	327	354	3	354	3
3	EM5OBF	252	301	276	3	301	2
4	HVPGZH	398	.	.	1	398	1
5	2V1E4D	365	.	.	1	365	1

Example Overview

This example shows you how to shift the nonmissing values in a series of variables that have a mix of missing and nonmissing values to the left end of the series.

The DATA step defines an array of the variables that have the mix of missing and nonmissing values. An iterative DO loop moves the nonmissing values sequentially to a new array of variables.

The data set in this example contains test scores for five applicants to a program. The tests could be taken up to three times in six months. The goal is to move all the nonmissing test results over the testing period to the elements of the new array. Because each applicant is limited to three tries, the new array SCORES has only three elements.

The iterative DO loop uses two index variables, I and J. Index variable I references the elements of array MONTHS. Index variable J tracks the elements of array SCORES. It is initialized to 1 prior to the DO loop.

The DATA step also includes three assignment statements that summarize the testing for each applicant.

Program

Create data set ADMISSION_TESTS.
Read the observations in
TESTMONTHS.
Define array MONTHS to contain the
scores in chronological order.
Define the new array that will hold the
nonmissing test results.

Initialize the index variable that will
identify the next element in SCORES to
which a nonmissing value in MONTHS
can be moved.
Execute an iterative DO loop the
number of times equal to the number of
elements in MONTHS.
Execute the DO group when the
element in MONTHS that is currently
being processed is nonmissing.
Move the nonmissing value from
MONTHS to the currently available
element in SCORES.
Increment index variable J by 1 so that
it will point to the next available
element in SCORES to which a
nonmissing value in MONTHS can be
moved.

Determine the number of times an
applicant took the test by counting the
number of nonmissing values in the six
variable array MONTHS.
Of the possible three attempts,
determine the highest score.
Identify which of the three testing
attempts was the one with the highest
score.

```
data admission_tests;
  set testmonths;

  array months{6} sept09 oct09 nov09 jan10 feb10 mar10;

  array scores{3} score1-score3;

  drop sept09 oct09 nov09 jan10 feb10 mar10 i j;
  j=1;



  do i=1 to dim(months);

    if months{i} ne . then do;

      scores{j}=months{i};


      j+1;




    end;
  end;
  ntimes=n(of months{*});



  besttest=max(of scores{*});

  besttry=whichn(besttest,of scores{*});


run;
```

Related Technique

The following DATA step is nearly identical to the preceding one. The difference is that the first three elements of the two arrays MONTHS and SCORES are the same. It moves the nonmissing values in the series of variables within the series. If you don't want to create new variables, you can use this DATA step to produce an output data set that is identical to the one in the main example.

The DATA step still uses index variables I and J. Instead of creating variables SCORE1, SCORE2, and SCORE3 within the DATA step, it puts the first three elements of MONTHS also in the SCORES array. These three variables, SEP09, OCT09, and NOV09, are renamed to SCORE1, SCORE2, and SCORE3 in the DATA statement.

For each observation, the DATA step first determines the number of times the applicant took the test and the applicant's best score. This is done before the iterative DO loop because the loop rearranges the values in the series of test score variables and does not set the value in the element's originating position to missing.

Create data set ADMISSION_TESTS. Rename the first three elements of MONTHS since these three elements will contain the nonmissing test results. Read the observations in TESTMONTHS.

```
data admission_tests(rename=(sept09=score1 oct09=score2
                             nov09=score3));

   set testmonths;
```

Define array MONTHS to contain the scores in chronological order.

```
   array months{6} sept09 oct09 nov09 jan10 feb10 mar10;
```

Define array SCORES that will hold the nonmissing test results.

```
   array scores{3} sept09 oct09 nov09;
```

Drop only the last three elements of MONTHS since the DO loop will move the nonmissing test results into the first three variables of array MONTHS (the same variables in the SCORES array).

```
   drop jan10 feb10 mar10 i j;
```

Determine the number of times an applicant took the test by counting the number of nonmissing values in the six variable array MONTHS.

```
   ntimes=n(of months{*});
```

Determine the highest score.

Initialize the index variable that will identify the next element in SCORES to which a nonmissing value in MONTHS can be moved.

```
   besttest=max(of months{*});
   j=1;
```

Execute an iterative DO loop the number of times equal to the number of elements in MONTHS.

```
   do i=1 to dim(months);
```

Execute the DO block when the element in MONTHS that is currently being processed is nonmissing.

```
      if months{i} ne . then do;
```

Move the nonmissing value from MONTHS to the next available element in SCORES.

```
         scores{j}=months{i};
```

Increment index variable J by 1 so that it will point to the next available element in SCORES to which a nonmissing value in MONTHS can be moved.

```
         j+1;
```

```
      end;
   end;
   besttry=whichn(besttest,of scores{*});
```

Identify which of the three testing attempts was the one with the highest score. Look at the elements in SCORES, which at the bottom of this step has all the nonmissing test results for the applicant.

```
run;
```

Example 9.8 Generating Random Numbers within a Range of Values

Goal

Generate a specific number of random numbers within a range of values.

Example Features

Featured Step	DATA step
Featured Step Options and Statements	CATS, CEIL, CHAR, FLOOR, RANUNI, and SUBSTR functions

Resulting Data Set

Output 9.8
GEN_IDS
Data Set

```
                            GEN_IDS

                      Obs        id

                        1      TY773
                        2      DX963
                        3      CE942
                        4      ED565
                        5      QL714
                        6      MF854
                        7      SA711
                        8      PX734
                        9      PL994
                       10      AD925
                       11      KA798
                       12      VK794
                       13      YD539
                       14      CI706
                       15      KI724
                       16      XZ719
                       17      NM940
                       18      HC724
                       19      UY685
                       20      YA649
                       21      PX665
                       22      YI986
                       23      ZZ725
                       24      KL981
                       25      CJ543
```

Example Overview

This example shows how to use the RANUNI random number function to generate random numbers within a range of values. The RANUNI function generates a rational number noninclusively between 0 and 1 by using the uniform distribution.

The single argument to RANUNI is a seed value. This seed serves as a starting point from which to generate the random values. The seed must be an integer. A seed of 0 causes RANUNI to use the system clock time as the starting point, which generates a different stream of random numbers every time the program is called. A seed not equal to 0 generates the same stream of random numbers every time the program is called.

By multiplying the value that is returned by RANUNI and applying SAS functions CEIL or FLOOR, you can generate integers within a specific range of values.

The UNIFORM function is an alias for the RANUNI function.

Data sets used throughout this book are comprised of fabricated data. Many data sets require ID values. The DATA steps that fabricate the data frequently include the RANUNI function in creating these IDs.

The following DATA step shows a way to fabricate 25 5-byte ID values. It randomly picks characters from variable FULLSTRING, a 26-byte character variable. FULLSTRING is a constant with its 26 bytes equal to the 26 letters of the alphabet.

The seed value that is supplied to RANUNI is specified in variable SEED. Because this value is not 0 in this example, every time the DATA step executes, RANUNI generates the same stream of random numbers. If you make no other changes to the DATA step and keep the value of SEED the same, you would generate the same set of ID values each time you execute the DATA step. If you want a different set each time that can't be reproduced, specify 0 as the seed value. On each execution of RANUNI, the current seed is updated internally, but the value of the seed argument that is stored in SEED remains unchanged.

In this example, the requirement is that the ID values must have letters A-Z in the first two bytes and a number between 500 and 999 in the remaining three bytes.

An iterative DO loop selects two letters at random to place in the first two bytes of variable ID. The value that is returned by each invocation of RANUNI is multiplied by 26 and the CEIL function is applied to the result. The CEIL function returns the smallest integer that is greater than or equal to the argument. The values that are returned by RANUNI and multiplied by 26 will be rational numbers greater than 0 and less than 26. Applying CEIL to these values returns integers from 1 to 26 inclusively. The CHAR function picks the single character from FULLSTRING in that integer's position.

The other invocation of RANUNI returns a value that is multiplied by 500. With the CEIL function applied to the result, random numbers between 1 and 500 inclusively are generated. The value 499 is added to each random number, which results in a list of random numbers between 500 and 999.

You can use the FLOOR function instead of the CEIL function if you want to obtain the largest integer that is less than or equal to the argument, but you would need to modify any multipliers or additive adjustments so that you obtain the required range of values.

The following DATA step generates observations and does not read in a data set.

Program

Create data set GEN_IDS.

```
data gen_ids;
```

Define variable ID.
Initialize LETTERS to equal the letters of the alphabet.
Initialize variable SEED that will be supplied as the argument to RANUNI.
Execute an iterative DO loop 25 times to generate 25 values for ID.
Initialize ID at the beginning of generating an ID value.
Fill the first two bytes of ID.
Generate a random number. Use the value of SEED as the seed value to the function. Multiply the random number by 26 and apply the CEIL function to the result to obtain an integer between 1 and 26 inclusively.
Fill the first two positions of ID.

```
drop i j letters seed pos value;
length id $ 5;
retain letters 'ABCDEFGHIJKLMNOPQRSTUVWXYZ'

      seed 3713;

do i=1 to 25;

  id=' ';

  do j=1 to 2;
    pos=ceil(ranuni(seed)*26);




    id=cats(id,char(letters,pos));
  end;
```

***Generate a random number. Multiply it
by 500 and apply the CEIL function to
return an integer between 1 and 500.
Add 499 to the integer, which results in
integers from 500 to 999 inclusively
that are saved in variable VALUE.*** It is
not necessary to change the seed value
that is specified in this invocation of
RANUNI. The stream of random
numbers was initiated in the first call to
RANUNI and continues from there. It is
not reset in this DATA step.
***Put the three-digit integer in the last
three bytes of ID.***
***Write each ID value to a separate
observation.*** Because this DATA step is
generating data and not reading a data
set, it is necessary to explicitly output an
observation on each iteration of the DO
loop so that there will be 25
observations in GEN_IDS.

```
value=ceil(ranuni(seed)*500)+499;




 substr(id,3)=put(value,3.);

 output;




    end;
run;
```

Example 9.9 Selecting Observations at Random from a Data Set without Replacement

Goal

Create a subset of a data set by randomly choosing observations from the data set. Do not allow an observation to be selected more than once. This method is commonly referred to as simple random sampling without replacement.

Examples 9.9 and 9.10 show different methods of sampling observations from data sets.

Example Features

Featured Step	PROC SURVEYSELECT
Featured Step Options and Statements	PROC SURVEYSELECT statement options: METHOD=SRS, OUT=, SAMPSIZE=, SEED= options
Related Technique 1	DATA step with RANUNI function and PROC SORT
Related Technique 2	DATA step with RANUNI function, OUTPUT and STOP statements, SET statement with NOBS= option

Input Data Set

Data set STUDY_POOL contains demographic data on 443 patients with a disease who are eligible to be included in a study. The first 25 observations are shown.

```
                         STUDY_POOL (first 25 observations)

                                           disease_
     Obs  studyid          dob  dx_age       years  duration      gender  age
       1  PK773Q    10/26/1960      40           9  late              F    49
       2  XU878R    05/06/1961      47           1  early             F    48
       3  FV465N    10/20/1977      23           9  late              F    32
       4  JP518G    04/16/1973      35           1  early             F    36
       5  PV818S    05/25/1974      25          10  late              M    35
       6  PV176X    07/19/1973      35           1  early             M    36
       7  QJ683W    11/23/1957      45           7  late              F    52
       8  QF971X    06/15/1975      33           1  early             M    34
       9  XW767L    05/27/1955      53           1  early             F    54
      10  IB738B    08/18/1962      45           2  intermediate      M    47
      11  DQ570Z    03/02/1978      30           1  early             M    31
      12  SU192H    02/14/1987      20           2  intermediate      M    22
      13  SW758U    03/05/1955      51           3  intermediate      F    54
      14  AW080T    05/04/1962      45           2  intermediate      F    47
      15  QO391M    11/04/1971      33           5  intermediate      F    38
      16  KK571Z    09/08/1962      45           2  intermediate      F    47
      17  GM905F    08/05/1959      45           5  intermediate      F    50
      18  GJ437V    01/12/1986      22           1  early             F    23
      19  OG052C    06/11/1971      37           1  early             M    38
      20  YP992Q    06/30/1972      36           1  early             M    37
      21  UN028V    04/22/1979      20          10  late              F    30
      22  SE317H    01/21/1948      55           6  late              M    61
      23  GZ756K    08/25/1953      55           1  early             M    56
      24  RZ619Q    12/03/1960      48           1  early             F    49
      25  VK658B    11/12/1986      20           3  intermediate      F    23
```

Resulting Data Set

Output 9.9a
SAMPLE25
Data Set

```
        Example 9.9 SAMPLE25 Data Set Created with PROC SURVEYSELECT

                                   disease_
       Obs  studyid       dob  dx_age   years  duration      gender  age

         1  IB738B  08/18/1962    45        2  intermediate      M    47
         2  SW758U  03/05/1955    51        3  intermediate      F    54
         3  YP992Q  06/30/1972    36        1  early             M    37
         4  QX762Q  06/17/1948    59        2  intermediate      M    61
         5  MF193R  09/14/1954    52        3  intermediate      M    55
         6  AG642K  01/18/1987    21        1  early             F    22
```

```
                         7 CH513Z  04/07/1951  57   1   early         M   58
                         8 FT520R  11/25/1951  53   5   intermediate  F   58
                         9 BT232M  07/11/1985  20   4   intermediate  M   24
                        10 LS696T  10/18/1981  26   2   intermediate  F   28
                        11 EI188W  06/12/1945  61   3   intermediate  M   64
                        12 QN271N  06/22/1985  23   1   early         M   24
                        13 QI177T  08/27/1948  60   1   early         M   61
                        14 EC092I  02/16/1987  21   1   early         F   22
                        15 NR337X  06/25/1955  53   1   early         F   54
                        16 AO783K  01/05/1964  40   5   intermediate  F   45
                        17 AT949T  08/14/1970  27  12   late          F   39
                        18 LQ219I  01/27/1948  59   2   intermediate  F   61
                        19 JV329F  05/12/1945  63   1   early         F   64
                        20 DU189X  05/02/1969  39   1   early         M   40
                        21 IQ901W  08/09/1956  52   1   early         F   53
                        22 JB893X  11/17/1947  57   5   intermediate  F   62
                        23 YV984F  08/24/1949  57   3   intermediate  M   60
                        24 AT193G  05/29/1984  17   8   late          M   25
                        25 UU780P  07/12/1945  62   2   intermediate  M   64
```

Example Overview

The following PROC SURVEYSELECT step illustrates simple random sampling without replacement. A specific number of observations are selected at random from a data set with the condition that an observation can be selected only once.

PROC SURVEYSELECT has multiple options that can customize the sampling of a data set. This example specifies two options, METHOD= and SAMPSIZE=, that tell the procedure to select 25 observations at random from data set STUDY_POOL without replacement. A third option, OUT=, saves the selected observations in data set SAMPLE25. A fourth option, SEED=, specifies a seed value to the random number generator so that the sampling is reproducible.

Program

Select observations at random from STUDY_POOL.
Select the observations by using simple random sampling, which is selection with equal probability and without replacement.
Save the selected observations in data set SAMPLE25.
Select 25 observations.
Specify an initial seed for random number generation so that the selection is reproducible. If you want SURVEYSELECT to use the clock to initialize the seed, do not specify the SEED= option or assign the SEED= option a value of 0 or a negative number.

```
proc surveyselect data=study_pool

              method=srs



       out=sample25

       sampsize=25
       seed=2525;




   run;
```

Related Technique 1

The following program randomly selects 25 observations from a data set without replacement. It starts by assigning a random number to every observation in data set STUDY_POOL. The resulting data set is sorted by the random numbers. A DATA step then creates the random sample of 25 observations by selecting the first 25 observations from the data set sorted by the random numbers.

While PROC SURVEYSELECT performs simple random sampling without replacement, you might want to use a DATA step instead if you need to modify the selected observations with programming statements.

The program in Related Technique 2 also uses a DATA step to select 25 observations at random. It does not require sorting of the data set and reads the data set only once. While the DATA step in Related Technique 1 is easy to understand, depending on your computer resources, it might be more efficient to use Related Technique 2 when you need to select a small sample from a very large data set.

Create data set STUDY_POOL2. ***Read the observations from STUDY_POOL.***	``` data study_pool2; set study_pool; ```

Assign to variable RANDOM a random number drawn from the uniform distribution. Specify a value greater than 0 for the seed so that the stream of numbers is reproducible. If you want to produce a stream of numbers that is not reproducible, specify the seed as 0 so that the random number generators initialize the generation process by using the clock time.	```
	  random=ranuni(54918);
	``

	``` run; ```

Sort the observations by the random numbers.	```
	proc sort data=study_pool2;
	  by random;
	run;
	``

Create the sample data set. ***Save the first 25 observations from STUDY_POOL2 in SAMPLE25. Do not save the variable that contains the random numbers.***	```
	data sample25;
	  set study_pool2(obs=25 drop=random);
	``

	``` run; ```

Output 9.9b
SAMPLE25 Data Set
Created with PROC
SORT and DATA Step

```
        Example 9.9 SAMPLE25 Related Technique 1 Data Set Created with PROC SORT and DATA Step

                                             disease_
   Obs    studyid          dob     dx_age     years     duration         gender     age

     1    VK162Z     12/31/1963      34         12       late               F        46
     2    YB377F     02/21/1950      58          1       early              M        59
     3    IB557W     11/29/1968      40          1       early              M        41
     4    CS710N     08/10/1960      48          1       early              F        49
     5    WI301T     09/17/1958      40         11       late               M        51
     6    EW595I     02/07/1986      21          2       intermediate       F        23
     7    VZ638C     08/16/1947      61          1       early              M        62
     8    JB893X     11/17/1947      57          5       intermediate       F        62
     9    QL460E     06/13/1973      33          3       intermediate       M        36
    10    BG914M     01/19/1984      24          1       early              F        25
    11    UV157Y     09/10/1967      41          1       early              F        42
    12    RM904X     10/16/1979      28          2       intermediate       M        30
    13    DT459U     01/28/1977      30          2       intermediate       M        32
    14    KP962X     11/04/1970      33          6       late               M        39
    15    VK949Q     11/13/1959      45          5       intermediate       F        50
    16    AY000Y     09/20/1963      42          4       intermediate       F        46
    17    SJ380M     03/23/1968      37          4       intermediate       M        41
    18    KN379R     10/28/1971      35          3       intermediate       M        38
    19    TP259E     03/31/1987      19          3       intermediate       F        22
    20    UW581J     10/24/1958      49          2       intermediate       M        51
    21    QF115M     03/20/1971      29          9       late               F        38
    22    IN550Y     04/01/1983      18          8       late               M        26
    23    CO796N     09/11/1971      37          1       early              M        38
    24    ME619D     09/03/1959      46          4       intermediate       M        50
    25    UL539V     05/30/1971      33          5       intermediate       M        38
```

Related Technique 2

The following DATA step reads all the observations from STUDY_POOL and computes a probability conditional on the number of observations that remain in the data set and the number that is needed to complete the sample. For example, if 50 observations remain to be processed in the data set and you need five more in your sample, you select the next observation with probability 5/50.

The DATA step assigns the total number of observations in STUDY_POOL to variable N. Variable K tracks how many observations still need to be selected. When an observation is selected, an assignment statement decrements the value of K by 1. The value of N is decremented by 1 with each iteration of the DATA step. The probability of selecting the observation that is currently being processed is K/N. If the value that is returned by the RANUNI function is less than or equal to that value, the observation is selected and output to SAMPLE25.

Create data set SAMPLE25.
Read the observations in
STUDY_POOL. Assign the total
number of observations in
STUDY_POOL to temporary variable
TOTAL.

```
data sample25;
   set study_pool nobs=total;
```

Retain the values of variables K and N
across iterations of the DATA step.
Initialize K to be the number of
observations to select from
STUDY_POOL.

```
   drop k n;
   retain k 25 n;
```

On the first iteration of the DATA step,
copy the value of temporary variable
TOTAL that has the total number of
observations in STUDY_POOL to data
set variable N.

```
   if _n_=1 then n=total;
```

Compute the probability of selecting
the observation that is currently being
processed by dividing the number of
observations that need to be selected
(K) by the number of observations that
remain to be processed, including the
current observation (N). Obtain a
random number from the uniform
distribution not inclusively between the
values 0 and 1. If the random number
is less than or equal to the probability,
select the observation for output.

```
   if ranuni(381705) <= k/n then do;
```

Write the selected observation to the
output data set.

```
      output;
```

Decrement the value of K by 1 because
one less observation is needed to be
selected from STUDY_POOL.

```
      k=k-1;
```

```
   end;
```

Decrement the number of observations
yet to process in STUDY_POOL by 1
with each iteration of the DATA step
after the processing of the current
observation has been completed.

```
   n=n-1;
```

When all the observations needed in
the sample have been selected, stop the
DATA step.

```
   if k=0 then stop;
```

```
run;
```

Output 9.9c displays the results of the preceding program.

Output 9.9c
SAMPLE25 Data Set
Created with
DATA Step

```
          Example 9.9 SAMPLE25 Related Technique 2 Data Set Created with DATA Step

                                              disease_
     Obs    studyid           dob    dx_age     years    duration        gender    age

       1    PV176X     07/19/1973       35          1    early              M       36
       2    OG052C     06/11/1971       37          1    early              M       38
       3    YP992Q     06/30/1972       36          1    early              M       37
       4    SE317H     01/21/1948       55          6    late               M       61
       5    WH928R     01/01/1951       57          1    early              F       58
       6    GA537T     10/13/1945       62          2    intermediate       F       64
       7    FO764G     08/14/1959       48          2    intermediate       F       50
       8    ZD500L     10/13/1973       35          1    early              M       36
       9    VD401X     08/30/1964       44          1    early              M       45
      10    GA105Z     03/21/1961       45          3    intermediate       F       48
      11    JX876R     09/05/1954       54          1    early              F       55
      12    AO783K     01/05/1964       40          5    intermediate       F       45
      13    SP922W     10/29/1978       20         11    late               F       31
      14    DC238T     09/16/1954       53          2    intermediate       M       55
      15    BF950R     12/14/1953       52          4    intermediate       F       56
      16    WW597U     08/15/1949       59          1    early              F       60
      17    KA204V     01/24/1971       36          2    intermediate       F       38
      18    NM423D     06/04/1954       53          2    intermediate       M       55
      19    WL948D     05/03/1985       21          3    intermediate       M       24
      20    JE523E     02/13/1968       37          4    intermediate       F       41
      21    LC395W     04/26/1968       40          1    early              M       41
      22    GR407P     11/02/1950       53          6    late               F       59
      23    TP462Q     07/11/1956       52          1    early              M       53
      24    VX080R     10/14/1953       52          4    intermediate       M       56
      25    UU780P     07/12/1945       62          2    intermediate       M       64
```

Example 9.10   Selecting Equal-Sized Samples from Different Groups

Goal

Randomly select the same number of observations from different groups in a data set. Do not allow an observation to be selected more than once. This method is commonly referred to as stratified random sampling without replacement and with equal allocation.

Additionally, create replicate samples by repeating the process of randomly selecting the same number of observations from different groups.

Examples 9.9 and 9.10 show different methods of sampling observations from data sets.

Example Features

Featured Step	PROC SURVEYSELECT
Featured Step Options and Statements	PROC SURVEYSELECT statement options: METHOD=SRS, OUT=, REPS=, SAMPSIZE=, SEED= STRATA statement
Related Technique	PROC SORT and DATA step with RANUNI function

Input Data Set

Data set JINGLE_WINNERS contains information on 208 winners of an advertising jingle contest for three products. The first 30 observations are shown.

```
                         JINGLE_WINNERS (first 30 observations)

        Obs    contestant     address                        category
          1    Adams BK       Osseo, WI 54758                Energy Bar
          2    Adams OT       Morganfield, KY 42437          Energy Bar
          3    Alexander IE   Columbus, WI 53925             Energy Bar
          4    Allen WN       Norfolk, VA 23518              Sport Drink
          5    Anderson EL    McIntire, IA 50455             Energy Bar
          6    Anderson FW    Reelsville, IN 46171           Energy Bar
          7    Anderson GC    Augusta, ME 04330              Sport Drink
          8    Anderson VU    Greensboro, NC 27416           Sport Drink
          9    Bailey DA      Branson, MO 65615              Protein Shake
         10    Bailey IA      Glen Mills, PA 19342           Sport Drink
         11    Bailey NJ      Dover, OK 73734                Protein Shake
         12    Bailey VI      Atkinson, NE 68713             Protein Shake
         13    Bailey ZO      Fleetwood, PA 19522            Sport Drink
         14    Baker KE       Oxford, MD 21654               Sport Drink
         15    Bell FK        Temple, ME 04984               Sport Drink
         16    Bell MQ        Burdick, KS 66838              Protein Shake
         17    Bennett QB     Mount Enterprise, TX 75681     Protein Shake
         18    Brown FU       Browning, MO 64630             Protein Shake
         19    Brown QD       Catlettsburg, KY 41129         Energy Bar
         20    Brown TF       Carnelian Bay, CA 96140        Protein Shake
         21    Brown TX       Walthourville, GA 31333        Sport Drink
         22    Brown WG       Crenshaw, MS 38621             Energy Bar
         23    Brown ZZ       Tilden, IL 62292               Protein Shake
         24    Campbell ZB    Beaverton, OR 97077            Protein Shake
         25    Carter KC      Antimony, UT 84712             Protein Shake
         26    Clark DA       Cawker City, KS 67430          Protein Shake
         27    Clark DO       Lake Worth, FL 33466           Sport Drink
         28    Collins QN     West Memphis, AR 72303         Protein Shake
         29    Cooper GP      Claudville, VA 24076           Sport Drink
         30    Cooper PM      Jackson, NC 27845              Sport Drink
```

Input Frequencies
Output 9.10a
Frequency of
CATEGORY in
JINGLE_WINNERS

```
                                JINGLE_WINNERS

                             The FREQ Procedure

                                              Cumulative   Cumulative
          category       Frequency   Percent   Frequency    Percent
          -------------------------------------------------------------
          Energy Bar         56       26.92        56        26.92
          Protein Shake      82       39.42       138        66.35
          Sport Drink        70       33.65       208       100.00
```

Resulting Data Set
Output 9.10b
GRANDPRIZES
Data Set

```
              Example 9.10 GRANDPRIZES Data Set Created by PROC SURVEYSELECT

                                                            Selection Sampling
        Obs   category     Replicate contestant  address        Prob    Weight

          1 Energy Bar        1     Adams OT     Morganfield, KY 42437   0.089286   11.2
          2 Energy Bar        1     Alexander IE Columbus, WI 53925      0.089286   11.2
          3 Energy Bar        1     Smith UC     Raymond, IA 50667       0.089286   11.2
          4 Energy Bar        1     Ward EN      Elberfeld, IN 47613     0.089286   11.2
          5 Energy Bar        1     Wright BR    Silver Star, MT 59751   0.089286   11.2
          6 Energy Bar        2     Adams BK     Osseo, WI 54758         0.089286   11.2
          7 Energy Bar        2     Green KX     Milwaukee, WI 53220     0.089286   11.2
          8 Energy Bar        2     Harris EL    Le Grand, IA 50142      0.089286   11.2
          9 Energy Bar        2     Hernandez GB Scott, MS 38772         0.089286   11.2
         10 Energy Bar        2     Jones IL     Pontotoc, MS 38863      0.089286   11.2
         11 Protein Shake     1     Bennett QB   Mount Enterprise, TX 75681 0.060976 16.4
         12 Protein Shake     1     Garcia FR    Aimwell, LA 71401       0.060976   16.4
         13 Protein Shake     1     Green DN     Seattle, WA 98111       0.060976   16.4
         14 Protein Shake     1     Johnson XJ   Larkspur, CO 80118      0.060976   16.4
         15 Protein Shake     1     Lewis RE     Imperial, MO 63052      0.060976   16.4
         16 Protein Shake     2     Hill LH      Sherrill, AR 72152      0.060976   16.4
         17 Protein Shake     2     Martin IZ    Dallas, TX 75379        0.060976   16.4
         18 Protein Shake     2     Ramirez QF   Sparks, NV 89435        0.060976   16.4
         19 Protein Shake     2     Robinson CL  Lincoln, NE 68522       0.060976   16.4
         20 Protein Shake     2     Smith TM     Camp, AR 72520          0.060976   16.4
         21 Sport Drink       1     Jackson CP   New Kingstown, PA 17072 0.071429   14.0
         22 Sport Drink       1     Rivera BK    West Willow, PA 17583   0.071429   14.0
         23 Sport Drink       1     Robinson KO  Auburn, NY 13021        0.071429   14.0
         24 Sport Drink       1     Smith HQ     Newtonville, MA 02460   0.071429   14.0
         25 Sport Drink       1     Washington FG Kingston, PA 18704     0.071429   14.0
         26 Sport Drink       2     Garcia IK    West Poland, ME 04291   0.071429   14.0
         27 Sport Drink       2     Johnson TS   Colts Neck, NJ 07722    0.071429   14.0
         28 Sport Drink       2     Miller SV    Hanover, PA 17333       0.071429   14.0
         29 Sport Drink       2     Thomas OF    New York, NY 10003      0.071429   14.0
         30 Sport Drink       2     Thompson YV  Allison Park, PA 15101  0.071429   14.0
```

Resulting Output
Output 9.10c
Frequency of CATEGORY in GRANDPRIZES

```
              Example 9.10 GRANDPRIZES Data Set Created by PROC SURVEYSELECT

                                    The FREQ Procedure

                                                       Cumulative    Cumulative
         category        replicate    Frequency  Percent  Frequency     Percent
         ---------------------------------------------------------------------------
         Energy Bar          1            5       16.67        5         16.67
         Energy Bar          2            5       16.67       10         33.33
         Protein Shake       1            5       16.67       15         50.00
         Protein Shake       2            5       16.67       20         66.67
         Sport Drink         1            5       16.67       25         83.33
         Sport Drink         2            5       16.67       30        100.00
```

Example Overview

The following PROC SURVEYSELECT step illustrates stratified random sampling without replacement and with equal allocation. A specific number of observations are selected at random from each stratum in a data set with the condition that an observation can be selected only once.

PROC SURVEYSELECT has multiple options that can customize the sampling of a data set. The STRATA statement names the variable whose values partition the data set into groups that do not overlap.

Input data set JINGLE_WINNERS has 208 observations. The observations contain the names of winners of a jingle contest for three product categories identified by the values of variable CATEGORY. Two rounds of prizes will be awarded with five prizes awarded in each category each time.

Variable CATEGORY has three values. Therefore, a total of 30 observations will be selected. The process of selecting five observations for each value of CATEGORY is performed twice.

In the following program, the two PROC SURVEYSELECT statement options, METHOD= and SAMPSIZE=, in conjunction with the STRATA statement tell the procedure to select five observations at random without replacement from each group that is defined by the three values of variable CATEGORY in data set STUDY_POOL. A third option, OUT=, saves the selected observations in data set GRANDPRIZES. A fourth option, REPS=, tells the procedure to perform the complete selection process twice. A fifth option, SEED=, specifies a seed value to the random number generator so that the sampling is reproducible.

Within one replicate of selection, observations are selected without replacement. However, the observations are not selected without replacement across the replicates. Therefore, it is possible for a winner in the first round to also be a winner in the second round.

The input data set must be sorted by the variables that are named in the STRATA statement before executing PROC SURVEYSELECT. The procedure does have additional statements and options that can be used to tell the procedure to do the sorting. For more information about the sampling methods, statements, and options that allow this, see SAS documentation.

Program

Sort JINGLE_WINNERS by the variable named in the STRATA statement.

Select observations at random.
Within each stratum, select the observations with simple random sampling, which is selection with equal probability and without replacement.

Save the selected observations in data set GRANDPRIZES.

Perform the stratified random sampling process twice.

Select five observations from each stratum that is defined by the values of variable CATEGORY.

Specify an initial seed for random number generation so that the selection is reproducible. If you want SURVEYSELECT to use the clock to initialize the seed, do not specify the SEED= option or specify it as 0 or a negative number.

Name the variable whose values define the groups in which to randomly select the five observations.

```
proc sort data=jingle_winners;
   by category;
run;

proc surveyselect data=jingle_winners
                  method=srs


                  out=grandprizes

                  reps=2

                  sampsize=5


                  seed=65;




   strata category;

run;
```

Related Technique

The following program randomly selects without replacement 10 observations from each BY group. The first five observations selected within a BY group are assigned to replicate 1, and the second five observations are assigned to replicate 2.

The first DATA step assigns a random number to every observation in data set JINGLE_WINNERS. The resulting data set is sorted by the random numbers. The second DATA step then selects from the data set that was sorted by the random numbers the first 10 observations in each of the three BY groups.

The preceding PROC SURVEYSELECT step selected observations without replacement only within the replicate. An observation could be selected again in the second replicate. The following program does not select a person more than once across the replicates.

Create data set WINNERS2.
Read the observations from JINGLE_WINNERS.
Assign to variable RANDOM a random number drawn from the uniform distribution. Specify a value greater than 0 for the seed so that the stream of numbers is reproducible. If you want to produce a stream of numbers that is not reproducible, specify the seed as 0 so that the random number generators initialize the generation process by using the clock time.

Sort by the random numbers within each BY group.

```
data winners2;
   set jingle_winners;

   rn=ranuni(6209193);










run;

proc sort data=winners2;
   by category rn;
run;
```

Create the sample data set.	```data grandprizes;```
	``` set winners2;```
Process WINNERS2 in BY groups.	``` by category;```
	``` drop count rn;```
Tally the number of observations selected with the COUNT variable. Initialize COUNT to 0 at the start of each BY group.	``` if first.category then count=0;```
Increment the COUNT variable by 1 each time an observation is processed.	```count+1;```
Assign the first five observations selected to replicate 1.	```if count le 5 then replicate=1;```
Assign the remaining observations to replicate 2.	```else replicate=2;```
Save the first 10 observations in each BY group.	```if count le 10 then output;```
	```run;```

Output 9.10d displays the results of the preceding program.

Output 9.10d
GRANDPRIZES
Data Set Created by
PROC SORT and
DATA Step

```
          Example 9.10 GRANDPRIZES Related Technique Data Set Created by PROC SORT and DATA Step

     Obs      contestant      address                          category       replicate

       1      Green KX        Milwaukee, WI 53220              Energy Bar         1
       2      Moore AH        Twin Brooks, SD 57269            Energy Bar         1
       3      Miller IC       Vadnais Heights, MN 55127        Energy Bar         1
       4      Adams OT        Morganfield, KY 42437            Energy Bar         1
       5      King FT         Rockford, IL 61103               Energy Bar         1
       6      Rivera JT       Bath, OH 44210                   Energy Bar         2
       7      Davis VH        Ten Mile, TN 37880               Energy Bar         2
       8      Brown QD        Catlettsburg, KY 41129           Energy Bar         2
       9      Johnson CJ      Edmonton, KY 42129               Energy Bar         2
      10      Johnson BT      Alexandria, SD 57311             Energy Bar         2
      11      Morris LI       Wamego, KS 66547                 Protein Shake      1
      12      Miller SZ       Ferriday, LA 71334               Protein Shake      1
      13      Sanchez DJ      Geronimo, TX 78115               Protein Shake      1
      14      Moore GG        San Rafael, CA 94903             Protein Shake      1
      15      Hernandez GS    St. Louis, MO 63115              Protein Shake      1
      16      Lee JJ          Garrison, UT 84728               Protein Shake      2
      17      Carter KC       Antimony, UT 84712               Protein Shake      2
      18      Hill LH         Sherrill, AR 72152               Protein Shake      2
      19      Edwards SX      Bosler, WY 82051                 Protein Shake      2
      20      Torres JL       Lacey, WA 98503                  Protein Shake      2
      21      Clark DO        Lake Worth, FL 33466             Sport Drink        1
      22      Smith UL        Minden, WV 25879                 Sport Drink        1
      23      Flores ZA       Patten, ME 04765                 Sport Drink        1
      24      Garcia IW       Springwater, NY 14560            Sport Drink        1
      25      Washington FG   Kingston, PA 18704               Sport Drink        1
      26      Johnson TS      Colts Neck, NJ 07722             Sport Drink        2
      27      Washington NV   Tampa, FL 33672                  Sport Drink        2
      28      Richardson QY   Sparkill, NY 10976               Sport Drink        2
      29      Cooper GP       Claudville, VA 24076             Sport Drink        2
      30      Jones WQ        Milton, WV 25541                 Sport Drink        2
```

Example 9.11 Creating SAS Datetime Values and Computing the Difference between Two Datetime Values

Goal

Create a new variable that contains a SAS datetime value by combining SAS date values and SAS time values. Compute the difference in hours between two datetime values.

Example Features

Featured Step	DATA step
Featured Step Options and Statements	DHMS, INTCK, and MDY functions

Input Data Set

Data set OCT2009_ORDERS contains order placement and shipment information about eight orders. The orders were placed in October 2009, and only the day of the month was recorded. The shipment date and shipment hour were recorded.

```
                                  OCT2009_ORDERS

                                   order_    order_                  ship_
     Obs   customerid   orderid     day       time     ship_date     hour
      1     XXV0NW      C10761       22       23:04    10/24/2009       7
      2     5MY0CJ      P18204       25        7:25    10/25/2009      18
      3     JEFL0M      O84093       26       15:42    10/30/2009       9
      4     E322GA      I02764       26       15:58    10/27/2009      12
      5     IGQTE1      U96795       28       14:03    10/30/2009      14
      6     FXM1EK      T76448       29       10:53    10/29/2009      15
      7     LEN8UV      J74397       29       16:14    10/31/2009       8
      8     JTRCY7      Z30952       30        8:13    11/01/2009      19
```

Resulting Data Set

Output 9.11
ORDER_STATS
Data Set

```
                          Example 9.11 ORDER_STATS

     Obs customerid orderid            ordered              shipped   prephours

       1    XXV0NW    C10761      22OCT2009:23:04:00    24OCT2009:07:00:00     32
       2    5MY0CJ    P18204      25OCT2009:07:25:00    25OCT2009:18:00:00     11
       3    JEFL0M    O84093      26OCT2009:15:42:00    30OCT2009:09:00:00     90
       4    E322GA    I02764      26OCT2009:15:58:00    27OCT2009:12:00:00     21
       5    IGQTE1    U96795      28OCT2009:14:03:00    30OCT2009:14:00:00     48
       6    FXM1EK    T76448      29OCT2009:10:53:00    29OCT2009:15:00:00      5
       7    LEN8UV    J74397      29OCT2009:16:14:00    31OCT2009:08:00:00     40
       8    JTRCY7    Z30952      30OCT2009:08:13:00    01NOV2009:19:00:00     59
```

Example Overview

This example creates two SAS datetime values from date and time data that are stored in separate variables in a data set. The program also computes the difference in hours between the two SAS datetime values.

The following DATA step uses the DHMS function to create the datetime values. The DHMS function accepts four numeric arguments that provide values for date ("D"), hour ("H"), minute ("M"), and seconds ("S"), respectively. The function returns a single value in the form of a SAS datetime value.

The DATA step uses the INTCK function with the "HOUR" argument to calculate the difference in hours between the two datetime values it constructs. The INTCK function returns the integer count of the number of interval boundaries between two dates, two times, or in the case of this example, two datetime values. The function accepts a variety of different intervals such as HOUR, YEAR, and DAY. The first argument can be further customized to accept multiples of an interval.

Data set OCT2009_ORDERS contains order placement and shipment information about eight orders. Because it is known the orders were placed in October 2009, the data set saves only the day of the month it was placed in variable ORDER_DAY. The time of day the order was placed is saved in variable ORDER_TIME. The date of the shipment is saved in variable SHIP_DATE. The hour of the shipment is saved in variable SHIP_HOUR.

The DATA step first computes a SAS datetime value for order placement and a datetime value for order shipment. The MDY function computes a date value for order placement.

An assignment statement then uses the INTCK function to compute the number of hours it took from receipt of the order to the time of shipment. Because the exact time of shipment was not recorded, the less precise determination of hours to prepare the order is computed rather than hours and minutes.

Examples 9.11, 9.13, 9.14, and 9.15 use the INTCK or the INTNX function. The INTNX function increments a date, time, or datetime value by a given interval or intervals, and returns a date, time, or datetime value. For more information about the many ways to use these two functions, see SAS documentation.

Program

Create data set ORDER_STATS.
Process the observations in
OCT2009_ORDERS.

```
data order_stats;
  set oct2009_orders;

  format ordered shipped datetime19.;
  keep customerid orderid ordered shipped prephours;
```

Compute a datetime value for order
placement. Determine a SAS date value
for the order date by using the MDY
function. Specify the time to DHMS as
the SAS time value that is stored in
ORDER_TIME, which is the number
of seconds since the previous midnight.
Because the hour and minutes of the
order placement time are available in
the SAS time value in ORDER_TIME,
specify 0 for hour and minutes to
DHMS.

```
  ordered=dhms(mdy(10,order_day,2009),0,0,order_time);
```

Compute a datetime value for order
shipment. Specify SHIP_DATE as the
date argument to DHMS. Specify
SHIP_HOUR as the hour argument to
DHMS. Specify 0 as the argument for
minutes and seconds since the exact
clock time was not recorded.

```
  shipped=dhms(ship_date,ship_hour,0,0);
```

Compute the number of hours between
ORDERED and SHIPPED. Indicate
hour as the interval to use in
determining the difference between the
two values.

```
  prephours=intck('hour',ordered,shipped);
```

```
run;
```

Example 9.12 Creating a SAS Time Value from a Character Value

Goal

Read a character value that cannot be read with an existing SAS time informat or function to create a SAS time value.

Example Features

Featured Step	PROC FORMAT and DATA step
Featured Step Options and Statements	PICTURE format, INPUT and PUT functions

Input Data Set

Data set INCIDENTS has power supply information for five incidents. Character variables IN_NOTED and RESP_NOTED records the times each incident was noted and responded to. The time values are not stored in a way that can be read with a single time informat.

```
                                INCIDENTS

Obs      location    type           in_noted      resp_noted
 1       SW009A      Surge          33.49         38.01
 2       N0003Q      Drop           9:13.69       12:15.02
 3       ESE01C      Transformer    8:00:00.33    10:21:06.43
 4       NW503K      Linkage        9:31:09.      10:18:18.
 5       ESE01D      Transformer    13:00:00.33   14:48:32.08
```

Resulting Data Set
Output 9.12
INCIDENT_TIMES
Data Set

```
                        Example 9.12 INCIDENT_TIMES

    Obs location type          in_noted     resp_noted     time_in     time_resp

     1  SW009A   Surge         33.49        38.01          0:00:33.49  0:00:38.01
     2  N0003Q   Drop          9:13.69      12:15.02       0:09:13.69  0:12:15.02
     3  ESE01C   Transformer   8:00:00.33   10:21:06.43    8:00:00.33  10:21:06.43
     4  NW503K   Linkage       9:31:09.     10:18:18.      9:31:09.00  10:18:18.00
     5  ESE01D   Transformer   13:00:00.33  14:48:32.08    13:00:00.33 14:48:32.08
```

Example Overview

This example shows how to create a SAS time value from a character value. The character values in variables IN_NOTED and RESP_NOTED in input data set INCIDENTS cannot be read with an existing SAS time informat or function such as the TIME*n*. informat or the HMS function.

The program uses a picture format that is defined by PROC FORMAT to structure the value in a form that the SAS informat TIME*n*. can interpret as a time value. A series of assignment statements that contain INPUT and PUT functions transform the character value into a numeric value and then into a SAS time value.

Program

Define picture format TIMECHAR.

Create data set INCIDENT_TIMES.
Read the observations in INCIDENTS.

Assign the TIMEw.d format to the two
new variables that will hold the two
time values.
Define array NOTED to hold the input
time values. Define array TIMES to
hold the results of converting the input
values to SAS time values.
Execute an iterative DO loop the
number of times equal to the number of
values to convert to SAS time values.
Convert the elements in NOTED to
SAS time values.
Remove the colons.
Create a character value that is saved
in a way that can be read by the
TIMEn. function. Convert the value in
TEMP1 to numeric by reading it with
the INPUT function and the numeric
informat 11.2. Next convert this
numeric value that is returned by the
INPUT function back to character by
using the PUT function and the picture
format TIMECHAR, which writes out
the value in a way that can be read by
the TIMEn. function.
Assign a valid SAS time value to the
corresponding element in TIMES by
reading the value of intermediate
variable TEMP2 with the TIME11.
informat.

```
proc format;
  picture timechar other='99:99:99.99';
run;
data incident_times;
  set incidents;
  drop temp1 temp2 i;
  format time_in time_resp time11.2;


  array noted{2} $ in_noted resp_noted;
  array times{2} time_in time_resp;


  do i=1 to dim(noted);




    temp1=compress(noted{i},':');
    temp2=put(input(temp1,11.2),timechar.);












    times{i}=input(temp2,time11.);



  end;
run;
```

Example 9.13   Calculating a Person's Age

Goal

Determine a person's age by using his or her date of birth.

Example Features

Featured Step	DATA step
Featured Step Options and Statements	FLOOR and INTCK functions
A Closer Look	More about Calculating Ages and Anniversaries

Input Data Set

Data set MARCH_HIRES has the names and dates of birth for 10 employees hired on March 1, 2009. Variable DOB is a SAS date value. It is displayed with the WORDDATE20. format.

```
                    MARCH_HIRES

Obs    name                            dob
 1     JK Allen            March 1, 1972
 2     RT Brown         February 28, 1980
 3     WI Carter           March 29, 1980
 4     LG Johnson           March 1, 1980
 5     MH Johnson       December 12, 1980
 6     PO Phillips      February 14, 1971
 7     TR Smith         November 9, 1967
 8     AG Rodriguez          July 2, 1955
 9     EW Washington        July 30, 1960
10     NA Young            April 22, 1984
```

Resulting Data Set
Output 9.13a
HIREAGE
Data Set

```
                    Example 9.13 HIREAGE Data Set

     Obs    name                          dob      hiredate     age

      1     JK Allen           March 1, 1972     03/01/2009      37
      2     RT Brown        February 28, 1980    03/01/2009      29
      3     WI Carter          March 29, 1980    03/01/2009      28
      4     LG Johnson          March 1, 1980    03/01/2009      29
      5     MH Johnson      December 12, 1980    03/01/2009      28
      6     PO Phillips     February 14, 1971    03/01/2009      38
      7     TR Smith        November 9, 1967     03/01/2009      41
      8     AG Rodriguez         July 2, 1955    03/01/2009      53
      9     EW Washington       July 30, 1960    03/01/2009      48
     10     NA Young           April 22, 1984    03/01/2009      24
```

Example Overview

This example computes a person's age by subtracting the SAS date value of the date of birth from another date. The following DATA step computes the age at hire for a group of employees hired on March 1, 2009.

To accurately compute the employee's age, the DATA step uses the INTCK function to count the number of months between the date of birth and the hire date. The number of months is divided by 12 to produce the number of years. An adjustment might need to be made if the day of hire is after the day of birth. The assignment statement that computes the age uses Boolean logic to return a value of 0 or 1 when testing if the day of hire is before the day of birth. If it is, a value of 1 is returned by the Boolean expression and the number of months is reduced by 1.

Last, the FLOOR function is applied to the number of years so that the age is represented as an integer. The FLOOR function returns the largest integer less than or equal to the argument.

Program

Create data set HIREAGE.
Read observations from
MARCH_HIRES.
Define the hire date, which is the same
for all employees in MARCH_HIRES.

Compute the age at hire for each
employee. Count the number of months
between the employee's date of birth
and date of hire. If the month of hire is
the same as the month of birth and the
day of hire is before the day of birth,
subtract 1 from the value that is
returned by INTCK.

```
data hireage;
  set march_hires;

  retain hiredate '01mar2009'd;

  format hiredate mmddyy10.;
  age=floor((intck('month',dob,hiredate) -
      (day(hiredate) < day(dob)))/12);




run;
```

A Closer Look

More about Calculating Ages and Anniversaries

The preceding DATA step demonstrates that there is no simple way to compute the age of a person or the anniversary of an event. The assignment statement that computes the ages of the new hires uses three functions (FLOOR, INTCK, and DAY), a Boolean expression, and arithmetic. The structure of the Gregorian calendar requires a complicated statement because it must take into account the rules that govern the lengths of months and years. The calculation of age or anniversary must produce an integer that is incremented by 1 on the person's birthday or anniversary date.

Commonly, programmers have computed age as shown in the following assignment statement, and most of the time this statement calculates the correct age.

```
age=floor((hiredate-dob)/365.25);
```

Inaccuracies can occur associated with leap year calculations. For example, data set MARCH_HIRES does have one observation, "JK Allen", where the two methods of computing age produce different values. The following DATA step is modified below to compute AGE_NOTACC with the formula immediately above. Output 9.13b shows the different values for age for "JK Allen".

```
data twoages;
  set march_hires;

  retain hiredate '01mar2009'd;
  format hiredate mmddyy10.;

  age=floor((intck('month',dob,hiredate) -
      (day(hiredate) < day(dob)))/12);
  age_notacc=floor((hiredate-dob)/365.25);

run;
```

Compute AGE_NOTACC by using the
common method of age calculation.

Output 9.13b lists the observations in data set TWOAGES.

Output 9.13b
TWOAGES
Data Set

```
                             Example 9.13 TWOAGES Data Set

                                                                    age_
                 Obs  name                      dob   hiredate  age notacc

                   1  JK Allen         March 1, 1972 03/01/2009   37   36
                   2  RT Brown      February 28, 1980 03/01/2009   29   29
                   3  WI Carter        March 29, 1980 03/01/2009   28   28
                   4  LG Johnson        March 1, 1980 03/01/2009   29   28
                   5  MH Johnson    December 12, 1980 03/01/2009   28   28
                   6  PO Phillips   February 14, 1971 03/01/2009   38   38
                   7  TR Smith      November 9, 1967 03/01/2009   41   41
                   8  AG Rodriguez     July 2, 1955 03/01/2009   53   53
                   9  EW Washington   July 30, 1960 03/01/2009   48   48
                  10  NA Young       April 22, 1984 03/01/2009   24   24
```

The INTCK function with the "MONTH" argument in the main example is used because it can count the number of months between two dates.

```
intck('month',dob,hiredate)
```

This specification returns the number of times the first day of a month is passed between the two dates that are specified as the second and third arguments to INTCK. This result will not be accurate if the day-number of HIREDATE is earlier than the day-number of DOB.

For example, using two dates close in range, the number of times the first of a month is passed between April 15, 2009, and April 4, 2011, is twenty-four times, which would return two years when 24 is divided by 12. However, when computing an age or anniversary using these two dates, you instead want the number of months to be 23 so that the division by 12 and application of the FLOOR function returns a value of 1. Therefore, when the day-number of the third argument is less than the day-number of the second argument, subtract a 1 from the number of months.

A Boolean expression is embedded in the assignment statement that tests whether the day-number of the date in the second argument is before the day-number of the third argument.

❑ When the day-number of the date in the second argument is *before* the day-number of the third argument, the Boolean expression evaluates to 1 (true), which causes the statement to subtract 1 from the number of months that are returned by the INTCK function. The final result is then divided by 12.

❑ When the day-number of the date in the second argument is *after* the day-number of the third argument, the Boolean expression evaluates to 0 (false). The number of months that is returned by the INTCK function is not changed and it is divided by 12 to obtain the age.

Example 9.14   Incrementing a Date by an Interval

Goal

Increment a date by a specific interval such as days, weeks, months, or years. For each starting date, specify the number of times to increment the starting date and the interval to increment it by.

Example Features

Featured Step	DATA step
Featured Step Options and Statements	INTNX function
A Closer Look	Understanding SAS Date and Time Intervals Understanding the Processing of the INTNX Function in This Example

Input Data Set

Data set SCHED_APPTS has a list of appointments for nine patients and information about scheduling new appointments for them. The values of variable APPTDATE are SAS date values, and they are formatted in the listing with the WORDDATE format. The other variables are described in the Example Overview.

```
                                       SCHED_APPTS

Obs  patient            apptdate  interval  units  nappts  alignment
  1  CVM4     Wed, Feb 20, 2008    week         1     3     same
  2  JD3A     Fri, Jan 25, 2008    week2        1     3     same
  3  QI1U     Tue, Feb  5, 2008    week        10     2     same
  4  W23V     Mon, Jan 21, 2008    weekday     10     2     same
  5  AB5U     Wed, Jan 30, 2008    month        1     2     same
  6  PO6I     Fri, Feb 15, 2008    month        7     1
  7  JA1L     Fri, Feb 15, 2008    month        6     1     end
  8  U21B     Fri, Feb 15, 2008    semiyear     1     1
  9  TN62     Thu, Jan 10, 2008    qtr          1     3
```

Resulting Data Set
Output 9.14
NEXT_APPTS
Data Set

```
                                Example 9.14 NEXT_APPTS

Obs  patient       apptdate          nextappt1          nextappt2          nextappt3

  1  CVM4     Wed, Feb 20, 2008  Wed, Feb 27, 2008  Wed, Mar  5, 2008  Wed, Mar 12, 2008
  2  JD3A     Fri, Jan 25, 2008  Fri, Feb  8, 2008  Fri, Feb 22, 2008  Fri, Mar  7, 2008
  3  QI1U     Tue, Feb  5, 2008  Tue, Apr 15, 2008  Tue, Jun 24, 2008      .
  4  W23V     Mon, Jan 21, 2008  Mon, Feb  4, 2008  Mon, Feb 18, 2008      .
  5  AB5U     Wed, Jan 30, 2008  Fri, Feb 29, 2008  Sat, Mar 29, 2008      .
  6  PO6I     Fri, Feb 15, 2008  Mon, Sep  1, 2008      .                  .
  7  JA1L     Fri, Feb 15, 2008  Sun, Aug 31, 2008      .                  .
  8  U21B     Fri, Feb 15, 2008  Tue, Jul  1, 2008      .                  .
  9  TN62     Thu, Jan 10, 2008  Tue, Apr  1, 2008  Tue, Jul  1, 2008  Wed, Oct  1, 2008
```

Example Overview

The following DATA step shows several applications of the INTNX function, which can increment date and time values by specific intervals. It uses the INTNX function to schedule appointments.

Data set SCHED_APPTS has appointments for nine people. The DATA step schedules one or more new appointments for these nine people based on information that is supplied in each person's observation.

Variable APPTDATE stores the initial appointment date and it is the starting point from which to generate new appointment dates. The second argument to the INTNX function call in the DATA step is APPTDATE.

The following four variables control how the DATA step generates new appointment dates. Three of the variables, INTERVAL, UNITS, and ALIGNMENT, are arguments to the INTNX function.

❑ INTERVAL, which contains the date interval in which to increment APPTDATE. It is the first argument to INTNX. The values of INTERVAL are keywords that are recognized by INTNX. The interval value that is supplied to INTNX can include a numeric suffix that serves as a multiplier of the interval value.

❑ UNITS, which specifies the number of intervals of the type that are specified by variable INTERVAL to increment the date. It is the third argument to INTNX.

❑ ALIGNMENT, which specifies the position within the interval in which to select the new appointment date. It is the fourth argument to INTNX. The values of ALIGNMENT are keywords that are recognized by INTNX.

❑ NAPPTS, which is the number of new appointments to generate. The DATA step is written to expect the value to be between 1 and 3 inclusively.

The DATA step can create up to three new appointments. The new dates are saved in variables NEXTAPPT1, NEXTAPPT2, and NEXTAPPT3.

"Understanding the Processing of the INTNX Function in This Example" in the "A Closer Look" section provides details about how the specifications that are supplied to INTNX determine the new appointment dates.

Program

Create data set NEXT_APPTS. Read the observations in SCHED_APPTS.

```
data next_appts;
  set sched_appts;
```

Specify an array that contains the starting appointment date and the new appointment dates.

```
  keep patient apptdate nextappt1-nextappt3;
  array allappts{*} apptdate nextappt1-nextappt3;
```

When an alignment within the date interval is not specified, default to the beginning of the interval, which is also the SAS default for INTNX.

```
  format nextappt1-nextappt3 mmddyy10.;
  if alignment=' ' then alignment='beginning';
```

Iterate a DO loop the number of times equal to the number of appointments to make.

```
  do i=1 to nappts;
```

Using the current element of the ALLAPPTS array, generate a new appointment date and save it in the next element of the APPAPPTS array. On the first iteration of the DO loop, start with APPTDATE. On iterations after the first, use the previously generated appointment date as the starting date. Determine the next appointment date based on the date interval in INTERVAL. Increment from the starting date the number of units of the date interval as specified in

```
    allappts{i+1}=intnx(interval, allappts{i},
                  units, alignment);
```

UNITS. Position the new date within the interval according to the value of ALIGNMENT.

```
                 end;
             run;
```

A Closer Look

Understanding SAS Date and Time Intervals

A SAS date or time interval is a unit of measurement that SAS can count within an elapsed period of time, such as days, months, or hours. SAS determines date and time intervals based on fixed points on the calendar, the clock, or both.

Functions INTNX and INTCK both accept date and time intervals as arguments. The interval specifications are coded the same way for both functions. The INTNX function as shown in this example's DATA step shifts a date value or time value based on the interval that is supplied to it. The INTCK counts the number of intervals between two date or time values. Example 9.13 showed how to use INTCK to determine a person's age by counting the months between the date of birth and another date.

Coding of intervals that are supplied to these functions can be complex. An understanding of how SAS determines the start of an interval is necessary to correctly shift a date or time value and accurately count the number of intervals between two date or time values.

SAS defaults to the beginning of the interval in which the starting date value or starting time value falls. Depending on the other arguments to the function, this point might not be the actual starting date. For example, if you are shifting a date by months, SAS determines the starting point of the interval to be the first of the month of that date regardless of where the date actually is within that month. For example, when using MONTHS as the interval, SAS determines that the number of months between March 31, 2009, and May 1, 2009, is 2. The following DATA step shows how to write the INTCK function to calculate the number of months between these two dates.

```
data _null_;
  nmonths=intck('months','31mar2009'd,'1may2009'd);
  put nmonths=;
run;
```

When the INTNX function shifts a date or time value by an interval, SAS by default aligns the new value to the beginning of the interval. You can override this default and align the value instead to the middle or end of the interval by using either the "MIDDLE" or "END" keywords. Additionally, when you use the INTNX function to shift dates, you can specify the alignment to be the same calendar date after computing the interval increment. The keyword for this specification is "SAME".

Multiples of intervals can be expressed different ways. With INTCK and INTNX, you can add a suffix to the interval keyword that specifies the multiplier of the interval. The third argument to INTNX can also be used to shift multiple intervals.

The two methods of shifting multiple intervals do not work identically so it is important to understand how SAS defines intervals and think through how you need to shift dates. They might or might not produce the same results. The following DATA steps illustrate how the methods differ.

The next DATA step produces the same shifted dates because the three calls to INTNX specify the "SAME" argument for date alignment. For DATE1 and DATE2, the "SAME" keyword causes the alignment to be based on the interval's shift period, which is three months from March 29, 2008, not the interval, which is months.

```
data _null_;
  date1=intnx('months','29mar2008'd,3,'same');
  date2=intnx('months3','29mar2008'd,1,'same');
  date3=intnx('qtr','29mar2008'd,1,'same');
  put (date1 date2 date3 ) (=mmddyy10.);
run;
```

The SAS log shows the values of DATE1, DATE2, and DATE3:

```
date1=06/29/2008 date2=06/29/2008 date3=06/29/2008
```

Omitting the "SAME" argument causes the INTNX function to default to the beginning of the interval when determining the shifted date. The first call to INTNX has a different value for the beginning of the interval from the other two calls.

```
data _null_;
  date1=intnx('months','29mar2008'd,3);
  date2=intnx('months3','29mar2008'd,1);
  date3=intnx('qtr','29mar2008'd,1);
  put (date1 date2 date3 ) (=mmddyy10.);
run;
```

The first call to INTNX where the interval is "MONTHS" places the beginning of the interval at the first of the month, which is March 1, 2008. Shifting three months and aligning to the beginning of the next interval assigns June 1, 2008, to DATE1.

The second call to INTNX where the interval is "MONTHS3" places the beginning of the interval at the first day in the three-month interval, which is January 1, 2008. Shifting three months to the beginning of the next interval assigns April 1, 2008, to DATE2.

The third call to INTNX where the interval is "QTR" places the beginning of the interval at the first day in the quarter of the starting date, which is January 1, 2008. Shifting one quarter to the beginning of the next interval, which is the beginning of the second quarter, assigns April 1, 2008, to DATE3.

The SAS log shows the values of DATE1, DATE2, and DATE3:

```
date1=06/01/2008 date2=04/01/2008 date3=04/01/2008
```

You can also add a "shift-index" to your interval specification. A shift-index shifts the start of the interval. The default starting point for an interval is "1". That means, for example, that the keyword "YEAR" causes the starting date to be January 1, and the keyword "HOUR" causes the starting time to be at midnight. If you wanted to define a fiscal year that runs from October 1 to September 30, you can write the interval as "YEAR.10".

As you can see, coding intervals can quickly become quite complicated. It is important to think through and test the kind of intervals and increments to use so that you produce correct results.

For more usage information about SAS date and time intervals, see SAS documentation.

Understanding the Processing of the INTNX Function in This Example
Table 9.2 describes how the appointments should be made for each observation in data set SCHED_APPTS.

Table 9.2 Description of the Calls to INTNX: This Example's DATA Step

Patient	Action	Interval	Beginning of the Interval
CVM4	Starting on Wednesday, Feb 20, 2008 (APPTDATE), schedule 3 (NAPPTS) appointments that are 1 (UNITS) week (INTERVAL) apart on the same day of the week (ALIGNMENT).	1 week	Wed, Feb 20, 2008
JD3A	Starting on Friday, Jan 25, 2008 (APPTDATE), schedule 3 (NAPPTS) appointments that are 2 weeks (INTERVAL and UNITS) apart on the same day of the week (ALIGNMENT). Apply the multiplier of 2 to the interval of WEEK to produce an interval of 2 weeks. Shift by single intervals (UNITS=1) of 2 weeks.	2 weeks	Fri, Jan 25, 2008
QI1U	Starting on Tuesday, Feb 5, 2008 (APPTDATE), schedule 2 (NAPPTS) appointments that are 10 (UNITS) weeks (INTERVAL) apart on the same day of the week (ALIGNMENT).	10 weeks	Tues, Feb 5, 2008
W23V	Starting on Monday, Jan 21, 2008 (APPTDATE), schedule 2 (NAPPTS) appointments that are 10 (UNITS) business days (INTERVAL) apart on the same day of the week (ALIGNMENT).	1 work week (five days from Monday to Friday)	Mon, Jan 21, 2008
AB5U	Starting on Wednesday, Jan 30, 2008 (APPTDATE), schedule 2 (NAPPTS) appointments that are 1 (UNITS) month (INTERVAL) apart on the same day of the month (ALIGNMENT). Because Feb 30 does not exist, SAS assigns the closest date, which is Feb 29, 2008. It then uses that day of the month to determine the second appointment, Mar 29, 2008.	1 month	Wed, Jan 30, 2008
PO6I	Starting on Friday, Feb 15, 2008 (APPTDATE), schedule 1 (NAPPTS) appointment that is 7 (UNITS) months (INTERVAL) away. Because no value for alignment is specified, default to the beginning of the interval that is seven months away when determining the appointment date.	1 month	Feb 1, 2008
JA1L	Starting on Friday, Feb 15, 2008 (APPTDATE), schedule 1 (NAPPTS) appointment that is 6 (UNITS) months (INTERVAL) away. With "END" as the alignment, make the appointment at the end of the interval 6 months away.	1 month	Feb 1, 2008
U21B	Starting on Friday, Feb 15, 2008 (APPTDATE), schedule 1 (NAPPTS) appointment that is 1 (UNITS) semiyear (INTERVAL) away. Because no value for alignment is specified, default to the beginning of the semiyear interval when determining the next appointment date.	1 semiyear	Jan 1, 2008
TN62	Starting on Jan 10, 2008 (APPTDATE), schedule 3 appointments that are 1 (UNITS) quarter (INTERVAL) apart. Because no value for alignment is specified, default to the beginning of the quarter interval when determining the three appointment dates.	1 quarter	Jan 10, 2008

Example 9.15 Determining the Number of U.S. Business Days between Two Dates

Goal

Determine the number of business days between two dates. Do not count specific holidays as business days.

Example Features

Featured Step	DATA step
Featured Step Options and Statements	HOLIDAY, INTCK, and WEEKDAY functions

Input Data Set

Data set DAY_RANGES has two date variables, DAY1 and DAY2.

DAY_RANGES

Obs	day1	day2
1	07/01/2008	07/05/2008
2	06/23/2008	06/27/2008
3	05/19/2008	05/19/2009
4	04/01/2008	04/05/2011
5	01/23/2009	01/25/2009

Resulting Data Set
Output 9.15
BUSINESS_DAYS
Data Set

Example 9.15 BUSINESS_DAYS

Obs	day1	day2	totaldays	workdays	holidays
1	07/01/2008	07/05/2008	4	2	1
2	06/23/2008	06/27/2008	4	4	0
3	05/19/2008	05/19/2009	365	255	6
4	04/01/2008	04/05/2011	1099	771	18
5	01/23/2009	01/25/2009	2	0	0

Example Overview

The following DATA step calculates the number of business days between two dates by using the INTCK function and the "WEEKDAY" interval. It also includes code to test whether the range of days includes holidays that occur on business days. For each weekday holiday that is found within the range of days, the number of business days is reduced by 1.

Data set DAY_RANGES has two date variables, DAY1 and DAY2. The DATA step determines the following within the range of days between DAY1 and DAY2:

❑ the number of days (variable TOTALDAYS)

❑ the number of business days minus any holidays that occur on a business day (variable WORKDAYS)

❑ the number of holidays (variable HOLIDAYS) whether or not they occur during the work week

The DATA step uses an iterative DO loop to look for holidays that occur on business days within the range of days between DAY1 and DAY2. It uses function WEEKDAY to determine whether a holiday occurs on a business day.

SAS function HOLIDAY returns the dates of specific U.S. and Canadian holidays. The first argument to HOLIDAY is a character value that references one of the specific holidays. The second argument to HOLIDAY is the year. For the full list of holidays that HOLIDAY recognizes, see SAS documentation.

Temporary array HOLIDAY_LIST contains the list of holiday keywords for which the business day total should be adjusted if the holiday occurs on a business day.

Program

Create data set BUSINESS_DAYS.
Read the observations in DAY_RANGES.
List the holidays that you want the DATA step to check whether they fall on business days.
Specify the holidays for which to check if they occur on a business day. Specify the values in the form known to function HOLIDAY.

Calculate the total number of days.
Calculate the total number of business days Monday through Friday.
Initialize the number of holidays.
Check all the holidays in HOLIDAY_LIST between the year of DAY1 and the year of DAY2.
Execute this DO group when the current element of HOLIDAY_LIST falls within the range of days between DAY1 and DAY2.
Increment HOLIDAYS by 1 since the current element of HOLIDAY_LIST is within the range of days between DAY1 and DAY2.
If the current element of HOLIDAY_LIST for the year that is being processed occurs on a weekday, decrement WORKDAYS by 1.

```sas
data business_days;
  set day_ranges;

  array holiday_list{6} $ 25 _temporary_
    ('NEWYEAR','MEMORIAL','USINDEPENDENCE','LABOR',
     'THANKSGIVING','CHRISTMAS');

  drop i y;
  totaldays=intck('days',day1,day2);
  workdays=intck('weekday',day1,day2);

  holidays=0;
  do y=year(day1) to year(day2);
    do i=1 to dim(holiday_list);

      if (day1 le holiday(holiday_list{i},y) le day2)
        then do;

          holidays=holidays+1;

          if (2 le
              weekday(holiday(holiday_list{i},y)) le 6)
              then workdays=workdays-1;

        end;
    end;
  end;
run;
```

Example 9.16   Counting the Occurrences of a String

Goal

Count the number of occurrences of a set of character strings in the value of a character variable.

Example Features

Featured Step	DATA step
Featured Step Options and Statements	COUNT, COUNTC, and COUNTW functions

Input Data Set

Data set QUIZ_GRADES has quiz grades for four students. The grades are stored in one variable, QUIZ_STRING, and the grades are separated by commas.

```
                    QUIZ_GRADES

Obs     student       quiz_string
 1        431         B+,B-,A,I,A+
 2        501         A,A,B,P,C,U,F
 3        289         A,A,B,A,A-,U
 4        130         C+,B-,I,?,W
```

Resulting Data Set
Output 9.16
QUIZ_SUMMARY
Data Set

```
                         Example 9.16 QUIZ_SUMMARY

Obs student   quiz_string   n_quizzes super good fair bad no_grades invalid

 1    431    B+,B-,A,I,A+       5       1    3    0   0      1         0
 2    501    A,A,B,P,C,U,F      7       0    3    1   2      0         1
 3    289    A,A,B,A,A-,U       6       0    5    0   1      0         0
 4    130    C+,B-,I,?,W        5       0    1    1   0      2         1
```

Example Overview

This example shows how to count occurrences of words and specific text strings in a character variable. A DATA step applies the three SAS functions, COUNT, COUNTC, and COUNTW, to examine the contents of a character variable.

Data set QUIZ_GRADES contains quiz grades for four students. The grades are stored in one variable, QUIZ_STRING, and are separated by commas. The goal of the DATA step is to count the number of grades per student and tabulate the grades in specific categories.

The COUNT function counts the number of occurrences of specific text in a string. The DATA step uses it once to find the number of A+ grades per student.

The COUNTC function counts the number of occurrences of specific characters in a string. The DATA step uses it multiple times to tally per student the number of quiz grades in the several categories.

The COUNTW function counts the number of words in a string. The DATA step uses it once to count the total number of quiz grades per student. The function specifies a comma as the delimiter between the quiz grades. A "word" in the context of the

COUNTW function refers to a substring that meets at least one of the following conditions:

❑ bounded on the left by a delimiter or the beginning of a string

❑ bounded on the right by a delimiter or the end of the string

❑ contains no delimiters unless specification is made by using the Q modifier as described in SAS documentation for the function

Program

Create data set QUIZ_SUMMARY.
Read the observations in QUIZ_GRADES.
Count the number of words in QUIZ_STRING. Specify that a comma is the delimiter between words.
Count the number of occurrences of 'A+'.
Count the number of occurrences of the character 'A' and the character 'B'. Because an A+ grade is counted by COUNTC and it is also represented in the SUPER variable, subtract the value of SUPER from the result that was returned by COUNTC to obtain the total number of good grades that range from B- to A.
Count the number of occurrences of 'C'.
Count the number of occurrences of 'U' and 'F'.
Count the number of occurrences of 'I' and 'W'.
Determine the number of quizzes that do not fit into any of the five valid categories.

```
data quiz_summary;

  set quiz_grades;

  n_quizzes=countw(quiz_string,',');


  super=count(quiz_string,'A+');

  good=countc(quiz_string,'AB')-super;











  fair=countc(quiz_string,'C');

  bad=countc(quiz_string,'UF');

  no_grades=countc(quiz_string,'IW');

  invalid=n_quizzes-super-good-fair-bad-no_grades;

run;
```

Example 9.17   Extracting a Character String without Breaking the Text in the Middle of a Word

Goal

Extract from a variable a character string that is no longer than a specified length and that does not end in the middle of a word.

Example Features

Featured Step	DATA step
Featured Step Options and Statements	ANYPUNCT, ANYSPACE, LARGEST, and SUBSTR functions

Input Data Set

Data set WORKPLACE has comments from six employees.

```
                                    WORKPLACE

            Obs    comments
             1     Cannot discuss work-related issues with my supervisor.
             2     Need flex scheduling&job-sharing options.
             3     Add closer parking areas.
             4     Love the cafeteria
             5     More programs for career advancement
             6     Mentoring? Coaching? Either available?
```

Resulting Data Set
Output 9.17
TRUNC_COMMENTS Data Set

```
                        Example 9.17 TRUNC_COMMENTS

    Obs  comments                                                truncated

     1   Cannot discuss work-related issues with my supervisor.  Cannot discuss work-
     2   Need flex scheduling&job-sharing options.               Need flex scheduling&job-
     3   Add closer parking areas.                               Add closer parking areas.
     4   Love the cafeteria                                      Love the cafeteria
     5   More programs for career advancement                    More programs for career
     6   Mentoring? Coaching? Either available?                  Mentoring? Coaching?
```

Example Overview

This example demonstrates how to use several SAS language functions to extract a text string at a word boundary so that the length of the extracted text is less than or equal to a specified length and as close to that length as possible.

Data set WORKPLACE has comments from six employees. The goal is to extract a string up to 25 characters in length from the comment variable COMMENTS. The string should not end in the middle of a word.

The DATA step uses the two functions ANYPUNCT and ANYSPACE to determine the column where to extract the text from COMMENTS. Both functions start from column 25 in COMMENTS and work backward to the beginning of COMMENTS.

The ANYPUNCT function returns the first position at which a punctuation character is found. The ANYSPACE function returns the first position at which a whitespace character, such as a blank, is found. The second argument to both functions is −25, which tells the functions to start at column 25 and work backward to column 1. Searching right to left from column 25 ensures that the maximum amount of text will be extracted.

The LARGEST function then picks the larger of the two values that are returned by the two functions. This value is the length of the extracted text and is specified as the third argument to the SUBSTR function.

The values of COMMENTS for the third and fourth observations are less than 25 characters in length. The DATA step assigns the full value of COMMENTS to TRUNCATED.

The punctuation characters that ANYPUNCT searches for are dependent on your operating system. In this example, the text for observation 2 breaks at the hyphen (-) punctuation character.

The whitespace characters that ANYSPACE searches for are dependent on your operating system. In addition to blanks, ANYSPACE searches for horizontal and vertical tabs, carriage returns, line feeds, and form feeds.

If you need to be more specific about the characters than that provided in this example's code, you could use the FINDC function. For information about its usage, see SAS documentation.

For more information about functions such as ANYPUNCT and ANYSPACE, see "Understanding Functions That Evaluate the Content of Variable Values" in Example 9.2 of the "A Closer Look" section.

Program

Create data set TRUNC_COMMENTS.
Read the observations in data set WORKPLACE.
Define a new character variable whose length is the maximum length of the string to extract from COMMENTS.

Search right to left for the first punctuation character. Start the search in column 25.
Search right to left for the first whitespace character. Start the search in column 25.
Determine the length of the text string to extract from COMMENTS. Specify 1 as the first argument to LARGEST so that the larger of COLPUNCT and COLBLANK is saved in CUTCOL, ensuring the maximum amount of text will be extracted.
Extract text from COMMENTS that has the length of the value of CUTCOL.

```
data trunc_comments;

  set workplace;

  length truncated $ 25;


  keep comments truncated;
  colpunct=anypunct(comments,-25);


  colblank=anyspace(comments,-25);


  cutcol=largest(1,colpunct,colblank);






  truncated=substr(comments,1,cutcol);

run;
```

Example 9.18   Cleaning Character Data Values

Goal

Apply several data cleaning rules to a character variable. Modify the case of words according to value and position in the value.

Example Features

Featured Step	DATA step
Featured Step Options and Statements	Hash object in the DATA step COUNTW, LOWCASE, PROPCASE, and SCAN functions
Related Technique	DATA step, macro variables

Input Data Sets

The five observations in data set UNEDITED_TITLES have one character variable.

```
            UNEDITED_TITLES

Obs    titletext
 1     of interest to all
 2     up at the crack of dawn
 3     the best of ?
 4     anything but...
 5     OUTSIDE-IN AND INSIDE-OUT
```

Data set LCWORDS contains the words that should be lowercase in the edited text value.

```
           LCWORDS

Obs      lcword
 1         a
 2         an
 3         the
 4         at
 5         by
 6         for
 7         in
 8         of
 9         on
10         to
11         up
12         and
13         as
14         but
15         it
16         or
17         nor
```

Resulting Data Set
Output 9.18
EDITED_TITLES
Data Set

```
                         Example 9.18 EDITED_TITLES

   Obs  titletext                 proptitletext            edited_title

    1   of interest to all        Of Interest To All       Of Interest to All
    2   up at the crack of dawn    Up At The Crack Of Dawn  Up at the Crack of Dawn
    3   the best of ?             The Best Of ?            The Best of ?
    4   anything but...           Anything But...          Anything But...
    5   OUTSIDE-IN and INSIDE-OUT  Outside-In And Inside-Out  Outside-In and Inside-Out
```

Example Overview

A common data cleaning task is to edit text values to make them uniform in structure. This example shows a way to standardize the contents of a text variable so that the first letter of all words in the value are uppercase except for a set of conjunctions and prepositions that should be entirely lowercase unless one of those words is the first or last word in the value.

Data set UNEDITED_TITLES has five observations with one variable, TITLETEXT. The values of TITLETEXT do not conform to the structure needed.

The first DATA step creates data set LCWORDS, which contains the words that should be lowercase in the TITLETEXT values.

On its first iteration, the second DATA step defines hash table LC and loads data set LCWORDS into LC. It defines variable LCWORD as both a hash key and data.

For each observation, the COUNTW function determines the number of words in the TITLETEXT value. The PROPCASE function converts the words in TITLETEXT to proper case and saves the result in PROPTITLETEXT.

A DO loop then iterates the number of times equal to the value that is returned by COUNTW to evaluate each word in PROPTITLETEXT. On each iteration of the DO loop, the SCAN function extracts a word from PROPTITLETEXT. The SCAN function uses a space as the delimiter to determine words. If the word is not the first and not the last in PROPTITLETEXT and its lowercase form is found in hash table LC, the LOWCASE function converts it to lowercase. Otherwise, the text remains in proper case.

As each word is processed in the DO loop, the CATX function concatenates the edited or unedited word to the previously processed words in the title. The new variable EDITED_TITLE contains the revised values of PROPTITLETEXT.

Notice some of the actions taken by the functions that rely on an understanding of how the functions determine words and delimiters.

❑ <u>Observation 3</u>: COUNTW counts four words with the question mark (?) the fourth word. The last alphabetic character word is "of", but because the IF statements do not distinguish between alphabetic words and nonalphabetic words, the word "of" is converted to lowercase.

❑ <u>Observation 4</u>: COUNTW counts two words. The second word ("But…") includes the three periods. Even though the alphabetic characters of this last word are in the LC hash table, the three periods that are concatenated at the end of the word prevent a match from being made to any key value in the LC hash table.

❑ <u>Observation 5</u>: COUNTW counts three words, and with the space that is specified as the delimiter in the SCAN function, the SCAN function extracts three words. However, the PROPCASE function converts the text that follows the hyphen to proper case because in addition to the space, the hyphen is one of the PROPCASE function's default delimiters. Even though the text after the hyphen in the first word (Outside-In) is in the list of words in the LC hash table, it is not converted to lowercase because it is not examined separately from the entire first word.

Program

Create data set
EDITED_TITLES.
Read the observations in
UNEDITED_TITLES.
Assign lengths to character
variables that are defined in
the DATA step.

Define the hash object on the
first iteration.
Declare hash object LC. Load
LC with data set LCWORDS.

```
data edited_titles;

  set unedited_titles;

  length lcword temp $ 50 proptitletext edited_title $ 80;


  keep titletext proptitletext edited_title;
  if _n_=1 then do;

    declare hash lc(dataset: 'work.lcwords');
```

Define key variable LCWORD in LC.

```
lc.definekey('lcword');
```

Store one data variable in LC.
Complete the key and data definitions for LC.

```
lc.definedata('lcword');
lc.definedone();
```

Initialize to missing the variable that is defined as key and data to the LC hash object. This action prevents notes about uninitialized variables from being written to the SAS log when there are no explicit assignment statements in the DATA step for the variable.

```
call missing(lcword);
```

```
end;
```

Count the number of words in TITLETEXT. Specify a space as the second argument to COUNTW to indicate that a space is the delimiter between words in TITLETEXT.

```
nwords=countw(trim(titletext),' ');
```

Convert the words in TITLETEXT to proper case.

```
proptitletext=propcase(titletext);
```

Execute an iterative DO loop the number of times equal to the number of words in the current value of TITLETEXT.

```
do i=1 to nwords;
```

Extract the ith word.
If the current word is not the first and not the last and its lowercase form is found in the hash table, concatenate the lowercase form of the word to the value in EDITED_TITLE.

```
  temp=scan(proptitletext,i,' ');
  if i ne 1 and i ne nwords and lc.check(key:lowcase(temp))=0
     then edited_title=catx(' ',edited_title,lowcase(temp));
```

When the word does not meet the conditions of the previous statement, make no changes to its form and concatenate it to the value in EDITED_TITLE.

```
  else edited_title=catx(' ',edited_title,temp);
```

```
  end;
run;
```

Related Technique

The following PROC SQL step and DATA step create a data set similar to the one that was created by the DATA step in the main example.

The program does not use a hash table to look up words that should be lowercase. Instead the PROC SQL step puts all the words that should be lowercase in macro variable LCWORDS. Trailing blanks are trimmed from the words and they are enclosed in double quotation marks. The intention is to put the LCWORDS macro variable value in an IN list. This macro variable is referenced in the IF statement in the DATA step. The value of LCWORDS is shown here in the lines copied from the SAS log. The %PUT statement displays the values of macro variables.

```
1     %put &lcwords;
"a","an","the","at","by","for","in","of","on","to","up",
"and","as","but","it","or","nor"
```

An iterative DO loop in the DATA step examines each word and checks to see if the word is in the list of values that are saved in the macro variable. When it is in the list and is also not the first word and not the last word, the lowercase form of the word is put in variable EDITED_TITLE.

*Save all the values of
LCWORD in macro variable
LCWORDS. Separate the
values with commas. Trim
trailing blanks from each
value of LCWORD. Enclose
each value of LCWORD in
double quotation marks.*

```
proc sql noprint;
  select quote(trim(lcword))
    into :lcwords separated by ','
    from lcwords;
```

```
quit;
```

```
data edited_titles;
```

*Create data set
EDITED_TITLES.
Read the observations in
UNEDITED_TITLES.
Assign lengths to character
variables that are defined in
the DATA step.*

```
  set unedited_titles;
```

```
  length temp $ 50 proptitletext edited_title $ 80;
```

*Count the number of words in
TITLETEXT. Specify a space
as the second argument to
COUNTW to indicate that a
space is the delimiter between
words in TITLETEXT.
Convert the words in
TITLETEXT to proper case.
Execute an iterative DO loop
the number of times equal to
the number of words in the
current value of TITLETEXT.
Extract the ith word from
PROPTITLETEXT.
If the current word is not the
first and not the last and its
lowercase form is found in
macro variable LCWORDS,
concatenate the lowercase
form of the word to the value
in EDITED_TITLE.
When the word does not meet
the conditions of the previous
statement, make no changes to
its form and concatenate it to
the value in EDITED_TITLE.*

```
  keep titletext proptitletext edited_title;
  nwords=countw(trim(titletext),' ');
```

```
  proptitletext=propcase(titletext);
```

```
  do i=1 to nwords;
```

```
    temp=scan(proptitletext,i,' ');
```

```
    if i ne 1 and i ne nwords and lowcase(temp) in (&lcwords)
      then edited_title=catx(' ',edited_title,lowcase(temp));
```

```
    else edited_title=catx(' ',edited_title,temp);
```

```
  end;
run;
```

Example 9.19 Validating and Standardizing Complex Character Data

Goal

Validate character data values that can be stored in multiple patterns. When valid, reformat values to conform to one pattern.

Example Features

Featured Step	DATA step
Featured Step Options and Statements	Regular expressions and associated functions: PRXCHANGE, PRXMATCH, PRXPARSE, and PRXPOSN CATS function
A Closer Look	Understanding the Regular Expressions Defined in This Example

Input Data Sets

Data set NEWCONTACTS contains contact information about eight people. The values for each variable are not uniformly specified.

```
                                       NEWCONTACTS

Obs        contactname         contactphone    contactemail
 1   Young Wilson, Karen      (315) 555-3210   karen.young.wilson@big-agency.gov
 2   Denise M. Morris         (607)555-0123    denise morris@college.edu
 3   Bonita Ann Henderson     920-555-6719     bahenderson@college3.eud
 4   Brown, Anne-Marie        9255554031       amb!1@more.net
 5   Butler, L. William       612--555-7171    lbb_@state.info.gov
 6   Davis-Lee, Kim           111-555-4444     K.D-L@business.edu
 7   Joseph Mitchell          (505)555-5432    joe_mitch@allwork.com
 8   Sanchez,    R. T.        334   5551234    sanc001@schooledu
```

Resulting Data Set
Output 9.19
CONTACTS_EDITED
Data Set

```
                        Example 9.19 CONTACTS_EDITED

    Obs   contactname              contactphone   contactemail

     1    Karen Young Wilson       (315)555-3210  karen.young.wilson@big-agency.gov
     2    Denise M. Morris         (607)555-0123  **Invalid**
     3    Bonita Ann Henderson     (920)555-6719  **Invalid**
     4    Anne-Marie Brown         (925)555-4031  **Invalid**
     5    L. William Butler        (612)555-7171  lbb_@state.info.gov
     6    Kim Davis-Lee            **Invalid**    K.D-L@business.edu
     7    Joseph Mitchell          (505)555-5432  joe_mitch@allwork.com
     8    R. T. Sanchez            (334)555-1234  **Invalid**
```

Example Overview

Character data can sometimes be collected in a free-form manner that is difficult to work with unless you modify them to conform to a specific structure. Values that are collected this way are usually not checked for errors either.

Many SAS functions and SAS language statements can be used to check and modify your data. Functions such as INDEX, VERIFY, SUBSTR, and the series of concatenation functions commonly are used in a series of IF-THEN-ELSE statements to check and revise character data. However, when you want to verify and edit complex data values, it might be more efficient and require less code to work with the set of Perl regular expression functions and CALL routines. With these expressions, you can match multiple patterns to your text values so that you can validate, modify, and extract data.

This example works with complex character data values. Each variable's values record the same type of information, but not necessarily the same way.

Data set NEWCONTACTS contains three variables of information about eight people. It contains the person's name, phone number, and e-mail address. There are differences in how the values for each variable are stored. For example, some of the names are written first name first followed by last name, while others are last name first followed by a comma and first name.

Some of the data values are also invalid. For example, the area code for one person starts with a 1, which is invalid. Some of the e-mail addresses are also invalid because they include invalid characters or site names.

To make a regular expression, you must first understand the patterns that you want to match and those you do not want to match. You describe the patterns in your data with alphabetic characters and special characters that are called metacharacters. Description of the many ways of specifying regular expressions is beyond the scope of this book. For more complete information, see SAS documentation. The following example will present just a few ways of specifying patterns to validate and edit the data.

Working with regular expressions is usually a two-step process. First the regular expression is compiled with the PRXPARSE function or CALL routine, which assigns a regular expression ID to a variable. Next the identifier variable is referenced by other PRX functions or CALL routines.

Usually your expressions need to be compiled only once. You can either put your PRXPARSE calls inside a DO group that executes only on the first iteration of the DATA step, or you can add the "o" option to the PRXPARSE call. The "o" option tells SAS to compile the regular expression only once.

After defining your expressions, statements in your DATA step that call PRX functions can then reference the regular expression ID variable.

Instead of making this a two-step process, you can specify your regular expression in functions such as PRXCHANGE that use them. However, this style might make reading your code more difficult because many regular expressions can be long and complicated to read.

In this DATA step, the PRXPARSE function defines a regular expression for each of the character variables. The calls to PRXPARSE are placed in a DO block that executes only on the first iteration of the DATA step. The regular expressions are compiled once.

❑ The regular expression that is used with CONTACTNAME is NAME_RX. Its definition specifies that contact names in the output data set that are last name first, first name last, and last and first names separated by a comma will be rearranged to be first name first and last name last.

❑ The regular expression that is used with CONTACTPHONE is PHONE_RX. Its definition will be used to validate telephone data and reformat valid telephone data to one style.

❑ The regular expression that is used with CONTACTEMAIL is EMAIL_RX. Its definition will be used to validate e-mail address specification.

"Understanding the Regular Expressions Defined in This Example" in the "A Closer Look" section describes in more detail how the regular expressions in this example are coded.

Following the first DO block, the DATA step then performs these actions:

❑ Uses PRXCHANGE to rearrange CONTACTNAME so that values that are last name first, first name last, and last and first names separated by a comma will be rearranged to first name first and last name last.

❑ Uses PRXMATCH to determine whether the value of CONTACTPHONE is a valid phone number. When it is valid, calls to PRXPOSN determine the positions of the three parts of the telephone number. The CATS function then concatenates the three parts and encloses the area code in parentheses so that all telephone numbers are specified the same way. When it is not valid, the value of CONTACTPHONE is replaced with the text "**Invalid**".

❏ Uses PRXMATCH to determine whether the value of CONTACTEMAIL is valid. When it is not valid, the value of CONTACTEMAIL is replaced with the text "**Invalid**".

The complex patterns and modifications would be challenging to write in a series of IF-THEN-ELSE statements so writing regular expressions is appropriate for this example.

Program

Create data set CONTACTS_EDITED. Read the observations in NEWCONTACTS. Retain across all iterations of the DATA step the values that are assigned to these variables on the first iteration of the DATA step.

```
data contacts_edited;

  set newcontacts;

  retain name_rx phone_rx email_rx;
```

Execute this block on the first iteration of the DATA step.
Build with PRXPARSE a regular expression whose ID number is assigned to NAME_RX.
Build with PRXPARSE a regular expression whose ID number is assigned to PHONE_RX.
Build with PRXPARSE a regular expression whose ID number is assigned to EMAIL_RX.

```
  drop name_rx phone_rx email_rx areacode prefix extension;
  if _n_=1 then do;

    name_rx=
prxparse('s/([a-z]+[-.a-z\s]+),\s*?([a-z]+[-.a-z\s]+)/\2 \1/i');

    phone_rx=
prxparse(
      "/\(?([2-9]\d\d)\)?\s*-?\s*([2-9]\d\d)\s*-?\s*(\d{4})/");

    email_rx=
    prxparse("/(\w+[.-\w]*)@(\w+[.-\w]*)\.(gov|com|edu|net)/i");

  end;
```

Modify the values of CONTACTNAME according to the regular expression NAME_RX. Specify -1 as the second argument so that the process of matching patterns and replacing text continues until the end of the value of CONTACTNAME is reached.

```
  contactname=prxchange(name_rx,-1,contactname);
```

Execute the DO group if the pattern of the current value of CONTACTPHONE matches that of the regular expression that is identified by the value of PHONE_RX.

```
  if prxmatch(phone_rx,contactphone) then do;
```

Because the regular expression that was identified by PHONE_RX was defined with three capture buffers, one for each of the three parts of the phone number, extract the first and assign it to AREACODE.

```
    areacode=prxposn(phone_rx,1,contactphone);
```

Extract the second capture buffer from CONTACTPHONE and assign it to PREFIX.

```
    prefix=prxposn(phone_rx,2,contactphone);
```

Extract the third capture buffer from CONTACTPHONE and assign it to EXTENSION. Concatenate the three parts of the telephone number. Enclose the area code in parentheses. Insert a hyphen between the prefix and extension parts of the telephone number.

```
        extension=prxposn(phone_rx,3,contactphone);



   contactphone=cats('(',areacode,')',prefix,'-',extension);
```

When the value of CONTACTPHONE does not match the pattern in the regular expression that is identified by PHONE_RX, replace the current value of CONTACTPHONE with a specific text value.
When the value of CONTACTEMAIL does not match the pattern in the regular expression that is identified by EMAIL_RX starting in column 1, replace the current value of CONTACTEMAIL with a specific text value.

```
  end;
  else contactphone='**Invalid**';




  if prxmatch(email_rx,contactemail)^=1 then
              contactemail='**Invalid**';




  run;
```

A Closer Look

Understanding the Regular Expressions Defined in This Example

This section describes in more detail how the three regular expressions that were defined in the preceding DATA step were coded. This section does not explain in general how to build your own regular expressions. For more information, see SAS documentation.

When you use regular expressions, you compactly describe expected patterns in your data and add programming statements to perform specific actions based on the results of matching your data values to the expected patterns coded in the regular expressions.

Forward slashes enclose regular expressions. Within each expression, you can match specific text to specific positions in a string. Regular expressions also support wildcard specifications so that your coding can indicate specific characters in one part of your string and any character in another. Ranges of values such as all alphabetic characters or digits from 0 to 9 can be specified. Coding can indicate how many times a pattern can repeat itself. Parts of an expression can be grouped with parentheses.

Table 9.3 describes the metacharacters in the regular expression that is associated with CONTACTNAME. The patterns that are defined in this regular expression are used to find values of CONTACTNAME that are stored last name first, first name last, and first and last names separated by a comma. When a value of CONTACTNAME matches the patterns, the value is rearranged by using the PRXCHANGE function so that the value is stored first name first and last name last.

When the value of CONTACTNAME does not match the patterns in the regular expression, the value remains unchanged. For example, values of CONTACTNAME that are already stored as first name first and last name last are not modified. These values do not have commas and thus do not match the regular expression.

The part of the regular expression that is being described is highlighted and enlarged.

Table 9.3 Description of Metacharacters in Regular Expression Associated with Variable CONTACTNAME

```
name_rx=prxparse('s/([a-z]+[-.a-z\s]+),\s*([a-z]+[-.a-z\s]+)/\2 \1/i');
```
Use the regular expression in a substitution. Place the pattern to be matched between the first two slash characters. Place the pattern of the result of the substitution between the last two slash characters. Indicate that case of the patterns is to be ignored by placing a lowercase 'i' after the last slash character.

```
name_rx=prxparse('s/([a-z]+[-.a-z\s]+),\s*([a-z]+[-.a-z\s]+)/\2 \1/i');
```
Group the contents of the regular expression by enclosing the metacharacters in the two groups in parentheses. These groups then become capture buffers that are referenced by the metacharacters between the second set of slash characters. The first capture buffer corresponds to the last name. The second capture buffer corresponds to the first name.

```
name_rx=prxparse('s/([a-z]+[-.a-z\s]+),\s*([a-z]+[-.a-z\s]+)/\2 \1/i');
```
Specify metacharacters identically for both the last name and the first name. Enclose in square brackets the allowable characters in each name.

```
name_rx=prxparse('s/([a-z]+[-.a-z\s]+),\s*([a-z]+[-.a-z\s]+)/\2 \1/i');
```
Specify in the pattern at least one letter as the first character in the first name and in the last name by placing a plus sign (+) following the square bracket. Place the range of characters that are allowed within the square brackets. Because an 'i' is placed at the end of the substitution expression, case of the alphabetic characters is ignored and specifying just "a-z" includes both uppercase and lowercase versions of the letters.

```
name_rx=prxparse('s/([a-z]+[-.a-z\s]+),\s*([a-z]+[-.a-z\s]+)/\2 \1/i');
```
Specify in the pattern that after the first letter in the first name and in the last name, there should be an alphabetic character, a hyphen (-), a period (.), or a space (\s). Indicate a space with the \s metacharacter. Including a space and a hyphen in the pattern allows matches when the value has two first names, two last names, or hyphenated names. A period allows initials in a matching value.

```
name_rx=prxparse('s/([a-z]+[-.a-z\s]+),\s*([a-z]+[-.a-z\s]+)/\2 \1/i');
```
Specify in the pattern that a match must have the two parts of the name separated with a comma and optionally one or more spaces. Indicate a space with the \s metacharacter. Indicate that there can be in a match none, one, or many spaces with the asterisk (*) repetition factor metacharacter.

```
name_rx=prxparse('s/([a-z]+[-.a-z\s]+),\s*([a-z]+[-.a-z\s]+)/\2 \1/i');
```
Indicate the arrangement of the results of the substitution. Place the second capture buffer before the first capture buffer. Place a space between them. Precede the capture buffer number with the backward slash escape character so that the number is not interpreted as text.

Table 9.4 describes the metacharacters in the PHONE_RX regular expression that is associated with CONTACTPHONE. The patterns that are defined in this regular expression are used to find valid telephone numbers in the values of CONTACTPHONE.

When a value of CONTACTPHONE matches a pattern in PHONE_RX, the three parts of the telephone number, which are the area code, prefix, and extension, are extracted from the value by using PRXPOSN. The CATS function then concatenates the three parts so that all the matches have telephone numbers stored the same way in the output data set.

When the value of CONTACTPHONE does not match the patterns in the PHONE_RX regular expression, the value is replaced with the text "**Invalid**".

The part of the regular expression that is being described is highlighted and enlarged.

Table 9.4 Description of Metacharacters in Regular Expression Associated with Variable CONTACTPHONE

```
phone_rx=prxparse("/\(?([2-9]\d\d)\)?\s*-?\s*([2-9]\d\d)\s*-?\s*(\d{4})/");
```
Place the pattern to be matched between two slash characters.

```
phone_rx=prxparse("/\(?([2-9]\d\d)\)?\s*-?\s*([2-9]\d\d)\s*-?\s*(\d{4})/");
```
Make two groups in the regular expression by enclosing each of them with parentheses. The first group corresponds to the prefix part of the telephone number. The second group corresponds to the extension part of the telephone number. The parentheses in the first part of the expression do not form a group; they are instead part of the pattern to match the area code and are described next.

```
phone_rx=prxparse("/\(?([2-9]\d\d)\)?\s*-?\s*([2-9]\d\d)\s*-?\s*(\d{4})/");
```
Specify the pattern of the area code part of the telephone number. Allow matches to optionally enclose the area code in parentheses. To prevent the open and close parentheses from being interpreted as metacharacters, precede them with the backslash escape character. Follow the open parenthesis and the close parenthesis with a question mark (?) to indicate that a match can be made if the parenthesis character is present one or zero times. Allow matches to have only digits from 2 to 9 in the first position of the area code. In the second and third positions of the area code, allow matches to have any of the 10 digits from 0 to 9 by placing the metacharacter \d in each position. Metacharacter \d means any digit from 0 to 9.

```
phone_rx=prxparse("/\(?([2-9]\d\d)\)?\s*-?\s*([2-9]\d\d)\s*-?\s*(\d{4})/");
```
Specify the same pattern between the area code and the prefix and the prefix and the extension. Allow matches to have one or zero hyphens (-?) between none or any number of spaces (\s*). The asterisk (*) repitition factor metacharacter that follows the two space metacharacters (\s) allows matches to have zero or more spaces.

```
phone_rx=prxparse("/\(?([2-9]\d\d)\)?\s*-?\s*([2-9]\d\d)\s*-?\s*(\d{4})/");
```
Specify the pattern of the prefix part of the telephone number. Allow matches to have only digits from 2 to 9 in the first position of the prefix. In the second and third positions of the prefix, allow matches to have any of the 10 digits from 0 to 9 by placing the metacharacter \d in each position. Metacharacter \d means any digit from 0 to 9.

```
phone_rx=prxparse("/\(?([2-9]\d\d)\)?\s*-?\s*([2-9]\d\d)\s*-?\s*(\d{4})/");
```
Specify the pattern of the extension part of the telephone number. Require that a match must have four digits each ranging from 0 to 9. Indicate a digit from 0 to 9 with the \d metacharacter. Indicate the exact number of digits by following the \d metacharacter with the number of digits in curly brackets.

Table 9.5 describes the metacharacters in the EMAIL_RX regular expression that is associated with CONTACTEMAIL. The patterns that are defined in this regular expression are used to find valid e-mail addresses in the values of CONTACTEMAIL.

When a value of CONTACTEMAIL matches a pattern of EMAIL_RX, the value of CONTACTEMAIL remains unchanged.

When the value of CONTACTEMAIL does not match the patterns in the EMAIL_RX regular expression, the value is replaced with the text "**Invalid**".

The part of the regular expression that is being described is highlighted and enlarged.

Table 9.5 Description of Metacharacters in Regular Expression Associated with Variable CONTACTEMAIL

`email_rx=prxparse("/`(\w+[.-\w]*)@(\w+[.-\w]*)\.(gov|com|edu|net)`/i");`
Place the pattern to be matched between two slash characters. Indicate that case of the patterns is to be ignored by placing a lowercase 'i' after the last slash character.

`email_rx=prxparse("/`**(**`\w+[.-\w]*`**)**`@`**(**`\w+[.-\w]*`**)**`\.`**(**`gov|com|edu|net`**)**`/i");`
Group the contents of the regular expression by enclosing the metacharacters in the three parts of the e-mail address in parentheses. The first group is the user name. The second group is the subdomain name. The third group is the set of valid domains.

`email_rx=prxparse("/(`**\w+[.-\w]***`)@(`**\w+[.-\w]***`)\.(gov|com|edu|net)/i");`
Specify identically the pattern of the user name part and the subdomain part of the e-mail address. A match must start with at least one word character (\w). A word character is any alphanumeric character plus the underscore (_). The plus sign (+) repetition factor metacharacter specifies the match must be made at least one time. The remainder of each part of the e-mail address can be missing or can be any combination of one or more periods (-), hyphens (-), and word characters (\w). The asterisk (*) repetition factor metacharacter allows matches to have zero or more of these characters.

`email_rx=prxparse("/(\w+[.-\w]*)`**@**`(\w+[.-\w]*)\.(gov|com|edu|net)/i");`
Specify that a match must have an at sign (@) between the user name and subdomain parts of the e-mail address.

`email_rx=prxparse("/(\w+[.-\w]*)@(\w+[.-\w]*)`**\.**`(gov|com|edu|net)/i");`
Specify that a match must have a period (.) between the subdomain and domain parts of the e-mail address. To prevent the period from being interpreted as a metacharacter, precede it with the backslash escape character so that it is interpreted as text.

`email_rx=prxparse("/(\w+[.-\w]*)@(\w+[.-\w]*)\.`**(gov|com|edu|net)**`/i");`
Specify that a match must have one of four domain names. Separate the four choices with the vertical bar character (|) to indicate that they are options and one must be present in a match.

Index

W

Symbols

CPSIA information can be obtained at www.ICGtesting.com
Printed in the USA
LVOW09s2015190515

439131LV00002B/10/P